WOMAN MARINE

WOMAN MARINE

A Memoir Of A Woman Who Joined The U.S. Marine Corps In World War II To "Free a Marine to Fight"

THERESA KARAS YIANILOS

La Jolla Book Publishing Company

Published in the United States by: La Jolla Book Publishing Company
P. O. Box 569, La Jolla, California 92038

Library of Congress Cataloging-in Publication
Yianilos, Theresa Karas
WOMAN MARINE, A Memoir Of A Woman Who Joined The United States Marine
Corps In World War II "To Free A Marine To FIGHT"
1. United States—Armed Forces—Women
II. Title
ISBN 0-9621142-4-3

Dedication

To all the magnificent women
who joined the United States Marine Corps
and served in World War II.

To the bunkmates with whom I served;
I remember each and every one of you.

SEMPER FIDELIS

THE MARINES' HYMN

From the Halls of Montezuma
To the shores of Tripoli,
We fight our country's battles
In the air, on land and sea;
First to fight for right and freedom,
And to keep our honor clean,
We are proud to claim the title
Of United States Marine

Our flag's unfurl'd to every breeze
From dawn to setting sun
We have fought in every clime and place
Where we could take a gun;
In the snow of far-off Northern lands
And in sunny tropic scenes
You will find us always on the job
The United States Marines

Here's health to you and to our Corps
Which we are proud to serve
In many a strife we've fought for life
And never lost our nerve;
If the Army and the Navy
Ever gaze on Heaven's scenes,
They will find the streets are guarded
By United States Marines

MARCH OF THE WOMEN MARINES

Marines!
We are the women members
of our fighting Corps
Marines!
The name is known
from burning sands to ice bound shores
Marines!
We serve that men
may fight on land and air and sea
Marines!
The Eagle, Globe and Anchor carry on
To make men free

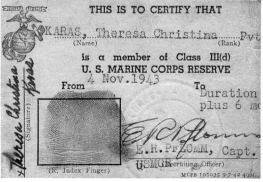

THIS IS TO CERTIFY THAT

KARAS, Theresa Christina........Pvt
(Name) (Rank)

is a member of Class III(d)
U. S. MARINE CORPS RESERVE
From 4 Nov.1943 To
Duration
plus 6 mo

E.R. PFLOMM, Capt.
USMC (Recruiting Officer)

(R. Index Finger)

(Signature) Theresa Christina Karas

MCPB 103035 9-7-42 40M.

Private Theresa Karas, USMCWR, February 1944

Acknowledgments

The author wishes to thank those who have contributed, without remuneration, who reviewed and edited the manuscript and assisted the author to make these memoirs as historically correct as was possible concerning events that occurred fifty years ago.

As in all memoirs, the personal experiences, memories and perceptions expressed in this book are mine, for which I claim full responsibility. My interpretations of Marine Corps orders, regulations and policies, my opinions and impressions of Marine Corps Administration at Quantico and Camp Lejeune and my descriptions of the conditions in the barracks and at work are solely my own.

It is not my intention to offend. Any reader of my book who disputes my memoirs and finds instances that do not concur with her experiences should keep in mind that this book is a personal memoir.

For review and verification of the historical content pertaining to the women Marines, I sought the editorial critique of two women whose opinions were of paramount importance to me, former Directors of the Women Marines, Colonel Julia E. Hamblet and Colonel Margaret Henderson. These women served with distinction in World War II and are today active participants in the Women Marines Association. My gratitude and appreciation to them is enormous. My admiration is boundless for these fine women whose honor and dedication has been an inspiration to all who served with them.

To Julia E. Hamblet, Colonel, USMC (Ret.), Director of the USMC Women's Reserve, 1946 to 1948, and Director of Women Marines, 1953 to 1959, who was my commanding officer in Quantico, Virginia, from, June 26, 1944, to May 22, 1945, I am forever in her debt. She shared her memories generously with me and was gracious and accessible. Her comments were invaluable. She, in turn, jogged a vein in my memory bank and I was able to make the vital changes in the nick of time. The book is better for it. She wrote:

"I have read with much interest your memoir WOMAN MARINE. It jogged my memory about the joys and disappointments, the headaches and heartaches, the enormous pride and sense of fulfillment in being a Woman Marine in World War II—in living up to our motto to "Free a Marine to Fight". It was particularly poignant for me because I served at Quantico

during much of the period about which you write. It is evident that a great deal of research and work went into this book. I'm happy you had the patience, the perseverance—and the knowledge—to write it. Good luck!"
Julia E. Hamblet, Col. USMC (Ret.)

To: Margaret M. Henderson, Colonel, USMC (Ret.), Director of Women Marines 1959-1964, and a veteran of World War II, I am eternally grateful. She wrote:

"Your book WOMAN MARINE is the most authentic book I have read depicting women in the Marine Corps during World War II. This book will bring nostalgia to women who were in the Marine Corps during World War II. It will also show active duty women Marines the evolution of women in the Corps. Indirectly, the book gives any reader a better idea as to how the Marine Corps instills "Esprit de Corps".
Margaret M. Henderson, Col. USMC (Ret.)

Lt. General Victor H. Krulak, USMC (Ret.) devoted his life to the Marine Corps and served with great distinction. After he retired from the Corps, he matched his illustrious career with brilliant success in the field of journalism. He is the author of FIRST TO FIGHT, a book that has won acclaim and literary awards. For his encouragement, his reading of my manuscript and making suggestions to improve it, I am sincerely appreciative.

Of the book WOMAN MARINE, A MEMOIR, he wrote:

"I have read your book—all of it. It is good. The text is fresh and disingenuous. Its freshness is important and should not be tampered with."
V.H. Krulak, Lieutenant General, USMC (Ret.)

Kay Miller, (a fellow neighbor in La Jolla), served in the Women's Reserve from, August 1944 to October 1945, in Quantico, Va., in the Air Squadron at Brown Field. She has worked tirelessly for three decades to make the Women Marines Association an important and permanent organization in American society. She served as the president of the San Diego Chapter for six years and was the chairman of the 1992 convention in San Diego.

I thank her for her review of the manuscript, for her enthusiasm for it and for saying: *"It's all true. It's just as it happened. I had forgotten so much and you brought it all back to me. I had such a good time reading WOMAN MARINE."*

To many others who assisted along the way to the completion of this book, I wish to express my gratitude.

My son, James Spero Yianilos, a business man and journalist in his own field and author of GLOBAL ACCESS, who taught me how to use the Macintosh word processor and weaned me away from my one-horse thirty-year old IBM typewriter. Thank you, thank you.

Olga Bullock, former WR, who served in World War II, who now volunteers so much of her time to the Veteran's Hospital here in San Diego at La Jolla, CA, who is a charter member of the Women Marines Association and one of its pivotal members and former officer, I wish to say, thank you, for all the years I could come to you to refresh my memory and talk "Marine Corps".

Mary Pedersen at the University of California at San Diego, who teaches computer classes, for working with me so diligently in putting my manuscript together.

The young Marines, the men and women in the Marine Corps museums at San Diego, Oceanside, Quantico and Washington D. C., who assisted me in my research. They were doing their duty but it was done with esprit and I appreciate their efforts in my behalf.

Author's Note

WOMAN MARINE, A MEMOIR is an autobiographical novel which is based upon the author's experiences as a United States Marine during her enlistment from 1943 through 1945 in World War II. During the war, while serving as an enlisted Marine, she wrote eight pages daily of her observations and life of these times in the form of letters to her husband. He carried them while serving as an infantryman, through the fighting in Germany, through Belgium, Holland and France, through the mud and snow and the taking of Berlin. These letters served as the archives that enabled Theresa Karas Yianilos to recreate the mood and times of the Women Marines in Quantico during World War II authentically.

It is a book that describes an era about women in the Marine Corps which has not been previously documented fully. WOMAN MARINE, A MEMOIR is a major contribution to the literature which records the historical significance that women have played in the history of the United States Armed Forces.

Her memoirs are based on true incidents, but some of the characters are composites. The author has taken literary license to change the chronological order of events and the naming of certain characters.

The historical characters are real.

There was really a Captain Katherine A. Towle who became a Colonel and Director of the Women Marines in 1948 until 1953.

Colonel Julia E. Hamblet was the author's commanding officer in Quantico from 1944 to 1945. She then became Director of the Women's Reserve from 1946 to 1948 and a Director of the Women Marines in 1953 until 1959. She is an active member and a beloved mentor to the women in the Women Marines Association.

Also real were General Philip H. Torrey, Colonel Karl I. Buse, Senator (President) Harry S. Truman, General Alexander Vandegrift, and Colonel John W. Thomason, author and illustrator.

The names of Captain Bungle and certain characters have been changed although the incidents are true enough.

The author actually did get married on the day the Japanese surrendered, August 12, 1945. The news that the enemy had finally capitulated did ring out as described. The papers and radio stations retracted their news and said they had been premature. Two days later, on August 14, the media made the same announcement. Either way, the war had ended.

WOMAN MARINE
A Memoir of a Woman Marine who joined the
U.S. Marine Corps in World War II
"to free a Marine to fight".

THERESA KARAS YIANILOS

Table Of Contents

Illustrations

Theresa Karas Yianilos

Introduction

WOMAN MARINE, A MEMOIR by Theresa Karas Yianilos is an evocative autobiographical story of a naive young girl who answered her country's call in 1943 during the height of World War II as did twenty thousand other young courageous women. She joined the U.S. Marine Corps full of patriotic fervor, anxious to travel, looking for adventure and love, hoping to find that handsome Marine who was perpetually marching on the recruiting posters. Instead she matured into a woman who eventually recognized her own worth to her country and to the Corps. As the battles for the Pacific Islands against Japan raged on for four years claiming thousands of Marine lives in casualties she realized what it really meant to *"free a Marine to fight "*.

Here is the true story of Marine Corps training in the Women's Reserve in the era of World War II from an enlisted woman's perspective. She tells of the women's pride, dedication and joy in becoming Marines. She describes how women were recruited from every village and city in the United States into hometown platoons and of the troop train that took them to Boot Camp in Camp Lejeune, North Carolina. Her detailed recounting has the ring of authenticity that could only have been written by someone who was there. Author Yianilos served as a corporal and received her honorable discharge in October 1945.

Her perceptive observations are astute as she describes how the women and men reacted to each other as they came together for the first time in the history of the United States Marines Corps to work, fight and love while wearing the same uniform. She has recorded the battle of the sexes between male and female Marines with humor and compassion. She describes the bonding that occurred between the women with truth and honesty.

It is a recorded fact that in 1942, the *Old Breed* in the Marine Corps, from the Commandant down through the ranks, resisted the enlistment of women. It is also true, that they were puzzled as to what purpose women could serve in the Marines. When they finally gave in to public clamor and political realities and included women into the Corps, the men in command had initial difficulties in determining where and how these women Marines were to be used, what they were to be called, what jobs they would be given to do, where they were to sleep and what kind of uniforms they would wear.

In 1942, there was another serious over-riding factor in the Corps' reluctance to bring in the women besides the obvious male chauvinist reasons. The women did not know that behind closed doors in the new Pentagon Building, the Corps was fighting for its own future existence as a separate fighting arm of the Armed Forces. It was this preoccupation with their survival that made the Corps delay its actual enrollment of women into the Corps as much as their antithesis to the idea.

The Corps was part of the Department of the Navy as authorized by Congress.

The pre-war inter-service rivalry that existed between the various branches of services was tempered with the declaration of war on December 8, 1941, against Japan, Germany and Italy, the three nations that had signed a pact of aggression. Both Army and Navy commands sought to consolidate the Corps' manpower resources and amphibious capabilities. A few persons in high offices of power sought to minimize the role of the Corps in this Second World War as they had attempted to do in the First World War in 1916.

In July 1942, Congress authorized women in the Navy. In November 1942, the Commandant, having to face political realities, signed the papers which allowed women to enter the Marine Corps as Reservists for the Duration of the War and Six Months.

The women were aware of the fact that the men did not welcome them wholeheartedly, but they were prepared to overcome this resistance by the force of their dedication to participate in winning the war against, Japan, Germany and Italy.

The women were not privy to military secrets nor the policies which had been made at the highest levels of military command. They did not know that the powerful Joint Chiefs of Staff of four men had made the decision that Marines would not be used in the European War and were to be confined only in the Pacific Theater of Operations, an area of 5000 square miles of ocean. The Corps did not have the authority to command its own destiny nor could it make decisions of where to fight, with which weapons or with what numbers of men.

(The Commandant General of the Marine Corps was not included in this decision making forum although at the time it was formed President

Roosevelt had expressed his wish to Commandant General Holcomb that he be made part of this group. Not until 1978 was the Corps made a member of the Joint Chiefs of Staff.)

In August 1942, the Corps was caught in a double bind. While the Commandant General of the Corps fought a quiet struggle in Washington D.C. to keep itself as a separate amphibious fighting force, the First Division of the Marines was engaged in a desperate battle in the first U.S. offensive attack against the Japs in the Pacific on an island called Guadalcanal. America needed a victory badly in this first year of declared war.

The Japanese seemed invincible as they scored their victories on one island in the Pacific after another and conquered the lands of South East Asia which included British Malaya, Dutch East Indies, and the shipping lanes to Australia. Americans had begun to question our country's ability to stop the "Japs".

For four months the outcome was in doubt. The turning point did not come until November. The island was not secured until February of 1943.

It was during this period of chaos that the birth of the Women's Marine Corps was conceived and executed.

By the time enlistment was opened to the women, in February 13, 1943, the Marines had won Guadalcanal and the Corps received the accolades of a grateful nation for the return of its self-respect. Not since the battles of Belleau Wood during World War One had the Corps enjoyed such high esteem. Women who qualified, 20 to 35 years of age for enlisted and 20 to 49 years for officers, who were white, educated and healthy, enlisted in droves, rushing into the Corps from all parts of the United States to fill up the quota of 18,000 enlisted and 1,000 officers. *(America in 1943, was a segregated society and black women did not enlist). (The recruiting posters "Free A Marine To Fight" depicted a woman of the white race.)*

The women who were inducted entered a military world that had been the exclusive domain of the male for almost two hundred years, where interaction between the members of a military society was conducted under the strictest rules within a prescribed set of laws and rules against fraternization.

The democratic philosophy of equality under which these women had been raised, written in the Declaration Of Independence which granted them inalienable rights, had to be set aside when they took their oath of allegiance. Rules of conduct that were spelled out in the *Articles For the Government of the Navy* and *Letter of Instruction #489* were quickly issued to discourage fraternization between males and females (*both Caucasian*) on and off military posts. The difference in gender was a matter of great concern and the problems it would generate were an unknown element.

The Corps sought to diffuse what was perceived as an explosive situation by taking the position that these women were Marines first and females second. They were to be handled the same way men inductees would be handled. Gender was to be ignored. They would be called Marines and given the same training that the men received, albiet watered down. Military customs of courtesy included deference to women. (*Letter of Instruction #489*)

The Corps demanded instant obedience and adherence to all rules and regulations. Traditions that had been followed for over a century and a half by the male Marines were also imposed upon the women. Esprit de corps meant fidelity and loyalty. The motto of the Corps is *Semper Fidelis*, Always Faithful. Many of the same demands made upon male Marines were also directed towards the women. Training in Boot Camp began the process of converting civilian women into military ones. Yet even here, in the domain of the drill sergeant, where boys were turned into men, gender had to be considered. The D.I.'s famous tirades, his colorful language and physical demands were tempered officially by the sex of his Boots.

That the Corps was successful in turning twenty thousand civilian women into fine Marines who enhanced the Corps with their grace, capabilities, commitment and loyalty is well documented. The traditions are maintained to this date by the women who now serve proudly as part of the regular Marine Corps.

PART ONE

The Home Front–Tonawanda, New York–June 1943

We both knew it. We'd never see each other again. I twirled his quaint sailor's hat with the letters H.M.S. on the band and he cracked jokes as we waited for the bus to take him to Niagara Falls and across the border. Back to Canada and his waiting ship.

"I won't forget you, Luv," he said, squeezing me right on Main Street. "Blimey! Your toilet water smells bloody peculiar!"

I hit his British Navy uniform playfully with the flat of my hand. "That's not me, you silly lambchop! That is the smell coming from all the defense factories around Tonawanda. You should really smell this place when the wind carries the stink of the chemical factories from Niagara Falls up the road."

He laughed because I fell for another of his jokes about my home town.

He gave me another hug which was about all he had coming since we didn't really know each other as we would have had he stayed an extra day or two. We had jitterbugged for hours the night before at the serviceman's dance at the American Legion Hall. He was the first English sailor I had ever met and he had taught me to do the Lambeth Walk which was the dance craze of all Liverpool and London.

"You promise to write?" He hollered as he jumped aboard the bus.

Of course I promised to write.

That made him number 17 on my list I had kissed good-bye right here at the same bus stop.

Seventeen boys who passed as ships in the night which didn't stay anchored long enough to be roped to the dock. That added up to ten soldiers, six of them home town boys, five sailors, two Coast Guards, and included the boy who had taken me to my high school senior prom who now wore the 82nd Airborne Division's *Screaming Eagle* patch of the paratrooper on his Army uniform.

Some were boys I had known since high-school, others I had met at the USO dances and church socials. They were all pen pals now to whom I sent cheerful letters on blue stationary soaked with

Blue Bonnet cologne from the Rexall Drug Store with a red lipstick kiss on the back of each envelope.

That was the trouble with the town of Tonawanda in Western New York State. There were no men. They had all gone to war.

It hadn't been so noticeable last year, but by the middle of January even the eighteen year old boys had been inducted into the armed forces to fight the Japs, the Nazi Germans and Mussolini's Italians.

The whole town had geared up for war. I, as everyone else, vibrated with patriotism and did my best to contribute to the war effort.

I sat on my home front dying to give my all but up to now that hadn't amounted to much. True, I had donated half a pint of blood to the Red Cross and they did make quite a fuss over me afterward because my type A was rare. The thought of knowing that somewhere a handsome brave soldier and I were sharing blood gave me goose bumps but that feeling didn't last long.

I volunteered for Civil Defense and took the noon watch as an air-raid spotter. I was ready but no one attacked, not during daylight and not in the moonlight.

I went to all the Saturday night dances at the American Legion Hall to entertain the troops. Tonawanda wasn't near any of the military camps and often we girls ended up dancing to the record player with each other for lack of men. I went to movies a lot, usually alone. Often the person sitting next to me was a female who was also alone. I'd sit in the dark, scanning the MARCH OF TIME or the newsreels for faces of soldiers I might recognize. I had danced with so many boys at the USO in Buffalo that according to the law of averages a few boys that I knew should have been caught on camera.

I had flirted with laughing fun-loving young men on furlough who had not experienced any fighting and had not been sent overseas yet. I didn't recognize the weary faces of Marines with empty sunken eyes that stared into space who were photographed in the Pacific Islands, nor the dirty tired soldiers in Sicily or North Africa. They all looked alike in their helmets and muddy uniforms.

Sometimes I would get a twinge of envy over those friends who had jumped into marriage soon after their high school graduation before all the good men were gone. One by one these brides were left alone as their young husbands marched off to camp.

As twenty started to slide into the home-stretch towards my twenty-first birthday and age began to creep up on me, I began to have these little nagging thoughts and twinges of anxiety about how "old maids" happened.

I had gone "steady", had been asked "to wait" and had heard a lot of wild promises which didn't hold up in the light of day. I gave each one of them locks of my curly brown hair. Consequently, I had quite a collection of lockets with pictures in them, a number of silver identification bracelets, and a few class rings. But no diamond ring. Not even a tiny one.

Uncle Sam got the cream of the crop and what was left, I dated.

I even went out with the handsome, big and overweight son of the richest family in our church. We saw a few drive-in movies together and had necked once or twice in his ice cream truck. His family owned confectionary shops in Buffalo where they sold home made chocolates and ice-cream. Whenever he had to make deliveries, he'd drive the ten miles from Buffalo to Tonawanda to visit me. But then, in 1942 he was plucked out of his third year at the University of Buffalo where he was failing a required course, German Language, for the third time.

Without any proposal on his part or promises on my part he had started to send me letters weekly which had filled my mother's heart with hope.

"Another box of chocolates arrived from Big Spero," Mama said with her mouth full. "I think you've finally got a chance to make a good marriage."

Poor Spero had been sent to the Army Cavalry in Fort Riley, Kansas, where he was miserable because all he did was shovel manure, give rub downs to a huge sweaty horse and clean out stables for six weeks. I suspected that the Army did not know that he considered animals a futile responsibility. When he was about ten years old he asked for a dog but his mother had given him a canary instead. The bird promptly caught a chill and died. Now the Army had given him a horse to take care of. Fortunately for the war effort the Army became mechanized and the horse was put out to pasture. He didn't look as romantic sitting in his Jeep in the second picture he sent me but his letters had silenced Mama's nagging me to marry.

But none of these boys were dream boats. Not one of them made me tingle down to my toes with the kind of kisses I saw in the movies, the kind Rhett Butler gave Scarlett. No one in Tonawanda kissed like that. I had been kissed many times, starting from the Spin

3

the Bottle games in the sixth grade up to the a little bit of necking at Mayor's Park which was a patch of green grass and old trees at the edge of town by the Erie Canal. But that didn't count. 'No touching below the neck' was number one necking rule.

I never had to fight off any of the nice boys I had dated.

I was waiting for true love—real love—the you-know-it-when-it-happens kind of love. But, that special magic—that big bang—that sudden recognition of Mr. Right that I had seen happen between boy and girl in all the movies, never hit me.

I tested a lot of boys but, so far it hadn't happened.

Until it did I was willing to wait. Wait and write and wait and write.

Now everyone of my sailors and soldiers was gone; shipped off to far away places: The Naval Base, San Diego; Camp Carson, Colorado; Fort Dix, New Jersey; Fort Riley, Kansas; Laramie, Wyoming; Georgia, California, and someplace overseas called APO which meant combat area, and that could be anywhere: Sicily, Italy, England, North Africa or the Pacific.

I watched the bus pull away and joined the crowd of people pushing against the closed doors of Woolworth's Five and Dime.

"What are we in line for?"

"I don't know."

"I hope it's silk stockings and not those 51 gauge rayons."

The man behind me said, "I bet they won't have any left of whatever it is by the time we get in." He looked at my legs and said in a loud voice everyone in line could hear, "You got a run in your legs, Honey."

That was the trouble with wearing leg paint. It clogged up the pores and the perspiration ran funny lines down the calves.

I smiled politely at his corny attempt at flirtation. I didn't want to hurt the old man's feelings. He was at least 38, probably 4-F or married with 4 kids, a reject from the draft. A man had to have a very good reason to be excused from being inducted into the Army and that meant he was no prize.

Who could have predicted all the things that would become scarce in the year and a half since the Japs struck at Pearl Harbor? Anyone who had been able to foretell the future and had stocked up merchandise of any kind was able to make a lot of money on the black market charging ten times the worth of anything they had to sell with no questions asked.

I never realized how much of my life was held up by those rubber trees in the Amazon. I'd see the piles of old rubber tires on the empty lot on the corner ready for the rubber scrap drive but all I could contribute was the elastic in my panties. Just as I lifted a tray of doughnuts at the Canteen, the elastic snapped and I felt my bloomers swish past my thighs down to my ankles. They weren't worth wearing after that. After a while, I became used to going without panties as well as stockings and it wasn't noticeable if I kept my knees together when I sat down. I wasn't giving anyone the chance to sing-song *I see England, I see France, I see your under pants.*

Losing my panties was just a small sacrifice. Things were a lot worse for our boys who were fighting at the Front. Each of us had to do her part and put up with the inconveniences and shortages. Our country was getting ready to open a Second Front against the Nazis any day now, if the rumors were true. A lot more sacrifices were necessary to win this war to beat the Germans and Italians to the east of us and the Japs to the west of us at the same time.

Hoarding was a treasonable offense. Anyone caught doing it was in big trouble, not only with the government but with the neighbors as well.

So many ordinary everyday items had disappeared from the shelves of the stores and were all gone: alarm clocks to autos, butter, bicycles to bobby pins, candy, cigarettes, gasoline to fountain pens, sugar, skates, shoes, skis, tires, tin, cotton, wool, whisky. Every day another necessity of life was no longer available. Everything went into the war effort. Factories had stopped making everyday things and had converted to making guns. Guns for butter. Sugar for alcohol. Alcohol for dynamite. The strangest ingredients went into the recipe for war.

The baker couldn't get enough lard, butter, eggs, flour and would close his shop just as it became my turn to be served although it was 10:00 a.m. and all I wanted was a breakfast roll for coffee.

The butcher wouldn't have any meat and would scold if I showed disappointment, "Don't you know there's a war on? It's meatless Tuesday." As you'd leave his shop Mr. Krause would yell, "Save your fats for soap. I pay two cents a pound." He had become very patriotic after we declared war on his Germany. He had gone to a German Bund rally at Madison Square Garden, and was so shocked by the violence of the brown shirt American Nazi sympathizers that he returned frightened and claimed that he was really from Austria and flew the American flag in front of his shop and stuck little flags in his knockwurst and bratwurst.

Since I worked part time at the Sugar Bowl Fountain Shop I knew all about the problems they had trying to get enough sugar on their allotment quota to keep the cases filled with the chocolate candy they made. Sugar had gone to war to be made into alcohol. Lines of customers would form outside the door the minute they had filled up their glass cases with chocolates and they would be sold out in a matter of minutes. Whatever candy there was went to the boys overseas and to war workers in the factories who needed it for their "breaks" and to keep up the pace of the graveyard shifts.

I had spent a great deal of my after school hours leaning against the green marble soda-fountain counter there, drinking Coca-Colas and eating hot fudge sundaes, while I talked to Helen, my best friend, who had to work after school. Her parents owned the Sugar Bowl.

Ever since I dated their nephew, Big Spero, his aunt and uncle treated me as family and would call upon me to help wait on customers in their shop since waitresses were so hard to get in this war time. All the small shops in Tonawanda had problems keeping clerks and waitresses. The whole town had disappeared into the defense factories where people could make big money working the swing shift.

My regular job was typist and proof-reader at the TONAWANDA NEWS which came out once a week. It didn't pay much, fifteen dollars a week, but that job put me right where the action was—in a newspaper office with the smell of printer's ink to inspire me. Writing classified ads wasn't immortal prose but at least it was real journalism. When I asked the police reporter if he would let me accompany him on his stories as the famous girl-reporters, Dorothy Kilgallen and Brenda Starr did, he turned me down.

"A pretty little thing like you shouldn't be down at the jail house. It's dirty and depressing. There's nothing there but drunks and burglars. Nothing exciting happens in Tonawanda," he said.

Well, I could have told him that myself.

Mostly, I was sent out for coffee a lot. Anyone who wanted to break into the field of journalism had to drink a lot of coffee.

My secret ambition was to go to California and live and work in Hollywood. I had seen every movie I could and knew deep in my heart that I could dream up love stories as good as the ones I saw on the screen.

People got very touchy if anyone tried to crash ahead of the lines that formed outside of shops the minute news spread of goods arriving. And for some who had a lot of defense pay to spend, the black market was one of the ways of getting things that were rationed. The only other way to get a hold of something scarce or rationed was to know someone who worked in a store who could put merchandise behind the counter in exchange for whatever you had they wanted. I wasn't one of those people who had anything to trade either so I waited in lines a lot. I came home with a great many things I wouldn't have bought if there had been no line. Still, I didn't have defense pay to throw around.

Tonawanda had two main streets, each about four short blocks long. Main Street was our best street for high class shopping. It had Zuckmaier's, our one and only good department store, and many other gift shops and clothing stores as well as the Rexall Drug store where I bought cologne in the drug store part and ate banana splits at the tables in the soda fountain section. Young Street, the other most important street in our town, was parallel to the Erie Canal and ran right into the bridge that took you over to North Tonawanda, where most of the factories had been built that gave Tonawanda such a peculiar smell when the wind blew in certain directions. I think the boundary line between the twin cities was somewhere in the middle of that bridge.

Young Street had a bakery with the best glazed donuts owned by a Czech family, a movie theater owned by a Jewish man, the Sugar Bowl owned by the Greek family of my best friend, a Chinese restaurant owned by my classmate's father, Jennie Chang; the Mohican Market, Mr. Krause's butcher shop, and a small general store where a fat Lebanese lady named Mary sold penny candies. If she knew you, she'd bring out a board with holes in it, and for a penny, let you take a stick and poke out small tightly wound pieces of paper which had winning numbers that would let you win ten cents to one dollar. I never won anything.

Changes came to Young Street in 1942. The barber shop and a pool hall, which used to have guys hanging around who whistled when I walked by now had old men for customers. The young men were clustered near the Army and Navy recruiting stores instead.

1942 had been a very bad year for America.

The Atlanctic Ocean was filled with German U-Boats and they patrolled our shores which put the whole Atlantic seaboard on alert. Tonawanda was only four hundred miles from Boston or New York and the Atlantic Ocean. Two of our neighbors had lost sons in the Merchant Marines when German subs had sunk their boats. We knew subs were lurking out there attacking and sinking our ships and we didn't feel safe from the Germans.

Japanese submarines patrolled the Pacific Ocean. Japanese soldiers and marines seemed invincible and were able to occupy one Pacific Island after another without any opposition. Our fleet had been sunk at Pearl Harbor. There was nothing to stop the Japs and we knew that too. Americans on the Western shores of the United States were just as fearful of the Japs landing in California, Washington or Oregon as the Easterners from Portland to Miami were scared of the Germans landing.

War had come to the United States in 1942 and we weren't ready for it.

Belatedly, the factories converted to war production. Our auto industry went into the manufacture of tanks and military vehicles. Our boat industry now rushed to build warships and submarines. All the factories around Tonawanda were working night and day.

Still we all lived in fear; fear of the invincible Japs and the Nazis, fear of the Fifth Column and the spies among us, fear of bombs that might come over any day. A blackout curfew was strongly enforced. We closed our curtains at night and our streets were dark and scary with no street lights to guide our way.

England had gone to war in 1939. We tried to stay out of it.

There was a lot of grumbling about this was England's war. President Roosevelt had promised in his campaign in 1940 for his third term that no American boy would fight on foreign soil. We would send guns and butter to England and even to Russia but not one American boy.

But that was before Pearl Harbor. The whole country got behind the war effort after Japan bombed Pearl Harbor on December 7, 1941, in an unprovoked attack which killed Americans, sank our ships and crippled our Navy and Air Force

Up until that minute, everybody was more concerned about America keeping out of the war in Europe. No one wanted to get involved with what was going over there when Germany and England started shooting at each other over Germany's invasion of Poland in September, 1939. Most of us Americans were *Isolationists* and voiced strong objections to any American involvement with England and Germany's war. Even our hero, Charles Lindberg, was one of those who called for us to stay out of that fight. A lot of hot headed young men joined the RAF (Royal Air Force) and went into Canada and volunteered to fight for England. There were voices that said America had to help but they weren't many.

The memory of World War One was still too strong. After all, it had been only twenty-three years since the last war and too many American boys had died in the trenches of France. A lost generation lay under fields of white crosses in France. Mothers, fathers, wives and sweethearts who had lost family and women who were left to wither on the vine had not forgotten the pain of that war. Feelings ran high.

Americans didn't care what happened on the other side of the Atlantic nor the Pacific. It wasn't any of our business.

We never expected to get socked in the West by Japs.

In truth, anyone with any sense could see this new war was inevitable, that we had to fight sooner or later. It certainly was odd that we weren't better prepared and the Japs had been able to catch us with our pants down.

The war began long before England and Germany started shooting at each other.

Italy, Germany and Japan had certainly made their intentions known for years before they marched into their neighbors' territories.

Italy and Japan had rattled their sabers first. Italy grabbed Abysinnia in Africa in 1935 then marched into Albania in 1939. Nobody, not even the League of Nations, where tiny King Haille Salassi of Ethiopia had gone to plead for help, stopped the Italians.

In the Far East, Japan invaded Manchuria in 1931; marched into China in 1937 and grabbed Nanking and then went into French Indochina in 1940. Nobody stopped them either despite the news of Japanese atrocities.

Germany started the aggression, first by defying the terms of the Treaty of Versailles of World War One and arming herself. Then Hitler, crying *anschluss*, the word for unification, claimed for her own those sovereign countries on her borders which Germany had lost in

9

World War One. For starters he marched into neighboring Austria and Czechoslovakia and grabbed them. England was scared into letting them get away with it. The agreement England's Prime Minister Neville Chamberlain signed with Hitler which was called the Munich Pact wasn't worth the paper it was written on.

Within weeks the Germans marched into Poland and tore the peace all to pieces.

England went to war to defend Poland as she had promised to do.

After that, the Nazis rolled its tanks and flew its planes over the supposedly invincible Maginot Line into Paris and conquered France with new military tactics called the blitzkreig. The whole French Army was simply passed over and the men left in their underground bunkers. France surrendered in a matter of weeks.

Other countries, Belgium, Holland, Denmark, Finland, Greece and all the countries around them fell swiftly to the swastika of the marching Germans within a few weeks also. Sweden and Norway tried to stay neutral but Germans controlled them.

But, by June 1943, the tide had begun to turn.

The Marines won one island in the Pacific after another.

The Allied Armies had finally been victorious in the North African desert over Germany's General Rommel, whom they called The Desert Fox, because he had been so wily.

American boys had reached within a few hundred miles from Rome in Sicily with hard fighting all the way. The fall of Italy was imminent.

The people of the United States had gone to war and patriotism filled everyone's heart and resolve! We were going to fight until the enemy surrendered unconditionally.

The red white and blue American flag, with its forty eight stars, showed up everywhere, on every thing, in shops, windows, homes, on autos and in the color combinations of our clothes. Love for our country was shown in every way possible.

Songs about America were played over and over, some of which were old and left over from World War I. It had taken our song writers quite a while to come up with catchy new tunes for this war so we borrowed songs from England and one from Germany. Our poor soldiers stole a tune called *Lily Marlene* from the Germans.

Irving Berlin's songs were resurrected and sounded good to us. I caught myself singing:

America, I love you, You're like a sweetheart of mine. From ocean to ocean, I pledge my devotion..
I'm a Yankee Doddle Dandy, A Yankee doodle do or die...
Over there, Over there, Tell them the Yanks are coming, the Yanks are coming...

Kate Smith sang a song we all loved but it wasn't easy to sing it or whistle by yourself.

God bless America, land that I love. Stand beside her and guide her through the night with the light from above. From the mountains, to the prairies, to the ocean, white with foam...

New posters appeared on the recruiting offices on Young Street and now there were pictures of women in uniforms. I watched as a Civil Defense volunteer pasted the latest one on the sidewalk sandwich board.

A woman in blue stared out of it straight at me with white letters urging *"SAIL WITH THE NAVY WAVES"*. I stared right back at her. I truly envied that woman in uniform. She got to go everywhere.

That was the day Mama and I really started to argue over every little thing.

From the first day of my "period" seven years before, she worried every time I went out on a date. She always waited up for me and opened the front door the minute she heard the loud creak which the first step on the front porch made when stepped upon to make sure I didn't linger too long in saying "good night."

"No one will buy the cow if the milk is free," was Mama's favorite phrase. In the next breath she would remind me not to stay out later than 11:00 P.M. or the door would be locked. After that hour all sorts of things could happen to a girl.

She warned, "Just remember Poor Prudy!"

The whole neighborhood knew about Poor Prudy.

Poor Prudy was engaged for seven years to the same boy and they often sat necking in her front porch swing long past eleven o'clock which always shocked the neighbors. Then he was drafted and he married another girl he had met outside of his Army camp after he had known her for only a few weeks and jilted Poor Prudy leaving her high and dry.

Prudy's mother told her best friend who told my mother in strictest confidence that Prudence was still a virgin. But, that didn't change what anybody really thought. Her reputation was ruined forever and now Prudence, who was twenty-seven years old, was going to be an old maid for the rest of her life as sure as snow falling in April in Tonawanda.

"Who's going to want to marry soiled goods?" sighed Mama.

Mama played the same message constantly. She might as well have recorded it.

"Your reputation is all a girl has. Once that is ruined, it doesn't matter how late she stays out. She'll never get a good husband. Her whole family is ruined. Her sisters will never be able to hold their head high and they won't get good husbands either."

My three sisters were all under twelve. I had been older sister and baby sitter to them since they were born: I was the eldest by eight, twelve, and sixteen years. They really didn't care whom I dated just as long as I brought home the little presents of gum and candy. They adored me. The responsibility for their future weighed heavily on my conscience.

"It's too late to close the barn door after the horse is gone," Mama said. Mama always worried about the wrong things and she would sometimes get the cart before the horse or put it in the wrong barn.

First, there was no one to whom I wanted to give milk. Second, I wasn't about to throw away the privilege of wearing a white wedding gown. It was a known fact that you had to be a virgin to wear white. *God* was watching each bride as she walked down the aisle and *He Would Know.*

I planned to wear a wedding dress just like the one Scarlett O'Hara wore at Fair Oaks except mine was going to be all white organdy with white roses and a veil that fell all the way to the floor. My life was going to be exciting and fun, not wasted on silly boring chores such as making beds and washing dishes every day. Tonawanda had no part in the plans that awaited me in my glorious future.

I didn't have a picture in my head of the man I was going to marry but I knew all about him. It would be someone I would probably meet in California. He would be a good dancer like Fred

Astaire, and he would grab me instead of Ginger Rogers and we'd dance *The Continental* while the boat sailed the Atlantic Ocean to London.

Or he'd be a lover like Jon Hall where he would grab me instead of Dorothy Lamour and we'd make love right through the hurricane under the palms trees on the island of Manakura somewhere in the South Pacific.

Or like Buster Crabbe (who was a more handsome Tarzan than Johnny Weismuller), where he would grab me and swing me through the jungle and offer bananas and tropical fruits to me, his Jane, as we lay on a bed of leaves high in the forest canopy.

And, oh yes, forceful like John Wayne where he'd grab me instead of Gail Russell and pull me up onto a horse and ride us off into the sunset to Tucson.

I was the heroine in all the movies that played in my head.

Yes, Mama didn't have to worry about her cow. *I knew someday, he'd come along. The man I love. And he'd be big and strong. The man I love.*

Well, maybe not in Tonawanda.

When I voiced some of my thoughts about how much fun it would be to join the Navy and see the sea or enlist in the WAACS and see the world, Mama got one of her headaches and plopped down in the easy chair. I ended up making dinner for Daddy.

"I'd like to do something for our boys overseas," I said.

"You're doing your share. You've used up the whole month's sugar and butter quota on those cookies you made to send to your service men. Almost all of the coupons in the A, B and C ration books are gone and the month isn't up yet."

"You serve donuts at the service man's canteen in the American Legion Hall. This family may not have a son in the service but we do our part." Mama added loudly to make sure Dad got the point. "God knows I've done my part."

This was usually about the time Dad left the house to go to the corner saloon for his glass of beer. He didn't like arguments and he didn't need much of a reason to spend the evening with his fellow workers from the factory. Mama never accepted the blame for having borne only females. She was sure somehow it was Dad's fault that we had no brother and no one to defend our country at war.

She continued her lecture after Dad had left.

"Those girls are in the service for one reason. Their reputations are ruined now. Embroider your initials on those towels I bought for your hope chest. You will need them when you marry."

Mama handed me some empty cans to flatten for the junk man as every bit of tin helped to fight the Japs, the Germans Nazis and the Italians.

More and more posters appeared around town of beautiful young women in uniforms urging us twenty to thirty-five year old eligible women to join up.

Mama wouldn't discuss the possibility of my enlisting for a second. She simply didn't want to hear it. "Nice girls don't go into the service. Good girls don't leave home before marriage. Get a job in a defense factory before the war is over and depression hits this country again," she said.

I took Mama's advice.

I hated my new job from the very first day.

I applied for defense work at the Remington Paper Box Company in North Tonawanda which was across the Erie Canal, about a twenty minute walk from our house down a dirt path and across a windy bridge.

I was interviewed in a comfortable chair in a large cheerful room filled with friendly office girls who were typing at their Remington typewriters.

After I signed a contract of employment and was hired, I was shown a narrow side door that was the entrance I had to use. I was told not to go through the front doors as the office girls did because I was "factory". I had to punch a time clock whenever I arrived for work and departed at the end of the day after the whistle blew. I entered a grey dirty factory building with four floors that was to be my workplace.

Congress passed a law freezing employees to their jobs in all defense plants throughout the country for the 'Duration of the War'. It was right there in very fine print. It was a federal offense, punishable by imprisonment along with spying and treason for any defense worker to strike, quit or switch jobs.

So there I was all wrapped up in red tape in a factory which made red tape for the government. I regretted my latest move. I had traded the smell of newspapers rolling off the presses for the rancid odors of a damp factory that made paper.

Mama thought the twelve dollars raise in pay was worth it all.

"Oh, sure, they gave me a fancy title: *Running Inventory Supervisor Clerk* for the *KARDEX FILE SYSTEM*," I griped. "It's nothing but blue collar factory work. All I am is a clerk, sort of a bookkeeper. They call my pay a 'salary' so they don't have to pay me a defense worker's wage with double time and all that."

"You're getting $28.34 a week. For a girl that is good wages. Before the war a man was lucky to make that kind of money! You can put some of it away in your cedar hope chest I bought for your eighteenth birthday!"

"But Mama! The place smells bad and the walls are grey! Crossing that bridge is miserable. It's so cold and damp when the wind blows over the canal."

"You never know a good thing when you see it. Look at how you treat Big Spero. He's such a nice boy and he's always sending you chocolates. I bet he'd ask you to marry him if you gave him half a chance. He's even the same religion as us. What more do you want?"

"His family owns a candy store. That's why he sends chocolates! And he doesn't know how to dance."

I did not tell Mama what really bothered me. It was not the sort of thing you confided in a Mother. Big Spero didn't know how to kiss. He didn't know what to do with his hands. He didn't grab or hug hard. He had no experience at all with women. He was twenty-one and I was certain I had been his first date. He didn't know how to dance either. What was worse, on our last two dates, just before he left for camp, he had forgotten to put money in his pants pocket and I had to pay for the drive-in movie and the hot dogs. He didn't have a chance but I wasn't about to dampen Mama's hopes.

Every time I talked to Mama it ended up in an argument about why I wasn't married. She had a way of twisting the conversation to the same subject.

"I had two babies when I was twenty," she boasted. "When you have crying hungry babies you won't have time to go dancing," she yelled after me as I ran out the door late for my duty to serve donuts at the American Legion USO.

You might think that because I had failed Business Arithmetic in my senior year in high school that I wasn't qualified for such a position as *Running Inventory Supervisor Clerk* in a defense plant.

On the very first day I reported for work the factory foreman took me through the warehouse and introduced me to all the stock boys.

The foreman was tall and skinny who did not use deodorant and had false teeth that clicked as he talked. He told me about his wife who didn't understand him and repeated the same gossip several times about the number of girls in the factory he had been able to comfort who were lonesome for their servicemen. He explained nothing about the work I was to do.

"You'll like it here. It's a big job for a little girl but we're one big happy family. Remember, I'm here anytime. If you get lonesome, call me," he said.

He handed me some papers which had long rows of numbers on them and seals with big red letters that said *RUSH*.

"These are orders. We call them *Requisitions*. It is your job to check the balances on the cards and see that there is enough in the inventory to fill them."

"What do I do if there isn't enough to fill an order?"

"You put the slip on this pile and go on to the next one. Got it?"

Then he was gone. I never saw him after that throughout the whole day.

He showed up each morning for a few moments when he would drape his arm on my shoulder and glance over my head to see what I was writing. Once his dangling fingers hit the nipple of my breast so I got in the habit of jumping up whenever I heard his footsteps. He liked that and told me it wasn't necessary to show so much respect and that we were all in this war together and I had a good attitude but all the time I wish he'd get the flu that was going around that would keep him home for a week or two.

Although I left Remington Paper Box Company six months later, I never did find his hiding place. But then that wasn't so strange. It was easy to get lost in this dreary building.

The second and third floors of the factory were a Fun House maze of corridors, aisles, alleys and little rooms formed by large sheets of cardboard used to make boxes, huge pads of paper, tree size logs of rolled corrugated paper and aluminum sheets, from which thousands of clips were to be stamped out by the girls on the fourth floor assembly line.

I was given three small desks, one on each floor. They were squeezed into odd corners with towering stacks of cardboard boxes forming walls on three sides giving me just enough room to work in.

The old brick warehouse smelled of old railroad cars and damp paper.

The freight elevator was dirty and old, creaky slow and scary with no walls so you could see the inside of the building as it groaned up and down. I wasn't allowed to use the nice clean passenger elevator since I was "factory" so I chose instead to run up and down the gray stained wood stairs from floor to floor as I made my rounds, meeting everybody who worked in the factory along the way, all the factory workers and all the stock boys.

The color grey was painted on everything, walls, desks, chairs. The little bit of sun that managed to shine in this part of Western New York never got through the windows which were painted solid. No light penetrated in or out, because of blackout regulations. Blackout curtains stayed in place even in the daytime over the few windows that hadn't been painted. Not that the German Luftwaffe would ever get this far inland. But still we weren't taking any chances in case the Japs or Germans sent their bombers over Buffalo, the big city next to us, and hit Tonawanda instead.

My job was simple enough. I was to keep a running inventory of all the merchandise in the factory.

First I wrote figures on little black lines onto little cards. The cards were 5x7 inches and they were stuck into drawers which were all lined up in a strange looking filing cabinet that was tall and narrow. This was the nucleus of the famous *Kardex Inventory File System* which the Remington Company had invented.

I had to sit in front of this cabinet, pull out each long slim drawer and since it was hinged in a strange way it would come out straight then drop into my lap with a thud.

I hated it the first time it bounced off my chest and ended somewhere down below my belly button hitting me straight in the pelvis. I never did get used to that thud as it socked me. And I always jumped at the clanging noise it made when it fell against the cabinet even though I knew it was coming.

Next, I was supposed to look at my cards, take a few of them out of their jackets, then go to the bins or rooms and make a determination whether the balance on the cards and the items in the bins even came close enough to fill the orders in my other hand. These orders came from companies and defense factories throughout the United States who needed paper clips, folders, all kinds of office supplies, and boxes of typing paper and empty file boxes, record sheets, and just plain lined sheets of paper with three holes in them. This was all vital material.

On my shoulders, and on my shoulders alone, rested the total war effort. Unless I filled these orders, no one could keep records of anything anywhere in the whole country. My job was very important. It sort of made up for the poor pay.

The stock boys would accept the *Requisition Orders* from me and load up large flat-bed carts after which they rolled these clumsy heavy carts through a big gaping doorway to an outside platform. Each day a train would come puffing up the siding next to the factory, wait until filled, then roll away to deliver these goods to important exciting places such as the new Pentagon Building in Washington D.C., the Navy Supply Depot in Philadelphia, or to companies such as the United Steel Corporation and General Electric that had been given great big defense contracts from the government.

Although Remington Box Company was classified as a defense plant and received scarce rationed material of paper and aluminum, it wasn't a war plant such as Bell Aircraft where they were building the secret fighter plane, the *P-39 Airacobra* and where everyone was working double-time earning double pay for every extra hour over the basic forty-eight.

Still, there were posters all over the factory's walls which warned against spies and other Fifth Columnists. *"If you must talk, tell it to the Marines!"* and *"Loose Lips Sink Ships"*.

At least, my job description impressed the soldier boys I danced with.

"So you're a real Rosie the riveter?"

"No, not a riveter. I'm the *Chief Running Inventory Supervisor Clerk* for *the Kardex Inventory File System* at Remington. I'm in charge of all the red tape in the government."

That was always sure to break the ice between us every time.

I tried to quit. But the plant manager wanted to keep all the employees he could.

"You see, my dear. We are all important here," he said jiggling his chair a little closer to mine.

I tried to pull my defense skirt down a little without his noticing my awkward movement.

"Now, we'd all miss you if you left us," he said.

But I knew differently. I was one little unimportant cog in a big war machine. One unimportant screw.

So that was how the first half of the war year of 1943 went for me.

I lived my nights at the movies. I saw *"CASABLANCA"* three times. How did the movie makers know to make that picture at the same time Churchill, Roosevelt and Stalin met in that city? It mystified many of us and was a topic of conversation for weeks.

Tunis fell in May and there were more pictures and stories in TIME and LIFE magazine of tired happy and victorious soldiers, British, Americans, Australians.

Every newsreel at the beginning of every movie showed our B-17's bombing factories in Germany. How could there be anything left standing in those German cities? Surely the war would be over soon.

Victorious Marines had kicked the Japs off Guadalcanal, which was an island somewhere in the Pacific Ocean and had begun fighting on another island called Bougainville. It was very difficult keeping all these battles or these islands straight. We didn't even have a map of the islands of the South Pacific in our Tonawanda library.

The frustration of my job at the factory subtracting five figure numbers from six figure numbers began to take its toll on me. I worried as the war progressed and the pile of orders that couldn't be filled no matter what the balance showed on the cards grew higher and higher. Even orders with red stickers of *A-1 PRIORITY* or *URGENT* or *TOP SECRET* that were to be shipped first, straight to vital military installations and defense factories didn't get filled after a while.

The stock boys no longer consulted the files before filling the orders. They began to answer any inquiry about orders labeled *Priority* with a shrug. "Ask Terry. No use looking at her records. She's the only one who can read them."

Secretly, I must admit I could not always read my own writing either but it was good to have their confidence in my work.

Being an important cog in the war effort should have been satisfying for me but it wasn't enough to quell the stirrings of patriotism all the songs, the movies, the posters and newsreels were awakening in me.

On those mornings when I overslept and punched the time clock late, I'd catch myself singing words to British War songs as I ran to work that lingered all day.

"When the lights go on again, all over the world..."

"There'll be bluebirds over the White Cliffs of Dover..."

"We'll meet again, don't know where, don't know when..."

"Praise the Lord and pass the ammunition, Praise the Lord and pass the ammunition..."

At night, as I crossed the bridge back to Tonawanda, as twilight turned into night, the tunes in my head would switch to lonesome ballads.

"I'll walk alone, and if they ask me, I'll tell them I'd rather. I don't mind being lonely..."

"When the deep purple falls, over sleepy garden walls..."

"It had to be you, it had to be you. I wandered around and finally found somebody who could make me be true, could make me feel blue just thinking of you. It had to be you, it had to be you..."

I was scrupulous about staying after hours in the factory to make up for my tardiness and to catch up on my posting. I wasn't alone because there was the night shift on the fourth floor and a skeleton crew on the warehouse floor. Since I was classified as factory, I could get in and do my office work anytime as long as I punched the time-clock.

Besides, that was the only time I could phone my friends as we had no phone at home. Now that my family could finally afford a telephone, we couldn't get one. No private phones were being installed until the end of the duration.

Everyday, I made my rounds, greeting everybody with the *V for Victory* sign with my forefinger and middle finger if I didn't have time to chat.

I had made friends with a few of the girls from the factory pool on the fourth floor with whom I shared my half hour lunch breaks.

Those friendly looking girls in the office that smiled at me the day of my application weren't so friendly after all. To them, I was classified as 'factory' and 'office' didn't fraternize with 'factory'.

They should have seen what was left of my pay check after all the with-holding was subtracted—$2.70 for tax, 75 cents for health insurance, 28 cents for Social Security, fifty cents for the Red Cross fund and $5.00 for a Victory Bond, buying one a month. That wasn't bad for an unmarried girl. But having to contribute fifty cents for a shower gift every time a girl got engaged or pregnant became a burden since there were at least 400 girls in this factory, most of whom I didn't even know and a lot I didn't like.

The stock boys still gathered daily for their coffee and cigarette breaks away from the 'No Smoking' signs. They usually hid in one of the numerous aisles made by the towering rows of various paper goods.

One of them stuck his head beyond the bins and whistled as I went by. I didn't mind one bit. It was all clean fun and they were either too young or too old.

"Meet cha in No. 5," called Louie who was scrawny with no chest. He had broken his engagement to a sweet little Polish girl named Leucadia who worked on the stamping machine that made grommets out of aluminum. He had discovered that getting married wouldn't defer him from being drafted so he decided to play the field.

I tried to tell Leucadia how lucky she was but she didn't listen and insisted on moping out in the open where Louie could see her long face and red eyes. Now he considered himself quite a lady-killer, even making a half-hearted play for me. That was the sad part of this whole war. So many drips and jerks were catching girls who wouldn't have looked at them twice if there were any real men around.

The whole factory knew I wanted my release.

"Don't vorry, Babushka," said old man Petronsky, who was too old to be a stock boy but couldn't quit because the company didn't have a retirement plan. "A purty gel like you, get married, no more trouble wit bosses. The Bolshevik will come and Uncle Joe make us all straw bosses."

That was always the time the senior man in the group would break them up and shoo them back to work. He always became nervous when Petronsky talked about the Russians. He still didn't trust the Commies, although personally I never met one in Tonawanda.

Stalin had switched sides after Hitler had broken their pact and attacked Russia. Hitler had conquered all the other countries to the west and south of Germany and did the same sneaky thing to the Russians that the Japs had done to us.

Supposedly the Communists were now our allies. President Roosevelt had added Stalin's Russia to the list of countries that America's Lend-lease program was assisting. They received food, guns and war material from us just as England did.

Russia may be at war with Germany but Stalin still hadn't declared war on Japan, the country that was our enemy in the Pacific. If Russia were really our ally, you'd think they'd go all the way as we had done for Great Britain.

With over fifty countries at war with each other, it was sometimes hard to keep track who was friend and who was foe. Nobody trusted Russia. It was full of *pinkoes* and *Commies*. We Americans had to be careful about the Communists.

Our government worried most over the German sympathizers that lived in our country. Warnings posters about the Fifth Column among us were on walls everywhere, on buses, street cars, and trucks and in public places. We were warned constantly to watch out for these sinister spies who listened for any piece of information that could be transmitted straight to Hitler by secret radios that could be hidden anywhere.

Who were they? Where were they these Fifth Columnists?

They were all around us.

Some of these subversives could be our German born friends and neighbors who might have been members of the German-American Bund before our government made it an Act of Treason to belong to the Bund when we went to war against Germany. These were the American Nazis. Those who had been officers and members were easily identified and arrested and separated from the general population and put into a camp.

But, not all of the American Nazi Bundists had been taken away by Federal agents. German-Americans looked like us and could hide their origin more easily than the Japanese whose skin color and slanted eyes gave them away.

Nobody really worried about the Italians here or there. In July 1943, Mussolini was deposed by the Italian people. Roosevelt appealed to the Italians to surrender. Italian soldiers did give up in droves when Sicily capitulated. The Italian soldiers weren't fanatics or very good soldiers and they had not put up the same kind of fight the fanatic Germans did. Newsreels showed them with their hands folded on top of their heads as Americans stood casually next to them holding their guns. They didn't look fearsome; they grinned happily at the camera and their obvious relief at being captured invited ridicule and pity.

But the Jap was different. He looked dangerous and hateful. It was easy to hate the Japs. Our fear extended itself and encompassed the Japanese families that had been living around us. When the Federal Government passed a law that forced all Japanese to move to internment camps most Americans, who didn't know any Japanese people personally, were relieved. There could be spies among them. They looked like the enemy and had the same slanted eyes.

Few people tried to challenge the policies of the Federal Government. Anybody who asked the question how could the government jail American citizens and their whole families, including children who had been born in this country, who had done nothing, wasn't heard. We were at war! We were fighting to save our country.

The Town Council called a meeting on what to do about our only Japanese family in Tonawanda, Mr. and Mrs. Yamada and their children. They owned a little farm and always grew the best tomatoes which they sold from a little hut, by the side of the road near the old airport, on the way to Buffalo. But Federal agents showed up one day and made the family pack up as much as they could carry. After they left, one of the councilmen bought their land for a hundred dollars which was cheap.

The agents also questioned my classmate Jennie Chang's father, who owned the Peking Family Restaurant where you could get great hot dogs for ten cents and roast pork dinners as well as delicious hot spicy Chinese food that Mrs. Chang cooked which took the roof off your mouth. It looked like trouble for them, until the very same councilman who bought Yamada's farm intervened in Mr. Chang's behalf. After that he ate in Mr. Chang's restaurant all the time for free. You see, anyone looking Oriental was suspected of espionage and had to prove he wasn't a Jap. All Orientals looked alike but it was best to be Chinese, since China was one of our Allies. China had declared war on Japan and Germany two days after Pearl Harbor. Chiang Kai Shek, their famous general, was fighting and killing Japs as we were.

Theresa Karas Yianilos

Recruited In Buffalo–September 1943

Autumn falls gently in Western New York. September nights usually give slight warning of the chill that will follow. The days are warm and glowing and the gold and red in the leaves of the birches and maples lulls a person into a general sense of well-being. It is a season that is known as our Indian summer. On such a rare lovely day the goddess of fate stepped into my life, spun me around and set me on a new path.

I had gone to Buffalo to shop in the middle of the week. I reported in sick which was just a little white lie since I really did have a tickle in my throat.

I also had *V-letters* to mail to all the boys I was corresponding with overseas. I preferred to write my letters on blue stationery doused in cologne but all letters going overseas had to be written on those dehydrated impersonal *V-forms* put out by the Federal government. The censors opened all letters, read them first and photographed each page and reduced it to a 4 x 5 inch black and gray picture that was difficult to read. I had to be very careful what I wrote; anything considered classified information would be blacked out. Warm romantic words were acceptable and I became an expert at saying *"I miss you"* and *"Wish you were home to get hugged"* twenty different ways.

But decoding a serviceman's V-letters was no fun at all. When I received *V-mail* from my soldier pen-pals who were overseas, half of the sentences and sometimes whole paragraphs were blackened out. What if one of the cut out spaces had been a proposal? I'd never know! No wonder my romances were going nowhere. I comforted myself with the thought that at least I wasn't married to a stamp and envelope as some of the women whose husbands had been overseas for two years fighting in North Africa, in Sicily, in Guadalcanal and the South Pacific, or worse, a prisoner of war in Germany or in the Philippines.

As I entered the Five and Dime store to buy talcum powder as a substitute for my favorite cologne which had become another war casualty, I saw two young women magnificently dressed in hunter green suits that were uniforms of some kind. They breezed briskly past me, laughing and chatting, oblivious to all the admiring and curious glances from other customers and clerks who had stopped in the midst of their transactions to stare after them.

Recruiting Posters 1943
United States Marine Corps Women's Reserve

*Recruiting Poster World War I,
September 1918*

Women Reservists "Marinettes" being
sworn in two months before the
Armistice in WWI.

They were beautiful. Their matching hats were trimmed with red cord and cute bronze bird pins and they looked stunning. Chic brown kid gloves and pumps with a flat bow and a fine quality leather shoulder bag hanging from their shoulders completed their charming outfits. They were in the height of New York city fashion, from their rayon stockings to their short skirts hitting just at the knee cap. One girl had three red V-shaped braid decorations on her left arm. The other girl had only two of these colorful accents.

I hurried to catch up with them and stopped them just outside the door. "May I ask what you girls are?"

"Marines! Women's Reserve, United States Marine Corps," they said in unison and kept walking.

At last I knew how to help my country! This was it. My country called. I had to be a Marine!

"What does it take to join? I want to join," I said eagerly.

The one with the three stripes seemed bored, as if she had heard the question many times before. She said, "You don't look old enough."

The other Woman Marine rattled off very quickly the words as if she knew them by heart.

"You have to be twenty years old, a United States citizen, have good vision and teeth, two years of high school for enlisted. College for officers. Not less than sixty inches—that's five feet—and not less than ninety-five pounds.

"You won't be taken if you're married to any Marine, or if you're married to an officer in the Navy, or if you have children under eighteen."

I wasn't married to anybody

"I want to join." I repeated. "Where do I go?"

"Why don't you go home and think about it a little bit?" said the sergeant, for that's what the girl with the three stripes was.

The corporal, the girl with the two stripes said, "The Marines don't take everybody. You may be disappointed."

"Yes. Go home and think about it a couple of days," agreed the sergeant.

That's how I met the Buffalo Recruiting Sergeant for the Women's Reserve of the United States Marine Corps in the month of September 1943. She didn't seem anxious to snap me up.

I was left standing there alone. I watched them walk away lost in a camaraderie I longed to share.

I didn't feel like shopping anymore so I went to mail the V-letters. I suppose I might have forgotten the whole incident but for the old Customs building in Buffalo that housed the Post Office. It had many corridors lined with doors. I turned down the wrong corridor or perhaps I was guided by my protector, the Greek goddess of fate whom I knew very well. She could be blamed for a lot of things that happened to me, not only on that day but, thereafter.

There, at the end of the hall, propped up against the wall, stood a full sized picture of a tall handsome dark haired man in a beautiful blue jacket with bright red trimming and glorious California-sunset blue trousers with a red stripe running down one side.

Above his head was the motto:

"The United States Marines Builds Men."

On the door were lettered the words

"United States Marine Corps - Recruiting Sub Station - Room 502."

The door was ajar. Inside the room were three Marines dressed exactly like the man in the poster. In a corner dominating the room was a flag of the United States.

On the wall was another poster of a lovely girl in the same deep green visored hat which was trimmed with a scarlet cord. She was wearing a dedicated smile. Underneath her necktie were the words:

"Be A Marine...Free A Marine To Fight"

It wasn't to be that easy.

Filling out the application and taking the aptitude test was simple enough. After all, I was an educated woman. I had a high school diploma. Even the personal interview with the officer presented no problem.

They asked for a physical statement from the family physician after giving me a physical examination, where they checked my eyes, ears and the rest of me. I didn't know how I was going to get that piece of paper from old Doctor Fairbanks of the record of my childhood diseases when he'd be sure to tell Mama the minute I asked for it, but, I'd think of something.

The following week I was able to complete all my tests at the old Custom House along with thirty or forty women. These sessions included having a complete physical and having to fill out a two hour psychological questionnaire where I had to answer questions about who hated me and whom I hated. It was quite obvious that some of them were trick questions. There were at least four hundred items to answer and not enough time to even think about them.

I expected they would outfit me immediately in one of those smart uniforms and send me home to say good-bye to my family. In my mind's eye, I had it all planned. I'd be so patriotically beautiful that Mama and Daddy would be thrilled speechless.

Instead, the sergeant said, "Go home! Wait until you're notified! Do nothing until you hear from us."

One of the Marines said, "Don't call us. We'll call you."

Two weeks went by; still no word from the Marine Corps. Four weeks crawled by with my heart leap-frogging over its own beats every time I intercepted the post man.

Finally, six weeks later my application was processed by Marine Headquarters in Arlington, Virginia, and the F.B.I. cleared me. What a relief to discover I was mentally sound, physically fit and had eyesight, teeth and hearing good enough for the United States Marine Corps Women's Reserve.

The day finally dawned and I sneaked off to Buffalo alone to pledge my troth to my country.

I stood next to the American flag with my right hand up before me and my other hand over my pounding heart repeating the words of the Marine Lieutenant:

"I do solemnly swear or affirm that I will bear true faith and allegiance to the United States of America; that I will serve them honestly and faithfully against all their enemies whomsoever; and that I will obey the orders of the President of the United States and the orders of the officers appointed over me, according to regulations and the uniform code of military Justice."

Tears filled my eyes as the Marine Lieutenant shook my hand and handed me an Identity Card which read:

This is to certify that
THERESA KARAS, PRIVATE is a member
*   of Class III 9d*
U.S. MARINE CORPS RESERVE
From 4 Nov. 1943 to DURATION PLUS 6
*   MONTHS"*

I was a MARINE! Well, not quite. The lieutenant gave me some papers and told me to go home again.

I was now on *"Inactive duty, awaiting traveling orders to Boot Camp."*

I was not given the uniform I had been expecting.

Now to tell Mama I was a Marine. I didn't look like one. I was still dressed in my pleated Stewart clan plaid skirt, sloppy Joe sweater, 36 inch pearl necklace, saddle shoes and bobby socks!

I dashed through the back door and it slammed hard before I could catch it. Daddy hadn't been able to get parts to fix the spring so even a burglar would have had trouble getting into the house unannounced.

Mama looked up from another box of chocolates that had arrived. She had been pushing the centers in to find the soft ones. Her mouth was full.

"Did you finally buy what you wanted in Buffalo? That was your fifth trip this month."

I gave her my Identification Card.

Mama didn't seem to understand. She turned the card upside down and over, smearing some chocolate on it, then she read it again.

"Where in the Lord's name did you get this?" She yelled.

"Mama, you are looking at a *Marine!*"

When she understood, her face clouded. "It wasn't enough that I ran a USO here in this house practically with you dragging in every service man you met. Now you have to join this—to service— every—ohhh!" She sat down and reached for her apron.

Dad said, "Sam Barrows, my supervisor head at the factory, has got some pull at the draft board. He'll get her out."

Mama brightened. "Do you think so? How could she do this to us? Respectable girls from good families don't join the army."

"Lots of girls have joined up. Little Maria Meliano who was a sophomore when I was a senior is now a sergeant in the WAACs and she's overseas in London now." I was defending myself but this was not the way it was supposed to turn out.

Mama didn't answer me. She continued to direct her conversation to Dad.

"They have to do something after what their relatives in Italy are doing to our boys," Mama sniffed scornfully. She had her own set of standards of who was her social equal.

"Mama! The Marines need women!"

"I bet they need women! But you're a girl not a woman!" She turned to Dad and cried louder, "She'll come home *pregnant!* Do you hear me? *Pregnant!* We'll never be able to hold our heads high ever again in Tonawanda!"

Later that evening at the corner saloon Dad treated his boss, Sam to a *Boilermaker*, that is a shot of whiskey with a beer chaser, while he told him about the family problem. But it turned out that Dad had wasted his money. Sam couldn't help. Sam couldn't get me out even if he wanted to, which he didn't, because I had done a very patriotic thing. He told him I now belonged to the Marine Corps for the *Duration and Six Months* and I was of legal age having passed my twenty first birthday and he couldn't do a thing about it.

"It's too late, Mama," Dad said. "We've lost our little girl."

Mama didn't cook supper that night and no one talked. Dad drank several cups of stale coffee. My little sisters went to bed without saying a word.

Once you're in the Marine Corps, nothing but nothing can get you out. I felt so safe, secure and warm in the blanket of the flag of my country. I belonged to the government and all of Mama's screaming and yelling couldn't get me out. I was going to fight for my country or at least, I was going off to war *To Free A Marine To Fight,* which was the next best thing since I was a female and couldn't get into combat.

The next day, Henry Martin came over. He used to be the pimply faced kid next door but he joined when he was seventeen and was now an eighteen year old salty sailor home on leave.

"I hear you went and joined. What made you do it?"

"You did too," I reminded him.

"When they were breathing down my neck and I was sure the draft was gonna get me. I thought the Navy would be the safest place to be in. I sure as hell didn't want to be drafted into the Marine Corps. Those *Gyrenes* are getting killed every day in the Pacific. That's not for me."

Henry was wounded while on duty at San Diego, one of our outlying naval bases on the shores of the Pacific Ocean. He got hit by a car while hitch-hiking on a dark rainy night on Pacific Highway. He was returning back to base after he had gotten a tattoo in one of the parlors on Broadway Street. Now he was home on a thirty day leave.

We sat on the front steps just like the good old days.

"Say, Kid," he said in a big brotherly fashion although he was younger than I. "Remember the time your mother said you were too young to date and I sneaked you out the window to go see Gene Krupa and Benny Goodman playing at Crystal Beach?"

I laughed at the memory.

"Say, Kid," he said, "remember the time you wanted to go see that stage play in Buffalo at the Erlanger Theater with your class and your mother wouldn't let you go unless she could be one of the chaperones? Didn't I talk her out of it?"

I remembered and relived the embarrassment of that incident all over again for a moment.

"Uh, since you're stuck in the Marines, I might as well let you have the benefit of my experience." A thought just struck him. "Hell! The Marines! Why didn't you pick the Navy?"

"I'm going to free a Marine to fight. They're first on land and on sea."

"Well, it's too late to tell you never volunteer for anything. I might as well give you the word!"

"The word?"

"You're going to have to learn to talk Navy. It's a whole different language. So you won't buy any sea-going Leatherneck's snow job."

Henry had a lot of experience in his eight months at San Diego which was so far away from Tonawanda it took five days by train or seven days by bus to get there.

"I've never met any service women. Is it like joining a sorority? Are they friendly?"

"The broads in San Diego that I met on C Street and Market Street are very accommodating." Henry smiled as he chewed on a memory.

I waited.

"Oh, you mean WAACS and WAVES? I never got to know any of that kind. A dame in a uniform? Hell! Who needs her!"

Sometimes Henry made me mad. This was one of those times. "Listen, Squirtball!" I used his ten year old nickname that he hated. "I am not going to run wild as Mama fears just because I will be living alone. I know that there is a percentage of bums in every step of life, but I bet they are not Marines!"

Henry leaned over and said in a low voice, "Did you ever hear of *Spanish Fly*? No? It's a drug that the guys smuggle into the country and the sailors sneak it into a girl's beer—"

"I don't drink beer," I interrupted.

"Into a girl's Coca-Cola." Henry continued. "It's tasteless and once she takes a sip. It makes her wild. She gets hot. She's got to have *it!*" He leaned back and watched my reaction to his words.

Didn't bother me. The solution was obvious. "I'll never drink Coca-Cola from a glass," I promised. "I'll drink it only straight from a bottle."

Henry said, "Lights out. Time to go in."

Mama opened the door and said, "Did you talk to her?"

Henry said, "I'm not sure." He went home to the house next door.

The girls at the factory were thrilled to learn the Marines had accepted me. The news spread like wildfire from the office to the fourth floor.

Everyone knew how particular the United States Marine Corps was; they didn't accept just any body that walked into the recruiting offices. Only the creme de la creme, the elite got in. I was now one of the few and I was so proud!

The plant manager pumped my hand up and down and patted my back hard as if I had the hiccups. He was being such a good sport about losing me. "So you're going to the *Devil Dogs?*" he said, which is what they called the Marines in his day in World War I.

"Yes, Sir. It's the best fighting outfit in the world, you know," I said proudly, holding my release for him to sign. He could have prevented me from going into the Corps by writing *"with prejudice"* on my release form since I was a defense worker. I was grateful that he hadn't done that.

"They are going to have to be," he said, smiling.

I smiled too. I had cleared the last obstacle to going into the Marines and had the signed release in my hand. My moment of anxiety was over.

I smiled at the girls in the office for the last time and walked out with my head held very high and proud. I wouldn't have lunch with them now even if they asked me.

The girls from the whole third and fourth floor assembly line went around collecting for a gift for me in my behalf. They chipped in on a going away present just as they did for the girls who were going to be married for whom they always gave a shower. They grinned as I gasped at the monogrammed stationary set with the real leather cover and the embossed insignia of the Marine Corps: an eagle clutching a globe with an anchor piercing right through the middle of North and South America.

The card said, "Use ink. Roosevelt needs the lead."

Inside the case was another present and I squealed with delight. "Where did you ever find a new pen?" Fountain pens had disappeared with the war because the rubber tubes inside that held the ink and the gold on the pen points were unavailable.

"Where else? Black market. It wasn't easy."

They were sad that I would be leaving them. We knew I would never be going back to Remington. I would probably never see any of them again. I was going to war and they weren't. And I was happy about that most of all.

They threw a wing ding of a going away party for me that was better than any wedding or baby shower. They took me to the most exclusive night club in Buffalo, the *Chez Ami,* where famous stars entertained. My boy-friends weren't the kind that went to such places. It was too expensive. An evening there could cost up to ten dollars for two.

The black and silver decor was very elegant and there was a cover charge just to get inside the club. I saw one of the girls sneak two dollars to the man in a tuxedo just to show us to our table.

Girls in short ballerina black skirts wearing little tables around their waists walked around selling cigarettes and gardenia corsages. A photographer snapped the eight of us as we sat around a ringside table next to the dance floor, where the man had put us, practically on top of the performers. We held up our glasses in a toast and smiled for the camera.

Just when the flashbulbs went off, the orchestra played a few bars of the Marine Corps Hymn. Just like that.

The master of ceremonies interrupted the music and announced, "Let's have a hand for this little girl! She is leaving for the Marines. How about that, ladies and gentlemen? Isn't she a pretty *Lady Leatherneck?*"

I gulped my rum and Coca-Cola so fast that m
in a squeak. "Not Lady Leatherneck! Woman *Mar*
sit down, embarrassed at being dragged to standii
"Whoops! Folks! The little lady says she's i
apologized elaborately. The crowded nightclub cla
enthusiastically.

"Woman Marine! Not Marinette!" I protested weakly but no one heard me in that din.

November passed by and December rolled in. Buffalo and Tonawanda were hit with two crippling snow storms that had closed down the schools and brought the city to a standstill for the usual three or four days. The kids loved it. Mothers and shop keepers didn't.

Still I waited for my traveling orders. The Marine Corps didn't seem to need me as desperately as the posters claimed.

The newspapers were filled with the brave exploits of the Marines in the South Pacific. They had captured Guadalcanal, New Georgia and the Central Solomons Islands. And now they had another victory on Tarawa Island in the Gilberts. When Mama saw the newsreel of that bloody battle and all the dead Marines and Japs, she turned silent. She never said another word.

I was afraid the Marines would win the war before I had a chance to do my part. That's what happened to the women reservists, those *Marinettes*, who joined the Marines in the First World War. They were inducted in September 1918 and two months later, in November, the Armistice was declared. Sure, they stayed for a year after the war doing the paper work of demobilization but it wasn't the same as actually helping to win World War One.

As the weeks rolled by and I heard nothing more, Mama relaxed a little, thinking Sam had used his pull at the draft board and had gotten my enlistment deferred or canceled.

Christmas was upon us and every radio station played Bing Crosby's record of WHITE CHRISTMAS incessantly over and over until I wanted to scream. Was I the only one left who couldn't stand to hear that song one more time?

"I'm dreaming of a white Christmas, just like the ones I used to know.
Where the tree tops glisten and children listen to sleigh bells in the snow...."

I was still in Tonawanda, still working at Remington, braving the cold windy walk across the bridge over the Erie Canal, dreaming of Spanish moss, cotton fields and warm sunny North Carolina and Camp Lejeune where I was to get my Boot Camp training. I lived with the thought that I may be lucky enough to be sent to San Diego, to Camp Pendleton in warm Southern California.

Several of my soldiers and sailors pen pals came home for the holidays. I saw a couple of the same movies twice and sat through HOLIDAY INN three times and listened to Bing Crosby sing his big hit, WHITE CHRISTMAS with Bob Crosby and his orchestra.

We held hands in the dark and they came out whistling that song. Each one said to me, "That will be *our* song. I'll think of you whenever I hear it!"

We went roller skating, drank sodas at the Rexall Drug Store, dropped nickels in the Wurlitzer juke box and danced at the American Legion Hall. We went to high school basketball games and Tonawanda lost to North Tonawanda again. I added a silver locket, an identification bracelet and a sterling silver anklet to my collection, kissed each one of them good-bye at the bus stop with the promise I would keep up the letter writing.

Big Spero came home for a seven day Christmas furlough just when another big blizzard hit. Mama greeted him as if he were her son-in-law and offered him all of her precious powdered sugared Greek wedding cookies she doled out to special guests.

He had lost a little weight but hadn't changed at all.

His manners towards Mama were formal and he used the words "Please" and "Thank you" with frequent regularity.

His politeness was another reason Mama considered him a good catch. His good breeding showed. After all wasn't his mother the president of the Ladies Aid Society and his father the richest man of all the members in our church who could count the mayor of Buffalo and two Municipal judges among his friends?

Spero was just too polite and he would have been stuck on Mama's couch all night if I hadn't grabbed his hand and made him go out into the howling wind with me.

Army life had been good to him. He had been transferred out of the Cavalry into ASTP, the *Army Specialist Training Program*, and had been sent to the University of Chicago. He had a room in the

36

dormitory that he shared with four other guys. Three ample meals a day were served to him by waiters in a dining room. Life in the military sounded great and I couldn't wait until I left for the Marine Corps.

Despite Spero's warm loving letters, he was reticent about kissing me or hugging me if there was a chance someone would see us. I waited for him to make the first move. Just as he moved towards me to give me a hug, Mama pushed the lace curtain aside to see if we had driven away. Spero stayed on his side of the truck.

"I sure missed you, Half Pint. It's so great to be back in Buffalo. Boy, do I miss home and you!"

"You missed Buffalo? You missed this snow?" That was incredible to me.

My teeth chattered and my nose ran with the cold. The heater in the ice cream truck was broken.

It was just too freezing to sit in the ice-cream truck to do anything, either to talk or to neck. Our breath turned to ice in front of our eyes.

He drove around the corner to the Rexall Drug Store where we planned to sit in the booths but the druggist was locking the front doors. He had closed early because of the storm.

He said, "Go home, kids." Then he saw Spero's uniform and apologized, "Sorry, Soldier. No one's out in this weather. We haven't had a customer all night."

We parked on one of the side streets and Spero made small talk about his new assignment. I didn't want to hear about his "Army" life and about people I didn't know. I wanted to hear about "us" and how much he cared for me, and how I was the only girl—the usual kind of sweet words that made dating so much fun. Spero did not flirt. He weighed his words as if they cost money.

So I followed the rules a girl had to remember when she was out with a man. The list was endless. Some had come from Mama. Others were just plain common sense that every girl should know.

Look interested in what interests *him*.!

Be a good listener! Let *him* talk!

Let *him* lead even if you are the better dancer!

Never call *him* up first. Wait for *him* to telephone!

Let *him* make the first move!

Don't be too anxious!

Always be agreeable!

Never let *him* think you are smarter than he!

Don't look bored!
Don't order the most expensive item on the menu!
A lady doesn't talk with her mouth full.
Never let *him* kiss you on the first date!
Keep your knees together!
Be in your own bed before midnight!
A man only wants one thing. Never give him *that!*
Always carry two dollars in your bra so you can get home.

"Your new assignment sounds too good to be true." I said. *Show interest in his work.*

"Sure you want to hear about it?" said Spero.

"Tell me all about it," I said. *Let him talk.*

"We wear uniforms during the week, but when we go off campus on liberty we have to take them off and wear civilian clothes. We can't tell anyone what we are doing. You know. Loose lips sink ships!"

"What are you doing?" *Be a good listener.*

"Me and ten other guys do problems in calculus and we do integrals. We're all college students who have been drafted. We've all had mathematics, physics and chemistry. We work out the same problems and then hand them in to our profs, Dr. Enrico Fermi and Dr. Leo Szilard. They have heavy accents. I can barely understand their instructions. But they don't say much. "

"What grades do you get?"

"That is what is so different from the schools I've been to. They don't grade us and don't give the papers back. It's solving the problems that is important."

"What are you working on?" *Never look bored. Ask questions.*

"Don't know. But it can't be too important. We have a lot of time on our hands and we play handball in the squash courts behind the stadium at Stagg Field. Dr. Fermi and Dr. Szilard have a project going in one of the courts at the far end. There are two guards posted at all times but they don't carry guns and when it gets below freezing in Chicago, they wear old raccoon coats. It's not G.I. like it was in the Cavalry."

I could use a raccoon coat myself. I turned on the heater and a blast of cold air came out. I turned it off quickly. My lips were chapped. Spero hated heavy red lips so I had applied lipstick on very lightly and now they felt worse since I didn't have the usual layer of protection. My lips started to go numb. My feet were frozen and stiff and my toes curled inside my heavy socks and saddle shoes.

I waited for Spero to grab me and take me in his arms. *Never kiss on the first date.*

"Our profs are working on something in that court. They usually leave the door open when they go in there and we can see there's nothing in the room but a pile of graphite bricks. The profs come out black and dirty after they work with that stuff. Their clothes, bodies, hair, everything, all black. That stuff is slippery too."

Who cares? I was bored with this conversation.

Dumb me! I finally caught on. Big Spero was shy and maybe a little afraid of me. After all, it had been over a year ago when we had dated last and necked at Mayor's Park. It was one thing to write of love and another to face it. The dope wasn't going to make the first move.

If I waited much longer for him to show me affection, I would turn into a frozen statue carved out of ice. I finally leaned over and grabbed him, took him in my arms and gave him a hug and a long kiss. It was about time and long overdue. He had wasted a half hour while I turned blue before his eyes.

Spero responded with gratitude and kissed me again and again. The dam of well-bred reserve had broken.

We shivered for about twenty minutes despite the heavy layers of clothes both of us were wearing as the wind howled and the snow piled up on the windshield. Then I kissed him good-bye and Spero drove home to his family.

I jumped into my flannel nightgown and into bed with a book about jungles titled "TYPEE' by Herman Melville who wrote about his adventures with the cannibals in the Marquesas Islands in the South Pacific.

Too bad the Marine Corps didn't send the Women Marines overseas. I would have loved visiting tropical islands and walking through tropical forests filled with palm trees and colorful parrots.

Spero came over once more after that as the storm of the century blanketed Buffalo. If he couldn't negotiate the ten miles of sleet and ice and twelve foot high banks of snow from Buffalo to Tonawanda, how did he expect to win me?

I did see him at church but he was flanked on either side by his stern father, the patriarch of their family clan and by his equally somber mother, the matriarch. She caught the looks that passed between us. Spero's obvious delight in seeing me seemed to annoy her. Her face did not change expression when my eyes met hers. I smiled and looked away. Since I had never spoken to her, she had no reason to dislike me until I remembered what I had done that might have displeased her.

The whole congregation knew I had joined the military. The men and boys who had answered their country's call, whether drafted, or volunteered, were considered patriotic, brave, heroic, and sacrificial. Some would probably be laying down their lives to save our democratic freedoms from the marauding Japs and Nazis.

By joining the Marine Corps, I had placed myself in the category of a camp follower and my reputation as a good girl had suffered.

The Ladies Aid Society knitted stockings, mittens, scarves and sweaters for the boys in the Armed Forces, not the girls. I knew I wouldn't be getting any Red Cross packages or home-made brownies from that group of charitable ladies.

My poor Mama. No wonder she cried a lot. She wanted to join that group. I probably ruined her chances of getting an invitation.

Spero's courtship manners left a lot to be desired. So was his choice of a Christmas gift for me. He gave me a record album of seventy-eights, with all the songs from the movie HOLIDAY INN, starring Bing Crosby, Fred Astaire and Bob Crosby and his Orchestra.

"*Our* song WHITE CHRISTMAS is in it," he said romantically.

My heart fell as he handed me the large package. I had expected a much smaller gift. From the number of times he had signed 'Love and Kisses' in his lonely letters, I had every right to think it might have been a sparkling ring. The thought of Mama's face when she would see the record album gave me the giggles.

"I knew it would please you," Spero said.

"I don't have a record player," I said.

"Oh, I'll get that for you by next year," he said.

The manufacture of all small appliances, including record players, had been suspended until after the war. Aluminum and steel had gone to war. I hadn't seen a record player, a toaster, a can opener nor even knives in any of the stores, much less something as big as a record player since the war began. Spero had forgotten what it was like to be a civilian. The Army took care of everything for him and gave him all he needed, food, clothes, cigarettes, a room, books, a lamp, schooling, whatever.

The way he took me for granted, as if there would be a next year for us, suddenly irritated me immensely. It would serve him right if I let him know that he wasn't the only opportunity in my life. He deserved to be made jealous.

"Do you know there are ten thousand, no, twenty thousand Marines to every Woman Marine? How do you feel about my joining the Marines?" I needled.

" That's okay. I trust you. I'm proud you joined. I told all my buddies my girl is a Marine."

I couldn't resist giving him fair warning. "Oh! I wouldn't be too sure if I were you." My disappointment was keener than I had anticipated and that surprised me. I expected a different kind of response and it bothered me that he didn't feel one pang of proprietary protection nor jealousy.

When I returned from our date on Christmas eve, Mama wanted to know what I had received as a Christmas present from Spero.

"Here, throw this in the Hope Chest you bought for me!"

She was more disappointed than I. Her plans for me had gone awry.

"He should have given you a ring. Then you would have stayed home, filled up your Hope Chest with linens and when he came back from the Army you could marry and start a family. Maybe I should talk to him."

She still didn't understand that I was now a Marine and belonged to my country and to the United States government for which it stands. The Corps could come and get me anytime, whether I was wearing a ring or not.

I checked in frequently with the Recruiting Sergeant, who was the very same Marine I had bumped into the Five and Dime store months before. She explained to me the reasons for the delay.

"You are just plain lucky to have gotten in when you did, Private Karas," she said. "Response to recruiting for the Women's Reserve has been so overwhelming throughout the United States that the quota of fifteen thousand, of whom you are only one, has been reached three months ahead of projections. Enlistment is going to be closed soon. You are going to Camp Lejeune, the new Recruit

Depot for women in New River, North Carolina. That is where our Fleet Marine Forces are training also," she told me.

"I'm ready to go now," I said.

"Your turn will come soon. They are graduating five hundred and fifty women every five and a half weeks. When they are through with you at Boot Camp, you will be a real Marine, not just a woman in uniform. You are classified as III 9d."

"What does that mean?"

"The Marine Corps has classified the appropriateness of jobs in respect to women's capabilities.

Class I denotes those jobs in which women are better and more efficient than men such as clerical and administrative, the fairly routine tasks.

Class II, is where women are good as men, one-to-one, like those assigned in Post Exchange, messengers, tailors and those women with technical dexterity.

You are *Class III*. That means you're going to be put in a job where women are not as good as men but since you are needed because this is wartime, you may be given Motor Transport and drive a truck or bus."

"I can't drive."

"I'm sure your officers will find something that isn't strenuous or physically tiring. You're *Class III*. That's a good spot to be in. You are expected to do whatever you are assigned cheerfully even if it is a duty you may not like."

"Is there more?"

"Sure, we have *Class IV*, but that is for jobs where women should not be used at all. That's combat and other heavy stuff."

The officer came over smiling and said, "We are assembling a whole group of you to form a *Buffalo Platoon*. You will leave with your neighbors. You will train together and represent your own home town as one unit. You will be with your own friends in your own home-town platoon."

"But I'm from Tonawanda. I don't know anybody from Buffalo. So take me now."

Here was my first order and I found myself objecting to what the Marine Corps had decided for me. The idea of being stuck with girls only from Buffalo didn't appeal to me one bit. I had been looking forward to meeting girls from all over the United States.

"You'll be trained at Boot Camp together and then assigned individually after the six week training period is over," the lieutenant continued. "Sergeant, give this Marine a list of clothing and items she'll need to bring with her."

I straightened up when I heard her call me "Marine". I took the list sheepishly and listened intently to the sergeant who went down the list with me. "You won't need to buy gizmos such as soap, toothbrush and toothpaste, or clothespins. The Marine Corps provides those things. They'll give you a box of sanitary napkins, and you'll get three towels and two face clothes and your own drinking cup. You will be issued shoe polish, a shoe shining cloth and a brush. Believe me, you'll get a lot of use out of those items. The rest of the items on the list you'll have to buy. And don't get hurt or careless. You belong to the Marine Corps now!"

"Okay," I told her.

"It's *General Order Number 20*," she said and her voice was different. It was stern and firm, not the kind you argue with. "You do not say "okay" to an officer. You say *aye aye*. Do you understand?"

"Yes," I said.

But she didn't like that either.

"It's *aye aye, Mam*. You do not say *okay* or *yes*, to an officer," she said.

Since Tonawanda is a very small town, people say "hello" even when they don't know each other because sooner or later you meet the same people over and over again. So naturally when different people I had seen around town but didn't know by name stopped me on the street to ask me how come I was going into the Marines, I'd puff up a little with the pride of it all.

I ran smack into old Mr. Hawks who sold life insurance to our family at fifty cents a week just as he was leaving the Younge Street Bar and Grill with four other men. The blue and gold Rotary flag was flying over the doorway just a little too low. That is why he didn't see me right off the bat.

"It's little Terry Karas all grown up. So our little town is losing you to the Marine Corps?"

Mr. Grave, the funeral director, standing next to him wasn't smiling as customary. He was tapping an empty package of Camels against his fingers. "Anyone got a coffin nail?" He inhaled and said to me, "We must be losing the war when the Marines need you pretty young girls to help."

I tried to set his mind at rest that we women Marines weren't going overseas like the Red Cross or the WAACs

"Women Reserves will free a Marine to fight. They don't want us to lay alongside them in the mud in the jungles holding their guns."

Mr. Koenig, of Koenig's Hardware, was someone I had served in the Sugar Bowl on Saturday nights where he had supper alone on milk and a tuna fish sandwich because Mrs. Koenig had enrolled in a Red Cross First Aid course. He said, "I said it before and I say it again. Women belong in the home cooking and taking care of our children. They are the foundation of our true Christian and democratic society. We don't need our women to do the fighting for us."

Mr. Clunker, the one who sold Dad his Model A, said, "Our country is in big trouble if Congress lets Roosevelt run for a fourth term. He's not telling us the whole truth about this war. When he ran for the third term, he promised there would be no boys on foreign soil. Then he lets the Japs bomb us so he could have an excuse for us to get into this damn war. Now the Army is at Anzio fighting the Germans for God's sake and Marines are getting killed at some god-forsaken island. Where the hell is New Guinea?"

I excused myself politely and rushed on but they didn't notice, so busy were they talking about the things the New Dealers were going to hand the Socialists on a silver platter.

I had the sergeant's list in my hand.

Tonawanda had one street for shopping: Main Street was only two blocks long. There was only one general store which carried the kind of quality clothes that were on this list. A girdle? Okay, I'd look for a pull on kind that had some stretch to it. Silk jersey lingerie? Never find that in Tonawanda not even at Zuckmaiers which had polished mahogany counters and drawers with porcelain knobs and porcelain labels and sales ladies who wore dark blue dresses with white lace collars. Silk of any kind was gone with the war. I did have one pair of silk stockings that I was hoarding that I had hidden in the bottom of my drawer. I wanted to wear them with that wedding dress with the white roses. The Marine Corps list said, cotton stockings. *Maybe that was a mistake.* No one wore cotton stockings except nurses. Did they really mean cotton stockings? *That must be a mistake.*

I also owned all the rest of the stuff I needed to take to Boot Camp: A warm coat, slacks, white shorts and blouse, pajamas, skirt, sweaters, simple dark suit, gloves, robe, housecoat, sneakers and a pair of dark brown dress shoes with heels that were no higher than two and a half inches with closed toe and heel. Thank goodness! I didn't need to use up my shoe ration coupon. I was saving that for open-toed burgundy pumps with four inch heels I had seen in a shoe store in Buffalo.

Mama really snorted when she went over my list. "Silk bloomers indeed! Next it'll be black lace chemises they'll want you to buy."

"Oh, Mama! No one wears chemises anymore. They're out of date. It's bras now. The Marine Corps recommends silk undies because they don't need ironing."

"So? What else will you be doing with your nights?" She harped. "You better be in by eleven just as if you live at home, hear me?"

A few weeks later when I heard the corporal yell, "Lights out" at 10:00 p.m. in Camp Lejeune, North Carolina, I remembered Mama's words. It would have made her very happy to know the Corps had the same moral standards as she did.

PART TWO

The Buffalo Platoon–January 1944

The day was typical of January in Buffalo, cold, crisp and chilling to the bone; the kind of day I was happy to leave behind.

The time came for me to join the Buffalo Platoon at the Buffalo railroad station. We were departing at nine o'clock in the evening and were going to sleep aboard the night train.

The excitement exhilarated my family while I experienced a calm that surprised me.

I had my bag all ready, filled with clothes hangers, notebooks, Kleenex, and air-mail stamps although as a serviceman, I could send letters *Free* just by writing the word in the right hand corner. I had fifteen dollars in my money belt and lifted my blouse to check it twice to assure Mother.

"Mama, I've got plenty of money. The government is going to pay for everything, the meals and the train ride."

Still she insisted on packing a lunch box with ham sandwiches, a jar of black olives, oranges, cookies and bananas.

The neighbors came over and each one had a piece of advice to give me.

Mrs. Martin said, "Be a good girl, Terry. Preserve thy honor."

Harvey Martin said, "Don't lose that cherry, Honey. Watch out for those sea-going Bellhops."

Mama had crying spells intermittently that whole week so I had my hands full and all I could do trying to reassure her that I'd write every day and go to church every Sunday although at home Daddy and she skipped Sunday services often when he had to wash the car or clean out the rabbit cages.

My little sisters clung to me and I hugged and kissed them often to reassure them I would be back with presents.

We entered the waiting room of the railroad station and found it packed with people. Numerous young ladies and their assorted relatives all milled about the stuffed bison on a pedestal in the middle of the lobby. It was the mascot of Buffalo and had been dead for years having come from the Dakotas sometime after eighteen ninety.

Two very tall Marines with one stripe on the sleeves of their forest green uniforms guarded the gate, their feet apart and a rifle at the side, braced straight up and out.

Somehow that sight gave Mama a great sense of relief.

After I kissed her and Dad good-bye I heard Mama say to some one, "Did you know our girls have to be in bed by ten o'clock?" The last glimpse I had of Mama was of her waving a little flag with a star on it. All mothers who had a son in the service had these flags hanging in their parlor windows.

At last, I was on my way to Boot Camp, Camp Lejeune, North Carolina.

The date read January 10, 1944.

I put the newspaper in my bag to save it forever.

Our group of thirty girls had a whole car to ourselves all the way to Washington D.C. with two women as shepherds, a lieutenant and a sergeant who led us directly to our Pullman car, past sleepy civilians and servicemen. They watched us intently from lighted windows as we boarded in single file. Even the engineers had left their throttles to peer at us through the steam that puffed from below their impatient engines. Fog formed the moment the vapor hit the freezing cold of a normal winter night in Buffalo.

A group of very young sailors, about seventeen or eighteen years old, attempted to follow us into our car but the lieutenant chased them away firmly but with tolerance for their condition. The adolescent sailors smelled of stale beer and didn't seem to believe her when she informed them we were Marines and incommunicado, like nuns. Still they kept returning and continued their attempts to peer into our area.

They didn't seem to comprehend that she was also an officer. They simply couldn't believe their eyes, that we females were Marines, on our way to Boot Camp. They clustered together, pushing each other, straining to get a better look at us. Their awe for the Marine Corps showed through their disbelief.

"BAMS? We don't believe it. All of them? BAMS?"

The girl next to me asked, "What are BAMS?"

One of the buoyant sailors yelled gleefully loudly and clearly.

"A BAM is a Broad-Ass Marine."

47

Several of us heard them and in minutes everyone in the Buffalo Platoon knew that the women Marines did indeed have a nickname after all.

We entered into the tight cozy quarters of a boxcar forty feet long. Thirty bunk beds, three decks high, were all made up, ready for us to pop into. The space allotted for our bodies was minimal. The sheets were stiff and crisp with starch.

"What kind of Pullman car is this?" The girl standing next to me asked.

I looked the other way while she struggled to undress and put on her nightie in the narrow aisle that remained between the parallel rows of bunk beds which had taken up most of the space. There wasn't much privacy here.

"It is one of those new Jeeps that fit on top of a railroad, a flatbed just made especially for troop movements," the sergeant answered.

She assigned bunks and I got a lower one which made me very happy until I watched the springs of the mattress above me sink lower and lower until it was inches above my head.

The lieutenant who escorted us sat outside one end of the car. Whenever the porter came through, she gave a warning cry of "Man aboard!" to herald his approach.

It was all very noisy and very exciting, very collegiate just as I envisioned one big sorority slumber party to be like.

The lieutenant gave another set of instructions. "Please, stay in this one car. You are to remain here until I tell you otherwise."

The train sped noisily past sleeping towns that glowed in eerie moonlight.

I couldn't sleep. I didn't know whether my insomnia was caused by the bumpy hiccuping train or the fear that the bobbing buttocks right above me were going to come down any moment.

Perhaps it was the sudden realization of all that freedom from Mama. I could do anything I wanted to. I was free, white and twenty-one. That thought was exhilarating all by itself and affected me as the caffeine in Coca Cola or dad's Turkish coffee.

I spent the whole night watching the passing panorama of dark shadows, the outlines of snow covered hills and the pine trees of New York State and Pennsylvania.

Many of the girls had begun the process of getting to know each other. Somehow I didn't feel like joining into any conversation in the dark.

The thoughts of silent dark houses lying under the white winter blanket with their inhabitants snug in their beds while we girls were on our way to war to help secure our American way of life kept me wide-awake. I wasn't the least bit tired.

Tears came to my eyes filled with the emotion of patriotism. I loved my country so.

It was the blizzards of Tonawanda and Buffalo I hated. I never wanted to see snow again. And now I was headed for the South, North Carolina, the *tropics*. I would get to taste sugar-cane and see cotton growing in the plantation fields and Spanish moss growing on oleander trees. The tune of a Hoagy Carmichael song, hummed in my head: *Memphis in June and sweet oleanders*.

I climbed out of my bed, into my robe and went for some water.

The lieutenant patrolling the corridor noticed me. She asked, "Homesick already?"

"Oh, no!" I assured her quickly. "The thought just came over me how we are on our way to make democracy safe for the world. I'm so proud to be a United States Marine."

The lieutenant reflected for a moment. "You really did read all that literature that was given to you when you signed up. It is not all glory you know."

"Yes, Mam. Isn't it true that we Marines were the first to fight on land and on sea and didn't the Marines prove that the Japs weren't supermen when they stopped the Japs in their tracks on Guadalcanal?"

"True. True."

"And Marines are amphibians?"

"*Amphibious*. Not amphibians. Amphibians are a kind of reptile. Marines are *amphibious*. They can operate on land and on sea. The Fleet Marine Forces are a balanced force of Marines with land, air and service elements that are integrated with our Atlantic and Pacific Fleets. They are trained and equipped to seize or defend naval bases to fight as far inland as the Navy wishes." She smiled. "You have six weeks of Boot Camp in which to learn this. So conserve your energy."

The slumber-party chatter and debates continued well past lights out as the impact of the men's real attitude toward us was understood and analyzed.

At 8:00 A.M. we were ushered into the dining car for breakfast, past wolf whistles, calls of *"BAM"* and offers from the sailors to join them for a game of craps that seemed to be a continuous activity that engaged the servicemen.

They addressed the Women Marine officers familiarly and did not seem to understand the importance of their rank: lieutenant, sergeant or corporal. Our officers in turn treated these service men as being of no consequence shooing them away from their charges as if they were naughty children who had learned a bad word and were testing how far they could get away with it before getting slapped. I got my first lesson in Marine Corps diplomacy in dealing with the Navy. These WR's had a job to do and they were doing it very well with quiet Marine dignity and great patience.

This was also the first chance to become acquainted with each other since the lights were turned off the evening before at eleven o'clock.

Some of the girls had actually gone to sleep.

Surprisingly few of us claimed Buffalo as our home town. Many of the girls were from surrounding small towns. Yet here we were in the Buffalo Platoon.

I found great rapport with several of my fellow Marines; one a girl six feet tall with the sweet name of Zoe.

"Are you of Greek descent?" It would have pleased my Mama so much to know I wasn't the only good "Greek" girl that had joined the Marines.

"No! My mother is a Grecophile," she said. "She loves the classics."

"Did you know your name, Zoe, comes from the Greek word meaning joy or life?"

Our friendship for life began at that moment.

We were all about the same age. We seemed to be in our early twenties and had the same educational background. Four of the girls were teachers; several had been secretaries or had worked in offices; quite a few had been sales girls or worked in restaurants; others had service jobs, three had been in college and one had been a hairdresser.

We all seemed to share the same patriotic motivation for being in this railroad car. We expressed the same desire—to do whatever job would be needed to end this war.

***Washington, D.C.,
War-time 1944-45***
Top: The streets are
crowded with people and
autos.
Center: Union Station
filled at all hours with
travelers.
Bottom: Toursits and
service-men on bicycles
sight-seeing.

Washington D.C.–January 11, 1944

We arrived in Washington D.C. at mid-day.

The strong odor and taste of coal fumes in the train yard coated the lining of my throat as we walked two by two past row upon row of chains of trains, all puffing steam and smoke, ready to go. Many of the trains were old and dirty; resurrected out of mothballs for the war.

The tumultuous activity and commotion was fascinating and deafening. Every train in the United States must have been gathered into this station.

The weather was delightful. After the cruelty of Buffalo's cold wintry weather, the sun touched crisp air of a January day in Washington D.C. was like a spring breeze. I breathed in great gulps of it.

We chattered, giggled and laughed, thrilled with all the new experiences and sights: the people, the buildings, the uniforms, the activity, the crowds.

"Stay close," commanded the lieutenant. "Orient yourselves. This is the USO Lounge. It used to be the Presidential Room. It is now yours. Civilians aren't allowed in there but with these bands on your sleeves you are welcomed anywhere a serviceman is. You are WR's now. Wear them! We will meet here. If you get lost, come back here."

She grouped us into a cluster in a corner of the waiting room of Washington's huge Union Station and gave us our instructions as she passed out dark blue arm-bands for us to wear at all times inscribed with the white letters USMCWR which stood for *United States Marine Corps Women's Reserve.*

Throngs of people milled about, walking aimlessly; sitting patiently on long polished wood benches. There were thousands of people packed in this huge Union Station: soldiers, sailors and women in uniform who were WAACS, WAVES, SPARS, Red Cross.

I saw colorful uniforms of foreign nations: Chinese soldiers, dark Indians in British uniforms, Australians with their hats turned up on one side, Free French sailors. Navy men were in great abundance and not all of them were Americans. I recognized the uniforms of the English Navy.

Coming and going, in total confusion were women with babies in their arms and civilians holding packages, suitcases or bags. The men looked alike as if their dark three piece suits, overcoats and fedora hats were a business uniform they had purchased at the same store. I noticed the women were dressed in fur coats or wool coats and they were in style also, many of them wearing fur hats that matched their coats.

Washington D.C. was a very sophisticated cosmopolitan city. People from all over the world had congregated here. And I was here in the middle of it all.

I was not the only girl who was overwhelmed by this scene.

We all were so thrilled that our heads swiveled trying to take it all in while at the same time we tried to obey the lieutenant's orders not to talk. We grinned at each other and shared our delight without saying a word.

Many people were crushed against each other in front of various numbered gates that had large metal numbers of one to thirteen over them. A group of civilians were bunched together, separated behind a rope all by themselves to wait until the uni-formed men and women who had *Priority* boarded the trains first.

There were scores of Navy people in front of a gate with a sign that read:

QUANTICO—RICHMOND—NORFOLK.

Standing near them, in a special group of their own, were Marines, wearing those beautiful blue dress uniforms with the white belts. Only a few of them were tall and looked as if they could march straight out of the Marine Corps recruiting poster.

"I thought all Marines had to be six feet tall," said Zoe who towered over everyone and was quite conscious of this fact.

"That rule doesn't apply anymore since November 1942 when the draft went into effect. The Corps has got to take what they get now."

The Marines cupped their hands around their mouths and sang in a baritone chorus, "You'll be sorry-ee!" in a camaraderie greeting.

We yoo-hooed to our Nelson Eddys back in the same manner singing "You'll be sorry-eee-rr!" in our prettiest Jeanette MacDonalds.

They yodeled back, "We already are-ee!"

The lieutenant dismissed us and we listened carefully as she gave instructions and granted permission to leave for sight-seeing:

"You *People* will travel in groups of six. You *People* will return by *twenty hundred*. You are ordered to be careful. You belong to the Corps now. Lunch and dinner is arranged for you at the Continental Hotel near-by. It's within walking distance."

"What's *twenty hundred?*" No one was sure.

Washington D.C.

At last I was in that magic city to see all my American History classes come to life. A whole day to see the Capitol, the Smithsonian, Washington's Monument and Lincoln's Memorial. The White House. Jefferson's Tomb. Cherry trees.

Several of us in the Buffalo Platoon discovered we shared the same passion to see these monuments. Not only that, we even had the same kind of school girl crushes on certain historical figures that had become more than dry bones in history books.

"I had such a crush on Thomas Jefferson when I was a junior in high school. He wrote the Declaration of Independence—that all men are created equal with inalienable rights. He was so brilliant and handsome. I read he had a slave for a mistress. I don't believe that for a minute." I confided to Zoe. "It can't be true.

"My secret crush was Abraham Lincoln. He was so tall and had such sad eyes. Did you know his first love died and he married Mary Todd on the rebound?" Zoe said.

Washington D.C. What a romantic city! What secret untold love stories it held. And we were here in the city of love.

The White House was a disappointment. Visitors couldn't go inside as tours had been stopped for the duration of the war. We couldn't gaze at it from the outside or peer at it beyond the iron gates because the whole block was closed off with guards who were posted at all entrances.

The cherry trees were naked. The dome of the Capitol building was not sparkling white.

From the rear window of the Capitol I could see a colony of the most ramshackle houses I had ever seen. We didn't have anything as bad as these in Tonawanda.

I interrupted the guide's lecture as he was pointing out the Howard Chandler's painting of the SIGNING OF THE DECLARATION OF INDEPENDENCE, a document which entitled everybody to life, liberty and the pursuit of happiness for which I got an A in my senior year when I wrote a paper on it.

"Who lives in those huts?"

"Gove'ment workers. Those are *tempos* built for all the new people who come here last two years."

"I don't mean those two-story wooden buildings with the gray shingles on Constitution Avenue." I pointed to the tar-paper shacks over there a short distance from the nicer *tempos*.

"Nigras."

"The climate in Washington must be very mild. You couldn't have anything like that in Tonawanda," I said.

Tonawanda didn't have any *'Nigras'* anyway so we didn't have the problem about where to put them.

The guide hurried to reclaim his tour group which had dispersed to stare at the slums in the back of the Capitol.

An elderly man of about fifty turned to him and said, "Why the hell isn't something done about that eyesore? Why are niggers living so close to the Capitol?"

A woman next to him said soothingly, "Hannibal, you can ask our very own Senator Harry Truman when we go to the Senate building to watch our government at work."

The idea of seeing our democracy at work and getting a look at real action sounded exciting. We tagged along with Hannibal and his wife.

The visit to the Senate turned out to be the most boring part of our sight-seeing. It was like visiting the zoo in the afternoon when all the animals are asleep. Nothing was happening. Nobody was doing anything. I didn't get to see a filibuster although we had spent a whole week on that subject in American History class and had to take a test on it.

We walked in as someone stood at the podium talking in a monotone but no one seemed to be paying attention. It didn't bother him that many seats were empty. A goodly number of the people's duly elected representatives seemed to be in deep reverie or asleep in their padded seats. It was difficult to tell from our vantage point what was going on.

We rushed through the rest of the monuments. Six hours were not enough to see all there was to see in Washington. I would have to return someday by myself.

The crowds of people who were tourists, as we were, jostled us on the sidewalks. They were gawking, rushing, not paying attention to where they were going, just like us. So many men and women were on bicycles riding along the Potomac and Tidal Basin it looked like the 7-Day bike races. Everyone seemed to be wearing some kind of uniform, many of them foreign: British, Free French, Dutch, Greek. I heard strange tongues. Russian, French, Chinese, Spanish.

At Jefferson's Tomb, we met a Marine Private First Class (he had one stripe) in dress blues who was flabbergasted when he discovered we were on our way to Boot Camp.

"Women Marines? My buddies have got to see this!"

He pleaded with us to accompany him to his Marine barracks at 8th and I Street which was a short walk from the Capitol building to show us off to the rest of the Marines there. "You gotta come. The *Commandant's Own* have got to get a look at you to see you are for real."

The *Commandant's Own* turned out to be the famous Marine Corps Band that was stationed permanently at Washington D.C. Our guide was a field music in it who played the bugle.

He was so thrilled to be our guide that he crammed a lot of facts into every breath he took.

"I've got the duty between reveille and taps. I have to strike the ship's bell at the gates to the Commandant's house. I'm part of the *Commandant's Own*. Our band plays at all special occasions, the inaugural of the president, funerals and at all the parades. We give concerts.

A barracks detachment of *Eighth and Eye Marines* always accompanies President Roosevelt when he vacations at Warm Springs. They do parades, funeral and special guard details. This used to be Marine Corps Headquarters until 1941. Now HQ is at Arlington, Virginia. So all we have is the band and the Marine Corps Institute here."

Eighth and "Eye" turned out to be a Corps' landmark. This was the oldest post in the Marine Corps, since 1801 and it took up the whole block in the heart of an old historical section of Washington. He had brought us to a charming park known as the Marine Barracks Quadrangle that stood between Eighth and Ninth Streets.

The commandant's house was anchored at one end of the quadrangle and was a historical gem of Colonial architecture. It was built in American Georgian style with a mansard roof. Its second story had double round dormers in a sea shell design and an attic with many dormer windows which had arches above it. A fence had been built around it. The symmetry of the round bays of an enclosed verandah with many windows on the first floor was formal and inviting. The front door was round with glass panels, and there were so many windows with shutters on each side that you knew it would be light and airy inside. It was grander than any house I had ever seen in the best part of Tonawanda on Elmwood Street.

A row of brick buildings that were three stories high, with covered walk-way with arches, where trees stood all in a soldier's row, were on one side of the square. Houses stood on the other. All together they made a quadrangle around a parade ground where sunset parades were held every Friday for anyone to attend.

The Marines were very proud of their post.

"See this plaque? The house was built in 1806. You know the British burned down all of Washington D. C. except for this building!"

We were thrilled with all the attention and the experience of having set foot on a real Marine post the very first day of being Marines. We were allowed to pass onto the post only after showing our ID cards to the guard although our arm bands would have been enough. The Marines here were more as we expected them to be: tall, over six feet, handsome, some wearing undress blues, white belts, hats and gloves.

"These must be the show-case Marines," I said.

The Marines clustered about us and we lapped up the attention. They were young, about our age.

"It's beautiful. And so peaceful."

"You WRs should be here on Fridays for our sunset parade."

"You are so fortunate to be stationed here."

This was the wrong thing to say to these Marines.

They responded quickly to dispel any assumption on our part that being assigned such "good duty" which was the envy of every Marine in the Corps meant they didn't have some of the same hardships as those Marines in combat. They rushed to let us know they had it "tough" too.

"A guy can get *Asiatic* with duty right here in D.C. We've all got the *gooney bird* stare just keeping up with the spit and polish of this new Commandant, General Vandegrift. He moved in eleven days ago to replace General Holcomb. "

I tried to apologize for my stupid remark but several more Marines joined our entourage.

"We heard about women coming in but you're the first ones we've seen."

A couple of them sang the now familiar greeting, *"You'll be sorry-ee."*

One of the Marines said, "We are glad to see you. Hurry up and relieve us."

Others nodded their heads in agreement.

Zoe whispered to me, "I don't want to relieve him. I'd rather stay here with him."

He grinned his appreciation but said, "We will all get relieved as soon as you WRs come in. Commandant General Vandegrift has given the *word, "There will be only two kinds of Marines, those going to the Pacific and those coming back."* It is straight to combat for every Marine in the States."

Suddenly the men stiffened. Their bodies shot straight up, their hands at a salute with better precision than any chorus line in a Busby Berkely Hollywood musical. Their attention was no longer upon us but riveted at a stern faced straight backed man in officer's uniform which had three stars on the shoulders and a red and green cord around the left shoulder. He was a general of some sort, I knew that much. Why they stayed frozen in that uncomfortable position so long, I couldn't understand; he seemed pleasant enough and there was a gentle smile on his face.

"At ease. Well!" he said, noting our armbands. "Welcome aboard." He walked on as the men relaxed and breathed again. I caught the gentle soft tones of a Southern accent. Our Commandant was a Virginia gentleman, that was easy to see.

"Better not let old Archibald see you," said one of the Marines when the general was out of earshot. Their relief was thick enough to cut with a knife.

"Archibald? Who is Archibald?"

The men were so eager to tell us a "true" ghost story that they fell all over themselves to make sure all the details were included.

Archibald was General Commandant Archibald Henderson and a ghost. He was the fifth Commandant of the Marine Corps who ruled for thirty-eight years, from 1820 to 1859, who had died about a hundred years ago while in office. He patrolled the corridors of that beautiful house and watched over the Corps. So when General Holcomb signed the papers on November 1942, which let the women come into the Old Corps, he had made his displeasure known in the only way ghosts were able.

"That old ghost knocked his portrait right off the wall as soon as General Holcomb announced it at the dinner table. My bunkie here says he had to swab up the mess."

"What mess?"

"All the pieces of the broken Japanese tea set that Commodore Perry had brought back when he opened up Japan. It was on the sideboard when it crashed down."

We giggled simultaneously. Men! They always draw the wrong conclusions.

"Are you sure it wasn't the Nippon tea set that upset Old Archibald? After all we're at war with Japan. You can solve the whole problem of the ghost in the commandant's house by changing to an English sterling silver tea set."

One Marine stared at me for a moment and said; "You'd make a good officer. You think like one. That is exactly what they did. There's a silver tea set in the center with candelabras on each side on that sideboard credenza right now."

I would have loved to have seen the inside of the house and look at the decor and furniture. We were told that it was closed to visitors since the Commandant and his family lived there. How wonderful it would be to be a Mrs. Commandant and live in that beautiful house. Could wives help decorate it or did they have to live in it the way they found it and not touch a historic thing?

The mood was convivial and the conversation spirited and honest.

"The ghosts of the *Old Corps* aren't the only ones unhappy about you women coming in. A lot of live ones don't care for the idea either. What are you women going to do that Marines haven't been doing for themselves since 1775?"

"Is that why you call us *BAMS?*"

They all broke into sheepish embarrassed grins.

"If we are to be called *BAMS,* then what names do the men get?"

"*Gyrenes! Leathernecks! Sea-going Bellhops! Devil Dogs! HAMS! Half-Ass Marines!* We've heard them all."

The battle lines between the sexes were drawn and we weren't anywhere near Boot Camp.

All in all it the visit to Eighth and Eye was an auspicious beginning to our careers in the Marine Corps. We had met our "brother Marines" and it was very good.

Hours later, at 7:00 p.m. (*Nineteen hundred*), we returned to the Continental Hotel for our supper.

There in the lobby was the Senator from Missouri, Harry Truman, whom we had glimpsed at the Senate building. You could tell he was from out West by the distinctive cream color western hat that he was wearing which had a wide brim. His wife stood next to him, bundled up in a fur coat even though the Washington night wasn't at all cold by my Buffalo thermometer.

Senator Truman stopped us and inquired, "What are those bands for, girls?"

"We're *Women Marines*," we chorused.

"Is she old enough? What's a sixteen year old doing with you?" The Senator had singled me out.

I drew myself up to my full five feet two inches and said, "Sir, I am twenty one and ready to *free a Marine to fight*."

"Give 'em hell, girls!"

"Come, Harry, we'll be late." His wife said patiently.

She acknowledged a greeting from a man who had tipped his hat as he passed by, "Good evening, Senator Truman. Mrs. Truman."

Harry waved his hand nonchalantly, engrossed with our group, particularly me. "Why did a half pint like you pick the Marines?"

"It's the best outfit!" I said proudly.

He turned to his wife and said,

"I tell you, Bess. The Marines have got a propaganda machine almost as good as Stalin's. It's about time they let the women join. The WAACs have been in since last May. Hell! What's good for the Army should be good for the goddamn Marine Corps!"

"Don't curse, Harry," said Bess.

The Troop Movement Of The Women Marines

It was very late. I dashed out of the lobby into the station, trying to catch up with my friends who had kept on walking, leaving me way behind, having to run to Union Station by myself.

The Buffalo Platoon was nowhere in sight.

The lieutenant had disappeared. Instead of our small platoon of thirty girls waiting at the USO lounge, hundreds of females were milling about. All were wearing Marine Corps bands on their arms.

Gigantic cards with letters of the alphabet nailed to posts bobbed high above all our heads. Under each of these posts stood a cluster of girls.

An arm grabbed mine and a voice commanded me to answer, "What is your last name?"

"Karas."

"That a C or a K? Stand here." I was shoved under the card with the letters K-L Car #11.

"I belong to the Buffalo Platoon and they are lost," I said to no one in particular. I didn't dare move from the spot I had been placed in.

Finally we were herded two by two in alphabetical order onto the train, each one of us hanging on to our suitcases, hats and other paraphernalia.

I was now part of a huge all female troop movement. I found a seat and arranged myself as comfortably as I could, still distressed about losing my newly found friends of the Buffalo Platoon, knowing I shouldn't be in this car, thinking any minute an officer would discover the error and I'd be pulled off the train and sent home.

A corporal walked through the cars and stopped at each seat as she assigned Pullman berths. She scheduled me into an upper berth and handed me a card.

"I'm supposed to be with the Buffalo Platoon," I said not wanting to start my Corps life dishonestly.

She was busy and ignored me. "You're K, aren't you? This is the J-K and L car. Stay right where you are."

"I'm not supposed to be here," I told the girl sitting across from me.

We each had a whole double seat to ourselves. She smiled and I noticed her eyes were green. Her hair was silky brown, worn smoothly away from her forehead, ending in a soft roll at the nape of her neck. It was a very sophisticated style with not a hint of a machine permanent nor even a suggestion of a pompadour roll on top. She had an olive Mediterranean complexion and was quite beautiful. She was wearing a black suit with a long sleeved blouse that had pointed collars and was made of a fabric I recognized as silk. Her manner was calm and soothing.

"Relax," she advised. "I'm Joan Ilario from New York City."

"I'm Terry Karas from Tonawanda, New York. You're beauti-ful. You should be a model," I blurted out like a star struck movie fan..

"Thank you. I am-was-a model. And you have the brightest blue eyes. Where did you get them?"

We smiled at each other in a sudden warm glow of mutual friendship and looked around to observe the other girls in the car.

The chatter was friendly, boisterous, noisy and it bounced off the walls all around. So many conversations were going at once that only a shrill remark here and there could be understood.

A girl with a prominent nose, straw textured blond hair, incongruous black eye-brows plucked too thinly, much too much rosy rouge, magenta lipstick and orange pancake make-up sat down next to us. Her ample figure bulged in her skirt and sweater.

"I'm Jean Kaplan from Brooklyn. Call me Blondie."

"Have you heard?" She giggled confidentially. "We can't talk to any men until Boot Camp is over. That is six weeks. Forty-two whole days with no men!" She rolled her brown eyes in mock despair, obviously enjoying the effect of her remark.

Snatches of conversation were picked up like a beach ball and volleyed from one seat to another throughout the railroad car.

"Men? What's that?" A southern drawl asked in mock igno-rance.

A western twang sang out, *"You'll be sorry—ee!"*

While the porters made up the beds we chatted with each other. Many ventured from their assigned seats as the process of getting acquainted began.

This Pullman car was typical of civilian passenger trains with the kind of sleeping arrangements that made up into seats during the day and beds during the night. It was not the same as the three-decks box car we had the night before that had been called "a cattle car" with bunks already made up. The seats in these Pullman cars were arranged to form the bottom berth and the top berth was pulled down from the ceiling to reveal a bed. There were only two bunks per unit.

I changed into my pajamas behind drawn curtains, then mod-estly put on my red flowered quilted housecoat before joining the long line waiting to get into the crowded dressing room and toilets at each end of the cars. There was good nature prodding because the lights were going to be turned off promptly at eleven whether we were ready or not. Military discipline had begun.

The next morning, breakfast was served in shifts at the dining car. As I walked through the cars, I realized for the first time the tremendous size of this troop movement.

I counted at least twenty cars. Averaging twenty-six girls in each car, it came to a total of over five hundred girls, all going to Marine Boot Camp in Camp Lejeune, New River, North Carolina. This was no haphazard transporting of women. This was a mass troop movement organized with precision.

Three women, a lieutenant, a corporal and a private first class were the only uniformed Marines on board supervising and escorting this all female troop movement. There were no men other than the railroad employees, the porters and the engineer on this troop train.

The enormity of this grand mass troop movement excited everyone with its historic importance. We discussed nothing else at breakfast and throughout the day.

"I counted nineteen cars," said Blondie whom we immediately named Brooklyn after she had spiritedly defended the Dodgers, its baseball team that was notorious for losing almost every game they played.

"There are exactly twenty-two cars. Some joined us after we left Washington," corrected Madelaine Fenton. She spoke with a clipped Boston accent and her sexy Betty Boop lips were inconsistent with the prim and all-knowing expression on her face. She wore her hair in a neat roll. All I knew about her at this point was that she had been a grade school teacher and was correct about everything. Later, when I knew her better, I learned she was a devout Catholic and wanted to be an officer more than anything else.

Members of the Buffalo Platoon walked through on the way to breakfast and spotted me at the same time I recognized them. "Terry! We've been looking for you. Where have you been?"

"In *Car 11*. Under *K*. How'd you all manage to stay together?"

"You have got to come with us," Zoe insisted grabbing my arm.

"How can I now? When we get to Camp Lejeune, it'll all be straightened out. We're in the Marines. They always have the *situation well in hand*."

The trek through the cars to the dining car had pried the more timid girls from their assigned cars and they joined the commingling of the girls in all the other railroad cars.

We soon discovered that every state of the Union was represented. In our car alone, there were girls from New York, Connecticut, Maine, Hawaii, West Virginia and California.

Not only was there a Buffalo Platoon aboard, but there were other All-Neighborhood Platoons from many other cities and regions of the United States which represented Albany, Houston, Seattle, Miami, Northern and Southern New England, Central New York, Dallas, St. Paul, Green Bay.

A Potomac Platoon had been sworn in on the steps of the Library of Congress and they were a tight knit bunch not like the rest of us who didn't know each other.

There were lots of Pennsylvania girls from West Moreland County, Fayette County and two platoons from Pittsburgh.

The girls from Georgia, North and South Carolina, Alabama, Kentucky, Florida and Texas all spoke slowly, softly with a slurring of the "r's" in the prettiest Southern accents. Each one had a distinctively different drawl and they could tell each other apart. I couldn't distinguish between their accents.

"I can see why you're called Southern belles," I told one group with whom I wanted to be friends. "Your voices are so melodious."

"Are you funnin' us?" asked Jenny Mae from Alabama.

"Never. Ah love your talk." My ear had picked up the rhythm of their sentences and words. I knew that it wouldn't be long before I would be speaking in a soft drawl myself.

Girls passed around and shared the candy bars, potato chips and chewing gum.

I walked up and down the aisles getting acquainted, offering the remainder of my box lunch of black olives and bananas. I was having the time of my life and I wanted everyone to like me.

I liked everyone in turn. I couldn't remember anyone's name. Somehow it was easier to remember where a girl hailed from than her first and last name. The solution to that problem seemed to hit us all at once. We began calling each other by the city or state she originated from. I was one of the exceptions. Tonawanda, an Indian word and a tongue twister, was just too difficult to say, so I was christened *Terry* immediately. If you couldn't remember the name or the place of origin, then the title of *Marine* would do.

"Would you care for an olive, Brooklyn?"

She roared with appreciation. "You're sure taking a chance, Marine. No men for six weeks and you are passing out passion fruit?" Brooklyn loved to make sex jokes which got tiring after a while.

When I pulled out a banana from the paper bag, she doubled over with high spirits. "I'm not ready for that!"

The girls joined her in laughter, after which no one would touch my olives or bananas.

Fenton called after me, "Terry! Come back! I'll have some olives. It is only a primitive pagan belief that they're an aphrodisiac."

Joan said, "Bananas are fattening, but I'm game."

We three munched unafraid, as we watched the panorama of the scenery swim by at forty-five miles an hour.

Our train kept a steady clip, never slowing down, stopping only for coal, water and perhaps a change of the crew. Occasionally we caught a glimpse of the tail end of the twenty-two car chain as we went around the Blue Ridge Mountains of Virginia. As we rolled past historic Fredricksburg, Richmond and tobacco country, we no longer saw snow nor ice-glazed earth.

Once in a while, someone would recognize a familiar landmark and shout and point out a home town or patch of land.

We would all rush to the window to voice our admiration for that particular section of the country. This ritual became a pattern that was repeated many times.

We passed Fayetteville and approached Wilmington, North Carolina. We could sense we were getting close.

As the corporal-in-charge went through the cars checking, rechecking and inspecting, we pelted her with questions.

"Isn't Kitty Hawk near where we're going?"

"Yes, about one hundred miles from where the Wright Brothers flew the first air-plane."

"When do you think we'll arrive?"

"Wednesday, some time, I hope."

"How come? That is almost three days from Washington. This train is going so fast we should make it in better time." Fenton had been making calculations all along.

"We aren't traveling in a straight line. We are zig-zagging across the country to foil the train watchers who may be spies or Fifth Columnists. No one knows our route."

Theresa Karas Yianilos

I shivered at the prospect of our troop train being derailed by saboteurs at the same time I noticed the aplomb manner of the corporal who stood there self-assured, magnificently confident in her Marine green uniform with the two red and green chevrons on her left sleeve. I resolved right then and there to be always faithful to the Corps. I vowed to become a corporal and live up to the Corps' motto—*Always Faithful, Semper Fidelis.* My vocabulary now had two more Latin words besides *Et tu Brutus* and *E Pluribus unum.*

Camp Lejeune, North Carolina, 1944
Top: The Sentry guard house at the entry of Post.

Bottom: A typical brick building in the Women's Compound.

Top: First meal in Mess Hall. Note metal trays.
Center: Cleaning the squadroom and making the sacks.
Bottom: A G.I. party means cleaning up and scrubbing.

PART THREE

Boot Camp–Camp Lejeune, North Carolina–January 1944

I was awakened Wednesday morning and immediately felt the change of speed. The train was now rolling at a snail's pace, past sparsely plumed pine trees with tall trunks reaching to a North Carolina sky that was a brilliant sapphire blue even in the early rays of the cool morning light.

Excitement ran high and necks craned to catch a glimpse of our new home and the new life we were about to start.

The landscaping was green and fresh without snow but the buildings near the tracks were shacks, tar-paper roofed huts with iron kettles in the yards and patches of greens growing next to them.

My heart dropped. Could these be the 'military housing' we were told about? They were the same sort of 'nigra' houses I saw in Washington D.C. behind the Capitol building.

Friendly natives came out of the houses and waved at the trains, their white teeth flashing big grins, dogs and children standing there staring at us.

We passed a clearing with live oaks draped with diaphanous shawls of Spanish moss. I had only heard about Spanish moss. I had never seen it. Now there it was before me. I had reached the South.

Nestled among the tall oaks and pines was a charming little octagon-shaped sentry house where two Marines stood guard. They were wearing gun belts, sun helmets and arm bands with the initials **MP** for military police. We waved joyfully to them.

A few red brick buildings came into view. All were of the same Colonial architecture, two stories high, with white trim, many windows, complete with cupolas and weathervanes on pale gray roofs.

The scramble for our suitcases was surprisingly orderly despite the confusion. As soon as we exited the train carrying our suitcases, a Woman Marine standing there gave a command so forcefully and loudly that each of us obeyed with surprising agility and alacrity.

"You are to exit in two's and line up immediately."

I hurried to follow instructions, tagging close to Joan and Fenton, all the while staring at the warm North Carolina sunshine which had a sky that was of such an intense blue color that I was completely mesmerized.

Our troop movement had been met by the Women's Reserve Marine Band of Camp Lejeune. A Woman Marine led them through a melody of songs as we had stepped off the train two by two. They were our first sight of women Marines in full dress uniform and they were beautiful.

They raised their instruments and welcomed us with the stirring music of the *MARCH OF THE WOMEN MARINES.* As I listened to the official song of the Women Marines for the first time I knew I would never forget it. It was a composition as inspiring to a woman Marine as *THE MARINE'S HYMN* was to the whole Corps.

A formation of Women Marines in full uniform stood at attention near-by and sang the words to the song that had been written just for the Women's Reserve:

Marines!
We are the women members
of our fighting Corps
Marines!
The name is known
from burning sands to ice bound shores
Marines!
We serve that men
may fight on land and air and sea
Marines!
The Eagle, Globe and Anchor carry on
To make men free.

A tall Woman Marine with one chevron on her green uniform which denoted she was a private first cass welcomed me rather forcefully, almost pushing as she touched my shoulder directing me to join a group of girls who were lined up in rows.

She yelled a command firmly and sternly, "*Knock off* the talking. Get in formation and follow me."

In three minutes she had collected twenty-eight of us. She started to walk very fast, increasing the pace to almost a run as she speeded up her foot steps.

We all tried to keep up, but I didn't succeed very well. My heavy suitcase occasionally brushed against Fenton who was ahead of me.

Groups of a motley assortment of women dressed in civilian clothing mismatched exactly like us were herded across flat widely paved streets towards red brick buildings with bright green roofs. The scene reminded me of old silent movies where the film had been speeded up.

I saw other groups of women, who were already outfitted in their Marine uniforms marching with precision. They were being led through their movements by shouting male sergeants. They were not oblivious to our arrival.

"You'll be sorry-eee!" they sang

As our platoon of twenty-eight girls approached the barracks in which we were to be billeted, a sound of yelling hit me as it bounced across the road. It was the whole Buffalo Platoon which had stayed together and were in one group of twenty-eight. They spied me and began to point and wave wildly.

"Hey! That's Terry. Terry! She belongs with us!"

Their platoon leader yelled back harshly, "*Knock it off*, Boots!"

They were thrown into confusion and stopped immediately. Zoe, threw her hands up in a silent gesture which said, "Looks as if we can't help you now."

I shouted to my platoon leader, "I belong with them."

She ignored me and commanded in Southern accents that were not melodious nor dulcet toned, "*On the double,* you Boots. And *knock it off!*" She started to run very fast.

Fenton, whispered without turning around, "That means shut-up, Terry." She limped a little.

It's not as if I had hit her with my suitcase on purpose.

We were led past a quaint foot bridge made of thin pine logs towards a compound where twelve H-shaped brick buildings stood, all with the same green roofs. Another group of twelve buildings had bright blue roofs. The pine green of the trees and the spring green of the grass framed the Colonial charm of the women's village in an inviting picture beckoning us to idle a while.

We marched past big red signs posted everywhere.

WARNING! OUT OF BOUNDS
RESTRICTED AREA!
FOR WOMEN RESERVE ONLY!

The men had put up a large sign that read: HADNOT POINT.

Hadnot Point had a juke box, a piano, and a soda fountain. It had a library and home town newspapers. It had sailing, canoeing, tennis, badminton, volley ball, archery, crafts and a theater with a different movie every night. It had religion: chapel services on Sunday for Catholics and Protestants, as well as separate services for Christian Scientists and on Friday nights for the Jewish faith. It had three mess halls, a post exchange, a post office, a uniform shop, laundry, beauty parlor, a theater, a service club with bowling alley.

What Hadnot Point had not was men. The men had named the compound accordingly in deference to their idea of their importance to the incoming women since it was out of bounds to all men. It was subtle but we got the point.

The nostalgic charm of the H-shaped brick buildings was lost in a blur of images as we were rushed into the barracks, past a corridor of closed doors with signs on them; Duty NCO, Mail Room, Officer In Charge; past open doors which led to showers, past a room with rows of toilets (to be called *the head*) thereafter, beyond laundry rooms with dryers and ironing boards. The hall funneled into a very large room with wings of narrow rooms on each end.

We entered a very large and long rectangular room, spartan in decor, with walls painted in a dull mint green color which I soon learned to recognize everywhere as Marine green. We were brought to an abrupt halt.

Thirty-one double bunks, with crossed metal bars at the foot and headboard, all painted a dark brownish Marine green, were lined up row upon row, one foot apart from each other and one foot from the wall. Across the room on the other side was an equal number of bunks. Thin mattresses, with striped ticking, were doubled over on the springs. The tall vertical windows which were covered with venetian blinds that rolled up and down were spaced at regular intervals. Not every bunk was near the coveted windows.

Separating the long rows of bunks in the middle of the room were unpainted clothes racks made from two by four wood with posts of four by fours. These were to be our closet hanging space for our civilian clothes then later our military uniforms.

In front of each bunk and in the aisle at the foot near the wall was a rectangular wood locker box, also painted in another shade of deep Marine Green.

Had I a choice, I would have taken the box at the front of the bunk but Jenny Mae, the tall Southern girl was assigned that as well as the coveted bottom bunk.

Now I knew where the first test of bravery was given in the Marine Corps. It started with the top bunk. I faced what was to be my sleeping accommodation for the next six weeks. It was at least four feet from the ground. I knew with certainty I'd roll off during the night. I'd be killed and my Marine Corps career would be cut short.

There was no time for reflection, regret, apprehension or going to the *john*—uh—the *head*.

Our NCO, which was the term that meant non-commissioned officer, and described anyone who had a rank above private, had no intention of waiting for anybody nor for any reason whatsoever. That became clear immediately. She didn't address any of us by any name other than *"Boot"*. Her instructions were loud, precise and succinct.

"If you wish to speak to me, state your name first and ask *'permission to speak'*. When I answer, *'permission granted'* you can then talk to me."

"I am your *platoon leader*. I am Private First Class Taylor but you will address me as *platoon sergeant*. My orders are to be obeyed without question. When I say *"Knock It Off"* I want complete silence immediately. When I call *"Muster"* you will fall into line instantly. Now *"Sound Off! Loud And Clear!"*

Thus we were introduced to our Mother Superior, our warden, the female equivalent to the Marines' drill sergeant, someone who was to be obeyed instantly.

We answered with our names as we stood by our bunks, suitcases tucked underneath neatly. She whipped past us, her head bobbing up and down as she checked off names on a roster. She stopped short and backtracked up to me.

"Terry Kerry? That really your name?"

"Yoe!" I snapped to attention. "It's Karas, Sir—uh—Mam—uh platoon sergeant."

"What kind of name is that?"

I was sorry to add to her troubles and make her more upset than she seemed to be already. "My grandparents are Greek and my—"

She wasn't interested in family trees as she strode past me.

"Irish, Polish, Italian, Greek—those don't count here. We are all Americans. Here you're nothing but a Boot, in for the *Duration and*

Six Months." It must have been one of her favorite sayings because she used it every time she gave an order or turned around.

I was billeted with one-hundred and twenty-four bunkmates in one squadroom with girls from Alabama, West Virginia, Texas, Oregon, South Carolina, Massachusetts, Wyoming and New York. And she was right. We didn't care about who was what. There was no time to find out. We were kept busy every minute.

First, the beds—oops, bunks—had to be made up. Silence had to be maintained while we stood in line at the linen room which was at the end of the hall. Noiselessly, we each signed up for two white muslin sheets, one pillow case, two terry cloth towels, one for face and body, and two closely woven wool blankets in two shades of moss green, also called Marine Green. Quietly, we all gathered around a bunk as the sergeant prepared to give a demonstration of how to make up a bunk which pleased me greatly because it was mine she was fixing.

"I'm going to explain this once only. In the Marine Corps you do things *by the numbers.* You make your *bunk* by the numbers. You *swab the deck* by the numbers. It's One-two. Three-four."

"Notice the distance between the bunks—twelve inches. That is one foot. You will not push it closer or further apart from the next bunk. Those on the top bunk will sleep facing the wall. Those on the bottom will alternate, heads against the *bulkhead.* That wall is not a wall; it's a *bulkhead.* Learn it."

"Place the bottom sheet on the bunk with the hemmed side up. Place the blanket six inches from the head. To make hospital corners," she raised her voice and it boomeranged against the instructions other NCO's were giving down the line. "Pick up the corner. Bring it tight against the mattress toward you. Hold it there firmly with youh palm. With youh other hand bring the edge over and tuck it in firmly. Pull the blankets over it tight. Fold youh other blanket from side to side, then from top to bottom; then in thirds with the open end inside. Place it at the foot of youh bunk."

The sergeant spoke rapidly and the combination of Southern drawl and speed, plus the echoes of other platoon leaders giving the same instructions to their Boots made it difficult to hear and understand. We hung on to her every word.

"Youh clothes are to be hung on that rack with the longest gear toward the front of the building facing B Street."

No one knew where B Street was and we turned around the room looking for it which was kind of silly and set us off into fits of giggling.

"The open part of the hanger will face East."

"We will now learn how to *stow our gear*," the sergeant continued. "Youh shoes will be lined on the racks, the toes facing the bunks and must be polished and tied whether *on* or *off* your feet."

She pointed behind her. "That is the rear of the building. Fold youh towel in thirds and youh wash cloth in half and hang them on the end of the bunk nearest the *bulkheak* acing it."

"What did she say?"

"Did you say something without asking permission, Boot? *Bulkhead!* The word is *bulkhead!* Boot! The Marine Corps is part of the Navy. Here you talk Navy. Learn it! Use it!"

The mimeographed sheet she gave to us had a list of shipboard terms: *aft* meant "in front; *starboard* was the "right side"; *ladder* for stairs, *deck* for floor. A few well known words that we had been introduced to in D.C. that were used by sailors and Marines were missing from this list. That included the word *BAM*.

The girls picked up the Navy jargon right away and were three sheets to the wind or sea-going before they got out of the showers talking instant Marine Navy Berlitz, calling each other *"Bunkie,"* saying *"Aye Aye"* instead of "yes" and *"gangway"* when they wanted room to pass to use the *heads* which were toilets and hollering *"Snap to it Mate"* if anyone lingered too long at the sink.

The NCO worried about being late constantly. She made us run everywhere, even inside from one room to another. "Move it, *Boots*! Hurry it up there, *Goons*!" She urged.

I panted along side a very tall lanky girl whom I knew only as Texas. With her twang and slow smile she could have been Gary Cooper's sister. She was my complete idea of how people grew in Texas. We became friends immediately. Her name was Lindsey and we began a friendship that was to last for many years.

Joan had been assigned across from me. I caught glimpses of her through the clothes hanging in the rack in the middle.

Madelaine Fenton, the grade school teacher, was my bunkie and she had drawn the top bunk next to mine. She wanted to be recommended for OTS, Officer Training School. She was determined to prove her mental alertness and superior moral qualifications. She displayed her superior abilities, initiative, intelligence and potential leadership every chance she had. She was generous with all kinds of information and asked questions incessantly to prove her sincere interest. I hoped with all my heart she could make OTS, so she could be happy in the service and relax.

Too bad the Women Marines no longer were commissioned directly from civilian life as they had been in the beginning in 1942 and early 1943. At this late date, in January 1944, with the quota almost filled, recommendations were made from the ranks and everyone had to complete Boot Camp first. Fenton would be with us all the way. Anyone could see she wasn't too happy about that miscalculation in her plans but she was determined to be a great Marine. Her spirit was good.

Several of the other girls were not as gracious about some of the disappointments they were experiencing. Signs of regret at their hasty marriage to the Marines could be detected in their griping as the noose of military discipline tightened.

Our NCO was often joined by a sergeant. They took turns yelling orders: *"Knock It Off!" "Now Hear This!" "Atten-Haut!"*

Their sentences always began with *"You will*—with nary a "please," as if they had already come to the conclusion you were going to give them an argument. I never met a nicer bunch of friendly quiet girls in my whole life. The minute the sergeant yelled, *"Knock it off, you goons,"* they shut up right away.

We weren't allowed to mill around. We were always in formation, lined up in neat rows or lines, always silent and quiet unless given permission to talk.

One of the first things we learned was to *"Fall out!"* That meant we had to run outside, get into position in a line, making sure our shoulders met the shoulders of the female standing next to us and stand at attention to await further orders.

As soon as we learned to *fall out* we were ordered to march *double time* which meant to walk at a fast pace, almost a gallop. That is the way we traveled from building to building, in formation, across the parade ground, never really knowing where we were going, being told nothing.

Many of us were out of shape and the wheezing and coughing we made as we collapsed in the seats of the auditorium was a cacophony of sounds.

A general silence prevailed as the senior commanding officer of the Women's Reserve Battalion, Captain Katherine A. Towle came into the room. She was of an indeterminate age, tall, thin, with a natural straight bearing, had soft blond hair and a charming manner. Now, she was my idea how a Woman Marine should be—warm, concerned, friendly, courteous, dignified and polite. I loved her immediately.

She was the antithesis of our sergeants and corporals. She spoke gently and softly. She told us we could come to her anytime we were troubled and wanted to talk. Our NCO corporals and sergeant should pay a little more attention to her ways and do a little imitating rather than yell and forget their "Please" and "Thank-you" each and every time every time they ordered us to do something. They called us by our given names only at roll call at reveille. Otherwise they addressed us as *Goons* and *Boots*. After all, we were living together, and twenty-eight names weren't that hard to remember.

The Hat

Immediately upon leaving the auditorium, we had to run all the way to the uniform shop.

A Woman Marine tailor put a tape around my head and yelled out, "Twenty-two."

She waved me down the line and another Woman Marine placed the magnificent hat on my head that I had been drooling over since September 1943, over five months ago. The Marine Corps hat of the Women's Reserve, with its bell shaped crown and red cord and brass emblem of eagle, globe and anchor, was made of the finest quality green covert cloth and of such skillful design that the transformation upon each of us was instantaneous and magical. I barely heard the instructions that were given at the same time so taken was I with my reflection.

"You will never tilt your hat. You may not wear hear pins, barrettes, hair ribbons or tiaras. You will wear your hat at all times when outdoors."

"You will salute all officers at all times when your head is covered except in church, at meals, indoors or in the theater."

A lesson followed on the proper way to salute. We practiced saluting each other while the NCO walked among us checking to make sure the forearm was at a forty-five degree angle with the wrist and hand straight over the right eye.

"You will salute all officers within six paces. When walking by him, prepare for the pass by saying, 'By your leave, Sir?' as you come along side of him."

"All officers?" I asked. "What if you don't want him to make a pass."

"Boot! You seemed to have missed the spirit of military courtesy. A salute is a friendly gesture. A token of respect for the rank. Rank takes precedence. You must render a salute to an officer with your head and eyes facing him at the same time."

Well! If this was the way the Marines wanted it, okay! But I knew a potential trouble making rule when I saw one.

The NCO said, "You need not worry about an officer making a pass. An officer is a gentleman. Commissioned officers and enlisted personnel will not, I repeat, will not, associate socially. That means no dating. Read the Commandant's *Letter of Instruction 489* on the bulletin board."

"No fraternization will be tolerated between officers and enlisted. Any enlisted woman caught dating an officer will be severely disciplined and discharged." She said it firmly.

"Aw! " said Brooklyn, "Everybody's got their shiksas. It's the same as home. All my ma could say to my kid brother was, 'What's the matter, couldn't ya find a nice Jewish girl'?"

Joan said, "I brought a Jewish boy home once and Papa said, "Wat kinda name is David? I told him he was named after a statue in Florence and he figured he was a member of the Sons Of Italy. His mother called me a shiksa and that broke us up."

Marines also ate with their hats on. That was the only Marine apparel we had anyhow. We weren't about to take them off.

Luncheon, now called *chow*, was served at 11:00 A.M., in a large building, the Battalion Mess Hall.

We were queued in double time into a double line, according to height. It made a neater and trimmer waiting line. I was teamed with Shauna, the Mormon from Utah, because we were both five feet two inches.

The aroma of food escaped from the mess hall and encircled me. I was starved. The train ride and breakfast seemed to have occurred in the distant past. So much had occurred in the past few hours.

Our group of twenty-eight girls was only one of many such groups. The line grew longer and longer as more platoons of dowdy, mismatched civilian-clad women emerged from the many barracks.

Near us but at a small distance, stood a formation of senior Boots who were outfitted in smart Marine uniforms, singing a tune I recognized as *"THE OLD GRAY MARE."* It was a silly sight too, because they were flapping their elbows like birds when they sang the words repeatedly:

Here we stand like birds in the wilderness
Birds in the wilderness, birds in the wilderness
Here we stand like birds in the wilderness
Waiting to be fed. Waiting to be fed

Another group came marching in from a different direction. They also were uniformed and a lively bunch, wagging their heads sideways singing a British song the *First Marine Division* had brought back from New Zealand and Australia. The Marines had been stationed there for many months after the assault at Guadalcanal to recuperate from that ordeal. The girls had changed the words and the song came out like this:

I've got six pence, jolly jolly six pence
I've got six pence, to last me all my life
I've got six pence to spend or six pence to lend
And no pence to send home to my wife. No wife
No cares have I to grieve me.
No pretty little boys to deceive me
Happy is the day I get my Marine Corps pay
As we go rolling home dead drunk
Rolling home dead drunk,
Rolling home dead drunk
By the light of the Carolina moon
Happy is the day
I left you home to stay
As we go rolling rolling home

Our platoon sergeant clapped her hands above her head for attention: "O.K. goon platoon! You sing too. And let me hear you!" She began a peppy tune that was easy to catch on to:

They say that in the Navy
The coffee's very fine
It's good for cuts and bruises and tastes like iodine
I don't like Navy life
Gee Mom I want to go
Right back to Quantico
Gee Mom I want to go home

By the second chorus, I was exhilarated, singing spiritedly, complaining and griping about the food I had yet to taste:

They say that in the Navy
The biscuits are mighty fine
One rolled off the table
And killed a pal of mine
I don't like Navy life
Gee Mom I want to go
Right back to Quantico
Gee Mom I want to go hooo-me

Food was served cafeteria style. I picked up a metal tray with six compartments and slid it on the rods in front of steaming pans of food.

There were at least six hundred women in this large room. Not a male in sight. The cooks, guards and mess personnel were all women. The *galley*, which was the Navy word to be used henceforth for the word kitchen just as if we were all aboard a ship, was staffed solely with women. The mess hall served only women and was staffed only by women called mess girls who were doing their mess duty.

Mess duty meant that each year, a Marine owed the Corps thirty days of kitchen chores. That was mandated for all enlisted Marines under the rank of corporal and we all had been forewarned that our time would come.

Good nature banter and laughter filled the air which increased in crescendo when the crew saw our motley bunch standing before them like birds in the wilderness with only our Marine Corps hats on.

We returned the laughter. Most of them looked like Charlie Chaplins in heavy boots that laced past the ankles and in white jackets that reached to the knees and flopped open, unbuttoned. They all had turbans on their heads and wore men's baggy pants made of white cotton twill with men's canvas web summer belts to hold them up. They had on men's skivvy undershirts with round knitted necks which were tucked inside the pants which made their bosoms look like watermelons placed sideways especially since a few of the mess girls were amply endowed.

"Here's another *chowhound*," one called as she ladled generous portions of food onto my tray. It looked delicious.

"I don't know why I'm so hungry," I apologized. "I never eat all this for lunch." I looked down at my stainless steel tray, each compartment filled to the brim with steak, mashed potatoes, buttered corn, rolls and butter and a Waldorf Salad of chopped apples, raisins and walnuts.

The mess girl laughed at my recruit timidity and added a piece of cherry cobbler. "You're a half-pint. There's plenty more."

"Keep this line moving," the Mess Sergeant commanded.

I hurried to the long wooden tables and benches where one half of a platoon sat, eight of us on each side. The condiments, salt, pepper, jars of orange marmalade and strawberry jam and stainless steel pitchers of milk and coffee were in the middle of the table. I filled my white heavy china mug with the last of the coffee. The blood went to my face, heating it with embarrassment as I found myself holding an empty pitcher to pass on.

"Go fill it and snap to!"

When I returned with it filled, there was no time to drink it. We had to eat fast.

Several lieutenants with silver bars on their shoulders were seated at tables and chairs, not benches as we were, on one side of the room. They weren't much older than our group. They hadn't gone through the line. They were served as we practiced it at home, at tables and chairs instead of friendly picnic type tables. Their portions were ladled onto china plates by a mess girl instead of handy metal trays. Their coffee was being poured into cups and saucers, not mugs.

"Seems as if we're having all the fun. Pity they can't join us since there are so few of them." I said.

Fenton said with envy in her voice, "They're officers. They live by themselves in their own rooms too. Things are better for officers."

Her voice was tinged with envy. She became impatient with me when I agreed with her and she nudged me to hurry with scraping off the tray before putting it on top of all the dirty trays as the Mess Sergeant watched. No doubt if a girl wasn't careful with her portions she could get very fat very fast.

"You can take as much as you want, Boot, but you have to eat it. No waste will be tolerated in this Corps!" This message was repeated by the Mess Sergeant several times.

Lunch over, we were assembled into formation and taken on a run to the W R uniform shop for the rest of our uniform.

The Marine Corps Women's Uniform

The WR Uniform Shop was manned by women and women tailors only, most of whom had one stripe on their sleeves which meant they had the rank of private first cass. The uniform shop was part of a complex of stores called the Post Exchange that was sort of a department store where all kinds of merchandise could be bought at extremely reasonable prices. It was one of the government's concessions for the low pay we earned as Marines. As military women we also didn't have to pay income tax, but at fifty dollars a month private's pay, who worried about that?

A clerk gave me a voucher for a lump sum of two hundred dollars and a written list of regulation clothing I was required to purchase with it. The officers received two hundred and fifty dollars which wasn't much of an allowance for their clothing either.

"You'll get twelve dollars and fifty cents quarterly clothing allowance after this as well. That and your Private's pay of fifty dollars a month. Do you want egg in your beer too?" The WR with the private first class stripe on her sleeve said the same thing to each Boot as she passed out the vouchers.

The tailor pulled off a forest green covert cloth jacket from a rack of jackets and quickly threw it on me.

She exhaled quite loudly as she pinned in two darts on each side, all the way from the welted slit pockets at the hip line to just below each breast. She turned me around and took in some more fabric in the four piece back. The side seams of the princess lines curved and met up at the top edge with the seams of the two piece sleeves. The jacket nipped in at the waist softly, ending at the hip bones.

I caught a glimpse of myself in the mirror and turned around on the small stool I was standing on, absolutely fascinated with the whole new procedure of being fitted. I had been a perfect size eleven in clothes from Lerner's or any of the shops on Main Street. Now I was a size 9 being pinned in all sorts of odd places to make it fit right.

The Marine Corps tailor worked quickly and silently. She pulled at the jacket which she called a uniform blouse, adjusted the slightly padded shoulders with the straps buttoned at the neck, and made certain the narrow set-in lapels lay flat against my body.

"Don't have to touch that" she said to the dart hidden under the lapel.

I bent my head to look and she admonished me immediately to "Look straight ahead, Boot!"

The two slashed and bound pockets slanted at each breast popped open as I took a deep breath.

"I don't believe it," she said. "For a little girl you've got two big problems. The hell with it. Let them pop. I am not going to put in one more pin."

I agreed with her about my problem. It was very difficult to find size 32-C cup bras. I had to send to California for the one I was wearing but she didn't want to hear that story.

As I discovered, the uniform *blouse* was not a blouse but a jacket. It had three brass buttons down the front and two smaller ones on the pointed ends of the shoulder tabs. The buttons were three dimensional with thirteen stars above an American bald eagle clutching a twisted fouled-up rope. A little hole on each corner of the collar was ready for two more of these pieces of jewelry. They gave the jacket just the right touch of sparkle.

"What darling costume jewelry!" I smiled at the tailor.

The tailor popped up to attention, pins in her mouth as the uniform lieutenant stood before me. Her eyes were sad but her voice was soft and gentle:

"Private! You will never refer to the *Marine Emblem* as costume jewelry. When you put on the *Globe and Anchor* it means you are a Marine. It is the most important insignia you will ever have in your lifetime. That *Globe* stands for the Marines who have worn honor throughout the world. Those thirteen stars stand for the original colonies when the Marine Corps was born in 1775. Do you know what a bald-eagle is? It is an American bird, our national symbol."

"Yes, Mam," I said. "No wonder the WR's don't have problems filling its quota. It's worth joining up just to wear this uniform." I really was quite smug with my reflection. "It's so much prettier than the ones the *WAACS* or *WAVES* have to wear. No wonder they are having trouble filling their quota."

The uniform officer smiled and said, "Carry on," and walked away.

We all knew that was true.

There was rivalry between the women's services, centered around the way we looked. We knew we looked the best and the most attractive. We were Marines! The best! First to fight! First in the air, on land and sea! First in fashion!

"We are a bunch of good-looking women! Do you think being attractive and pretty was one of the unwritten qualifications we had to have when we enlisted?"

It was true. None of us were too fat, too big, too tall or too short. Some of the girls were stunning knock-outs and others were very pretty. Each and every woman in this room would get a second look. With the uniform on, each one had been transformed into a woman of distinction.

"It's the uniform. It makes all of us look wonderful. I wonder who designed it," said Joan. She had modeled clothes of famous designers in New York, Mainbocher and Hattie Carnegie, and knew all about good fabric and exclusive designs. "Look at the great cut of this suit! It has got to be a *Mainbocher*. Every woman can wear it. And this hat! It was made by the Knox Company. It looks good on everyone. The only one who looks good in the an up-side down sauce pot hat the *WAACS* have to wear is Olvetta Culp Hobby, their commanding officer."

Fenton was standing on a stool at another mirror, getting her jacket fitted. There were very few pins. She had the kind of Boston figure that looked so great in cashmere sweaters and skirts, with no breasts to get in the way of the smooth line.

She said in that matter-of-fact prim way of hers, "Our women's uniform is a direct copy of the men's uniform, even to the khaki shirts and ties that go with it."

The corporal said, "There will be no mistaking us for any other part of the Armed Forces. We are Marines. It's a very wise decision on the part of Marine command."

The corporal's voice rose above the chatter of women who were thrilled with their new clothes as she restored discipline back into her fitting room.

"Hear this! Your Marine uniform is to be worn at all times except for sport. You are not to wear any part of your Marine uniforms with civilian clothes. Nor are you to be out of uniform at any time. You will wear it night and day for the *duration and six months.*"

"What about a wedding gown?" That question interested everyone and the room quieted down quickly.

"Even for a wedding gown. You must get special permission from the captain. You thinking of getting married, Boot?"

"If I find someone special," I said hopefully.

"Not in the next six weeks you won't. You, Boots, are prohibited from talking to any male. Not even on long distance calls. Forget romance. Concentrate on being a Marine."

The uniform corporal yanked the sleeve hard and I thought she was emphasizing her point but all she was doing was pulling it straight to check its length and to align the pointed overlay of the cuff into place properly as the men wore theirs. She pinned the six gored skirt which flared slightly at the bottom and it came to the middle of my knee cap. I had worn my skirts longer in conformance to the latest style and I pointed this fact out to her.

"You are lucky to be getting a Marine uniform, Boot. Some of us old enlisted salts that came in last March and April had to go all the way through Hunter College in New York in civilian clothing. At Mount Holyoke in Massachusetts WR officers had worn their civilian clothing with just an MC armband for identification."

Cordovan brown leather oxfords, with short Cuban heels, were fitted on me next. These were regulation which meant I had to wear them for parades and work. They were the kind of shoes I would never be caught dead in. Old ladies and old maids wore these. As I bent to tie the laces, I discovered they were surprisingly comfortable.

"They are a size larger and narrower than I wear," I told the corporal who had given me the shoes.

She smiled knowingly. "Wait until you start drilling and marching. You will thank me."

I waited in line again, this time anxious to receive the magnificent shoulder bag made out of crinkled Buffalo leather with a Facile spring clasp. I had never seen a purse that worked like that. You stuck your hand in it to push it apart to open and close. It was so much easier than zippers or snaps.

But there were no more purses in the supply room. A disappointed groan whooshed out of all of us.

The corporal didn't have any tolerance for our frustration. "There's a war on. Remember? We have our shortages right here in Camp Lejeune. But it's only temporary. So count your blessings."

"Supplies should catch up before you graduate from Boot Camp, but in case they don't, you will be able to use your allowance to buy many of the WR Marine uniform items, including your leather purse and gloves, later. Certain department stores throughout the United States are authorized to sell official regulation Marine Corps uniform apparel. New York, San Francisco and Washington D.C. have them for sure. Don't worry! Women's Reserve uniforms will be available at many stores and PXs. You aren't going to your duty stations in civilian clothes." She had answered most of our concerns, as one item after another was out of stock.

The let down from my disappointment was followed by a wave of guilt as I recalled how blithely I had abandoned all the Priority requisition orders from Marine Corps Depot of Supply in Philadelphia and left them unfilled, all in a pile on my desk, back at the Remington factory. I wondered on whose desk the order for Marine Corps Women's Reserve purses was sitting. Maybe that defense worker had quit and joined up too.

A cloth shell, called a purse cover, that was to be fitted over the leather bag (which none of us had received) was issued anyhow. It was green cotton twill and was to be worn with the summer uniforms and the *dress whites*. We were also given a plastic hat cover called a *havelock*, to protect our hat from the rain. Umbrellas were not an option.

But Marine Corps's supplies hadn't kept pace with the rush of enlistment of Women Marines. There were many official uniform items that couldn't be filled from the list. Sizes just hadn't caught up with demand either. Some of us were issued certain items while others didn't get them.

Three battalions, one thousand six hundred and fifty women in training all at one time, graduating every five and one half weeks had cleaned out the supply room.

Also out of stock was the most beautiful uniform of all the women's services, the one that everyone talked about, the one that made every Woman Marine simply the best-looking female where ever she went: *The dress white uniform.*

A general moan filled the room and the officers tried to shush us. Since it was winter, the absence of the summer dress whites in our lockers didn't constitute an immediate crisis. There would be plenty of time after graduation to buy the complete outfit which consisted of a cotton twill white dress jacket with gold *insignia,* a six gored white skirt, a green twill hat with the white cord and gold insignia that was a copy of the winter hat, white gloves and pumps. But, we did get fitted into the summer uniforms of green and white seersucker. It was a two piece suit with short sleeves, green insignias and white buttons.

"I'm so glad to get these," I said. "It's been surprisingly warm here in North Carolina."

"The commanding officer will tell you whether it is hot or cold. You will be told what to wear and your officer decides the uniform of the day. Not you!"

The only uniforms we could wear until we were given the order were our winter greens even if the North Carolina day turned out to be a scorcher.

We all giggled at ourselves in the green hats that were issued with the summer uniforms which made us look like Girl Scouts on patrol. Poor gawky country gal Jenny Mae who had a large head size was especially comical in the soft green hat with its round crown and stitched brim, down in front, up in back. This was our least favorite item of the Marine Corps uniform. We all looked a little too adolescent in these summer hats.

The line moved fast as the remaining items piled up in our arms: two khaki shirts, two ties, two slips and a girdle, two pairs of lisle hose in a neutral beige color with seams. It was true! We did have to wear cotton stockings.

"You *People* will wear a girdle at all times, under winter and summer uniforms!"

Of course! How else can you hold up those cotton stockings? Didn't matter how thin you were, a lady always wore a girdle, especially under a suit. No one took exception to this order.

The most expensive item was the double breasted trench coat with a removable wool lining. Even that had to be hemmed. It cost over forty dollars. A red wool scarf called a *field muffler* or *field scarf*, was issued at the same time with explicit instructions. It was to be crossed over in a fold and tucked inside and never tied, and at no time was the coat to be worn without it.

The item of apparel which delighted everyone was the slimming green twill fatigue dungarees jump suit with straight pant legs, to be worn for work and not sports. The outfit was the same as those worn by the Marines in the South Pacific. It buttoned up the back and had a bib top with shoulder straps two inches wide which crossed in the back and buttoned in front. The pant legs had no cuffs and fell straight and loose to the ankle. Even the bigger girls seemed thinner in them. The boxy loose four button jacket had a emblem stenciled on the square pocket on the left breast and there was room to stencil our name on it. A couple of white men's skivvies shirts went with them and a darling Pork Pie hat with a turned up brim completed the cute outfit. I couldn't wait to wear these dungarees.

My wish was answered within minutes. The platoon sergeant announced *"a field day"* and escorted us at a run to an empty class room which she considered filthy.

"This is youh first *detail. Swab down* the Venetian blinds, *deck, bulkhead* and desks. And polish the brass!"

The first week went by in a blur of frenzied cleaning, drilling, marching, filling out questionnaires and classes. We were up at 0545, fell into formation at 0630, ate breakfast at 0645, and went to classes from 0800 to 1130, marched to lunch and after all that, we went to more classes until 1600, all in Navy time. We hit the sack at 2200.

Translated into Eastern Standard time, that meant we were up at 5:45 A.M. and put to bed at 10:00 P.M.

Evenings were spent cleaning what was already spic and span beyond God's expectation. And we marched, marched, and sang and marched. The promised two hour visit at the week-end to the Post Exchange, the PX, became a beacon to each of us. Mess hall, where hundreds of women came together for breakfast, lunch and dinner became peak moments of joy and relaxation. I developed an appetite and capacity for food that astonished me.

We no sooner put on our long-awaited uniforms than wailing began and grew in crescendo throughout the squadroom. A vital and essensial part of our uniform was missing.

"Did anyone bring a bright red lipstick or nail polish? I'd like to borrow it, please." The same begging cry was on everyone's lips. No one offered. No one had it to share. No one had the foresight to bring a color that matched the red cord of the Marine hat.

The fashionable make-up colors of 1943 were corals, pinks, magentas and ruby. To be color correct it was important to match individual skin tones and hair color not clothes. Blondes wore pinks; brunettes wore ruby or coral and auburns wore magenta. In the Marine Corps, none of this mattered.

We couldn't wear any of the make-up we had brought if it didn't match the true scarlet of Marine Corps red, the regulation color of the red cord on the Marine Corps hat and the red muffler of the trench coat. Whether blonde, brunette or red-head, our lipstick had to be regulation and we now shared the same problem.

Bulletin Board Notice:

Commandant's Letter of Instruction 489 Paragraph H:
Lipstick must match the red cord of the Winter Service uniform and applied thinly. Mascara shall not be worn.

We checked with each other frantically. No one had anything that came close.

The promise that soon we could have our own special Women's Reserve lipstick, that chemists were working on a special Marine Corps red lipstick and nail polish, was of little comfort. The redder the lips were, the more fashionable and presentable a woman was. Being without lipstick or nail polish was a form of nakedness few of us had to endure since junior high school.

The corporal was sympathetic. She too had experienced our distress.

"You will be able to buy Elizabeth Arden's *"Victory Red"* and Revlon's *"Scarlet Slipper"* lipsticks at your visit to the PX in two weeks. They are not an exact match but they are acceptable for now. Make sure that none of you *people* foul up that will get the whole barracks restricted and privileges revoked."

A visit to the PX became the focus of our greatest desire. Two weeks now seemed an eternity. Woe unto the goon Boot who caused our squad or platoon to miss the reward. The corporal's threat had teeth in it.

Suddenly we were aware of how special that clear scarlet color was that was painted, woven, enameled and printed on every thing connected with the Marine Corps. It was on the chevrons on the sleeves of uniforms, the signboards, emblems, pouches, bandsmen's drums, slings, auto tags, officer's hat cords, aiguillettes, stripes on blue trousers, bandsmen blouses, blankets on dogs, and now on lipsticks and nail polish, on uniforms, on books, pamphlets and all printed material. There was no escaping the Marine Corps colors of red and its companion colors of egg yellow and marine blue.

Brooklyn had brought enough make-up to cover all the actors in a senior high school play. Her anxiety to buy more make-up finally caused Laramie, her bunkie, to ask, "Why do you need all that horse manure?" Laramie was a direct person, with a scrubbed look and a sunburned tinge, a former school teacher from Wyoming. In our squadroom were many former teachers.

Brooklyn wasn't offended in the least. "In case any of those Paramarines practicing out there on Onslow Bay get dumped in this no man's land by mistake, I want to be ready for them," she said flippantly. She never showed resentment at remarks. New Yorkers seemed to have a great resiliency.

"You should come out West. We've got lots of men in Wyoming who are ranchers and hungry for wives. They are lonesome and most of them are well off and own herds of cattle," said Laramie.

"Brooklyn, I think you don't mean half of what you say. I bet you have someone special back home."

Her black eyebrows, so incongruous with her blond peroxide hair almost met above the bridge of her nose as she winced. Tears welled in her eyes. "Yeah! He's home all right. We both joined up together. Only they accepted me. Not him!"

The Women's Barracks

Names were impossible to remember. The barracks rang with cries of "Hey, Texas!", "O, California!", "Hi, St. Louie". If two girls discovered they were from neighboring states it was "Howdy, Neighbor!". World War II was forgotten as Yank and Rebel discovered they were still fighting the Civil War.

The girls promoted everyone with grand titles of General, Colonel, Major or Captain, right down the chain of command.

"Hey, General! I forgot my razor. I need to shave my legs. Got one?"

"Hell, Colonel! Who will know the difference with those stinking cotton stockings. Don't you love the way they wrinkle so sexy on the legs?"

Outside the squadroom our name was "Boot" or "Goon". "Marine Private" was heard when disciplinary attention was forthcoming. Nothing could have drawn women closer together nor as fast as having a common enemy. We shed our civilian attitudes of competitiveness very quickly.

We soon realized that if any one of us faltered, the whole unit would be made to pay for the mistake of one person. A spirit of cooperation and unity prevailed and became the guiding force. It was to each person's advantage to lend a hand to any mate who fell behind in any chore to avoid the restriction that would be meted out to the whole group. Each one had become her sister's keeper. The clumsy girls who couldn't work fast enough or were inept in following directions or orders were given a helping hand very quickly, even to the point of helping them dress or find the item they had misplaced. A wall of cooperation, a spirit of sharing, a readiness to share goods and secrets forged bonds of friendships in each squad as a bulwark against the leaders who could dispense demerits, restrictions, punishments and award liberty. It was a method of indoctrination that worked with the training of men and it was successful with the women.

It was the beginning of what we would recognize as *esprit de corps*.

The platoon sergeant came into the squadroom every half hour and the cry of *"Atten-hut!"* went echoing down the long room. We had to drop everything to hear an explanation of another facet of military life and we'd be given more rules and regulations to memorize, many of which were petty or simple common sense.

"There will be no smoking in the laundries. Smoking is allowed in the squadroom only when the smoking lamp is lit," said the Duty NCO who was in charge of the barracks.

"You will walk to and from the PX or Recreation Hall in a group with one person in charge. You must log out and in for all activities," said the platoon sergeant who was in charge of our bodies.

"You will not be allowed to talk to any male while you are a Boot!" said the lieutenant who was in charge of discipline and morale. "There will be no fraternization with enlisted male Marines while you are Boots. There will be no fraternization whatsoever between officers and enlisted when you are out in the field after graduation."

"You will wear cotton stockings and a girdle at all times."

She carried a thick red book of rules and regulations as we all did.

The moments of peace and quiet that were granted to us were spent in sharing information, commenting on the observations we had made and trying to assimilate the regulations and read the *Commandant's Letter of Instructions* we had been told to memorize that had been posted on the bulletin board.

"Where are these men we're supposed to avoid? How about sending smoke signals to the pilots in the Douglas Dauntless planes we see above us?."

"Oh, they're around all right. Hear the guns?"

"That is the target field. There's a notice on the bulletin board that says we get to shoot guns."

"I hope my husband is as safe from attack as I am," said Sherry, nicknamed from Charlotte. Somehow no one called her by her state; Indiana didn't suit her. She was tall and dignified with excellent posture.

"Where is your husband?"

"Somewhere out there under the ocean in a submarine." Sherry confided he was a lieutenant, junior grade, and we were sworn to secrecy. She hadn't told the Corps.

"How do you expect to get away with it?" we asked in awe of her courage.

"There was no rule that said you had to give the rank of your husband when you notified the Corps of your name change. You can even keep your maiden name if you request it," Sherry explained. "So I didn't tell them he was a lieutenant in the Submarine Service. They didn't ask me."

Tears welled in Sherry's eyes as she produced a picture of a bride and groom out of her locker box. "We got married on his last leave, just before I left for Boot camp. He's going to be a professor after the war. If we had waited we couldn't have been married at all. He doesn't come home again for nine months."

"I thought the Marines wouldn't take you if you were married to someone in the Navy or the Marines?" someone asked.

"They changed that rule a month after they made it in March last year. You still can't get in if you're married to an officer but it's okay if he is an enlisted man."

"The Corps will not assign a married enlisted Marine couple to the same post. They warn you about that when you join in case you're enlisting because you think you'll be together."

"Falling in love with a Marine officer is totally against regulation. It's the worst thing you can do. No! I take that back— marrying him is the worst. The Corps considers marriage between officers and anyone who is enlisted, fraternizing. They don't care if what you want to do is make it legal. For the Marine officer dating, marrying or shacking up with an enlisted is really bad news. He gets a court martial. For us WR's, we just get kicked out."

"Read it. It's on the bulletin board. Paragraph H. No association socially between officer and enlisted."

Disbelief fell upon all of us like a school of fish caught in a net. Who could believe in this day and age such medieval rules existed anywhere in the United States?

"What can they do? Put you in the *brig* for breaking any of those rules in the red book of regulations?

"WR's aren't put in brigs nor prisons. WR's get *confined to quarters, loss of pay, reduction in rank* and *extra police duties* for breaking regulations. But the rule about marrying an officer gets both of you discharged."

"I can't believe what you are saying. It's one thing for a rule to be written in the book for peace time but this is 1944, *for God sake!* The Corps isn't going to kick a Marine out of the Corps in the middle of a war! After they spent so much money to train us and make us Marines? C'mon! Look at how much is invested in an officer! You can't take every rule in that red book or on the bulletin board *that* seriously."

Fenton was appalled at the flippant remark.

Nevertheless, the rules against fraternization seemed to worry everyone the most. It went against the grain.

"Forget it! No officer is going to look at a Woman Marine and risk his career."

"After all, an enlisted WR would be expendable. She isn't supposed to be dating an officer in the first place. She can always get pregnant, married or not, and go out on a *Four ninety nine!*".

"What is a *499?*"

"You don't know about *General Order 499?* Where have you been? Every WR knows that one! It says if you are pregnant you get an honorable discharge for medical reasons immediately. No strings attached. With all benefits."

The voices became indignant.

"No one tells me who to marry or who I can date! A good looking guy is fair game, providing he's not already married. Aren't we a democracy or what?"

"The military is *not* a democracy. The United States is a democracy. The Corps is not. Wake up and smell the Ovaltine!"

"Marines don't get a vote or a choice on anything! The Corps tells you where to sleep, when and where and what time to go to bed. So, now you discover they can tell you who you can't go to bed with. Is that news to you, Boot?"

Every Boot had a comment or complaint to make about one or another of the rules, regulations and the Letters of Instructions that had been posted on the bulletin board.

"I expected the Corps to send me wherever I was needed. And I'm ready to go. But to tell me how to apply my make-up and what to wear? That's really going overboard. I always wore my lipstick thick like Joan Crawford. Now I can't even put on mascara. Without eyelashes and eyebrow pencil, I will look all washed out!"

"I never owned a girdle in my life and now I've got to wear one every day! To hold up cotton stockings! *Holly cow!*"

"I *always* have a glass of blackberry wine before I go to bed. It's works better than hot cocoa!"

"You can't bring Mogan David into the barracks. And that's that! If you're caught with any wine in your locker, you're in serious trouble!"

"Officers can keep liquor in their quarters. The enlisted can't. Take it or leave it! You do things the Marine Corps way."

"Wine isn't liquor. The Priest gives it to us to drink in church for communion, *fer god's sake!*"

"We *always* have wine with dinner. Mother served champagne the night before I left for the Corps."

"Well, the Corps can't mean wine or beer. They're talking about whiskey. We are all over twenty-one years of age. Let's ask the

NCO about that rule. Is it only in Boot Camp or after we get out of Camp Lejeune?"

"I can live with that regulation about no booze in the barracks! But the rule that says a WR can't smoke on the street is downright wasteful. That means dousing out a good cigarette that hasn't been smoked down. Those packs cost fifteen cents!"

"That's a good rule! A woman smoking on the street doesn't look feminine or lady like. It's okay for the guys but a woman who smokes on the street looks so hard and low class. A Woman Marine smoking on the street makes the Corps look bad!"

The conversation stopped as the corporal NCO walked in.

She said cheerfully, "A slack ship is not a happy ship. *G.I. party* at eighteen hundred. In the Marines, we use Navy time. Learn it!" A G.I. party meant mops, brooms and pails.

She walked past each of us and made another profound observation. "Hair can not, I repeat, can not touch the collar. Some of you *goons* have hair that is below the collar! *Cut it off!*"

After an early supper of fried chicken, mashed potatoes, gravy, green beans, gelatin salad with finely chopped cabbage and carrots and a dessert of chocolate layer cake which was served at *sixteen thirty* or 4:30 P.M. Eastern time, I assembled in the *"head"* with the rest of the amateur barbers. Not all of us were cut out to be hair stylists.

"Your hair is not too short. I cut off only this much. It's off your collar, isn't it? Just be glad they don't use a lawn mower on us as they do the men Boots."

"God-damn it, Terry! You almost nipped my ear," yelled Pittsburgh who had a tendency to curse easily. She too had belonged to a home town platoon, the Pittsburgh one, but had been billeted with us accidentally. That happened to a lot of the girls.

I apologized, "A single blade razor is the best thing to use. It will give you curly hair like mine. Besides, I can hardly see, it is so smoky in here."

"Here, have a drag! Take it. I've got plenty."

"No thanks! Cigarettes make me choke."

"No kidding? You just didn't do it right. You've got to practice. Try mine. They are rum flavored."

Cigarettes were given free by many cigarette companies to all servicemen and women. There was never a shortage of different brands, Camels and Lucky Strikes being the most popular. There were even mint and rum flavored cigarettes which were passed around for everyone to sample as if they were chocolates from a box of candy.

The toilets and laundry room were blue with the haze and when the smoking lamp was lit, so was the squadroom.

"Do you have any vices, Terry? I bet you take your whiskey straight!"

"Liquor makes me break out in red blotches and beer tastes bitter. I like to kiss and neck. Is that a vice? And I can drink six cokes a day, easy." I had tried all the sinful vices.

"Stop picking on Terry," Laramie said. "I could go for a long cold draft right now."

It was wonderful being able to share one's short-comings with understanding friends.

Bits of conversation floated about as one hundred and twenty girls tried to use ten wash basins and ten toilets. Different routines, bathing rituals and habits in personal grooming were shared, compared and discussed. Intimate body secrets were disclosed with a frankness that was normally reserved for close family relatives of the same sex and maybe the family doctor.

"You've never shaved your legs before? Here's my razor. Stop looking like a hairy ape!"

"You never never cut your hair "down there"? You'd better unless you want to go to bed with curlers in both places."

"Here, try these Tampons. I wouldn't go back to sanitary napkins for anything. Don't be silly. Of course, you'll still be a virgin."

"I didn't tell you to shave it off. Wait until it grows out, you'll find out why."

"You put it in wrong—that's why it hurts. No! It's not stuck up there forever. Give it the old *Geronimo*! Pull the string!"

The woman gave the cry of the Paratrooper when he pulled the string to open his parachute.

The Boot did the same and everyone cheered for the girl who had been successful in getting her tampon out of her vagina.

In the Quiet Hour, which was a period of rest and relaxation granted to us daily, the talk was all about men. Those women who had men that were prisoners of war or had been killed said very little. They had joined the Marine Corps for the most patriotic of reasons.

As they listened to the jabbering of the romantic illusions of the unmarried girls their advice had one universal theme, "Don't waste time. Grab all the love you can. You may not have a tomorrow. Don't give up hope."

It was also true that for all the kidding and threats that the men had better run and hide when we got out of Boot Camp, practically every Woman Marine had someone special fighting overseas or stationed somewhere.

"Only twelve girls in the whole platoon do not go steady," said Joan.

"Yes," I said. "I'm one of them."

"Sure. I saw those snaps you were showing around," Joan scoffed.

"I gave them away. Shauna thought the English sailor was cute so she got him and Laramie is going to write the Coast Guard guy. I've got the Infantry at Camp Carson, Colorado left. Anybody want him?"

"I'll take the guy who sends you chocolates," said another Boot from the next squad who had heard I was giving away my pen-pals.

"I'm keeping Spero," I said. "My Mama likes his family's candy. His letters are long and too mushy. You'd get bored."

"One of these days, Terry, it'll hit you hard and you'll go out on a *four ninety-nine*," was Fenton's forecast.

At that barren point in my love life, I couldn't imagine myself getting a medical discharge for pregnancy under Marine Corps General Order Number 499.

Unlike all the mothers in Tonawanda, the Corps didn't care whether a pregnant Woman Marine was married or single. Pregnancy was a medical condition and not a moral dilemma. The Corps considered young motherhood and being a Marine incompatible unless the children were over eighteen.

Our very own director, Colonel Ruth Streeter had four children, three of whom were in the Armed Forces. Like Eleanor Roosevelt, who had raised a family and went on to serve her country, Colonel Streeter also answered the call when she was chosen to be the Director of the United States Marine Corps Women's Reserve.

The words in the song coming over Shauna's radio were saying just what I was feeling:
Will I ever find,
The boy on my mind ,

The one who is My Ideal

Pittsburgh started a jive step jitterbugging to Glenn Miller Orchestra playing *"Little Brown Jug"* on my favorite radio program, ASSEMBLY that played the best of the big band music. She stretched out an arm and grabbed me to dance with her. Our Ginger Rogers-Fred Astaire routine was amusing the whole barracks when a strong voice said,

"Knock it off! No radios are allowed. There is a radar school on base." The Duty NCO stood firmly in the doorway. Radar was something we had heard about. It was mysterious and secret. We knew very little about it except that it had something to do with invisible waves that could detect enemy planes.

Silence fell with a pall bearer's gloom. Radio wasn't something you turned off. It was the oxygen and the sun, as much a part of our lives as the air we breathed. I carried mine with me everywhere. Few of us had brought our radios since it hadn't been on the list. Mine had become community property which I was happy to share.

At 2200 *(twenty-two hundred)* or 10:00 P.M. to those who hadn't studied their Navy time, she stood once again in the doorway and yelled, "Hit the sack! Lights out!"

I debated whether a quick cross would be acceptable to GOD instead of a full kneeling prayer when Jenny Mae solved the problem for all of us.

She began to sing her Lord's Prayer ever so softly as they did in her Baptist Church. When she came to the "Amen" the whole barracks joined in with her. That started a couple of them sniffling a little.

Why? I didn't know. I liked the Marine Corps. It was the college life I had envisioned but could never afford because of the Great Depression. This life was like all the movies I had seen about college hi-jinks with sorority sisters singing songs and dancing. An empty hole and hunger was being filled in my life that had been opened by all the collegiate movies of the 1930's with the *Ta Ra Ra Boom Te Yey* of Notre Dame songs.

Darkness, pitch black, enveloped the barracks. Soft mournful sounds of a trumpet with the long plaintive notes of *TAPS* which I had always associated with the death of a soldier and never as a lullaby sent chills and tingles through me. My hairs stood up.

From a distance I could hear dogs barking.

From the bunks near-by the coughs and stirrings of restless bodies with tired and stiffening muscles added discordant harmony to the cacophony.

It was at this time I discovered the best part of being in a top bunk. Between the top slats of the Venetian blinds I could see the orange Carolina moon shining through the tall pine trees standing like Marine sentinels outside Area One, the very restricted women's compound.

Sleep would not come. My pink rayon pajamas, so comfortable to wear in my double bed at home, rebelled at the method I had used to slip into my sack. I had inched my body between the sheets without disturbing the blanket that was tucked so firmly with all the hospital corners intact. I hadn't been confident that I would be able to make the bed perfect enough to please the officer for morning inspection. My plan was sound. If I slept quietly without moving, then I wouldn't wrinkle the bed and in the morning all I needed to do was pass the flat of my hand to make it taut. The pajama tops choked me around the neck and the pants tightened painfully in the crotch.

Carefully, quietly, to avoid being caught in the hourly check up by the Duty NCO, I removed my pajamas and placed them on top within easy reach for the first thing in the morning. I fell asleep to the lullaby of exploding shells and bullets of Marines practicing night tactical landing maneuvers near-by.

"Hit The Deck!"

A shrill whistle pierced the dark. Lights flashed on. I tried to rise. Something was holding me down. It was my blanket and hospital corners that were still tucked in tight. Girls stood stiffly by their bunks and answered to the roll call of their last names. The Duty NCO walked rapidly past them roster in hand.

I fell out of bed, tearing the hospital corners every which way and sent my pajamas to the deck as I fell into formation.

"Karas?" she shouted.

"Here!" I answered. She marched past me, oblivious to stark naked me standing at attention. No one else cared either? Who had time to be modest?

Fenton was taking out the pins from the tight pinwheels of hair on her head as she rushed passed me to the *head*.

Whoever got there first didn't have to wait and the rush was fierce. Brooklyn was right behind her, clutching a bar of soap, clad only in a towel that didn't go all the way around her ample buttocks

Jenny Mae was obviously used to awakening at the rooster's hour of 0545 Navy time. She had returned from the gear closet with a mop and pail and was throwing imaginary flowers hither and yon as she prepared to swab the deck under our bunks which had to be washed daily in the first half hour of dawn, along with making the beds or sacks, dusting the Venetian blinds besides finishing any other assigned police duties. All that and getting dressed according to the uniform of the day.

I was supposed to help her but Jenny Mae was the ideal bunkie. She didn't mind doing it all. I found my beautiful new princess style housecoat to cover my nudity but half way up the zipper stuck and refused to budge.

"Did yo-all check the bulletin board, Bunkie?"

"Not yet," I said, still tugging.

"Bunkie, yo-all got the *head detail* this week. The toilets on the left side are youhs."

I rushed to scrub the five white sinks and matching toilets before breakfast.

"Muster for chow in two minutes!" came the command.

The formation of all the platoons, including mine, was already waiting outside the barracks building for the march to the mess hall. I hoped my tardiness went unnoticed in the pre-dawn pitch black darkness as I joined the last girl in line. The NCO's were grouped in a conversation of their own discussing contests: "I'm bound to get the goon platoon award for sure this time," said one NCO.

"Not a chance," said my sergeant. "Ah've got the prize foul-ball in my squad. She won't let me down. She's bringing up the rear now. That's worth ten demerits. I'll just give her the ladder to clean with a toothbrush. That's sixteen steps to topside." I turned around to see who was behind me but there was no one except the next platoon, Company K, from topside—second floor squadroom keeping the required distance of ten feet between Company I, my platoon.

The chill morning spray hit my face with tiny astringent needles. "Mmmm! Smell that air!" I loved everything about North Carolina even the crisp pre-dawn mornings before the sun had a chance to warm up the earth. Compared to Buffalo climate this was mild. No snow on the ground meant the tropics to me.

"Yeah! Smell that Atlantic Ocean," said Brooklyn.

"And the Intra Canal Waterway, Onslow Bay and Neuse River," added Fenton.

"Utah was never cold like this! This is a damp climate. You don't feel the dry cold we have out West," grumbled Shauna, the words coming out between clattering teeth. "Half of the one hundred and sixty-seven square miles of this Camp Boggy-bottoms must be under water."

The tune of the STARS AND STRIPES FOREVER, the famous march that Marine Corps own John Philip Sousa wrote, had some new words and they floated down the chow line:

Be kind to your webbed footed friends
For a duck may be somebody's mother
He lives in a place called a swamp
Where it is always cold and damp
You may think this is the end
Well————It is

We joined in the singing just to keep warm, stamping our feet, which seemed to help to curb the hunger twinges that were aroused by the aromas. The women Marines were always singing.

The combined smells of country style sausages and steaming coffee escaped from the mess hall and blended with the scent of damp pine needles, stinging me to a sharp awareness of the ravenous appetite I had developed in the Marine Corps.

The sky lightened to a deep blue gray and I traced the shadowy outlines of the branches of the pine trees and the roofs of the buildings in the women Marines' compound here at Hadnot Point. The sky changed from pale gray to light blue as the sun rose higher and the line moved inside slowly, past the grapefruits, the tomato juice, small boxes of cornflakes, huge pans of oatmeal, cream of wheat, sausages, scrambled eggs, trays of toast and butter—a typical Marine's breakfast.

"Nothin' like chores to work up an appetite!" Jenny Mae said.

"Thanks, bunkie, for fixing my bunk and swabbing the deck and cleaning the blinds, Jenny Mae," I said. "I never would have made it if you hadn't."

"Ah'm sure happy youh mah bunkie," she said. "You tap dance great."

"What's that white lumpy stuff you're chowing down?"

"Youh never had grits?"

A quick look around the mess hall and it was easy to separate the Yankees from the Rebels. The girls from north of the Mason-Dixon Line had no mushy white cornmeal on their trays.

"I wonder," said Joan, looking down at her tray, "how were they able to scramble eggs for six hundred? They sort of smell funny."

"They're dehydrated powdered eggs. It's quite simple. The Mess cooks mix the powder with water and bake it."

Fenton had prepared herself for every eventuality to her getting a commission and knew a lot about the way things were done in the Marine Corps. We had come to depend on her a lot.

"I've got to tell my mom about this recipe. All she knows is knishes. Aren't these eggs the greatest?" said Brooklyn.

"Civilians can't get this egg powder. All of it goes to the men overseas." Fenton informed us.

A buzz of excitement always surrounded the bulletin board which was posted to the right of the front door at the entrance to the squadroom. Like the icons in a Greek Orthodox Church, the notices were the first thing you saw. Reading the bulletin board was crucial to the well being of every Marine. A crowd always stood in front of it.

Announcements were constantly posted on it that gave the latest notifications of schedules and lectures. Lists of duty assignments could appear on it at any time. It was the responsibility of every Marine to keep up with the notices on the ever changing bulletin board. It was also the source for much rumor and scuttlebutt.

Cries of "We get to see men!" and "Hooray! We get to shoot guns!" brought a cluster of girls running to confirm the good news that all Boots were to receive lectures and field demonstrations on combat, landing operations, tactics, aviation, amphibian tractors and paratroopers. We would get field trips to the rifle range and see demonstrations of hand to hand combat, infantry weapons, the war dogs, and the Paramarines Most of us had expected that as women Marines we would be taught how to shoot, but, rumors had spread that we wouldn't be given guns. It turned out to be true. It seems the only reason we women Marines were even going to be given an opportunity to shoot on the rifle range was due to our President's wife, Eleanor Roosevelt. She expected it.

Advanced training was offered to any WR who would be lucky enough to be selected after graduation from Boot Camp for further schooling in any one of the Specialist Schools. It meant two to four months of training right here at Camp Lejeune. That was an opportunity many of us wanted. Camp Lejeune had everything.

A cornucopia of opportunities in specialist training for many categories which were once available only to men was listed on the bulletin board.

Now that the men were being sent to fight and lay down their lives for our country, it was up to us, the women to hold up the rear. It was up to the women to show that we could do what the men could do. Everyone of us had the confidence that she would be able to take the place and be just as capable as any man. Secretly, some of us thought we could do the jobs better.

New careers dangled like ornaments on a Christmas tree. We were offered many intriguing possibilities and promises of being sent to different specialty schools for further education.

There were schools for *Cooks and Bakers, Motor Transport, Quartermaster, Paymaster, Message Center* and *Administration* and schools to become *non-commissioned officers.*

Nine thousand women were needed for aviation alone. Training would be given for various positions to make it possible to free the men to fight.

These women would be sent to schools all over the country for highly specialized training to become an *Aviation Machinist Mate at the Naval Training School* in Memphis, Tennessee; *Link Training Instructor* at Naval Air Station in Atlanta, Georgia; *Aviation Storekeeper* at Indiana University, Bloomington, Indiana; Quartermasters of *Aviation Supplies and Material.*

The list was exotic and fascinating to read, the opportunities danced like sugar plum fairies around women who had grown up during the stifling years of the Depression in the last decade when any job would do.

We would never have been offered anything as exciting as these jobs which were listed on the bulletin board if there had been no war: *First Sergeant, Paymaster, Signal, Parachute Rigger, Aerogra-*

pher, Clerical, Control Tower Operator, Aerial Gunnery Instructor, Celestial Navigation, Map-Maker, Secretary, Finger Printer, Draftsman, Machinist's Mate, Jeep Driver, Motion Picture Operators Technician, Aircraft Instruments, Radio Operator, Radio Material, Radio Material Teletypewriter, Post Exchange, Uniform Shop, Aviation Storekeeping, Automotive Mechanic, Carburetor and Ignition, Aviation Supply and *Photography.*

I read the list avidly. One job classification was missing and I breathed such a loud sigh of relief that Fenton, reading the bulletin board next to me, asked me about it.

"Are you talking to yourself, Terry? Did you just kiss that bulletin board?"

"I am so happy. You just don't know how relieved I am. There's no *Running Inventory Kardex Supervisor* on that list!"

"Is that what you did before joining? I'm surprised. It sounds very important."

"It wasn't. It was just a lot of little cards that I had to flip up and record balances of inventory on in a strange file cabinet that always fought back and made me black and blue. I told the Classification officer I'll do anything for the Marine Corps but that. I hated that job."

My attitude was not unusual. Many of us didn't like what we did in civilian life. Amelia Earhart and Jackie Cochrane had soared in the sky and showed women they could fly but there were millions of us forced to make their way in life on the ground as waitresses, salesgirls and factory workers. Before the war, there weren't that many opportunities for women outside of teaching, waitressing, office work or salesgirl. Many jobs in factories, in business, in the professional fields such as medicine, mechanical, science and university, that once were open only to men were now being done by women. This fact had not gone unnoticed by many of us. The topic was discussed in our bull sessions and frankly, some of the women were puzzled as to what would happen after the war when we'd have to give these jobs up.

"Do we have to go back where we came from?"

"I'll never go back to the Remington factory and do the same work." I said.

"I wouldn't be surprised if the Corps assigns you to do the same work," Fenton said with pessimism "They'll give you the exact opposite of what you requested. Look at me! A graduate of Massachusetts Teachers State College! I asked for officer's training."

"Not a chance. The Marine Corps doesn't use that filing system. Read that list over again. It's not on there."

All the same I took no chances. I knocked on wood, crossed my fingers and spat three times. Still a chill went through me. Thank goodness, I wasn't superstitious or I'd have been depressed all day.

Military School Days–The Making Of A Marine

The list of all the classes we were to be taught in Boot Camp was posted on the bulletin board and excitement ran high.

No high school in the United States offered a curriculum of such subjects as Military Customs and Courtesies, Navy and Marine History, Naval Law, Weapons, Chemical Warfare and Map Reading. We would be taken on field trips to learn about Amphibious warfare and hand to hand combat or the art of camouflage. This was a whole different world. And I liked it.

Classes began every morning immediately after chow. I jockeyed into a seat in the front row of the classroom. One glance at the rolled shade on top of the blackboard told me movies were to be shown.

The male, a First Sergeant, standing next to the desk noticed my eagerness to be near the fountain of knowledge. His face was expressionless. I smiled vivaciously at him and was rewarded with a gas mask.

"This is the way you put this mask on. Tight against your face. You must avoid suffocation. You won't be able to breath if you don't pay attention to me!"

I stood at attention, holding my breath behind the rubber tubes, groping for my consciousness against the claustrophobia as he droned on about *Chemical Warfare*. I swayed slightly and realized I was losing the battle before I even got to the gas chambers to sample the gases for identification. I ripped off my gas mask before he finished his demonstration and snuffed out my chances to be assigned as a *Toxic Gas Handler*, *Chemical Warfare Specialist* or even *Chemical Laboratory Technician*.

An old Gunnery Sergeant with three stripes above and "two rockers" below, with four hash-marks on his sleeve denoting his sixteen years service as a Marine replaced the first instructor. A hush fell as the weapons instructor, an impressive figure of a man, strode in carrying a weapon. He took a *parade rest* stance, feet apart.

He held the weapon up and parallel to his head with both hands.

"Dis is not a gun! Dis is a breech loading, magazine fed, bolt operated, shoulder weapon. Weighs 8.69 pounds less the bayonet. Popular name—da Springfield Rifle!"

He held the rifle higher. "It's da Marine's best friend. A Marine sleeps with it—lives by it. He's married to his rifle."

The whole class of women broke into giggles at the image of a virile Marine preferring his rifle over one of us.

The old Gunny focused his eyes on us, confused that his oft repeated lecture to Boots was greeted as witticism. "Wot's so funny? You think I like teaching you She-Marines?" His tone had become plaintive. "I want to be fighting the sneaky bastard Japs and here I am instead. You can bet, if it wasn't for dis lousy war I would not be here!"

The class giggled again. "If it weren't for this war we wouldn't be here either." We said it simultaneously in a chorus of soprano voices.

The old Gunny sighed sadly as if someone dear to him had died. "She-Marines! They're killing my Old Corps!"

He led our weapons class to the rifle range where we learned how to use the Marine's best friend.

Lying prone on my stomach, I held the rifle as he placed it properly in my arms. First he put it against my shoulder and then he adjusted the sling tight and high on my left arm. A sandbag in front of me gave some support to the back of my left forearm and wrist.

"Line up da sights! Put that bull's eye on da target right in da exact center. See the peep sight? Right where da lines cross. Keep your eyes on da target. Dat's 100 yards away. And hold your breath and squeeze. You won't hit anything, but that's okay."

The rifle weighed considerably more than I expected. I couldn't seem to keep it up and steady.

The Gunnery Sergeant noted my struggle and came to my aid, grumbling. "*She-Marines!* Is dis the way we're gonna win dis war?"

Nevertheless, he helped support the rifle with his little finger as I aimed at a white piece of paper.

"You don't pull da trigger. You squeeze it gently like da tits on da Honolulu whores on Hotel Street." The Gunny's phonograph record of instructions had not been updated for this new breed of Marines. The feminine snickers behind him made him turn around.

As he straightened up, I squeezed the trigger, a bang went off and the rifle socked me hard in the shoulder.

A white flag went up behind the target. The Gunnery Sergeant gave a low whistle. "I'll be damned! Pinwheel five."

"It's like embroidering a cross stitch. Just keep it neat and even. It's really easier than it looks," I told Jenny Mae awaiting her turn.

"Ah know," she said. "Ah go rabbit huntin' with my pa in the hills back home all the time." And another flag went up.

"I've been picking off coyotes outside my school house in Wyoming all last year," said Laramie as another flag went up.

"Mother and I won the Boston Skeet Club trophy for two years in a row," said Fenton as she pulled the trigger and another flag went up. "Do you know if it weren't for Eleanor Roosevelt, we wouldn't be here?"

Brooklyn aimed eagerly, "At least, I don't have to pay. It's cost me a lot of money to win all those stuffed animals and Kewpie Dolls at Coney Island."

The gunnery's manner changed drastically.

"*She Marines!* Dey can shoot. No *Maggie's drawers* for *my* Marines."

But despite our good showing, we did not get anymore lessons on the rifle range.

The Women's Reserve Boot platoons hurried on, ours along with the others, from class to class always on the double, running, running.

The next class, *Ships And Aircrafts*, demanded strict concentrated attention. Instant identification of aircraft from black silhouettes which were flashed on the screen for one tenth of a second was demanded of us. It was not as easy as one would think.

First we were given ten minutes to memorize the shadows and then split seconds to recognize them. The Jap plane, the Mitsubishi A6M Zero was easy to spot. I always got that one right. But even after six weeks, the split second timing required to identify these planes had me shooting down our whole airforce of P-36s.

Had I been very good and fast, I might have been picked to go to one of the *Aviation Specialist Schools* and end up in one of the elite Aviation Women's Reserve Squadrons that were posted across the country. Many of them were in California. I had requested a posting in one of them when I filled the form of where I wanted to serve. Visions of California sunsets at any one of the air bases in Southern California danced in my head. California had been my first choice.

Any of the posts in that state would have been fine for me: El Centro near the Mexican border, El Toro, Oceanside: Mojave, Twenty-nine Palms, Santa Barbara, North Island and Miramar in San Diego.

At least five hundred Women Marines had been assigned as *Aviation Storekeepers* who were involved in the storage and issue of all equipment in aircraft maintenance. A lucky few would become *Aerographers*, to observe and record weather conditions for Marine pilots. Scuttlebutt said they were all tall and handsome. It would be fun to be assigned as a *Link Trainer Instructor* who could teach young Marine pilots how to fly blind in a fuselage that never left the ground. That also wasn't in the cards for me. It seems I suffered from vertigo, a little dizziness.

The possibilities of what each of us could do in the Marine Corps were wonderful to imagine as we went from class to class. Our dreams made the hours fly and our attention to the instructors sincere.

The Chain Of Command And Fraternization

Until a Boot understood the concept of the chain of command and accepted the laws of fraternization, she remained a civilian.

The two hour classes on Naval *Law And Justice, Marine Corps Administration* and *Military Customs and Courtesies* were supposed to turn each one of us into a Marine who knew what to do, how to act and to obey and respect the traditions under which Marines had lived and died for one hundred and sixty-eight years, from 1775 to 1944.

This was very serious material.

This was not a class to dope off in, fall asleep, day dream or be inattentive. If a Marine broke any of the traditions, rules, regulations, general orders and laws, all of which had to be memorized, a Marine could be punished, dismissed, and face unpleasant consequences.

Familiar writer's cramps returned as I took copious notes.

Anyone who dozed off in this class while the rules of the chain of command and fraternization were spelled out was digging her own grave. We didn't have to agree or like what we heard, we just had to learn it and abide by all of them throughout our period of enlistment.

The military concept of class distinction, which promulgated the philosophy that one group of people was inherently superior to another group, originated with the Royal English Navy which in turn reflected English society, then and now. The division into two groups, the aristocracy and the peasants, was echoed in the creation of the officer class whose role was "to command" and the enlisted (or impressed or inducted) class who had "to obey".

When the American Navy and the Marine Corps were created in 1775, by authority of the Continental Congress which represented the citizens of a rebellious nation seeking its inalienable rights from Mother England, they incorporated all of the same old English traditions that had made England's Navy so invincible. While on land a revolution was being fought to prove that all men were created equal, the young American Navy was embracing and incorporating some of the very same old ideas that had given birth to the rebellion.

From the first few ships that were given to General George Washington to fight in the American Revolution, the American Navy had grown to a fleet of thousands of ships that included destroyers, submarines and air-craft carriers. From that time to the present war, the chain of command was enforced according to the English blue-print.

Each group was assigned certain rank and privileges. Instant obedience was demanded of the lower group to the commands issued by anyone of the upper group. No enlisted could countermand or disobey an order from an officer. That was tantamount to treason. No one could dismiss an order from the rank above. That was how the chain of command worked in England's Navy and that's how it was followed in the United States Navy.

The laws against fraternization were also rooted in the two-class society of England. The lords and ladies of England's aristocracy did not mingle socially with their inferiors. This attitude was perpetuated in the military in both countries. Rules and regulations were passed and enforced with vigor prohibiting any enlisted from social contact with an officer. When women came into the Corps, it included the act of marriage between officer and enlisted to be an act of fraternizing and cause for discharge without benefits. Navy rules

Theresa Karas Yianilos

and regulations took precedence over all other lines of demarcation, sexual, educational, religious, monetary, cultural and emotional.

We lived in a democratic nation where the most popular wise-cracks were "It's a free country, isn't it?" and "I'm free, white and twenty-one!" Free choice was an American Constitutional birth-right.

At the top of the list were two Marine Corps Commandments:
Thou shall be obedient to all military orders given by the rank above you, cheerfully and on the double.
Thou shall not fraternize.

In order to become a disciplined Marine each person had to forget what was common knowledge in a democratic nation that gave each individual the right of choice. In the military, there were no choices. There was only the Marine Corps way, done by the numbers. The first order of loyalty was to the squad, the platoon, the company, the battalion, the regiment, the division, the Corps and Country. You couldn't be a Marine if you didn't accept this basic philosophy that was the foundation upon which the Corps stood hard and firm.

One did not question the reasons for the chain of command. It was a force to be obeyed without question borne of a tradition hundreds years old. Without it, discipline could not be maintained. There was always someone superior in rank to each and every Marine, whether officer or enlisted, who must be accorded instant obedience without argument or refusal. Refusal to obey an order from an officer was mutiny at its worst. The rank above always had the right of way. A military person could not by-pass the immediate rank above him/her and go to the top if he/she wanted satisfaction. It didn't work that way in the Marine Corps because of the chain of command.

The enlisted group was on the bottom of the pyramid. They did not salute each other.
Privates had to defer to Privates First Class.
Privates First Class had to concede to Corporals.
Corporals had to jump for Sergeants.

110

Sergeants had to obey all Staff Sergeants who in turn answered to those sergeants above him, from Technical to Gunny, to First Sergeant or Sergeant Major.

All enlisted had to snap to for all officers, from the lieutenant to the top of the chain. Enlisted were required to show respect and render a salute the moment they saw an officer. The Chain of Command required that the lower ranking officer render a salute to the higher ranking officer. Rank was always worn on the collars, shoulders and sleeves and was highly visible, red stripes for enlisted and gold or sliver for the commissioned officers.

The Second Lieutenant deferred to the First Lieutenant.

The First Lieutenant answered to the Captain.

The Captain obeyed the Major.

The Major carried out the demands of the Lieutenant Colonel.

The Lieutenant Colonel walked on the left side of the full Colonel.

The full Colonel attended to the General.

But, the chain continued to the top.

The one star-Brigadier General had to acquiesce to the two star-Major General who had to defer to the three-star Lieutenant General. That is as far up as the Marines went in the year 1943-44.

But, these Marine generals had to obey the orders of the Joint Chiefs of Staff who were Army Generals and Navy Admirals in the rank of four stars.

They were in charge of the war and could tell everyone where to go and where to fight, including the Marines. Still they were not the last word.

President Franklin Delano Roosevelt was Commander In Chief and he was the last man in the chain.

Except for Congress. They had the ultimate power which was given to them by the electorate of the United States. Only Congress could declare war. Still they weren't the last link in the chain.

The people were. They had the last word.

A Marine was obliged to report all complaints, requests and information to his immediate superior. The superior was then obligated to pass it on to his superior and so on up the line. Sometimes a request or a complaint that was passed on would be stopped along the line. Too bad. There was no recourse to find out and by-pass the superior who stopped the chain.

For the enlisted or the bottom rank of officer, there was no reversal of this chain of command by vaulting over one's superior one step above and going directly to the officer three or four steps ahead. That ploy was not allowed and was so frowned upon that it was not an option. There was no going straight to the top with any complaint or request. Therefore, one never knew where the blockage or denial of request originated or at what rank. For Marines of lower enlisted rank, it was impossible to send a tracer to discover what happened to a request if it were denied or delayed.

An officer could resort to the good old boy's club of personal connections to make his case if there was a disagreement with another officer. The chain of command worked fine for the men.

Not so for the women. For women Marines the problem became most serious when a complaint needed to be reported to the very superior that was causing the complaint. It was a problem that never was touched upon nor discussed in Boot Camp. No classes were ever given on how to deal with men who had the power of promotions and rank over the women who used that power outside military protocol. The rules against fraternizing were supposed to take care that this didn't happen. It did not always work.

The American Navy and the Marine Corps had kept these traditions intact for almost two hundred years. They did not want and feared any erosion of this particular tradition and refused to change it to accommodate the females who were inducted.

When women entered the Navy and the Marine Corps, additional rules were added to protect the established traditions and not those inalienable rights which were specified in the Declaration of Independence about any pursuit of happiness. Intermarriage between enlisted and officers made love and marriage an act punishable by dismissal with loss of pension and other fines.

Being able to retain all this information was vital if a Woman Marine wanted to pass the exams which would place her in one of the administrative posts for which she was freeing a Marine to fight. She could become a *Legal Clerk,* an *Administrative NCO,* a *Secretary* or a *Stenographer,* a *File* or *Supply Records Clerk,* a *Messenger* or *Courier, Recruiter, Quartermaster* or a whole long list of other classifications.

I tried to stay awake, but the droning voice of the lieutenant WR instructor was so soothing. My fingers fell asleep with pencil in mid air, my elbow propped up on the wooden writing arm on the right hand side of the chair. I barely caught phrases of Marine Corps history here and there.

"The Constitution in 1787 gives Congress authority to decide the power of size.

National and naval policy—to seek the enemy and destroy—— maintain Navy—strength and readiness—

"Uphold National policies—guard the United States——...over-seas possessions—"

"1940—we had 20 planes—1943—were 2000 planes.

In 1936 we had—nineteen thousand Marines. In January 1944 we have 350,000 men and 14,000 enlisted women and 800 Women officers."

We stumbled from the classroom into bright sunshine exhausted from the bombardment of information. The Corsairs F 4 V's and Brewster Buffalo's from near-by Peterfield Airfield made curlicue's and beautiful patterns of smoke screens in the azure sky as our platoon ran across the compound to combine with other platoons as we all ran on the double to our next class.

The Navy commander at the podium introduced himself. "I'm Doctor Stork—uh—that is spelled Storch."

Giggles trickled over the room at his self introduction.

"I'm a real doctor—a proctologist. I am here to lecture on personal hygiene and venereal diseases."

One hundred and sixty-five women who filled the room were alert and attentive. Some were married; many were engaged; many were virgins and many were not.

The doctor said "uh" a lot. "Uh—the spirochete germ is—weaker today than it was five hundred years ago. In 1800 Napoleon sent uh French prost—uh—women to undermine uh the Italian troops....

Uh—the prophylactic is uh a chemical preventative applied to men for syphilis and gonorrhea. Uh the drug 914 is used to cure. It's an eighteen month slow long treatment....

Uh look for a hard sore uh not painful on the penis. It's visible upon—uh—inspection... "

Anxious whispers came floating down our row.

"Do we get monthly inspections as the men do?"

"Didn't you know? The men have to stand there naked every week and show *it* off?"

"Who has to look?"

"It's an officer's job."

"Who's going to ask him about us? Do we have to go through Show and Tell?"

"Pittsburgh, You ask him!"

"The hell I will. You're the one who wants to know."

The buzzing was quite audible.

"Are there any questions?" The doctor looked above our heads. The murmur stopped immediately. No one spoke up.

He continued, "Uh, many changes can affect the menstrual period-uh-nervous reaction, worry, fatigue, environmental and changes in the climate, changes in daily routine."

"Before menses," he consulted his notes, "the female is grouchy, blue, depressed due to endocrine glands. She must avoid fatigue and competitive sports. When bathing, she should take only a warm shower in a comfortable room...."

A tsunami wave of laughter hit the room. The doctor hadn't seen our squadroom of one hundred and twenty-four girls trying to take a leisurely shower in the cold concrete cubicles painted battleship gray with no doors nor shower curtains and exposed pipes from which rusty water flowed in a sharp stinging spray.

The doctor was visibly relieved when the class came to an end.

"If knowing all this is supposed to make you a Marine, then I have been one for years," said Laramie.

I didn't hear much of what was said in *First Aid Class*. We were shown how to wrap bandages and what to do for emergency injuries. Of course I sat in the first row which made it a forgone conclusion I would be chosen as the victim. After that it was difficult to take notes lying on my stomach while the Schaeffer Prone Pressure Method was demonstrated to show how to save a life after accidental drowning, electrical shock, carbon monoxide poisoning, blows to the head, exposure to colds or overdose of drugs. Forty-five minutes flew by and I dusted myself off and proceeded to the next class. It had been fun and I had made the class laugh playing the accident prone Marine.

A thin gentle woman Marine Lieutenant was the instructor in the *Map Reading Class*. It was obvious the material she presented was as new to her as it was to her students. Together we spent an hour trying to figure out how to read a field map for the movement of troops.

I saw numb blank looks cover the faces of my mates when she gave us problems of how to determine the visibility of the contours between *"low elevation B"* and *"30 mark"*.

"Use the aid of a prismatic compass to read the azimuth of a course," she offered generously. The best of you may be assigned as a *topographic draftsman* and you will work with such tools as a *stereoptical comparograph*," she promised in return for our undivided attention.

A suspicion grew that the women officers had been schooled only a short time before us and they were not totally familiar nor comfortable with their material.

No doubt about it, we preferred the Old Salts and the Gunny sergeants as instructors. They had been around and knew their subjects. They looked and smelled Marine Corps. These men were the real thing. They were the professional sea-soldiers who guarded our shores before 1940 when there were only 18,000 of them in the Corps. They were the nucleus of the cadre of Old Breed Marines here at Camp Lejeune who would pass down the traditions of the Marine Corps to the thousands of new Boots, both men and women.

There were no short five minute recesses between classes and no return to the barracks for a pit stop. The kidneys began to protest.

No one dared suggest the idea to the platoon sergeant who did not let up the chant for one second.

"On the double! On the double! Youh laft! Youh laft! Move it, Goons!"

We were led away from the buildings and when we reached the asphalt road which ended into the river, she commanded,

"Platoon! Halt! Fall into formation!

The Drill Instructor–The D.I.

Our next instructor was another male Marine and rather young, somewhere in his middle twenties. His hat was of World War I vintage with four dents in it. He stood there calmly and surveyed our fumbling efforts with a menacing stare. We had been brought before the infamous drill instructor

We assembled four abreast and with outstretched arms reached for each other's shoulders to judge our distance while this short stocky male Marine sergeant watched us carefully. His whole body conveyed his utter disgust and boredom with each and every one of us. We could see in his eyes that his judgment of us was not very high.

We had been prepared for this meeting with the D.I. the night before by our platoon sergeant. She had peppered her lectures with warnings that foreshadowed the trials that awaited us.

"After the D.I. gets through with you, you'll appreciate how soft I am on you *Goons*. He is straight from P.I." she said.

P.I. Parris Island!—the notorious Boot Camp for Marines, three hundred and twenty miles away—where they went in as boys and came out as men. I guess they were going to try to do the same to us.

Our platoon sergeant moved back with respect and reverence. The drill instructor replaced her at the head of the platoon.

He stared at us, measuring each of us, in what seemed to be an inordinately long time.

The suspense was uncomfortable.

He then lifted his red face with the sunburned nose towards the magnificent blue North Carolina sky and moaned loudly in great pain, "Holy Mother! First the dogs! Then the niggers! Now the women!"

Then he jutted his chin toward us and from the bottom of his throat came the voice of thunder, "*Knock It Off!*"

All the giggling and friendly chattering stopped as suddenly as if someone had clicked off a radio.

"Some of you *People* are chewing gum! Get rid of it. Don't throw it on the deck. It's yours!"

The wads of Wrigley's spearmint slid down in one gulp.

So this was the Marine Corps' secret weapon. The D.I., the one man responsible for turning out the finest sea soldier in the world.

The Uniform, 1943-1945
Top: Shining the
regulation oxfords,
a daily chore.
Center: Distributing the
seersucker summer
uniforms.
Bottom: All uniforms are
fitted and customized.

The Drill Sergeant, 1943
Top: Recruits in civilian clothes meet the D.I.
Center: The D.I. and a platoon of uniformed WR's.
Bottom: Woman Marines on parade

The two-hash marks on his sleeve proclaimed his eight years of service and the dulled insignia on his collar and hat had turned green from the salt spray of his sea duty.

He must have joined when he was seventeen. The Sharpshooter's Cross hung over his left pocket and dangling next to it were three bars and a wreath for pistol, machine gun, bayonet and automatic rifle marksmanship.

I eyed his insignia. Mine were so shining new, proclaiming that I was a Boot. I wish I had his salty antique ones.

"*Atten-Hut!*" His command vibrated across the field.

"Line up forty inches back to breast! In even rows. Square your rows!"

That was not so easy especially with all the big busted women in our row. Bertha came from robust Norwegian stock from Decorah, Iowa and had a bust measurement of forty-three inches, most of them fore rather than aft. And several of the Boots were tall. Lining up shoulder to shoulder was difficult.

He began his cadence count. "Fo'wd harch! Won Up Ah Reep! Reep foah youh laft!"

I didn't understand a word he said. I only felt the rhythm—one, two, three, four—the left. One, two, left, right, three, four. It was a dance. Not fast like the Jitterbug or the Boogie Woogie but more of a Lambeth Walk.

He began a chant in time with the steps:
Yoh had a good home and youh laft!
Yoh had a good home and youh laft!
Yoh laft!
Laft reet laft!

"All right! Platoon! Count cadence count!" his voice bellowed.

At first our chanting was timid, our soprano voices weak, as we chorused, synchronizing the words with the beat of our footsteps.
We had a good home
And we laft!
We had a good home
And we laft!
One two three four
One! Two!
Three. Four!

"I can't hear you!" He bellowed.

He must have been hard of hearing because we were shouting our heads off. That was not easy for some of us who had been taught since childhood that a lady never raised her voice. Nevertheless the chant grew louder and louder until the hypnotic rhythm and rhyme made it impossible to be on the wrong foot.

We marched on that asphalt pavement back and forth. Each time as we came perilous close to the river, he always commanded a *"to the reeh harch"* which meant "to the rear march". That called for placing one foot behind the other and twisting around and reversing the direction.

The road disappeared right into the river which had no beach and became deep immediately.

This was the road used by amphibious tractors and vehicles, LCVP for landing craft vehicle personnel, which was a combination boat and car. They could be driven by the Fleet Marine Forces from ships off shore directly from the water onto the land. That what the Marine Corps was all about; why Marines were called Sea-soldiers. They were amphibious and were trained to fight on land and on the sea. Special vehicles had been developed in order for them to make the assaults and establish beachheads.

Our platoon marched straight towards the river again.

We waited for the order to reverse our direction but the command wasn't given.

We approached closer and closer to the deep river's edge. Several ahead of me fell out of step and so did I in anticipation of the command of *"to the rear harch"* to place the right foot behind the left and swing around the moment it was given.

The tension mounted as the river loomed only a few feet away.

I broke first into a fit of giggles. Tension does that to me sometimes.

Glints of iridescent colors on the water made an image inside my head come alive that struck me so funny I could no longer hold in my laughter. My mind's eye saw twenty-eight hats floating on the water, as twenty eight-women, me included, were *one up-a-reeped* to our doom, obedient to the end, while the waters went glub-glub over our heads, drowning us all. It would solve the drill instructor's problem of how he'd like to see us disappear, along with the dogs and niggers, of course.

"Platoon! Halt! Right Face!"

We stopped dead in our tracks inches away from the water's edge. I was right. He had been testing for obedience. Not a muscle moved.

The D.I. glowered. We stood at attention staring straight ahead and I tried to look through him but it was impossible.

He stood three inches away. He was in my face, in my space. "You! Boot! Two steps forward!"

I did as I was commanded, a little frightened but unable to turn off that silly image in my head, which left a wide grin on my face as I tried to control the giggling.

"Put your hands akimbo on your waist!.'

I did so with the whole platoon watching, as puzzled as I. I didn't know what was coming next and neither did they.

"Wave them back and forth!"

I flapped my elbows.

"Now tell me! What kind of bird are you?"

I searched his eyes and red face for a clue. A long moment passed by. Bird? Was I supposed to answer? A bluebird of happiness? Another giggle hit me. A parrot? Polly want a cracker? Of course! The American eagle! The bird in the Marine Corps emblem!

"A wise bird! That's what you are! A wise bird!'

"Oh, no, Sir!" I said most sincerely.

He stared unsmiling. I returned his gaze the smile no longer on my lips.

"I wasn't laughing at you—" I started to explain.

"Who gave you permission to speak, Boot?" He was shouting but that didn't frighten me as much as the women officers who could dispense orders and discipline without raising their voices.

He stared right into my face and forced me to look right back.

I suppose this kind of approach might be effective with the male recruits but any female who hadn't learned how to stare down a boy by the fifth grade had better plan on being a spinster. I remembered that the only way I could get a boy's attention in the third row, fifth seat, across the room was to simply have a staring contest. It worked every time and soon he was carrying the books home from school, his and mine. But this was a different kind of staring contest and it was uncomfortable. With great relief, this game broke up after a long interminable minute.

I hastily obeyed his command to "Step back into ranks!"

I did a smart neat turn about-face and did exactly as I was told.

The D.I. made our platoon repeat the same marching drill over and over but he never took us that close to the river's edge again. His dented field hat that gave him a quaint World War One look sat square on his head and bounced up and down.

I caught his stern look watching me more than once. I would have liked to take his hand and tell him I would curb my silly imagination and not to worry about me but of course, that was impossible; the military discipline said no fraternizing.

The D.I. rode us hard. We saw him every day for one hour drilling on the parade ground. He was intense about his mission and assignment. He had volunteered to transform civilian women into Marines in forty-two days of Boot Camp. When he finished with all of us, we would have the military bearing of Marines.

After the first week, we could see how far we had come. Not that we had been given any kind of praise. It was something we had guessed at by ourselves just watching each other.

He always greeted us as if he had inherited Job's Lot when we came into his life. His uniform was always immaculate yet there was always a rumpled exhausted aura about him even before he spent the twenty minutes teaching us the intricate steps of *Close order drill.*

His day must have been very full teaching the many other groups as well as ours. He was one of several male D.I.'s teaching the Women Marines.

Close Order Drill was a ballet of graceful movements to the beat of *One-two. Three-four. Left foot. Right foot.*

Steps had to be in precision: everyone on the same foot at the same time. Sometimes fast as in a tap dance.

"Double time"—one hundred eighty steps a minute.

"Quick time"—one hundred twenty steps a minute.

We responded instantaneously to his commands—or tried to.

"Left flank! Harch!" This command was one of the most difficult but most graceful drill step.

Our flanking oblique movements pivoting to the guide at the end of our row opened like a hand painted fan to reveal a beautiful picture for a few moments then it closed. Timing was crucial and it took many days to do it right.

Our platoon had it perfect until one day a momentary confusion sent me in the wrong direction and gave the D.I. another cause for a display of apoplexy. I bumped into Jenny Mae who was the guide and confused her into thinking she had made the mistake and was on the wrong foot. She shuffled her feet. Our row did the same.

The row behind us shuffled their feet and everyone fell out of step. The beautiful flanking movement disintegrated before his very eyes.

Now we stood before the platoon, and once again he singled me out as he vented his frustration.

"You! Boot! You have gotten on the wrong foot with me from the beginning! You! Right guide! Don't you know your left foot from your right?"

My poor bunkie! Shy sweet Jenny Mae had been chosen guide because she was so tall. She died every time she had to stand there by herself. There was one thing about my Alabama buddy that we understood: she was very sensitive to her short-comings and wanted to please everyone. Her eyes filled with tears and she hiccuped a few sobs and then some heart-rendering ones.

The D.I. hurriedly ordered us back into the ranks.

Jenny Mae dissolving into tears because she had displeased him had thrown him into confusion.

I just knew the male Marine Boots did not react this way. Nor did the rest of us, generally speaking.

We practiced the same steps over and over day after day, but it was the drill command *"To the rear harch!"* that turned our formation into a Laurel and Hardy comedy routine just when we had it down pat.

Fenton got caught that time; Fenton who was bucking for officer's training, who was always perfect in obeying commands. She couldn't help it either.

The command called for putting the right toe behind the left heel and pivoting in the opposite direction without losing the beat and to continue marching in the opposite direction.

Six of these commands, given in rapid staccato in the middle of a march, had some of us going East, some squinting against the afternoon sun in the West, bumping into each other in a giant patty-cake baker's man routine.

Fenton couldn't restrain her guffaws. Seeing her lose control and break down, of all people, the one who was determined to follow each command with religious exactitude; who always asked questions at all lectures displaying intense interest, even at the impromptu informal talks held in the corner of our squadroom at night; who always sounded off in the correct manner, name first then asking for permission to speak. It was too much. I tried to hide my laughter but my shoulders gave me away and this triggered off the whole platoon. The laughter rolled liked waves on the Pacific shores, spreading from one to another as we milled about.

So now Fenton and I stood in front of the platoon with the smiles wiped off our faces. Fenton was mortified and contrite.

Our platoon sergeant continued the lecture that the D.I. had given all the way to the barracks. Her Navy language was nastier and her tongue was sharper than that of the D.I. who usually glowered without saying a word.

"Stupid! Dope Heads! Snafus! Sad Sacks! Knuckle Heads! Eight Balls! The Navy jargon was cute. No one minded hearing her call us those names. It wasn't real swearing as the men received from the badgering of their D.I.'s who lived with them and watched over them twenty-four hours a day.

Day after day, the D.I. found something wrong with one of us. I got more than my share of attention.

He didn't like anyone to smile at him and I learned *"to wipe that smile off my face,"* but his disposition remained stern and sour all the same.

"He just doesn't like Women Marines," I said. "I am just a symbol. I refuse to take it personally."

"One of us should bell the cat," said Fenton, the grade school teacher.

"I'd say his trouble is just the opposite," said Laramie. "When a bull is put out to pasture and can't get at the heifers, he gets ornery."

"You all know he can't talk to us. He's assigned to teach us military bearing and discipline through *close order drill* and nothing else."

"Teaching Women Marines is a volunteer assignment. They have to draw straws for it."

"You mean they put us in the same category as going on combat patrol?"

"I can see their CO now," said Brooklyn. "See here, Marines! I need volunteers! Who is going to teach the women which foot is their *loft! Their loft! Reep for your loft!"* She went into a burlesque of peg-legging it across the room.

A song that was very popular, especially with the men, came on the radio and I joined in with my alto:

A woman is two faced... A worrisome thing to let you to sing
The blues in the night

Joan said, "Terry, be serious. You're part of the trouble. He's got his eye on you."

"I don't care for his type," I scoffed. "I want someone like *Walking John*. So far I haven't seen any Marine like him. Well, maybe, a couple of those guys at Eighth and Eye in Washington. They were what I expected Marines to be."

"*Walking John?*" asked Pittsburgh as she pinned up her wet hair. It was a chore she had to do every night since the short hair-cut I had promised her hadn't turned it into a natural feather curl as mine had.

"He's that tall handsome Marine in dress blues on the recruiting rosters who is forever marching! I even have a crush on the sketch of the marching Marine in leggings that was done for World War I."

"C'mon Terry. Leave the tall ones for us big gals," said Texas who was sitting on her bunk playing solitaire across from Sherry who was always writing letters to her husband in the submarine service.

"I can't help it. I don't get little mice unless they have a certain look. Strong, determined, handsome, big. I can't describe him exactly. I'll just know when he happens to me!"

"Little mice? What are those?" Brooklyn asked.

"That feeling you get up and down inside when you kiss someone special—makes colors appear inside your head and feels like an elevator button got pushed."

"You'd be surprised how big some of these little guys are," grinned Brooklyn with one of her double entendre comments.

"Size doesn't matter where it counts the most."

Pittsburgh said, "I think the D.I. is cute."

"That's settles it. The D.I. belongs to Pittsburgh," said Laramie in a spirit of generosity.

"As soon as radio silence is lifted and restriction is over, and we can talk to the men around here, I'll try to make time with the D.I. I wonder if he's Catholic with the same Pope as mine?" Pittsburgh asked.

"He certainly seems to be. He's always saying "Jesus Christ" when we foul up."

"My Dad thinks if the Catholics keep having such big families they will take over the country and we'll have a Catholic president some day."

"That will never happen no matter how many kids the Catholics have. There are too many Protestants."

"The Mormons beat the Catholics any day or the Protestants on that score. My great-grandfather had seven wives, and thirty eight children," said Shauna. "He lived to be ninety-four. Everyone of his wives died before him and his last wife was only seventeen when he married her."

"What kind of men do you have out west?"

"It's the air around Salt Lake City. It is very pure and clear. Mormons don't drink alcohol. They don't smoke and they don't drink coffee either. That has got a lot to do with keeping a body fit."

"What do you do for recreation in Salt Lake City?"

"We dance a lot. Always having dances."

"That'll work it off every time," said Brooklyn.

We packed all our civilian clothes and shipped them back home in our suitcases. We were given duffel bags to hold our gear and spent the evening stenciling our last names on the green canvas bags.

Gone were the awkward mismatched gangling rainbow-clad saddle-shoed individualists.

We had metamorphosed into chic uniformed Marines, brisk and smart, professional from the highly polished cordovan brown oxfords, brown leather gloves to the brim of our red-corded hats and our *Victory Red* lips.

No longer could we be called dames, tomatoes, broads, chicks or any of the other terms of familiarity!

Like butterflies emerging from their cocoons, suddenly we were neat trim beautiful American Marines, One look at us told the story. We were a good looking outstanding group of women. We were definitely not *BAMS*.

A constant stream of women passed before the large full length mirror which was a fixture of every Marine barracks, It was nailed on the wall at the exit and entrance of each squadroom. Each Marine had to check his appearance before going before the public. It was an order.

The order for the uniform of the day called for winter greens. It said so on the bulletin board but that was one notice no one had to read. The excitement of putting on our uniforms for the first time vibrated throughout the barracks.

The first morning of the wearing of the uniform was almost a disaster for the platoon sergeant.

She called, "Muster! Fall out in formation! In five minutes!" Formation in front of the barracks was the first drill each and every morning.

Her platoon didn't make a move towards the exit. A silly problem had come up which no one had foreseen.

Five minutes later she yelled, "Move it! Move it! Why are you Boots standing around?"

The women had piled up at the mirror in the hall and had squeezed into the *head* in front of all the other mirrors. Our whole squadroom of one hundred and twenty-four women were immobilized in the barracks for the dumbest reason.

Only one or two girls knew how to tie a four-in-hand tie. They were trying their best to teach those who had forgotten the instructions from the night before.

We women knew how to pin a diaper three ways, do needlepoint, embroider, crochet, knit, crewel and bake cookies from scratch but none of us knew how to tie a man's four-in-hand tie that was to be worn with our khaki shirts.

"Who knows how to tie a tie?" The wail echoed through the barracks. We were all thumbs and the girls piled up trying to help each other.

"Not that way! You make the loop first. Keep your thumb in place."

"How come the men can do it so easily?"

We put our new khaki green trench coats on and folded the red wool field muffler over the knotted ties and marched out in rhythm to the cadence count. We were impressed with ourselves and wanted to impress the world. The only male who would see us that day was the drill instructor.

"Won Up A Reep—Reep Fo Yoh Laft!"

Heads high, shoulders back and arms lightly at the sides, we strutted proudly, the thrill of achievement and glory in ourselves visible in the briskness of our step.

"MARINES! You are ready for battalion review. "Now put that laft foot down!"

No one missed the inflection on the first word that the D.I. called out. He gave every one of us a shot of pride that had an instant effect. The joy of being called Marines, no longer *Goon* or *Boot* was overwhelming. A warm wave of love flowed invisibly but tangibly from all of us to our D.I., the man who had brought us to this point.

Our backs straightened up more. You could hear every one of the left feet stamping down hard as the heels of our oxfords punched ridges into the squishy asphalt made soft by the sun. Half of us got stuck and it spoiled the look of the formation.

"Jesus Christ and Holy Mother of Mary!" cried the D.I. who wasn't allowed to really curse as he could with the men.

"One good thing about taking the Virgin's name in vain, it proves he's Catholic," Pittsburgh said with great satisfaction at the discovery.

The daily marching and exercises in the North Carolina sun began to show on all of us. I never felt healthier, stronger, nor prettier, nor happier. I liked what I saw in the mirror, my new figure, my windburn complexion and firmer muscles. I no longer slouched.

"Look! I have Betty Grable legs," I boasted.

"Mine are Flat Foot Floogies!"

"It's these setting up exercises every morning, rain or shine, that is reshaping me," lamented Joan. She pressed her fingers together in front of her in a mocking of the NCO physical instructor. "This is going to put me into a B cup. I'll be ruined in the rag business."

"That particular exercise is supposed to make the upper arms strong enough to carry the M-1 rife in one hand above the water when you're storming the beaches," said Fenton.

"That's fine for the men. What do you think it's doing to the women?"

Joan brought out a tape measure immediately. Groans and squeals of delight alternated with each measurement that was announced. Not every girl was happy. Big breasts spoiled the lines of the Marine Corps uniform just as big hips did.

Laramie sat on the wooden deck and walked five paces forward and backward on her buttocks. "This one is great for your butt. It firms the rear and thighs so you can climb off the debarkation ropes off the sides of LCVT's. Of course, we're not going to have to do that."

"Well, you won't spread into a *BAM* with that exercise."

"How about this one, where you crawl on your belly and have to keep your fanny close to the ground so you won't get it shot off?" I knelt on all fours to demonstrate.

"If you do it properly, it will strength your pelvis for labor pains and to relieve menstrual cramps. If you kick your leg out like this it will strengthen your uterus." Someone fell to the deck to demonstrate.

Brooklyn flipped over on her stomach to show how to improve the inner thighs while getting shot at.

Other girls from the squadroom fell to the deck. With all the huffing and puffing and laughter, no one heard the sergeant call "Atten-hut!"

Our lieutenant stood next to her, smiling at our gyrations.

"At ease," said the lieutenant "What's that you are doing?"

"Sexercises, Mam!" I said forgetting to sound off my name first, trying to salute on my stomach and jump up to attention.

"That is the Marine Corps spirit," said our pretty senior officer. "We must be strong enough to meet all challenges."

Every day we mustered with enthusiasm and high spirits on the parade ground for the Marine Corps exercises under the warm North Carolina sky, so unexpectedly blue and sunny for the winter month of January. Some of the other earlier platoons wore peanut suits, which were made out of tan cotton fabric that wrinkled easily and had old fashioned bloomer shorts with elastic around the bottom. But, we were the 24th Training Battalion and we missed out when the supply ran short. We still were a motley group in our various white shorts and blouses.

Being called a *BAM, a broad ass Marine,* wasn't as bad as being one. We took the exercises seriously.

To be strong enough to carry on the traditions of the Marine Corps was the aim of every Woman Marine. The trick was to look as if we weren't able to "take over" otherwise the men would panic further. Since womankind had been playing the game of acting the weaker sex for centuries, the instructions to follow the male lead were more of the same.

It was going to be difficult to hide our strength and brains in the same old ways once we were called upon to prove our capabilities at the same time. The training companies that had preceded ours who were assigned to duty were showing the Corps what we women were made of and already they were doing jobs that had always been the bailiwick of the male Marine.

Women had taken over the bus system on Camp Lejeune and Cherry Point. They drove those six by six military trucks for Motor

Transport and had the responsibility of dispatching, as well as the maintenance and repairs, of the largest of those green dinosaur trucks that transported the men into bivouac areas in the deepest roughest boondocks. Yet their trim neat figures belied the work they did as bus and truck drivers.

We Women Marines had to tread softly and carry a big stick no matter what our duty was.

Captain Towle, our CO, made a special lecture on this very subject, and pointed out the pioneer terrain we were about to traverse. She was a hard-charger and G.I., as military as the new Commandant of the Marine Corps, Major General Alexander Vandegrift. But, she also was the prime example of the Woman Marine who hid her steel under a pretty face and a non-threatening soft voice.

"Our position requires diplomacy," she said. "We not only have to relieve the men for combat, we must demonstrate we are capable of doing whatever is required, cheerfully with a willing spirit. We must prove that the high standards of the Marine Corps shall be safe in our hands and prove to each Marine that women are necessary to help win this war."

The message came through loud and clear.

We women had to prove our worth but still know our place. We were equal but some Marines were more equal than others. The Corps could make it very hard if we asked for too much. We had to learn the written rules of the chain of command, but, the unwritten rules, the ones that were custom and tradition, had to be understood by intuition.

Men had the right of way. It wasn't much different in civilian life.

The Marine Corps was more restrictive than the Army or Navy towards the distaff side of its inductees.

"Women Marines will not be sent overseas, into combat areas nor will they serve aboard ships."

The WAACs, Navy nurses and Red Cross women were in London and in other parts of the world where they had gone once the Allies and Americans had secured the areas. The WAFs ferried planes from one place to another. But, the Women Marines were going to stay in the United States.

Camp Lajeune, 1943-1944
Top: Womens's Reserve Boots in class.
Center & Bottom: Women Marines, (WR's) watching Marines
demonstrate tactical maneuvers.

Camp Lejeune, 1943-1945
War dogs: Each dog has its trainer.
Dogs accompany Marines on patrols.

Two Kinds of Marines, 1944
Top: Marines in full combat pack on their way to the Pacific.
Bottom: Note the Company of Women Marines arriving as the men are being shipped out.

Two Kinds Of Marines: *THOSE GOING TO THE PACIFIC AND THOSE WHO HAVE BEEN OVERSEAS*

Camp Lejeune was the major training area for Fleet Marine Forces. It was ideal because it had a deep river, the New River, and forests of tall pine trees which were called the boondocks.

Here, Marines practiced assault landings with live ammunition and flame throwers and perfected the tactics of establishing beachheads. A beachhead was defined as enough land or territory to land troops and supplies. Theoretically, once the beachhead was won, Army reinforcements were supposed to back up the Marines and fight the rest of the way. That is what we were told in class and now we were going to see the actual way they did it.

Our company was herded on to buses and for the first time we saw the Atlantic Ocean and the sand dunes and scrub brush of the beaches of North Carolina.

The new Commandant, General Vandegrift had stated:
"There will be two kinds of Marines, those going to the Pacific and those who have been overseas."
There was no doubt where these men were heading.

We were here to watch Marines, dressed in full combat gear, go through some of their jungle training in preparation for the coming battles on tropical islands. This field trip would give us an understanding of what it meant *to free a Marine to fight*. Seeing the conditions Marines would have to face when we relieved them for front line combat was supposed to give us inspiration.

We clustered at a safe distance and watched as groups of men demonstrated what their training was all about. The ferocity of their masculinity made a deep impression on each of us.

They were acutely aware of our presence. We had sized each other up. We were not allowed to say one word to the men. Obviously they were under the same orders as we were.

The Marines were dressed in a splotched pattern of gray-brown-green fatigue dungarees. The same kind of cloth covered their steel helmets which were draped with net that was with flowers, leaves and branches like the Queen of May.

Their officer was our guide.

"This is called camouflage. It is an old American trick we have reintroduced in this war. Remember what happened to the British during the Revolutionary War?"

Of course! Every American child who had passed second grade knew about the dumb English soldiers that the Liberty men were able to pick off because their red coats were so easy to spot in the woods.

"We won our democracy with our forest green then and we'll preserve it with these Marine camouflage greens now!".

The men had draped these spotted cloths and vine covered nets over the artillery guns to make it difficult for planes to spot them from above as well. When the men positioned themselves among the trees and bushes they blended so well we girls truly couldn't see them.

"It's going to take more than a spotted suit to hide from me when this restriction is over. " A female's high pitched voice was carried by the wind to the men.

Male laughter ricocheted from every bush and tree. A warm family solidarity and friendliness filled the air. Our combined laughter said it all for both of the sexes—being deprived of each other's company was the worst part of Boot Camp.

We watched the *Marine Raiders* go up rope ladders laden with full combat pack on their backs, their rifles with them.

A wrestling of hand to hand combat in the newly introduced style of Ju-Jitsu by several pairs of Marines demonstrated the advantage this method of fighting gave the smaller or weaker individual over the larger opponent. This form of self-protection seemed to be ideal for women but they didn't offer to let us in on the secret.

We went to another secret training area, the Paramarine Battalion where Marines were loaded into a plane wearing full pack and parachutes.

"Marines have become part of the attacking infantry during an invasion or amphibious assault. We are very careful where and when we drop the paratroopers."

I knew just what the captain was talking about. My high school prom date was now a paratrooper in the 82nd Division. He had told me awful stories about the stupid things that kept happening during the training exercise. Some boys actually got killed.

"The *Screaming Eagles* were always getting dropped over water by mistake," I said out loud, forgetting my orders to ask permission first.

The captain noted my observation and so did the WR lieutenant.

"Private Terry will make a good volunteer," she said.

I was put into a shock-drop harness where I was dropped from a wooden paratrooper flyaway tower twenty feet high to experience the pull when the parachute open.

I crossed my arms near my chest and held my legs straight together and closed my eyes. The girls patted me on the back when my wobbly feet touched the ground but it was something I didn't care to repeat.

To think, I was going to relieve a poor Paramarine Raider who had to do this in the dark from an airplane thousands of feet in the air, and jump into the jungle of a Pacific Island behind enemy lines. I was glad I was a woman at the moment. When we females yelled "Geronimo!" and pulled the string it was for a different reason.

A picturesque squad of Marines came frolicking off the Landing Craft Vehicles (LCV) down the sandy shore with their dogs at their side.

As they came closer, there was no missing the look of war dogs. These Doberman Pinscher dogs were man's best friend, but that meant only one man—his trainer. These dogs had an alert coiled attitude about them, eyes narrowed, heads slightly down, short pointed ears straight up and were tuned to their master's slightest move. Choke chains around their necks were held firmly by the Marines.

I knew they wouldn't have taken food from me even if it were steak. Not that I wanted to offer any or even go close. There was nothing cuddly about these sleek black panthers.

"Aren't they ugly and mean! Ugh!"

"They are beautiful to the Marines whose lives they save," said the captain pointing out why we were here on a windy beach in North Carolina.

The hand to hand combat with short blade bayonets and judo tricks took a kind of courage that brought a quiet respectful hush from all of us.

It was raw violence and an unfamiliar territory that was difficult to even contemplate ever being a part of. It belonged to the world of men.

The Marines who demonstrated these killing techniques were baby face young. They were somebody's kid brother learning these combat techniques.

We became very quiet as we watched, thinking of the Jap who would be the other opponent.

"A man's stomach has to be pretty strong to sink that blade into living flesh. How can they bring themselves to do it?"

The captain said, "The Marine's philosophy is 'You live for your country—Let the other bastard die for his. We do not teach Hari Kari in the Marine Corps."

He spoke with solemnity. "The Asian mind doesn't regard death as we do. The Jap soldier is tricky but he is so anxious for the *Bushido* honor of dying in battle that he goes into a *Banzai* charge without reason—without the remotest chance of winning."

Most surprising of all was the sight of men in Army khaki lined up against the shore ready to go through amphibious exercises.

What were G.I. soldiers doing at our Marine base?

"These are Army personnel learning amphibious warfare, getting ready for the amphibious assault in Europe. The Second Front should be any day now."

Dogfaces was the name Marines had given to Army Soldiers. This was only fair since the Army had many names for the *Leathernecks*, making for a spirited exchange all the way around.

"It's my bet we will be opening up the Second Front in the next three months and these men will be invading the European continent," said the Marine captain as he offered his hand gallantly to our pretty second lieutenant to help her negotiate the hilly terrain.

"We've trained Army's lst, 3rd and 9th Infantry Divisions here for the North African landings.

From a safe vantage point, well out of the way, on a sandy hill with patches of scrub brush, we watched an awesome sight—an amphibious exercise of the Fleet Marine Forces. The "enemy" from Tent City were repelling the "attacking" Corps at Onslow Beach.

What a great show. We witnessed flame throwers, hand to hand combat, and the firing of mortars and bozookas.

Enemy and attackers consisted of men from the 29th Marines plus two Negro Defense Battalions, the 51st and 52nd from Montford Point, and a group of Dutch Marines, who had escaped from the Japanese and Germans. All were learning how to fight using Marine Corps tactics that had been perfected during the past three decades and written into the Fleet Marine Forces manual back in 1934.

"Those Marines are black! There are *Niggers* in the Marines!"

A loud whisper in a stunned voice with a Southern accent from one of the WR's behind me floated out for everyone to hear. "Are there *black* Women Marines too?"

The whole exercise was organized chaos.

While a landing party was shooting its way in under cover of gunfire from the Navy ships offshore, Marine planes dropped bombs of white powder on enemy positions. All kinds of military amphibian craft moved about in the water. Then they crawled onto the land as lumbering alligators.

A huge LST, a Landing Ship For Tanks, of tremendous size, about half a city block long, with great bow doors and tiny super structure making it look top-heavy, was parked on the beach as a large stationary target. Tanks, bulldozers, trucks and artillery rolled out of it while enemy bombers pummeled it with white powder.

Men debarked off a rectangular bathtub of a boat. This was the famous Marine Corps assault craft, the Higgins Boat, the kind the Marines used to hit the beaches in the Guadalcanal campaign. The boats rode high in the water and men in full combat regalia loaded down with equipment debarked by rolling over the side, landing on their faces in the surf. Those who were able to stand helped others to get up.

The captain's lecture was sprinkled with military and Navy jargon.

We all nodded our heads as if we understood every important word.

"Without the Higgins Boats," he explained. "Guadalcanal would have taken a lot longer to secure. We could have used a hundred more. It's a great craft! Great craft! We're replacing it with LCVP. It's faster, has a speed of nine knots, and can carry thirty-six combat equipped troops. We haven't got enough of them yet." He pointed to a slim craft, about thirty-six foot long.

He then directed our attention to a large tank with treads which gave it the appearance of a tractor.

"Those amphtracks have proven their worth. That newer model is the *Water Buffalo.* Replaces the *Alligator* which gets rusty in salt water."

A strange and ridiculous truck rolled out of the water. It had a propeller.

"That's the Army's DUKW. We're giving it a try out. Looks as if they have a winner there."

Being privy to such top-secret military plans and equipment had created its effect.

The Women Marines were awe-struck. Up to now we had seen the friendly rivalry and competition of the services when the men were on furlough and heard only the name calling, *Dogface, BAM, Sea going Bellhop, Swabbie,* to repeat a few. Now we had seen the cooperation that would save lives.

I said, "It's wonderful the way the services cooperate. All working together to win this war;, each one doing what he does best: The Women's Reserve, the Marines, the Army, the Navy!"

The captain had his back turned and wasn't even close but he heard my whisper. He said privately to our lieutenant behind a cupped hand, "Now, you'd suppose if a raw recruit can figure that out, so could the brass in Washington."

Watching this preview of how our men would storm the beaches at some designated rendezvous was a sobering sight and brought the meaning of the assignment of what it meant to be a Woman Marine.

A somber contemplative platoon thanked the captain formally.

The lieutenant said, "I'm sure these demonstrations have impressed upon each and every one of us the full meaning of our commitment as Women Marines."

The theatrics, the smoke, the guns, the planes, men running for cover, the explosions, all of the violence, while overwhelmingly impressive, made the whole operation seem like a war movie. There was a strange quality of deju vu, of familiarity.

"This is better than a John Wayne movie." A nervous comment floated out of the group and our officer heard it.

"There is a large difference here," she said. "When you left the movie theater you knew the heroes really didn't die and all that shooting and all that killing could be viewed as a lot of fun. Just remember the demonstrations here at Camp Lejeune, aren't rehearsals for a movie. Many of the men you saw today will not be coming back."

A pall of gloom followed us into the barracks and no one had to order us to be silent.

The girls from the Southern States had returned upset over something that had made them nervous and apprehensive. They had separated themselves and were clustered into a clique. My bunkie, Jenny Mae was among them.

"Are we going to get *Blackies* in the Women's Reserves? Are we going to have to sleep with *Nigger* WR's?" Georgia asked, speaking for Louisiana, Alabama and Mississippi beside her.

The Boots from the Northern States shrugged off their concerns as silly but the small group of the Southerners that had gathered around the NCO were united in their regional prejudice.

The corporal brought in the lieutenant to handle the problem. Both were young but it helped that the officer was a Southerner as well.

She tried to reassure the Rebels from the Confederate States.

"There are two all male Negro Units over at Montford Point. The men are separated into their own camp and their own facilities. They are enlisted and have white officers. There are no Negro women in the Women's Reserve at this time."

"Are they joining? They've got black Marines already."

"No! Not at this time. All you *People* can stand easy. The Women's Reserve do not have separate facilities to accommodate negro women."

The Southern girls were mollified and the barracks resumed its rehashing of the events of the day.

The consequences of what we had seen was not lost to any of us. *To free a Marine to fight* meant some of those men were going to die. Our own dedication came into focus as each of us faced the issue of combat.

"No wonder the men didn't want us to relieve them. Would you want to go into that fire and brimstone with shooting and bombs all round you?"

"Could you shove a bayonet into a real body?"

"Do you want to go into combat?"

The consensus was "No!"

Someone asked, "It must feel awful incinerating another human being with those terrible flame-shooters! How grisly. I feel so sorry for those soldiers in those caves."

"They're Japs, aren't they?"

There was no sympathy for the enemy from the Women Marines just as there could be no compassion from the Marine who was going to pull the trigger. The Jap soldier was not a human being. He was the *enemy*.

There was great relief we women did not have to go into combat, with or without flame-throwers. Not one Woman Marine said she wanted that job.

At night we were shown a silent scratched up yellowing film left over from World War I with Marines in leggings and field hats demonstrating tactical maneuvers and how to handle barbed wire and trench warfare. It was far afield from what we had seen that day. Our World War had bombs raining from the sky that killed women, children, and unarmed civilians indiscriminately and leveled cities to the ground. No place was safe.

The day's events had been so harrowing that some of the women actually fell asleep during the quaint out-dated irrelevant movie.

Immediately after morning chow we were sent to the barracks to change uniform. The call went out: "Uniform of the day will be dungarees. Fall out in five minutes."

It seemed such a waste of time to dress in full uniform just to go to breakfast and then undress again. But, like Englishmen who dress in formal dinner jackets and gowns for dinner in the jungle in darkest Africa we women Marines had to appear in the mess hall properly attired at all times.

We were loaded into Marine buses painted that dark green I have come to recognize forever as Marine green. The fumes of the diesel fuel combined with what had been a delicious breakfast of French toast and bacon into a nauseating mixture. Not even the recognition we were on our way to Area Three, the men's area, helped the nausea.

141

My vision blurred and I tried to focus on the company of men who were marching along the road in full heavy marching order pack, carrying everything from the heavy M-1 Garand rifles on their shoulders to knapsacks with pots and pans on their backs. Their D.I. tried to work some spirit into their step, counting the rhythm in a harsh nasal voice.

When the men saw we were women, they brightened up and began an enthusiastic cadence chant as loudly as they could:

Here we go
Up the Hill
Down the Hill
One Two Three Four

Their leader, the D.I., ordered "Double Time" and the men picked up their cadence and chased our bus with renewed energy. The women egged them on by waving their fingers.

Another group of Marines in dungarees that matched ours except the letter P was stenciled on their jackets stopped in the middle of their work of policing the area to stare at us.

One Marine yelled out loud and clear for all to hear.

"What do the big guns say?"

The men answered in chorus: "BAM! BAM! BAM!"

We were taken aback by their insolence.

"Don't they know they can be disciplined and restricted for that?"

"Didn't you see the letter P? They already are prisoners. They don't care."

"What for?"

"AWOL—Absent without leave, over leave, desertion, drunk and disorderly. You name it. Some Marines don't want to go."

"That is what they get for drafting just anybody. The Corps should take only those who appreciate what being a Marine is."

Selective Service and the draft took every able bodied man into the Armed Forces and assigned the inductees to whatever branch of the Armed Forces needed to be filled at the time. Men ended up in the Marines who hadn't volunteered for it. The Corps was no longer an all volunteer force as it had been before 1941 and the standards had been lowered to fill the quota of men needed to fight the Japs.

Our bus was loaded with *gung ho* Marines all of whom were volunteers. We had joined because we wanted to be here.

A group of Seabees, dressed in gray fatigues, halted their construction to wave from their bulldozers. These were the Navy engineers and construction workers who built roads, docks, air strips and bridges. We waved back. Their tremendous reputation for getting things done fast was well known to everybody. They were highly respected and held in awe. Their exploits in putting up bridges in one day, and finishing air strips minutes before the planes had to land had been documented in the news, newsreels and in National Geographic.

Camp Lejeune was an enormous place. The buses rumbled through forests of towering pine trees that stretched endlessly until finally we stopped at a cleared site where our group was greeted by a Marine officer, a captain.

I pushed my way out of the bus, so happy to be out into the pine scented moist air, that I gulped huge draughts of oxygen to get rid of the queasy feeling.

The Obstacle Courses

We were assembled near a playground of some sort which had strange wood contraptions built out of four by four lumber. There were horizontal ladders, vertical "A"—shaped ladders from which ropes dangled, and a series of strange looking bridges made of logs over ponds. One tall platform had nets dangling from it.

This was the famous Marine Corps obstacle course. Each exercise was called an obstacle stance.

My heart sank. Were we scheduled to swing on these playgrounds? The bacon and French toast turned over in my stomach.

Marine physical training was notorious. It was one of the reasons Marines were so tough. Every Boot had to pass these tests to become qualified as a Marine. Any Boot who flunked and couldn't cut the mustard was mustered out and sent back to civilian life.

The captain announced in a loud voice which carried above the noise, "This is a demonstration only. Women Marines are *not* required to tackle the obstacle courses."

An audible sigh of relief was released like air out of a balloon.

"Of course, if any of you *People* would like to give one of the stances a try, step forward," he offered hospitably.

A squad of Marines, about thirteen of them, went through their exercises, swinging through these complicated jungle gyms as easily as chimpanzees in trees.

One obstacle stance called the *Engineer Bridge*, required the fine balancing coordination of a circus performer on two tightropes strung ten feet above the ground. One rope went under the arm pits; the other rope under the feet. One handsome blond Marine maneuvered easily but slowly across and went on to tackle another problem that was more spectacular.

He climbed to a platform thirty feet in the air from which a rope was attached at a thirty degree angle to the ground. He stepped off the platform and holding on to a wheel, he went coasting down in a breathtaking ride.

"Any WR want to give the *Monkey Bars* a try?" The captain looked around for volunteers.

The *Monkey Bars* was a horizontal ladder, ten feet off the ground suspended over a bed of sawdust. It looked very difficult as the Marine swung hand over hand from one rung to another.

I caught the eyes of the handsome blond Marine, who obviously thought I was attractive, watching me. I smiled at him. He smiled back.

There was another obstacle stance called *Dry Nets* which had nets on the sides of a mock up of a Higgins Boat, going thirty feet up one side and down the other. Marines in full combat pack scrambled up and down them just as they would have to do when making an amphibious assault.

The *Vaults* consisted of four foot logs that had to be jumped over.

Once again I caught the eyes of the handsome Marine.

I was standing in front of the *Easy Balance Walk* which had round logs, about ten of them, laid over a water hole. Now that looked easy. Several women volunteered

"Are you volunteering, Private?" said the lieutenant. "Move it! You're holding up the line."

Brooklyn gave me a little shove to get a better view, she told me later, but it looked as if I had wanted to give it a try with the others.

And I found myself balancing on the logs. The *Easy Balance Walk* was as easy as—whoops! falling off the logs. I tried to get up but I flopped back into the water instead.

The blond Marine whose eyes had been following my movements dashed in to save me. The water was bath-tub deep.

At last, I was in the arms of a rugged handsome Marine. "Oooh! Thank you," I purred softly.

"That's okay," he whispered. "That is why we're standing by—to catch you *BAMS* as you fall off. I was making book you'd fall. Just won me two bucks."

"If I am a *BAM* we're both Marines what does that make you?"

"A *HAM.* A *half-ass Marine* for being here in the first place."

We both grinned at each other. He must have been one of the inductees. There were no hard feelings.

We returned to the barracks, exhilarated and happy, full of chatter, having thoroughly enjoyed the field trips which had taken us out of Hadnot Point into the world of men.

But the day ended on an unhappy note which sent shivers of fear through all of us.

A quiet request from the Duty NCO to see the lieutenant. was made to several individual girls.

Several girls in other platoons were informed that they were being discharged for medical reasons for the 'Good of the Corps'. One girl was pregnant much to her surprise. Another one was being mustered out for a mysterious reason of 'unsuitability'.

Brooklyn had also been called to the lieutenant's office and returned crying. She had buried her head in her bunk.

Pittsburgh, Laramie, Sherry, Joan and Fenton watched woefully.

Poor Brooklyn had received her mustering out slip—a medical discharge. The physical exam during the first two weeks of Boot Camp had disclosed something that hadn't shown up before.

"That's a sneaky way of getting out of the G.I. party and the General's inspection." No one laughed at my feeble joke.

"Your boyfriend will be thrilled when he sees you. Look how beautiful you are!" said Laramie in an effort to comfort her.

Brooklyn had stopped wearing heavy pancake make-up and no longer dyed her hair. Dark hair predominated and it was very short. Most of the blond was gone.

Brooklyn's tears started afresh.

"He won't know me. He's never seen me with my real face and hair!"

After we comforted Brooklyn, we went about our duties. Our Boot Camp schedule didn't allow any time to linger over the fate of any one but your own. By morning Brooklyn was gone and no one mentioned her again. I couldn't even remember Brooklyn's name after a few days. Friendships made in Boot Camp were not the everlasting kind that had been forged in all the years of grade school or high school.

There wasn't enough time.

Guard Duty

I had pulled guard duty with Fenton from 8:00 P.M. to midnight—I mean, from twenty hundred to twenty-four hundred Navy time.

She and I were given passwords and were instructed to stand guard and not let anyone pass who didn't say those exact words. We were to protect the women's barracks and the boondocks, a area of pine trees that was the spookiest place in the middle of woods in Camp Lejeune.

We walked the post, back and forth, sluicing in mud. Rain had begun at supper time and hadn't let up once. We resembled French Foreign Legionnaires in our plastic havelocks which protected our hats, not our necks. The water ran over the brim and my eyes crossed trying to see past the Niagara Falls as I searched the pitch black boondocks for "enemy".

We didn't have umbrellas. They were not military. The rain pelted our trench coats. The men had ponchos but we weren't given any to wear. They would have helped.

We carried a small wooden club. The men had guns. We didn't.

"This is silly," I said. "Who is going to break into the guard house, or the mess hall or the laundry? C'mon! A barracks filled with five hundred women? At this hour? In this rain?"

Fenton answered stiffly quoting the general orders from the Marine Corps Manual. "We are supposed to walk the post in a military manner, keeping always on the alert and observing everything that takes place within sight or hearing."

"Nothing's happening and I don't hear anything." I said.

"There's no talking except in the line of duty," said Fenton in her sternest officer's voice. I sure wished she would make OTS, Officer Training School. It was a shame no officer was around to see how G.I. she was.

"Gee, Fenton, when you talk like that, I forget you're a Boot like me." But she refused to join me in conversation and walked her side of the post in silence.

When I finally heard footsteps behind me, I was so happy for someone else to talk to that it clean slipped my mind to *'challenge all persons on or near my post'* and *'to allow no one to pass without authority'*.

I raised the flashlight on the person's face and saw Captain Towle.

"Whee! Am I glad it's someone I know," I sighed loudly. For a second I had a little fright. It was wonderful to see a familiar face. It was friendly of her to come out of that warm barracks at midnight to visit with me in that pouring rain.

She frowned and didn't say anything, just stood there blinking in the beam of the flashlight a very long minute.

I did forget something. Then I remembered the challenge, "Halt! Who Goes There?" I hollered.

"Friend!" she answered, closing her eyes.

Friend? I thought the password was "Semper Fidelis"? Was I being tested? Should I let her by?

She opened her eyes wide and gave me all the passwords at once: "Officer of the guard! Semper Fidelis! Friend!"

"Advance friend and be recognized!" I hollered loud and clear, right into her ear.

Still holding my salute in my most military manner I screamed out, "Post number three secure, Mam!"

"Stand at ease, Private. Thank God!" she said hurrying on to the next post.

After that encounter, my esprit de corps was so revitalized that I actually enjoyed waiting in the rain in the dark for another two hours to be challenged again.

No one came.

I tiptoed into the barracks and heard crying in the night. It was not Brooklyn. It was one of the Boots from another squad and she was sitting on the toilet.

"What's the matter?" I whispered with toothpaste in my mouth.

"I joined the Marine Corps to be with my husband. He's a Marine too and he came all the way from his base at El Toro in California to see me. They let me be with him for two hours and we couldn't leave the Chaplain's Office."

"Don't worry. You'll be seeing him in two weeks when you graduate."

"No! I won't be! He's been released for combat by a Woman Marine and he's leaving for the Pacific."

The next morning, every one avoided looking at Brooklyn's empty bunk with the rolled up mattress. It could have been any one of us. As we stood assembled before the barracks for muster, Brooklyn came out of Battalion Headquarters. She lifted her head in a subdued good-bye, closing and opening a fist.

Some one called out, "Once a Marine, always a Marine!"

We were a sorry looking group of women as we returned from another field trip united by one wish, to get to the showers first. But none of us would be collapsing into her bunk at the end of our Boot day. We were greeted by our NCO with news that spread mass consternation and galvanized us into action.

"Prepare for complete inspection and regimental review. There will be no doping off, gold bricking or snafu. This is a G.I. party to end all G.I. parties."

"Your barracks will be inspected by General Vandegrift, our new Commandant of the Marine Corps, and our very own Director of WR's, Colonel Ruth Streeter."

"Now move it! Put your backs into it. We must make them proud of each and every one of us!"

In translation, it was the same message my mother had been giving me for years when guests were on their way; "Clean up your messy room!"

The lieutenant said, "I will expect all hands to look alive."

The NCO used her tongue as a whiplash. "If I see one kitten on the deck, you *People,* will be restricted from the movie and the recreation hall. It's shape up or ship out!"

For two days, the chow was quite casual—one meal consisting of cold cuts, potato salad and jello. The Mess girls were exhausted but the galley as well as the barracks shone with the sparkle of spring housecleaning as only women can do.

Still the men were taking no chances. Colonel Arthur, himself, the commanding officer of the Recruit Depot, planned to inspect us the day before the Commandant General got a look at us.

The occasion was more than a graduating class of our platoons. This was the grand parade of the first anniversary of the Women's Reserve organization.

February 13, 1943, was our birthdate. The Women Marines were one year old.

Enlistment had opened on that date, and almost a year later, 15,000 enlisted and 1000 officers Women Marines were serving throughout the United States.

Three thousand of us would be on parade right here at Camp Lejeune.

The solemnity of the historic occasion was not lost to any of us as we polished, scrubbed and threw our mops into buckets of pine-scented soapy water. We even had to smell good.

Graduation, The Evolution Of A Marine

The day arrived for the battalion regimental review. As graduating Senior Boots, the honor of leading the Women's Reserve Recruit Depot went to us.

Thousands of Women Marines, both officers and the enlisted, waited in formation for that first note of music and the first command to march and pass in review. The tension created enough electricity that it could have turned a moonless night into day.

Even the usual sunny North Carolina sky was nervous, as dark clouds played peek-a-boo with the sun, now you saw it and now you didn't.

Somewhere, out of the line of vision, was the review stand, filled with the most important brass in the Marine Corps. The only person missing was the Commander-in-Chief, President Roosevelt.

The three thousand females ready to march represented all the Boots, both seniors and new arrivals, the Officer Training Class, the Specialist Schools and the Casual Company, which included those Women Marines that had already graduated and were awaiting assignments.

The whole Women's Reserve Schools had been turned out to greet the Commandant General of the Marine Corps, Alexander

Vandegrift and the Director of the Women's Reserve, Ruth Cheny Streeter, who been promoted to a full Colonel only days before. Both commanding officers had come from Marine Corps Headquarters in Washington D.C. to review us.

Standing next to them straight and tall was our very attractive blond senior officer, our C.O., Katherine Towle, now a Major (she too had been promoted from Captain).

This was an important day, a first for us, and a first for many of the officers. Every boot, enlisted and officer, quivered with the anticipation of the ceremonial solemnity of the occasion.

Reviewing a battalion of Women Marines was also a first for the fighting General Alexander Vandegrift, who had been in command of the First Marine Division in the Guadalcanal campaign in 1942. He was brought back from the Bougainville campaign in the South Pacific just four months ago in November 1943 to serve as commandant.

We were going to start his first year with a bang.

This was our big show and it was up to us to let him see what Women Marines were made of.

The reviewing stand was full of officers of the Old Corps and battle wise Marines of the enlarged war-time Corps. They were impressive men, ramrod straight, magnificent in their uniforms with full fruit salad of ribbons and medals covering the whole left side of their chests. They had flown in from every Marine Post throughout the country to inspect this battalion review of the Women's Reserve and had come from as far away as Washington D.C., Philadelphia, and California.

We had to show this group how effective the Marine Corps training had been when applied to Women Marines. We were about to demonstrate that we also had esprit de corps and knew the meaning of *Semper Fidelis*.

The sight of three thousand women, in uniform, assembled all together in formation, each company behind its own red dress guidon with the gold letters of USMCWR waving high in the air on the enormous parade ground was so overwhelmingly overpowering in its emotional impact that tears glistened the eyes of many of us. You could actually see the powerful spirit of patriotism well up in each of us as it took hold. Each head went higher, each chest raised further, shoulders pushed back further, bodies went ramrod straight.

The historic importance of this rare day was evident, every one aware that we were marching straight into the history books.

While we found our places in formation we stood at *parade rest,* as the general and our commanding officer with a flock of other officers visited the empty barracks and mess hall.

Parade rest meant holding a certain position: standing with hands behind the back and with feet apart to balance the weight of the body evenly to avoid fatigue. It worked. There was consolation in the fact that we didn't have to bother about any rifles or have to fool around learning commands such as *"Right Shoulder Arms!"*

We later found out that General Vandegrift told Major Towle, "That's the best Mess I've seen in thirty-five years."

Serious tight smiles on the faces of our women officers, told plainly how nervous our young lieutenants who were company commanders felt.

We each had something to prove, individually and collectively. There may have been other reviews, other parades, but what made this battalion review so important was the fact it was on the eve of the first anniversary of the birthdate of the Women's Reserve.

Women had been in the Corps for only one year. Our battalion carried a great responsibility. We were also aware that the men didn't believe we could walk a straight line and make a true column without wavering or falling off to the right or left. Of course, they would be magnanimous, being the gentlemen they were but we, on the other hand were seeking perfection not charity. We had been practicing for weeks now and had performed flawlessly on Saturday.

Our confidence was high.

"Now hear this" commanded Lieutenant Dill standing at the head of our company. "Listen for the first note of the Marine Corps Hymn. You hit the deck with your left foot and step out smartly at the same time."

It was critical for all of us to be on the same foot at the same time otherwise our heads would bounce like a calliope. When one person falls out of step, the next person automatically shuffles to get on the right foot and so on down the line. The cadence goes out of time and everybody ends up doing the 'shuffle off to Buffalo' dance step. The consequences of such an eventuality were too horrible to contemplate.

The sun reflected on all the gold and silver in the review stands and telegraphed machine gun sparks of light like tracer bullets.

Hundreds of officers stood waiting for us to march.

Thousands of us stood tensely waiting for that first note, not breathing, not a muscle moving, eyes straight ahead, shoulders back, chests out.

Dark clouds filled with moisture, rolled by blocking out the North Carolina sun. A strong wind came out of nowhere and all the flags, the American flag of the forty-eight states, the red and gold banners and the guidons each company carried, responded with vigorous waving.

Above us in an aerial salute flew F4 U Corsairs, TBF Grummann Avengers and a few old Voughts.

The forty-three Women Marines in the Women's Reserve Band raised their instruments and the very first note of the MARCH OF THE WOMEN MARINES rang out.

We stepped out smartly. Not a foot out of step.

At that very moment the clouds opened up, drenching us with the big drops of rain that signified the start of spring in North Carolina. No one missed the beat of the left foot.

As we passed the review stands the first row did a *Right Dress* and turned their faces towards the officers. The choir of our voices sang without prompting the words we all knew by heart so well:

Marines!
We are the women members of our Fighting Corps
Marines!
The name is known from burning sands to ice bound shores
Marines!
We serve that men may fight on land and air and sea
Marines!
The Eagle, Globe and Anchor carry on
To make men free.

Marine Barracks, Quantico Va. 1944
Top: The sentry at the guard house entrance to the Post.
Center: The statue of Iron Mike next to the Little Hall which houses the PX and Post Theater. Note the spring flowers.

Bottom: Marines marching.

**Marine Barracks,
Quantico Va. 1944**
1000 Women Marines are
assigned to the offices and
non-combatant duties.
Bottom: 500 Women
Marines are assigned at
Brown Field to the
Aviation squadron.

PART FOUR

Marine Barracks Quantico, Virginia–March 1944

Quantico, Virginia! The university and showplace of the Corps. Quantico! It was the dream post of every Marine. Only forty-five minutes from Washington D.C. and I had pulled what was "good duty". *Gee, Mom, I want to go, rright back to Quantico! Gee, Mom, I want to go hoooome!*

Now to free a Marine to fight!

I was now a "line" Marine and held a temporary Warrant.

That was a far cry from *Running Inventory Kardex File Supervisor.* I didn't know what my duty assignment would be in Quantico but at last, I was on my way to help my country win the war.

We were a contingency of twenty-nine graduated Boots and had traveled together carrying special orders since five-thirty Tuesday night from Camp Lejeune.

The train rolled into the small Quantico station on Thursday morning. The tracks formed the dividing line between the town of Quantico and the Post.

Passengers who disembarked on the right side of the train found themselves in the tiny town of Quantico, Virginia which had one main street and a few houses. The Quantico railroad station butted right up next to the tracks and it was an ill-kempt dirty wooden building with signs on doors that read "For Colored Only" and "For Whites Only". Just standing there a few minutes left a funny taste of coal dust that lingered in the back of the mouth.

Marines who stepped off the train had to walk across the tracks which were only a few steps from the gate of the Marine Post which was fenced off from the town of Quantico.

We passed a Marine with rifle posted at a neat freshly-painted octagonal guard house at the Sentry gate and entered the Post. He pointed the way to the Provost Marshall who is sort of a sheriff.

We walked into the provost's office with some uncertainty but that was dispelled the moment he saw us. The Provost's face broke out into a big grin and his greeting was hearty.

"It's good to see more of you WR's. You sure liven this Post," he said as each of us formally presented our papers to him in order to enter the Post.

The old provost said, "The WR compound is in that direction over the tracks past the underpass. Report to your CO."

Men were everywher. A company of rugged Marines marched right toward us in full pack. Off at a small distance I could see another company in forest green marching in drill formation.

A convoy of jeeps and military trucks, lights on in broad daylight as required of all convoys, barreled through the Post and out the gate. Women Marines were driving the trucks. Men were seated in the back under canopied covers carrying rifles which they held straight up.

Quantico Post was tidy and green with many pine trees, large shade trees and bushes. It looked more like a college campus with grass, flower beds, cherry trees and lilac bushes in bud filled with the promise of spring.

A bronze statue of a World War I Marine stood prominently as official greeter in the middle of a circular drive in front of a two storied stucco building which was the Post Headquarters where Commanding General Torrey commanded.

A flag pole visible from every part of the post held the Stars and Stripes of the forty-eight states.

Near it was an imposing brick building that took up a full city block. Two tiers of wide steps led up to many doors on two sides. This building housed the Post Exchange, the Hostess House which was a cafeteria as well as a hotel, and the Marine Corps Museum.

The Virginia sun was warm with just a hint of a breeze. I had draped my trench coat neatly on top of my green seabag on which I had stenciled my name. I lugged it with both hands, practically dragging it on the ground. It was stuffed with everything I owned and very heavy.

Marines passed by and greeted us with a howl at the end of their "hellos" but no one offered to carry any of the seabags for us. They were treating us as equals right off the bat.

Fenton and Sherry were with me, as well as Lindsey, the gal from Texas who reminded me of Gary Cooper. The rest of my Boot Camp buddies had stayed behind and were posted to various specialist schools at Camp Lejeune. Pittsburgh was assigned to Motor Transport School and she promised she'd land the D.I. before she graduated. She had discovered that not only was he a Catholic but he had ancestors from Poland as she did. He was a Polish Marine as she was.

Jenny Mae was thrilled with her assignment to Plumbers' School. She planned to get rid of the chicksales in her home town in Alabama when the war was over and give her family and all her cousins inside toilets.

Laramie was posted to Cooks and Bakers School to become a butcher but she wasn't too happy about that.

"All I know about beef is what I see on the range—the gas range. Not all Wyoming girls tend cattle." My last memory of Laramie was her singing, "Give *me a home where the Buffalo roam.*"

Joan, our beautiful model who should have been put on a recruiting poster, was going to Quartermaster School to learn how to be a supply clerk.

Shauna had traveled with us but she continued on to Washington D.C. with other Women Marines who were posted as administrative clerks to Henderson Hall at Marine Corps Headquarters, Arlington Annex, Arlington, Virginia.

"I guess they figure if I can keep track of all my Mormon relatives and ancestors, I can keep Marine Corps records straight," Shauna said when she got her assignment.

"*Semper Fidelis,*" I said as I waved good-bye to the only Mormon I had ever met.

One by one we stepped forward to present our papers to our commanding officer of the Women Marines Battalion here in Quantico.

We stood ramrod stiff in proper military bearing but I dissolved in the emotional rush of happiness at seeing some one I had known at Camp Lejeune.

I wanted to hug the officer who stood there welcoming us. How wonderful to see a familiar face from Camp Lejeune. She was one of the officers who had guided me through Boot Camp and had helped me become the Marine I was.

"Private Karas reporting for active duty, Mam!"

My CO smiled at my delight.

"Welcome aboard. You Marines will want to rest today before you go on your *seventy-two,*" said Captain Lloyd.

A gasp of surprise and pleasure came out of us in unison. Three days to do anything we wanted. Go anywhere. I really didn't know what to do with this new-found liberty and freedom.

"Now for the bad news. I am sorry to tell you, but I can't place all of you immediately. Seven of you will be assigned to Motor Transport. For the remaining WR's without assignment, you will be placed on mess duty and police duty in the women's compound." Her soft voice was filled with regret and her eyes reflected sympathy and understanding.

"That's all right." We all said it simultaneously.

"The men should see your esprit. Then they would make room quickly enough," she said.

I walked out with the group but I back-tracked to tell her how happy I was to be with her again, that I didn't mind police duty, and if she wanted anyone for guard duty that I was her man, that I would do anything she needed.

She was engrossed in talking to another Woman Marine officer. She sounded very determined and perhaps a little upset, but you really didn't know because officers seemed to always talk in an even tone. It was the corporals who raised their voices.

"Those battalion commanders think they will solve the whole problem of what to do with Women Marines by throwing those quota forms in the deep six. That maneuver won't help them one bit. I know Quantico can use well over one thousand WR's and they are going to get them by July. They will make room for us. I'll see to that!"

She jumped almost clear out of her cotton stockings when she backed into me standing right behind her.

I hadn't meant to give her a fright like that. I had been extra quiet because if there is one thing I learned in Boot Camp, it was not to speak to an officer without getting permission first. It only proved how silly that rule was because you ended up scaring the officers making it near impossible to have a heart to heart talk.

She stopped everything to thank me for my offer which I kept repeating to make sure she knew for certain I was sincere. She even saw me to the door and opened it for me, guiding me out, her hand on my shoulder kindly and gently. Her politeness was so profound that I was overwhelmed since it was my position rightly to open doors for officers. My heart was filled with love, admiration, and respect for my commanding officer. If I had been a male Marine, I would go into battle for such an officer and fight the Japs bare handed.

That is what esprit de corps meant. And I was full of it.

I loved Quantico right away.

For one thing, the corporals and sergeants started their sentences with "Please" and "Will you?" instead of ordering you without a cordial preamble. There was a lot of smiling and "helloing" and "hi's" from other WRs as I hurried to the barracks. It was the friendliest place I had ever experienced.

The buildings of the women's compound were built solidly out of red bricks as if we women were going to be a permanent part of the Marine Corps and not get kicked out after the duration and six months and the war was over. Four H-shaped barracks all in a row had been built for us, just waiting to be filled with Women Marines.

The Women Marines had their very own Post Exchange which was a new building with neat white porches flanking both sides of the entrance. The spacious mess hall had the feeling of a Southern plantation house with its six straight brick columns at the entrance. Next to it, workers pounded away building a new recreation hall just so we women could have a place of our own for get-togethers, dances, art and craft classes, to play ping pong or records and have parties. It was going to be one grand club house.

Around by the side was the Administration Building for the Women's Reserve. This was where all the Women Reserve Marine officers worked; where they ran the Women's battalion and published a small newspaper of our own.

Coming out of there, who should I bump into but my own recruiting officer from Buffalo who had escorted the Buffalo Platoon to Washington, the very one who had inducted me, who had watched me as I pledged myself to the United States of America and the Marine Corps so many months ago when I was a young naive civilian girl. I wondered if she could see the change in me.

I saluted her and grinned happily to see her familiar face once more.

"I remember you very well, Private. You look wonderful. That uniform is very becoming to you."

We chatted a while. She gave me the latest scuttlebutt which made me realize how lucky I had been to have joined when I did.

"Recruiting for Women Marines was closed in January 1944. We are nearly 15,000 Women Marines with at least 1000 officers. We

159

are authorized to go to 18,000 and it's only a matter of time until recruiting opens again. Women are clamoring to join the Marines. We were swamped with enlistments," she told me.

"Thank you, for letting me join. I love the Marine Corps." I gushed.

"You will love Quantico too," she said. "I am now the recreation officer here. This post has all the facilities. We can share everything the men have. You don't even have to leave the post to have fun. We have the men's gym for badminton and volley ball, their bowling alleys, tennis courts, their horses at Post Stables, their boats at Post Docks for sailing on the Potomac River, their swimming pools."

What a cozy happy family Quantico promised to be. There was even a diamond field for baseball games.

"But," she admonished. "Don't let me catch you in the bleachers after six for night games."

I knew she was joking. How can you play ball in the dark?

By the time I reached my billet, Company A, Barracks One, my Boot Camp buddies had picked up their linens, had selected their bunks and had made them up.

Once again luck was with me. No one had claimed the best bunk, the one in the middle of the squadroom next to the exit, around the corner from the hallway. The light in the hallway which was always lit provided a night light that suited me just fine. Anyone who walked in and out of the room had to pass this bunk. I would meet every one in the squadroom coming and going in and out of the squadroom.

Fenton's sack was six bunks away and she was stowing away her gear according to the chart she was given by the NCO. She scolded, "Terry! Can't you ever be anywhere on time? I tried to get you a better bunk!

"This bunk is fine. I get to see everybody who comes and goes. The shower lights won't bother me one bit. Did you see that handy dryer in the wall in the laundry room? All you have to do is pull out the rack, drape the wet clothes over the rods and in twenty minutes they are dry. We could use that invention in Tonawanda."

This squadroom was messy and littered. Morning inspection was over yet there was personal gear thrown everywhere. After the immaculate sterility of Boot Camp where a kitten of dust would cause panic, it was strange to see girls sleeping in bunks, sacks left unmade, a few stuffed toys scattered on top, locker boxes left opened.

Each single bunk had a locker box at the foot of the bunk and a locker closet against the wall. There were no ugly hanging clothes poles in the middle of the room.

The same Marine green colors were everywhere except in the *head*, showers and laundry room. These rooms were painted white and battleship gray, the standard Navy colors. Wood-framed mirrors hung over each sink. The eye-shade light fixtures were painted green which gave everyone's face a strange mint tint when make-up was applied.

Except for the new arrivals, and a few girls who were still asleep, the squadroom was empty.

"You can sleep as late as you want here?" I called out amazed at the sight of Marines in bed past 6 A.M. reveille.

A groan growled out of a tousled blond head of hair that was partially hidden under a Marine green wool blanket on the lower bunk next to mine. A pretty pink-faced doll with wide blue eyes and a perfect figure shook herself out of the sack and mumbled audibly, "How the hell can anyone get any goddamn sleep in this crummy barracks?"

She threw on her uniform and pinned a blue MP armband on her arm, looked at me directly and said, "Goddamn guard duty! Having to change into greens four times a day is *Semper Fi* bird shit! I'm Gerry Adams. Madison, Wisconsin. Say will you give Blanche a shove and tell her it's time for her goddamn supply duty!"

My delicate fragile bunkmate swore like a Gunny sergeant. Her manner bespoke of a nonchalant confidence, the kind that seniors possessed after many years of going to the same school. I knew I was looking at an old *Salt* and I was just a freshman. I liked her immediately.

I held out my hand and said, "I'm Terry Karas from Tonawa..."

But Gerry Adams was gone and out the door.

I did as I was told.

As I bent down to tap the other sleeping form, angry eyes opened up wide like Bella Lugosi in *Dracula* and stared right at me, scaring me right out of my cordovan oxfords.

"Don't touch me!" snapped Blanche.

Out rolled a female—about thirtyish—wearing a full length Mae West black corset with a pinched waist. She threw on a black and orange silk robe with an embroidered dragon on the back, picked up a douche bag and a towel with the name of HOTEL STATLER embroidered on it, and headed for the *head*. Her dog tags tinkled like wind chimes on her ample bosom and her heavy perfume followed her out the room. She did not greet any of us but we were equally rude staring at her like that. She wasn't your typical Woman Marine. Different as we all were, we were alike in a general way, our physical appearance was homogeneously the same. She was different: seasoned; older; buxom; worldly and sort of earthy.

True, we had to wear a girdle and slip at all times; that was part of the uniform. But this Marine was going beyond the call of duty with that black lace corset and red ribbon. Mother's generation was the only one who wore corsets that laced and had steel stays. Only very fast loose women wore black lingerie, black shimmies and black corsets where the breasts were pushed up. I never knew why this was so or who had told me that piece of information. I just knew it was true. All you had to do was look around for verification. Not one female in our eighty-man squadroom wore black lingerie. We had either white or flesh color panties, slips and bras. Our nighties were pink, blue or white always trimmed with white lace. A couple even had bunny-feet pajamas. No black. No red.

After late noon chow at 12:30 P.M., I saw Blanche again, walking along with stacks of linen sheets and towels in her hand which she was delivering to each barrack. She looked just as odd in her dungarees and pork pie hat balancing precariously on her rolled bun of shiny black hair slick with pomade. She, unlike most of us, had not cut off her hair. It was suspiciously and unnaturally black. Not many girls dyed their hair so I couldn't help staring again. There was no rule against it except that for identification purposes a Marine's hair had to match the picture that had been taken when she enlisted.

She acknowledged my warm smile with a cool glaze and didn't give me a chance to explain that I wasn't really going to shake her awake. I guess she wasn't friendly right off the bat until she got to know you better.

The WR's who were leaving on their *seventy-two's* had commandeered the ironing boards. They no longer looked like Boots, fresh out of Recruit Depot. The first thing they had done was press sharp non-regulation creases illegally along the seams of their six-gored skirts and along the back and front of their khaki shirts under each breast. Their rayon stockings which were turned inside out so the seams would outline the calves were also against regulation. They bagged anyway.

Gerry had returned, her guard duty temporarily over until the next shift. She took one look at them and gave a light warning. "Don't let any WR officer catch you out of uniform like that or you won't get off the post and you'll be restricted to barracks. The men won't bother you because they don't have jurisdiction over you, but the WR officers are strict about the uniform of the day."

Gerry was an *Old Salt* out of the first class at U. S. Naval Training School at Hunter College and had graduated in April 1943. She had her own code about which offenses should be reported.

"I'll be goddamned if I'm going put adult women on report because they are not wearing their girdles or have rayon stockings on before 4:30. What's that got to do with being a good Marine?" she said as she removed the MP band off her sleeve.

As military police she was supposed to keep the girls on their toes and turn them in for breaking regulations or were out of uniform. Bouncing breasts and buttocks were a dead-give away that a Woman Marine was not wearing a bra nor girdle under the uniform.

We became buddies right away. I liked her immensely and told her so.

Gerry had walked out of her class at the University of Michigan and into the Marine Recruiting Office at Ann Arbor the same day she was notified her fiancé's plane had been shot down and he had been killed. If she could have gone straight into combat and fought the enemy with her bare hands, she would have. Instead she was assigned to duties of policing the area, which was another name for cleaning-up and was made an MP(military police) in the women's compound which was for her, another name for 'snitch'. WR military police could only serve in the women's compound and they could only enforce the dress code and other minor infractions.

Up to now, she hadn't freed any Marine to fight. It left her cynical about the war and critical about the rules and regulations we women had to abide by. Nothing bothered her now. She was blasé about everything.

The core of her civilian code of behavior had been left untouched. She ridiculed certain aspects of military life and made caustic remarks about the war and what the Marines were fighting for. I found her fascinating but she either slept when off duty or disappeared as soon as she had liberty. She never seemed to stay in

Theresa Karas Yianilos

the barracks long enough for us to have a long bull-session and claimed that the squadroom gave her claustrophobia.

"It's all these 'females'," she explained. "They stink like women."

I took a deep breath but the only odors I could detect were the combined mixtures of all the different kinds of perfumes, bath powders, colognes and deodorants and occasionally a whiff of the scorched starch used to iron the uniforms and the disinfectant soap used to clean up the barracks. Oh, yes! Insect repellent of some sort was mixed in there. And the chlorine used to clean the *heads* and sinks. That was strong.

A noisy group of Women Marines who had been on mess duty trickled into the barracks. Their white clothes were stained with food. Each one flopped on her sack and picked up a magazine or book, without changing clothes. They couldn't do much else because they all had to report back to the mess hall in two hours to prepare for evening chow.

One of the girls carried a cherry pie.

"Here, bet you can use this!"

I thanked her, ready to chat, but she looked past me and cried out with loud irritation in her voice. "Oh! Moonbeam! Not more bottles! If they make noise again at captain's inspection on Saturday, we've had it. The whole squadroom will be restricted!"

A small thin dark hared girl walked by us balancing four empty gallon glass mayonnaise jars and vinegar jugs. She almost lost one but I helped her catch it just as it was slipping from her arms.

She thanked me gratefully in a twang of the Ozarks. One by one she slipped them under the bunk across from mine. They clinked together as they hit other bottles and jugs hidden under there.

"What are you going to do with those?"

"Jugs are hard to come by back home in Missouri," she said happily. She had a shy way of talking, ever so softly, squinting her eyes and smiling all the while that I thought maybe she wasn't too bright. "I'm sending them to my Paw to help 'im out. He is real happy I joined up. Now he's got all the jugs he can use." She sighed. "Ah won't be able to keep it up because I'm going off mess duty next week."

"Don't worry, Moonbeam. I'll save them for you. I start next week. Moonbeam? Is that your real name?"

164

"Yes, mam. My Paw named me that 'cause Ah was born by the light of the full moon. Yo' all will have to wash the jugs first 'cause they were filled with stuff like salad dressing and mustard, okay?" she said with fear that I would back out of the deal.

"Cross my heart. I'll do it." I promised sincerely and so I found another friend real fast.

Fenton saw I was preparing to go on the town, to Quantico Town.

"I'll go with you, Terry. I'll straighten my locker closet and locker box when we return. I can't let you get into trouble by yourself."

We reached *Iron Mike,* the bronze statue, and the flagpole next to Little Hall just in time to stand *Colors* at sunset. We snapped to attention and held our salutes until the last notes of the bugler faded away and the flag was neatly folded into a triangle under the Field Music's arm.

The whole post of Quantico had stopped dead in its tracks for the flag ceremony that went on twice a day at sunrise and sunset.

All traffic, both vehicles and pedestrians, halted immediately upon the first note. Engines were turned off.

Marines and civilians had stopped on the steps leading to the P X just as if they were playing the kid's game of 'One-Two-Three-Red Light'. After *Colors,* everybody moved at the same time as if a switch has been pushed on the movie projector.

We window shopped at all the counters in the PX. The first showcase we went to was the make-up counter and tested the new lipstick called *Montezuma Red,* which had been formulated especially for Women Marines. At last we had the exact shade of scarlet to match the red cord on our hats.

At the book and greeting card counter, I accidentally bumped into the officer standing next to me who was looking over the books as I had been. I bent down to pick up his book at the same time as he did and we bumped heads.

We laughed at our clumsiness.

I looked at the title of his book and couldn't resist flipping through it out of habit before I handed it to him. The title was AND A FEW MARINES by John A. Thomason. It was filled with illustrations and looked interesting. All about Marines in China before the war.

"I was going to buy that, Miss," the officer said politely.

His new lieutenant's bars were as shining bright as my Globe and Anchor insignias and his hair was cropped shorter than mine. He was about the same age as I.

"I'm not a Miss. I'm a Marine. Your book looks interesting. Is there another copy?"

He smiled, found another copy, gave it to me and smiled again.

"Did you just come out of Boot Camp?"

"Yes. Camp Lejeune. Did you?"

"OCS. Officers' Candidates School. Right here at Quantico."

"One of those 90-day wonders?"

He grinned at my saucy remark. "Where are you from?"

"I'm from Tonawanda, New York. You?"

"El Cajon, California."

"California! Do you know any movie stars? How close is El Kahone to Los Angeles?"

"Pretty close. A half a day's drive on Highway 1 from San Diego. I go there a lot."

I gave him a second long look and he perked right up at my interest in him. He could see I was impressed with his western origins. I knew a lot about that golden State from the hundreds of cowboy westerns and musicals I had seen during the last decade. Who didn't know about Hollywood? Where a girl could walk the streets and become a star overnight!

He told me he had graduated with an elementary teacher's degree and was in the ROTC program before he joined the Corps. We had been talking for at least five minutes when he realized he had tarried too long.

He lowered his voice to a whisper so no one could hear, "Will you meet me by the glass cages in the Marine Corps Museum on the second floor topside after the early movie? No one ever goes there and we can be alone."

He didn't invite me to go to the movies with him and I knew why. But that was all right. I did not want to go with him neither, not to a movie nor to a museum to look at dusty uniforms of another era. Besides he didn't know any movie stars at all so what would we have to talk about?

Fenton had just joined us and stood behind me clearing her throat.

She scolded me as we walked away. "Terry, you can't be seen walking with an officer on the Post. You can't go to a Post movie with one either. Officers have to sit upstairs and go out by the side exit while enlisted have to sit downstairs and go in by the front door." The movie ushers were M.P., military police, which meant we were guarded as we watched the movie. I wasn't about to rendezvous with any officer in any museum as long as there were so many rules against fraternizing to land a girl in trouble.

Marine Barracks Quantico was commanded by General Philip Torrey who was famous for enforcing his personal orders against fraternizing between the men and women Marines, particularly between enlisted and officer ranks. Our gender had introduced unprecedented concerns for the Marine Corps which led General Torrey to issue one post order after another.

About one thousand women Marines were stationed in Quantico and there were four barracks full of females who worked on the post itself. Although we were outnumbered by the men, we seemed to be more visible. Women were all over the place.

More women were stationed at Aviation Women's Reserve Squadron #21 at the Quantico Air Station at Brown Field. They had their own barracks, mess hall, and were almost a separate Marine Corps. Our group did not interact with that group. We could not go there, nor cross the lines into the air base without permission because of radar that was housed there. Their WRs, on the other hand, exited and entered Quantico from the same gate.

General Torrey's position adhered to the official Marine Corps' general policy: The men were to ignore the difference in our sex. Marines were Marines. There was no distinction between the genders.

But, every week another order by General Torrey would be posted on each and every bulletin board throughout Quantico as each new problem arose because of that difference in gender. Romance was to be stamped out by Marine Corps rules and regulations. It didn't stop love between the sexes or doing what comes naturally.

Some of the rules and regulations were unintentionally humorous. To anyone caught breaking them, they weren't funny.

General Torrey's latest orders were always repeated from Marine to Marine and kept the Post buzzing with his latest disposition.

Theresa Karas Yianilos

ALL COMMANDERS TAKE NOTE:
No Hand Holding Between Marines!
Married Marines Can Not Be Stationed On The Same Post!
No Fraternization Between Officers And Enlisted Will Be Allowed On
Or Off The Post, Either Walking Or Driving!"

Scuttlebutt rumor swept the Post constantly about who was caught doing what. Those couples in love or in lust became adept at finding new and different areas in Quantico to snatch a few private moments together.

General Torrey himself went out nights into the bushes to make sure there was no fraternization going on in the boondocks. Pine forests flanked both sides of the three and a half mile stretch of road that connected the Post to the main highway between Washington D.C. and Richmond. It was a favorite place for trysts.

One night he flushed out six couples like mallard ducks who had been billing and cooing on the pine needles under the large trees in the forest. Then the general saw one couple holding hands on a quiet Sunday afternoon while walking at Post Docks by the romantic waters of the Potomac River where Fleet Marine Forces had held amphibious assault training exercise and in less than twenty-four hours, they were transferred, she to Parris Island and he to Camp Pendleton and on to the Pacific.

The Hostess House Cafeteria was also in the same building as the PX and Post Theater and was always crowded with enlisted men and women. Marine Corps chow was delicious and plentiful but sometimes it was fun to eat in a restaurant with china dishes and cups instead of metal trays.

It was common practice to share tables and so we asked two baby-face Marines, each of whom had one stripe, which indicated they were private first class, if they minded if we sat at their table. Both of the Marines stood up immediately and pulled out two seats. Billy and Sammy paid the dime for our coffee and invited us to meet them later at the Enlisted Men's Club.

The line formed for the early movie at the Post Theater. A different movie played every night and it was free. I would be able to see every movie that Hollywood had ever made.

I would have enjoyed waiting in line but I had an errand to run.

I apologized to Fenton. "You can go if you want to but I'll have to miss this one. We'll never make it back in time. Early movie starts at 6:00 P.M. Once the MPs close the doors or if the movie is full, they won't let you in. I have to go into Quantico Town and find a drug store. I've got the curse."

Just as Dr. Storch had predicted, the change in climate did cause problems for me.

The Quantico Post Exchange hadn't geared itself for the monthly needs of female Marines. The PX sold everything, from wedding rings to albums, from lipsticks to sterling silver silverware, from cigars to shaving lotions. Women Marines had been in the Corps for over a year, but still it hadn't occurred to the Marine Purchasing Officer to stock such items as Kotex, sanitary belts and Midol. The men didn't need any of those things.

I waved at the nice old flirty provost as we walked off the Post which irritated Fenton a little bit. "Will you stop being so friendly with everybody! We'll have half the post trailing us."

As we walked into town, a Gunny sergeant and his buddy stepped up their pace and came alongside of us and matched our cadence.

I asked them about their *fruit salad* on their chests because you just don't ignore a slew of campaign ribbons as they had.

"This is the Blaze, and this is the Purple Heart. This is the Marine Corps Good Conduct Medal which I got before the war when it really meant something," they explained with well earned pride.

Both of them had a blue diamond patch on their sleeves with the number 1 in the center. They had been First Division and were billeted at Casual Barracks as out-patients while doctors worked to get their malaria under control.

By the time the Gunny told me about all the action they had seen on Tulagi in the Guadalcanal campaign and how all they had to eat for months was the dried fish and rice they had taken from dead Japs they had killed and how wonderful the Sheilas were in Australia, I had eaten two hamburgers and a chocolate milkshake at the Riverview Cafe. I also was wearing the Gunny's salty emblems. He had traded my insignia for his old ones and was as thrilled with my unblemished shiny new ones as I was for his corroded antique used insignia. I hugged his arm and gave him a grateful peck on the check.

I tried to slip away to buy my female necessities and slipped out the side door but the sergeant followed me and caught up to me at the cash register in the drug store.

He made a big thing about paying for my purchase and insisted upon carrying the package I had behind my back. I handed him the square shaped box with the bold letters KOTEX written on it.

A few of his buddies walked by just then. They whistled and woo-wooed him in a friendly manner. He suddenly remembered he had a game of snooker and disappeared into a pool hall down the street. That was the last I saw of him. I had forgotten to get his name.

All the way back, down the short Main Street of Quantico Town, past the snack shops, military store, barber shop, tattoo parlor and billiard parlor, past the gate and the sentry, into the Post, Fenton continued her commentary about our comrades in arms. Her voice bounced off the walls of the underpass that led us back to our barrack.

"Marines have a girl in every Port. You are either one more on a long string of 'Sheilas or they'll try to tie you down if you date them twice."

They were being shipped out so fast they didn't have much time to fool around. I understood their plight.

"They're trained that way, Fenton. To secure the beachhead," I said.

"You mean secure the maidenhead," said Fenton who had a natural streak of born suspicion. Must come from teaching in Boston.

On the map, Quantico was indeed a very large place with the Potomac River flowing along side the military reservation.

If you colored all the areas that were *out of bounds,* it became a very small place for the WR's.

Quantico swarmed with thousands of enlisted men but most of them were in training and were always in some kind of formation as they marched from one area to another, from one building to another. Hundreds of Marines could be seen at one time, loaded in trucks in convoys on their way to maneuvers. Battalions of men filled the barracks but those areas were *Out of Bounds.*

Five thousand *out of bounds* acres at the Guadalcanal training area were filled with men training amphibious and combat tactical maneuvers where live ammunition was used. Unless a WR was in Motor Transport and had driven a truck there, it was no place for a woman.

The Aviation Battalion at Brown Air Field was located at the one end of the Post. The Marines who flew planes or were assigned to keeping Marine Corps aircraft flying lived and trained in a separate unit of their own. Brown Air Field was *out of bounds* to everyone except the Women Marines who were stationed there because of radar. We never saw the men nor the women. They seemed to be a separate Marine Corps. We didn't interact with the WRs stationed there.

The Reserved Officer Candidates Schools which turned out a new batch of hundreds of college-aged ROC' officers every three months were also *out of bounds*.

Breckenridge Hall which was only a block away from the Women's Compound was absolutely forbidden territory where WR's could not walk unless they worked there. This was where the elite batch of impressive Marines and senior officers in the Marine Corps, attended Command and Staff courses. None of the enlisted women ever saw any of these magnificent creme de la creme specimens of manhood, the best of the Corps. They were way *out of bounds*.

You couldn't take two steps at Quantico without having to come to a snappy salute. Handsome officers, so straight and magnificent in their military bearing, with shining bars on the collars of their sharp uniforms were everywhere. On the sidewalks. Riding in cars. All *out of bounds*.

The officers had their own club known as the Officer's Mess. Officers were separated into two categories, married and bachelors.

The ones without wives lived at BOQ, Bachelor officer's Quarters. That was another *out of bounds* area. We enlisted Women Marines couldn't go there even if invited, not in the day-time nor night time.

Yes, Quantico wasn't as large as the acreage showed on the map. The orders against fraternization had made the Women's Reserve compound a small island in a sea of officers.

We the enlisted, did have our own clubs and our own separate places where we were permitted to go.

I would never have risked my reputation in Tonawanda by going into a place where they served mainly beer. Back home, we called those places 'saloons' and only old men like my dad went there, not respectable young girls. Yet here at Quantico, it seemed the acceptable thing to do.

"We've been invited to the Slopschute."

Fenton wasn't as curious as I. She sniffed scornfully at the invitation we had been given by the two Marines we had met at the Post Exchange.

"There's a good reason why it's called a Slopschute. It's strictly for the rank of privates and privates first class! Why don't we wait until we are invited to go to the one of the NCO clubs. There are two clubs, one for corporals and sergeants and another club for staff sergeants. This one is for privates. It can't be much."

"That is what we are, Fenton. Privates. Just out of Boot Camp," I reminded her.

The Slopschute wasn't hard to find. It was right off Barnett Street, across from the statue in one of the few wooden buildings on the Post that had been built before World War I. It had many windows, green shutters and matching color asbestos roof—a friendly cozy place even if the white paint was peeling off the slat sidings. Stairs led to double doors.

The moment I opened the doors I knew why the enlisted men called their club "Slopschute". A heavy peculiar order of stale spilled beer hit me in the face. So did the loud music from the juke box playing *DON'T GET AROUND MUCH ANYMORE...*
Missed the Saturday dance
Would have gone but what for?
Awfully lonely without you.
Don't get around much anymore.

We looked around for the young Marines we had met at the PX who promised to be our hosts. The place was packed with Marine green winter uniforms.

At one table sat a group of sailors of the rank of seamen second class and apprentice seamen, the Navy equivalent of private and private first class.

At another table, also by themselves, was a covey of WR's drinking and joking. Two of the girls were dancing with each other which seemed kind of odd since so many males were around. It reminded me of the American Legion Hall in Tonawanda. But there we had no other choice. Here men were in the majority.

Billy and Sammy broke into happy grins and didn't hide their surprise that we had kept our promise to show up. Proudly they escorted us across the dance floor, past the bar to a long wooden table and benches. They introduced us all around to the eight other Marines there. A dozen fluted glass pitchers—each one containing at least one and a half quarts of beer were on the table.

Billy said, "You've got a lot of catching up to do."

Before I could tell him "Never mind," he jumped up to fetch more 'buckets of beer'. So full of beer were the pitchers that some sloshed over. No one bothered to wipe it up. I guess it didn't really matter and the beer trickled between the slats on the table to the deck.

Fenton didn't say anything. She had become very quiet and she stared at the drops of beer that barely missed her legs.

I protested their generosity. Now was not the time to tell these Marines I didn't like beer and never touched the stuff.

Billy waved my upturned hand aside. "Drink up! It's only twenty-five cents. You can't get high on this *three point two* dishwater."

"Only the officers are allowed to bring real liquor on the Post," apologized Sammy.

He excused himself to go to the men's *head* again. Seemed there was a procession going in and out of there continuously and a line was formed outside the toilets.

I drank a few sips to be sociable and they made a big joke about me being *"One Brew"* after the cartoon character in the *MARINE CORPS GAZETTE*.

The Marines were very accommodating, making a big fuss over us.

I took turns jitterbugging with each one of them when they discovered I was a very good dancer. I did a rhumba to Xavier Cugat's *JUNGLE DRUMS* and a slow one to Harry James's *YOU MADE ME LOVE YOU* and a swing to Benny Goodman's *DON'T BE THAT WAY*.

Something was bothering Fenton. I could tell. After a while something was bothering me too. I couldn't put my finger on what it was at first.

There I was having fun and all that. Some of the jokes were corny. Especially the *BAM* jokes. Oh yes! These nice Marines had all kinds of versions of how the word *BAM* came about.

"Did you hear this one?

"There was this happy male rabbit and he was hop-hopping along until he bumped into a woman-rabbit.

BAM BAM! THANK YOU MAM!
He hopped hopped until he came to another woman-rabbit.
BAM BAM! THANK YOU MAM!
He hopped hopped until he came to a white house
where he met an iron woman rabbit on the lawn.
BAM BAM!
GODDAMN!"

We laughed together. They were all good kids. Every one of them. I suddenly knew what was wrong. They were all too young.

Our ratings were the same; private and private first class. They were fresh out of Boot Camp like us. But they were also only seventeen, eighteen and barely nineteen years old because that was how old the boys were who were being drafted into the Marine Corps. It was no longer an all volunteer service. Many of these boys had enlisted when they were seventeen in order to be able to choose the Marines as their service instead of waiting to be drafted and taking a chance on being sent into the U.S. Army. Their faces still had adolescent pimples and some barely had to shave.

We WR's had to be twenty years old with a high school education before we could volunteer for the Marine Corps. We simply didn't match. Their fuzzless baby faces just made us feel old and a little sad. No wonder the girls at that other table preferred to hen it alone.

Still, the uniform united us all in a camaraderie of brotherhood and sisterhood that made for a pleasant evening, one worth repeating.

At 10:00 P.M.—twenty-two hundred Navy time—the lights flickered on and off telling us it was closing time.

Fenton had been ready to leave almost from the moment we had entered the Slopschute.

The eight 'gyrenes' escorted us all the way back to the barracks and we marched in cadence, singing Boot Camp songs all the way.

Three more couples joined us.

When we halted in front of the barracks, one of the men started a football cheer from Michigan.

Someone else was from Michigan who had been kissing his date good-night and he turned around and shook hands with the cheering Marine. That started everyone else shaking hands with each other because they were from states just as good as Michigan.

Soon a big crowd had gathered around the doorway shaking hands.

Other Marines whose bodies were pressed against the building separated long enough to look up and watch.

One couple wasn't bothered by all the jolly goings-on. It was my bunkie, Gerry, kissing her Marine date good-night, their lips together as if they were in another world. So that is why she never stayed around the barracks.

The duty officer stood in the door and warned, "Fifteen minutes."

If that had been my mother, or anybody's mother in Tonawanda, there would have been a terrible scene at the mortification of all the gossip that would have resulted from having caught their daughters in such a compromising position for all the neighbors to see.

Taps was at 10:15 P.M. but 11:15 was absolutely the latest for checking in at week-ends. The boys had to return to their barracks before curfew. They would have lots of time to stay up all night when they got to the Pacific Islands.

Women's barracks, Quantico Va. 1944
Top: The chow line: Where buddies meet.. The author, Sherry Grose and a squadmate.
Center: The bulletin board: A gathering place for news and announcements.
Bottom: Mail call: Mail is distributed by duty NCO.

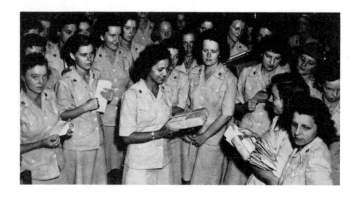

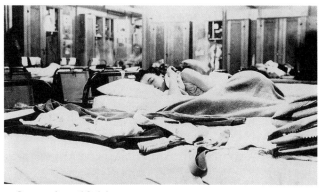

Women's Barracks, Quantico 1944
Top: Moonbeam asleep. Note she is the only one in squadroom.
Center: The Laundry Room: Ironing of shirts a required duty.
R. Bottom: Lindsey on Police Duty with sheets.
L. Bottom: Terry, in dungarees, also on Police Duty.

Theresa Karas Yianilos

Women's Barracks–Quantico

I whipped off my hat and uniform blouse; unbuttoned my skirt and shirt as soon as I swung the door open and bumped into an embarrassed male guest being shooed out of the women's lounge at the last possible moment.

Far from quieting down, the barracks became a beehive of activity.

As soon as the downstairs lounge emptied of men guests, it filled up with women in all kinds of night wear. My pink pajama tops were tied in the middle but the latest style seemed to be long romantic white gowns from the Gay Nineties period with long cuffed billowy sleeves and high lace necklines.

"Who would believe that you are a bunch of Marines. You all should be carrying candlesticks to complete the portrait," I said to the group in the laundry.

"Makes me feel absolutely virginal," said Smokey, waltzing around in a pirouette, a cloud of smoke from her cigarette following her.

She was about one hundred fifty pounds, a baker in the galley at the Mess Hall. She checked her girdle which she had stretched over a chair to dry wide enough to fit instead of using the dryer where it might have shrunk. It was still a trifle damp. So we talked a while swapping stories.

Smokey's troubles started at the same time as World War II. "I thought I'd be an old maid. I never had one date while I was in school. When this war started, my mother told me all about the Lost Generation from World War I and how all the young men had been killed in the trenches in France and left a whole generation of women unmarried without kids. That scared the hell out of me. I figured I was going to be an old maid for sure, especially since there was going to be a shortage of men."

"Well, there is."

"I married the first guy that said he wanted to marry me. We drove across the border to Maryland and got hitched for two bucks. No blood test, nothing. He went back to Fort Dix and we found we had nothing in common, except we liked the same beer so we had it annulled. Then I married a 4-F and he wouldn't leave me alone, not even to go to work. So I got that annulled too and decided I better join the Marine Corps before I made another mistake."

I agreed. "Smokey, you have done the right thing."

178

She wasn't too sure about that "To hell with that Semper Fi garbage. I've put on twenty pounds since Cooks and Bakers. I'll never catch another husband!"

I reassured her with an old saying of Mama's.

"It's the fat chicken that makes the best broth!"

The barrack was a bee-hive of activity at night. No one just sat around doing nothing. Everyone wrote letters, at all hours in the nooks and crannies of the barracks. There was no rule that someone writing a letter shouldn't be interrupted, and often the letters went unfinished as impromptu *bull sessions* began around the woman Marine who held a pen in her hand.

You could pick out which of the married women were being faithful wives; who didn't date other men in their absence. They wore their husband's pajamas for moral support and usually had their wedding pictures propped up before them when they wrote their letters, no matter where they chose to sit, the *head*, the lounge or the laundry which was the favorite place for many after 'lights out' had been shouted. It was the only warm room in the barracks.

There was one subject that wasn't discussed. Widowhood. Death and the loss of one's love was kept at bay with silence. It was not something that could be shared in any of the bull sessions.

Those who had joined because their husbands had been killed in the war didn't talk about it nor dissect their emotions. They had made their statement by enlisting. In fact, most of the girls in the squadroom didn't know who the widows were.

Those women Marines who had men that were prisoners of war kept up the letter writing just as if the letters were being delivered even though they hadn't heard from their spouses or boy-friends for years. It was the only way they could sustain hope. A few of them pursued wifely activities to maintain their illusions that everything would turn out all right. One WR was doing needlepoint, making covers for her antique chairs which she had put into storage. Others did embroidery on pillow cases, putting their married initials in satin stitch. I too had brought my embroidery. Mama had taught me how to use a needle since I was nine so I could fill that Hope Chest.

A day didn't go by without a Woman Marine announcing her engagement and flashing a ring.

Two girls in our squad had just married fellows they met here at Quantico only a few weeks before. One was such a quiet mousey girl. Who would have thought she could find someone so quickly, much less get pregnant, in that time? But there she was—out on a *four ninety-nine* waving her honorable medical discharge for the whole squadroom to see.

Everyone delighted in her coming motherhood. Having a baby was something many of us planned but not yet. It was for sometime in the distant future. Not today. Not tomorrow. Having "his" baby was wonderful when it happened. But most of us preferred that it happened later rather than sooner. The dream of wifehood, motherhood and a little house with a picket fence had been put on hold by most of us.

Yet, when a woman Marine announced her condition, we all oohed and gushed with the romance of "love" fulfilled. Our mutual joy for the pregnant Marine cast a pink glow onto the Marine green painted walls.

But, on the other hand, motherhood was also to be avoided since discharge from the Marines was the price that had to be paid.

To be pregnant was to forfeit a career as a Marine. It meant the immediate termination of enlistment. It was a consequence that many Women Marines didn't want to consider as viable and I was among that group. I certainly didn't want to take that route in life. Mother's lament that 'I would come home pregnant' still rang in my ears. Not me! I was married to the Corps!

There had been several discussions on that issue and we always divided into two camps. There were those who were willing to pay the price for motherhood and accept discharge but there was a surprising number of Women Marines who had decided on the Marine Corps as a way of life who wanted to have it as a career although our oath was given with the condition that our enlistment was only for the duration of the war and six months. The women who were inducted into the Corps during World War One in September 1918 had served only two months of war-time when the Armistice was signed in November. Within a year they were all discharged. A few stayed on in the Corps as civilian office personnel.

We were going to receive the same fate. Attitudes hadn't changed much in the two decades between the two wars. Women were useful in the military in time of war but not in peace.

An undercurrent of resentment could be heard in the comments about the unfairness of it all.

For some reason, the most intimate of subjects, *sex* and the mystery of pregnancy or rather *'How Not To Get Pregnant'*, was discussed in the *head*, which was the most uncomfortable room in the barracks. Women who hardly knew each other from different squads or platoons would venture their opinions as they went in and out the toilets. Eighty women living in one big room made personal intimate revelations you wouldn't dare voice to your own mother. At least, not my mother.

The concerns of thousands of mothers were repeated in the voices of their daughters who faced ancient dilemmas with an added dimension.

"My mother would *kill* me if I came home pregnant, unmarried, and *discharged* !"

"You are lucky. Mine would hardly talk to me until the day I left. She was mad I gave up a good job to become a Marine and warned me not to come home pregnant."

"Mine did that too."

"Why should we have to give up the Corps? The men don't get discharged if they become fathers!"

"The men want just one thing. If you give it to them, then it proves you are a slut and he's got something to brag about to his squad. If you don't, then you are a tease. It's not fair."

"Who said the Corps is fair? The men get jailed and put in the brig and the women get discharged. That's the way it is."

"Just don't get pregnant. That's the only solution."

"That is easier said than done. Sometimes a guy doesn't have a condom and then what do you do?"

"He's got to withdraw in time."

"If you don't say "No", you've got only yourself to blame."

"It's so hard to say "No" when he's being so loving and sweet and has bought you dinner and tells you he loves you and asks you to wait for him. Some Marines are so good at snowing a girl to get what they want. And now with the war, you know, it may be the last time you'll ever see him. He could get killed tomorrow."

"If a girl lets the petting get that far, she deserves what she gets. Pregnancy. Discharge. All of it."

Everyone groaned at the small town opinion that had been expressed by one of the bunkies. That was exactly Mama's attitude and all the righteous women in Tonawanda. I heard her say it plenty of times: a girl in trouble asked for it. It was always *her* fault. A man was doing what was natural. You can't blame a man for trying. A man didn't marry *that* kind of girl!

Mama's words bounced around in my head.

"Wouldn't it be great if we had a pill we could take the morning after and decide right then if we wanted to be pregnant or not."

"You can say that again!"

"We are at the mercy of men."

"That's how God planned it. Procreation is what makes the world go round."

"For God's sake! We're not talking about religion, Fenton! We're talking about how *not to* get pregnant before, not what to do after!"

"It certainly *is* about religion. A good Catholic can't use any contraceptives. It's God's law. Look it up. It's right there next to the one about adultry, and honoring your father and mother."

"How about asking Doc, one of the corpsman or a doctor if there is any other way?"

"The doctors are the last ones who will tell you anything about birth control. It's against the law. Especially if you're unmarried."

Most of us were about the same age, under twenty-five, and I realized my bunkies didn't have any real solutions to a moral and physical problem that each woman had to deal with herself. I suspected they didn't know any more than I did.

I hid the fact that I didn't know how to avoid getting pregnant.

Mama had harped consistently on how the only way to avoid pregnancy was to keep your virginity. Save yourself for marriage. It was the best and only method of birth control that I was taught. When I was younger, I believed that everyone got pregnant on their wedding night. Every mother in Tonawanda kept a score card of those brides whose babies were born in seven months. That was a sure sign she *had* to get married. Doing *it* once was enough to get a girl in the family way.

Obviously this was not exactly true.

Could there be another way? I didn't dare ask for fear of showing my ignorance but, there were many unanswered questions in my mind.

Everyone seemed to know what they were talking about, but there were gaps in how much I understood. Too many pieces were missing from this puzzle of sex between the sexes.

The subject never went away. Nothing brought a heated discussion or generated as much fear as the subject of pregnancy and its military and social consequences.

I perched on the table in the hallway under the night light to catch up on my letter writing too. I still kept in touch with a few of my old beaus and pen-pals and with Spero whose chocolates always made a hit with my bunkies.

I wrote home weekly. I didn't want Mama to take it into her head to visit me. If she worried too much she'd be liable to take a bus and drop in unexpectedly. She would never understand how you couldn't talk to an officer until you got permission from the First Sergeant and she would start her scolding lectures the minute she saw something that needed correcting. She would never respect nor understand the chain of command. I wrote letters home frequently and repeated in each letter how we had to be inside the barracks by ten o'clock.

Yes, I had chosen a good bunk to meet everybody. Those who had signed out ahead of time and had permission to return to the barracks trickled in as late as twenty-four hours (12:00 midnight in Navy time) in various state of mind and condition.

A *WAVE*, one of the many hospital corpsman who shared our Marine barracks, winced in pain as she passed me.

"Are you hurting, Doc?" I asked.

"Oh! My aching ears! I can use three stripes now so I could order that NCO Sergeant to knock it off and turn off that screeching soprano."

All the sergeants lived by themselves in the little rooms in the hallway that crossed between the squadrooms in the H-shaped buildings. The doors were closed but Lily Pons was coming through all the same.

"It's a good thing we Yanks outnumber the Rebels in our squadroom. We don't have to put up with hillbilly music. That's all you hear in Barracks Three over at Motor Transport."

"I could listen to Glenn Miller, Artie Shaw and Benny Goodman all day," I said, although to tell the truth some of the country music had a great beat.

My new bluejacket friend leaned against the table and loosened her tie and started to pick pine needles and prickle burrs off her uniform and bra.

"Boy! Is that ground chilly! It's too damn cold for boondocking maneuvers. That's all that gyrene wants to do. I have a brain and a mind too, but he hasn't gotten that far up yet."

"Boondocks. Maneuvers at this hour?" I asked. What was she talking about now? Weren't we discussing music?

"You mean a Leatherneck hasn't snowed you into taking a walk with him up Fuller Road? Three miles and half of pine trees and locust forest on both sides right up to the Main Gate to the Washington-Richmond highway. Just be careful where you step. It's so dark in those boondocks that you're sure to step on somebody if you don't watch it. Hell! It's the only place to go when you want to shack up."

I could tell Doc had much more experience than I did. Maybe she could give me some of the answers I sought. She was a hospital corpsman and all medical personnel knew a lot about the human body.

"That Marine wants me to wait for him until he gets back. What the hell does he think I'm going to do? Wear a chastity belt?"

"You have to be so careful," I said.

"You said it, bunkie. If you ever need a Marine's medical history to check him out, I'd be happy to oblige. Call Post Dispensary and ask for me. And carry condoms. Be safe."

I had never seen a condom. How would one begin to offer a condom to someone? When? At what moment. Why? What do you ask for in the store? What store? She saw my puzzled look but I didn't want to interrupt her stream of information with dumb questions.

She continued anyway, "You'd want to know if he had a social disease before going boondocking with him wouldn't you? Some of these guys come back with syphilis or gonorrhea more than once."

I had never met anyone who was so casual about the act of sex. I thought only men did the loving and leaving and had lust in their hearts.

Doc thought I hadn't appreciated her offer. "Look! I mean it. Don't go shacking up with any gyrene until you check with me. I do it for a lot of the girls. I've got to turn in. Sick call starts at 0800. That line will be a mile long of sick-bay Marines who want to make the binnacle list. Poor bastards! That won't keep them from getting shipped out to combat."

Gerry was the last to come in—just as the Duty NCO locked the door. One second late and she would have been checked off as AOL, Absent Over Leave, although she was just outside the door. That's the kind of thing Mama liked about the Corps. The strict adherence to curfew. Protecting the daughters of the Corps.

Gerry held up her left hand. On it was a small diamond ring. She flipped the empty maroon jeweler's box from the PX nonchalantly.

I squealed with delight. "You got a diamond? A real diamond?" I was so thrilled for her.

Gerry's smile was wan. "Goddamn! He talked me into it."

"Don't you love him?" Her reaction puzzled me.

"I'm not so sure now. He waited until I said 'yes' then he told me he's been transferred to Post Stables. Have you ever kissed a barn door that has been scrubbed down with Lifebuoy and sprayed with citronella oil?"

"He's in the Horse Marines? Aren't you proud? Aren't you excited? Will your Marine go on parades in Washington D.C. with full cavalry equipment, saddle bags, sword and rifle?"

I had splurged on that same book in the PX titled AND A FEW MARINES by John W. Thomason which the young lieutenant had dropped. It cost $3.00. But, now I would give it to Gerry as a wedding present because it had a short story about the Horse Marines in China during the 1920's and '30's.

"Do you know the Horse Marines date back to the turn of the century during the Boxer Revolution in China? The Mounted Detachment of the Legation Guard at Peking rode Mongolian ponies. They are the most romantic Marines in the Old Corps."

I turned her hand sideways to catch the light of the diamond and tried to make it bounce off the incandescent lights overhead.

Gerry threw bilge water on my bridal enthusiasm immediately.

She groaned, "He's a shit Marine. There are no more mounted left. The last detachment of Legation Guard was disbanded in China years ago. Even the officers have to walk now."

"What a coincidence that we two bunkmates should have boyfriends in the cavalry."

Little incidents like this only confirmed my belief that fate was the controlling force in life.

"Don't worry, Gerry." I said. "Maybe the Corps will issue your Marine a jeep the way the Army did to Spero."

185

"Not a chance! The Corps keeps horses for recreation just so some officer's wife can ride to hounds. War is hell!"

"Why did you take his ring, if you're not crazy about him?"

"What difference does it matter whose ring it is?"

Gerry's grief over her first fiancé who had been killed in the first year of the war was still fresh and it was obvious she had been won on the rebound. I had no way of comforting her. Once more she retreated into her sack.

I went to the mirror in the *head,* brushed my teeth, squeezed a whitehead on my temple and puzzled over Gerry's acceptance of a ring she didn't seem to have much enthusiasm for. A diamond was a diamond, no matter how small. I thought about how I would react to getting a ring from the man I had set my cap for. No doubt about it. I would be loud and sappy with my happiness.

I thought about the record album resting in the bottom of my Hope Chest. Had it been a diamond, I too, would have been engaged. Oh well! A girl had to be patient and play it cool before she hooked her man, but afterwards she had better keep the bed warm. That was another of Mama's sayings.

I tiptoed into the dark squadroom and slipped between the sheets. My legs cramped up half way in and stopped to a dead-end right in the middle of my bunk.

My sack had been short-sheeted. You know, where the bottom sheet is folded in half with both ends at the head of the bed. Not only that, it had been filled with newspapers, shoes, my perfume bottle and my stuffed toy mouse. I was delighted someone had short-sheeted me. It was a sign of welcome—somebody's way of having fun with me—probably Fenton.

Well! I had to come up with something good in retaliation.

I quietly pinned her into her sack with all the safety-pins I could find as she snored deep in sleep. I could hardly wait to catch the surprised look on her face when she tried to crawl out of her bunk for roll call at 6:00 a.m. reveille.

But I missed it. The Duty NCO stood next to my ear and yelled "Rise and shine!"

When I jumped out of the sack I forgot all the stuff I had quietly placed on the deck the night before and kicked the bottle of Blue Bonnet cologne into a perfect five yard field goal drenching the sergeant when the top fell off. The rest of the bottle trickled deep into the grooves of the wooden deck as the glass smashed. It drowned out the permanent odor of the disinfectant used to swab down the decks and bulkheads.

The sergeant said, "You are a gooney bird. An albatross." She also ordered me to get my hair cut short before Captain's Inspection and gave me EPD, extra police duty of GI cleaning.

The accident gave me a chance to meet the rest of my squadmates, all eighty of them. They bunched up to see what happened. Everybody held their noses and made faces as they passed by me.

Blanche smiled and said, "This place smells like a whorehouse".

"She should know," said Gerry.

Fenton handed me a dustpan and a broom with a smile of retribution on her face. She helped me clean up.

"You are a real buddy. After what I did to you. You swear you weren't the one who short-sheeted me?"

"Don't thank me, Terry. The two hours EPD I got for being in the sack at roll call? Add them to the two hours you got."

The Mess girls had departed in a noisy jubilant mood, not caring whether they woke everybody else up. This was the last day of their thirty day stint of mess duty.

I threw on my dungarees as did the other WR's who were awaiting assignment marking time on general duty, police duty or guard duty, patrolling the women's battalion in the WR compound. Guard duty was particularly boring. It meant being on call two hours on, two hours off and having to look for anyone who broke any one of the hundreds of rules. It meant being alert and saluting women officers with precise alacrity or risk being put on report. It meant being restricted to the women's compound.

The Women Marines who were assigned to duty in the offices throughout the Post were up early also, taking time out to apply mascara, very lightly of course, since it wasn't regulation, and lipstick which was, making sure the cotton seams in their stockings were straight, uniforms sharp, the Dyan-Shine polish on their cordovan brown oxfords as near to a spit shine as the one the men always managed to achieve on their GI shoes.

The Women Marines aimed for a spit and polish that would outshine a Post full of men.

Theresa Karas Yianilos

Mess Duty

"It's fouh-thirty. Youh won't fohget the jugs?"

Moonbeam's soft voice tore through my dream as I clung to the last shreds of it. Once I woke it would be gone. Gone from memory. I had seen his face. The man I would marry. Moonbeam woke me just as I was about to say his name. I rolled over and tried to call him back.

"Youh supposed to be at the Mess Hall by five."

The Duty NCO was quietly going from one bunk to another nudging the women scheduled for Mess duty, allowing the others to sleep until reveille at six o'clock (0600 Navy time).

I stumbled in the dark looking for my Mess clothes. It wasn't hard to find my stiff cardboard cotton dress. I wrapped the white turban over my hair while Moonbeam followed me to the *head* with instructions of exactly how to get the jugs and gallons.

I half heard her as she rambled on about this wonderful Marine she met on week-end liberty in Washington. When she described him he sounded exactly like my dream of a man—tall, quiet, strong, wise and handsome.

"He's from Arkan-saw. We're practically next door neighbors. And he saves jugs too!"

My dream popped like the cartoon balloons in the funnies.

"Does he care for you too?" I asked

"I don't rightly know. We didn't talk much."

"He made love to you?"

"Oh, yes. He held my hand all the while he looked at me."

"Kissed you?"

"Just once. I let him and he asked first."

"Sounds very serious. I think it's safe to let him know how you feel."

"I can't. I just look at him and get weak all over."

"Are you going to see him again?"

"We're supposed to meet at the USO on Saturday in Washington."

"Write him a love letter and send it to him. If he doesn't answer then don't go."

"I don't know how to write a love letter."

"Try some words of Tristan and Isolde. I found that poem in the library and it's very passionate. He'll never know they're not yours originally."

188

Women's Mess Hall, Quantico Va. 1944
Top: Terry dressed for Mess duty with turban and girdle under starched uniform.
Center: WR's waiting in chow line.
Bottom: Swabbing down the gallery after serving.

"Will you write a love letter for me? Then I'll copy it in my handwriting."

"Okay," I agreed. After all, I had lots of practice juggling all those soldiers and sailors at the end of my fountain pen all these years.

Moonbeam went back to her bunk happy and I went out into the dark black morning that was still night, anxious to get out of the cold and into the warm galley, looking forward to learning how to cook. The way to a man's heart is through his stomach. Mess duty was a wonderful opportunity to prepare for the future.

I liked the Marine Corps more and more as each day unfolded with new adventures.

There was a lot of hooting and hollering when some of the old salts saw who had been tagged as this month's Mess crew.

"Not you too!"

The Chief cook, a Woman Marine named Frenchy, a three stripe sergeant, handed out assignments.

It was just quieting down when Smokey saw me. She looked twice as big in her men's white trousers, skivvy undershirt and boondocker boots with flour all over her. Her clothes, including the boots, were part of the men's issue of uniform.

She let out a whoop and told the Chief Mess Cook to give me a special assignment.

I didn't have to wash garbage cans nor scrub pots and pans that hung from big hooks on a square rack in the middle of the ceiling. Nor swab out the deep steam vats that stood all in a row as if in a symphony orchestra. Nor swab the decks. Nor wait on women officers who ate in a room by themselves with china and cloth napkins.

All I had to do, three times a day, from 5:00 A.M. to 8:00 A.M. morning chow, and from 10:00 A.M. to 2:00 P.M., noon chow, and from 4:00 P.M. to 6:30 P.M. supper chow, was to slice bread. Forty loaves for nine-hundred women.

I would slice bread ahead of time, arrange it on trays, then wait for the cry of "Bread" when I would dash out with a tray and place it on the chow line. I didn't have to stand there and pass it out to anyone as the girls who ladled out the food from huge pans had to do.

It was the easiest and best duty in the galley.

Smokey showed me how to use this large carborundum steel knife. I was afraid of it at first but I soon had the knack of it. The

Marine Corps couldn't get a slicing machine because of the war. I kept slicing and slicing with this oversized knife. Some of it came out thick Texas style and some of the slices were paper thin, perfect for English High Tea. I just knew I'd get the hang of it if I cut enough slices.

The galley was staffed by women, serving women only, which just proved how much truth there was to the statement that two women in the same kitchen spelled trouble.

There was one male. He was a technical sergeant everyone addressed respectfully as Mess Sergeant. Even the WR lieutenant deferred to him. Probably because all his hash marks and zebra stripes proclaimed the many years of Mess he had served. He stayed in his office making up menus and didn't come out much. He never spoke to any of us mess girls directly.

The WR lieutenant went around tasting everything.

The Chief Cook Frenchy, passed on the cooking orders to all the PFCs and corporals who did the actual cooking.

There was so much to notice my head swiveled as I watched the cooks prepare chow. I concentrated on memorizing the recipes. When the time came for me to marry and set up houskeeping, I'd be ready. After a month of mess duty I aimed to be cooking as a Marine Mess Sergeant, ready and able to serve Marine Corps chow every day.

The Chief Mess Cook kept checking up on me. Once I didn't realize she was behind me and missed her by an apron string with the carborundum knife. She must have had more confidence in me after that, because she didn't come around.

I kept cutting and cutting. When I ran out of bread, I opened the big metal door and found more. Soon I ran out of the aluminum trays too. I was very proud of myself knowing I was ahead of the demand. I hadn't heard the call for "Bread man" in a long while.

I did hear a "Who told you to cut this much, Private?"

The Mess Sergeant was behind me staring at all the counters I had filled so artistically like a checkerboard, dark bread on one side, white in between.

"She's drunk from all the rye she's been slicing," said one of the little cooks who thought it was funny and giggled loudly.

He surveyed the artistic palette of bread and turned to the Chief Cook. "Change the noon chow to S.O.S."

I was very happy to have helped him with his menu planning. Waste not! Want not!

He took my carborundum knife away and said I could have it back tomorrow. There was no more bread to cut anyhow.

"What's that you're cooking?" I asked the chief cook, recognizing a French gourmet recipe when I saw the white sauce.

"S.O.S. Shit on a shingle. Start toasting all that bread you cut."

"Oh!" I wasn't sure I wanted that recipe.

She was impatient with my queasy look and shoved a spoonful at me like medicine. It wasn't bad. It was tasty.

"Recipe for this? Forty five pounds of dry chipped beef, thirty six gallons of milk, nine pounds of butter, eighteen pounds of flour, salt and pepper to taste. Got that?"

At the vats a WR who had a rating of private first class stirred a pudding mixture happily humming to herself over the steaming kettle drum:

"Toil and boil
Bubble and brew
Here's how I'm going to poison you."

"Sure, I can give you the recipe. Take fifty-four pounds of oatmeal, forty five gallons of milk, salt to taste and you've got enough cereal for a cozy family of nine hundred." She was amused by my interest.

I was classified as 'Bread Girl' so it wasn't as if I were *goldbricking* by going around collecting recipes. I wasn't supposed to work at any other duty other than I one I was classified for.

In the Marine Corps, unlike the Army, work in the kitchen was a thirty-day tour of duty performed by every enlisted lower rank Marine. Mess duty was not punishment to be meted out as it was done in the Army. When it was a Marine's turn, he or she went on Mess duty cheerfully and did the job that was assigned. That was it. This duty had to be fulfilled, as long as a Marine was a private or even a corporal, one month out of each year. Sergeants were excused. There was no grousing nor griping by any Marine because of mess duty. On the contrary, the galley was a place where mischief and humor made the preparation of three meals a day for one thousand women a lot of fun.

Smokey had finished mixing the meringue for one hundred and fifty lemon pies and let me lick the beaters.

The Lieutenant saw me and she tasted the meringue as well sticking her forefinger into the big batch itself. She went into the Mess Sergeant's office to tell him perhaps a little more salt. I thought so too but of course, I didn't dare say so.

Frenchy was the only temperamental one in the galley. When you do all the work and are the star it's expected. She gave most of the orders.

The cooks and bakers didn't seem worried about anything. They went about their duties in extreme confidence. They joked and teased at the same time they snapped to, obeying all instructions on the double, taking everything in their stride, as they lifted hundred-pound bags of flour or sugar, huge blocks of butter, five gallon cans heavy with oil or molasses, glass gallon jars filled with mayonnaise, mustard, honey or catsup.

Their confidence in performing their duty was inspiring to watch. Under their golden hands, the kitchen produced large pans of steaming hot foods, roast turkey, ham, beef and fried chicken, different kinds of salads, vegetables, crusty breads, rolls, cakes, cookies, cornbread, and pies; apple, pumpkin, blackberry, cherry, and lemon.

Still they found time to clown around which made all of us here on temporary assignment feel as if we had been invited to pitch in with preparations for an endless party.

Frenchy ordered her cooks to bear a hand with forty-five hams for supper chow.

Two tiny corporals, Tammy and Little Mo, pulled out big legs of whole hams out of the depths of the ice-box. They sat on the deck, cross legged as Indians do, and cradled the hams tenderly in their arms rocking them as if they were babies singing lullabies with funny words.

They put several legs in each pan, oiled the hams with a mixture of honey and mustard, patting them as if they were baby bottoms. The aluminum pans were so heavy it took two of them to lift them into the oven. Even that didn't slow them down.

"If you have so much piss and vinegar, start peeling," said the Chief Cook, interrupting their silly songs.

They just kept it up, talking back to her although they knew she was the sergeant and they had to do everything she commanded no matter what kind of tone she used or the manner in which she said it. The chain of command was in effect in the galley no matter how informal everyone was. The work had to be done and done right. There were over a thousand women Marines to be fed three times a day here at Quantico.

The next morning I woke to the first rays of the morning light. Reveille hadn't sounded but I knew I was late. I rushed to the galley dressing on the way, tucking in my hair under the turban and pulling down my girdle which had ridden up uncomfortably as I ran.

The Women Marines of Motor Transport from Barracks 3 were lined up and I could hear their mutterings. The late chow line had joined the early chow line and it grew like a tape worm and circled the building. Three buses idled at the curb.

The serving girls stood in front of the large metal pans but there was nothing in them. The main breakfast entree of French Toast was missing. The minute I entered through the double doors I heard the cry "Where is that Bread Man?"

"Yoe!" I shouted.

"Bread! More Bread! Snap to it, Bread Man!"

The Mess Sergeant came out of his office. His phone had been ringing right off the hook.

"Motor Transport is late. I've had two company commanders call. What is the snafu?"

"There's only one Mess Man classified as Bread Man. They are waiting for their French Toast you scheduled this morning."

By the time everyone had cleared out of the Mess Hall, I was too exhausted to eat my French Toast or even join the girls in barbershop harmony as they swabbed the decks afterwards.

The cooks managed to catch their breath but the chief cook was in a foul mood. All that rushing and double time had invigorated everyone except her. The cooks and bakers were on to the next meal.

"Throw me some chickens!" she yelled.

The cooks obeyed promptly. Plucked fowl went flying through the air, legs and wings flopping past her, landing in the big steam vats which had just been washed. The next thing you knew the Chief was chasing Little Mo and Tammy around the galley. Frenchy caught Little Mo and stuffed her into the steam vat. The humor of this scene straight out of the movie TRADER HORN with Harry Carey rescuing the hero out of stew pot from the cannibals perked her right up and she laughed as hard as they.

The Lieutenant repeated her commands, "Girls! Girls! Attention! Attention!" Her sweet school girl's voice didn't carry and she wasn't heard.

The salty male Mess Sergeant roared out of his office and everything went quiet which proved once more what a great help it is to have a man around the place.

The next morning, all three officers greeted me at my duty station at the maple block cutting board when I went to my Post: the lieutenant, the Mess Sergeant and the Chief Mess Cook. Exactly fifteen loaves of bread had been laid out for me all in a row.

The Mess Sergeant handed me my knife, handle forward, and said, "I'm going to keep an eye on you."

I pushed the knife against the loaf. If I believed in voodoo I would have panicked. A knife-like pain hit me in my own bread basket at the same moment. Was it hunger? Another pain, sharper and deeper hit me again and again. I keeled over right into the Mess Sergeant's arms.

Naval Hospital–Quantico

When I opened my eyes again I found myself looking at a doctor. I was in a hospital bed, not a bunk. Next to him stood a Navy nurse with lieutenant's bars on her white uniform.

"Where am I?"

"Naval Hospital."

"In Washington D.C.?"

"No! You are right here in Quantico. You have had acute appendicitis. You almost waited too long. You also had a few cysts on your ovaries. We removed them."

"The bread has to be cut for chow." I tried to move but my whole body from the waist down was bandaged.

"You don't have to worry about cutting bread for quite a while."

"How long will I be here?"

"At least thirty days. You won't be getting out of bed for at least two weeks."

Any and all sick Women Marines and WAVES for whatever illness, including surgical, gynecological and E cases, were bedded here with me in this long room. There was only one ward set aside for the enlisted women in Naval Hospital. Of course, the women officers had their own separate room.

The nurses, all of whom were officers, lieutenants in the Navy, and corpsmen, who were enlisted Navy personnel, wouldn't let me get out of bed although by the second week, I did become tired of the bed-pan. I did not question nor argue with their advice nor refuse any of the pills, although they insisted on giving me a sleeping pill every night, waking me up to make sure I swallowed it.

I did everything anyone in white told me. I had no reason to act otherwise. Doctors were to be obeyed and never refuted. They were next to God and nurses sat on the right hand of doctors. Not only were they officers, they were in charge of my life. I cooperated.

"You are our best patient," said the corpsman. "Not like some of the BAMS we have had in here that show no respect for the Navy."

The care I received at Post Hospital was excellent, thorough, and attentive. Since it was the first time in my life I had been sick enough to be in a hospital, I was no connoisseur of medical care. On the other hand, the room was filled with patients in the other beds who had a running commentary on every aspect of hospital life.

I had no complaints as I recovered except for the wobbliness of my legs when I took the first steps after being prone for two weeks. When they replaced the bandages I saw for the first time the Grand Canyon that was my incision and it appalled and frightened me. It meandered vertically up my whole right side and ruined the look of my once pristine body.

My dismay was so sharp that I blurted out, "Doctor! I can't wear a two-piece bathing suit now!"

"You're a Marine. It doesn't matter. If you had been an actress, I would have made that cut smaller," he said nonchalantly. The Navy captain didn't think my concern over my huge incision was worth discussing and he walked on to the next bed.

Women Marines and a few WAVES filled every bed in the ward. I was one of the four women patients who had surgery. One WAVE was there for a dislocated jaw she got when she fought off the attentions of a sailor who had escorted her back to her barracks through a short-cut in the boondocks.

Two women were from Motor Transport and they had broken their legs while wearing those high top men's boondocker boots. The Corps didn't issue any women's boots for field work. The men's sizes somehow didn't fit around the ankles, even when the women wore several pairs of socks to take up the space.

Most of the occupants of the beds had female and menstrual related complaints, and other gynecological problems.

The complaints, gripes and general dissatisfaction over the treatment from Navy doctors and nurses was the chief topic of discussion among the Women Marines and the Navy WAVES in the hospital beds. The minute the ward was all clear of all hospital staff the cacophonous litany began.

Everyone resented being forced to swallow pills they didn't want as the nurses stood by and checked each mouth to verify that the pills went down the gullet.

The minute we were left alone, the griping began again. Nurses were officers and therefore, not to be trusted with personal observations or complaints. Their first loyalties were committed to the doctors whom they served, all of whom were male.

Most of the doctors' expertise was oriented to the needs of the men. Among them were urologists, internists, surgeons and general practitioners who had been drafted out of civilian life. They were all men. A gynecologist to handle the illnesses of the women was as rare as a woman doctor.

There was total agreement among the patients that the Navy doctors knew very little about female illnesses. Their therapy for female problems was viewed with suspicion because they weren't gynecologists. Stories about the incompetent care and futile treatments were exchanged as proof of the doctor's lack of knowledge about women's illnesses.

"I've had this infection for six months and my vagina is itching so bad that I can't sit at my desk and do my work. So they paint it purple with Gentian of Violet and tell me to take a boric-acid sitz bath. It doesn't help. They give me pain pills and I still have it."

To be fair to the Navy doctors, I volunteered my personal medical history to the symposium. "Even civilian doctors can't cure that itch." I said. "I've had it off and on since I was thirteen. The doctor took me off meat for a year. It didn't work but it helps if you stick a thumb nail size piece of Ivory soap up there during the day."

"The Navy doctors can't cure it! It comes back every time!"

Everyone had experienced that misery at one time or another. No one knew what caused that horrible itch. I dreaded the thought that it might return while I was on duty here in Quantico. And now I was being told the learned Navy doctors couldn't cure it.

"Navy medical care goes to the men first. They can cure syphilis or gonorrhea! They've got that problem licked. But an itch where you can't scratch? Forget it! They can't be bothered."

"They know how to cure the diseases the men get, but they can't stop a monthly curse that goes on for thirty days," a voice across the room offered. Her period was into its second month.

I entered the debate to defend my doctor and started an argument as if I were waving a banner for Roosevelt at a Republican convention.

"How can you say your doctor saved your life? All you had was an everyday common little appendectomy. Look at what he left you with! You've got a Navy scar a mile long. That nice Navy doctor was a butcher. And insensitive. I heard him tell you it didn't matter because you are a Marine."

"I don't plan to be a stripteaser like Gypsy Rose Lee," I said, trying to make the best of what I wasn't too happy about. I was content that I had been taken care by the Marine Corps even if a Navy doctor did it. At home, I would have had to pay for this operation and it would have cost at least one hundred dollars and a loss of a month's pay.

"Have you seen any women doctors here at Naval Hospital?" One of the patients asked.

"Well, no."

"There aren't any. That's why you haven't seen a woman doctor. They are all men. What do they really know about women? They're not trained in gynecology. Not one of them has ever had the monthly curse. They don't even know what we mean by cramps. We need more women doctors. That's what."

"Where are you going to get more women doctors? You know it's next to impossible for a woman to get into medical school."

"These Navy doctors will give you a hysterectomy if you tell them you have monthly cramps. I bet they don't cut off a guy's penis because he has a pain."

That started a round of dirty jokes about penises and I fell asleep right in the middle of it all because of the sleeping pill.

The Great Debate continued on and off.

No one said a word when the doctors made their rounds. The chain of command didn't allow it. There was no other option nor redress other than griping to your buddies.

No one confided in the Chaplain when he made his rounds and visited each of us.

No one said a peep to the Red Cross volunteer who passed out writing paper and magazines.

No one said a word to the corpsman when he fixed the beds or the nurse when she changed our dressing.

We had been told when we joined that our bodies belonged to the Marine Corps. Well, I found that was really true. If a Marine didn't like the medical care and preferred his own civilian doctor or dentist at home, he or she could not seek outside medical consultation without a Special Release from his or her superior officer or from the Navy doctors. They didn't like to give a release to an outside civilian doctor. Few asked for it. Fewer still received it.

It wasn't until the medics dumped a patient into the bed next to mine that I began to worry if maybe what the other patients were saying was true.

Two burly Navy corpsmen brought in a limp form wrapped in a white sheet as tightly as a mummy and dropped her on the bed next to mine. They pulled the curtains around her. I heard blood curdling screams, crying and moaning.

The corpsmen carried on a conversation as if their patient wasn't even there yelling her head off.

"Do we have another E case like this one?" One of the corpsmen nodded his head towards the new patient across from me who had arrived that day.

"Naw, she's another *BAM* whose menstrual was upset by Boot Camp and it won't stop. I keep getting these pills mixed up. It's atabrine for the Gyrenes and ergot for the women. Right?"

"Right. At least in combat, we know what to do. There it's plasma or sufadiaozle. They're either shot or they're not. It is hard to figure out what is wrong with these females. Look at the trouble this E case gives us."

The corpsmen discussed their work as if we were all sedated and couldn't hear.

There was a stigma attached to E cases. E case was a mental condition, a "Nut" who had cracked up in the service. That was the label put on any Marine who broke under pressure and stress, who couldn't cope with discipline, who wouldn't obey, who refused combat and didn't want to kill or be killed and manifested other bizarre behavior. Usually, once the condition was recognized, the Marine Corps acted swiftly. The Marine was discharged quickly and quietly. If an E case had to be hospitalized first, he was put on a special ward away from surgical patients and discharged as soon as possible.

The Corpman saw I was watching him intently and he said to me, "Your bunkie won't give you any trouble. She'll be out cold for a while."

When the room was cleared, the Woman Marine next to me who had been screaming a few minutes before, pulled her curtain open and said very calmly, in a refined voice in a normal tone, "Hi! I'm Valerie from Coral Gables, Florida."

She was old. Too old to be a Woman Marine. She actually had wrinkled skin and thinning hair.

Curiosity consumed me. I pelted her with questions. "What are you in for? What did they do to you? Are you a WR?"

She brought out a wedding picture. In it a lovely girl stood next to a handsome tall Marine. Tears came to her eyes as she handed the snapshot to me.

"This is my wedding picture. I was married three months ago. Look at what these doctors have done to me. What is my husband going to say when he sees me now?" She began to cry softly.

I couldn't believe my eyes. "Is that you? What happened?"

"That is what electric shock treatments have done to me. They have turned me into an old woman. I had a hysterectomy fourteen years ago. I was nineteen years old. As long as I take hormones, I am fine. Otherwise I go into menopause."

"Hormone pills? I have never heard of them. Are they new?"

"No! I've taken them for over ten years. These Navy doctors refused to prescribe them. I ran out and they wouldn't let me go home to my doctor to get more. They don't believe in them. They are treating me as if I am crazy. I begged them to release me but they put me here instead. I am *not* crazy. These Navy doctors don't know anything about females in this hospital. I would be all right if I could have my pills." She repeated that over and over as she sobbed quietly in her desperation.

"Why won't they give you the hormone pills? Are they dangerous?"

"Of course not! These doctors just don't believe it them. They know nothing about them. They say they are experimental. I've been on them for over ten years."

"What made them bring you here in the first place? Did you get sick?

"Without those pills, I get hot and cold flashes. I get these crying jags. I can't concentrate. I get so nervous and irritable and so depressed I can't work. The lieutenant reported me and the first thing they did was give me an electric shock treatment. They are torture." She shuddered and moaned and tears welled up in her eyes again.

"Electric shock treatments? What are those?"

She described the treatments Navy Hospital doctors were giving her and she frightened me with her graphic account. The whole room became silent as she told her tale of horror as she described what they did to her in a special room where there were electrical apparatus and tubs for this sort of therapy.

"First they strapped me down. Then they put electrode wires on my head. Then they send low voltage electric volts through my body just like I'm Frankenstein. That is when I pass out. Then they plunge my whole body into a bath of cold water. The next thing I know, I am in this bed. The doctors insist this will calm my brain patterns and make me normal. There is nothing wrong with me. It is the doctors who are the monsters."

It seemed the women were being treated with a different standard of consideration as if we were a mysterious species whose physical problems were mental.

Outside the Naval Hospital, the Marine Band serenaded the patients with *Embraceable You*. It was their weekly concert to cheer up the boys.

For the next two weeks I listened to Valerie cry, moan and be tortured. We would always have a normal heart to heart talk after her shock treatments. I became very fond of her and I told her so.

"I'm praying for you. Tell the Chaplain. Please. He can help."

She cried and I held her hand until she fell asleep. I had been ambulatory and allowed to walk around for two weeks now, first in the ward and then on the hospital grounds. Inactivity had increased my anxiety to return to duty and free a Marine to fight.

Then one day, while still attached to Post Hospital, I returned to find her bed occupied by another Marine.

Valerie was gone.

When my thirty days were up, I was pronounced cured and fully recuperated for duty, and was returned to my barracks, with a six inch scar that was healing nicely.

Several months later, I saw my hospital bunkie in the PX. She was wearing the *Ruptured Duck*, the gold emblem, on her chest signifying a Marine who had been discharged. She had make-up that was applied skillfully and was no longer the crone who had slept next to me. Years had fallen off her face and the wrinkles had disappeared.

"Valerie, you look marvelous!"

"I'm going home. They finally let me go to my own doctor and I have been taking my hormone pills. You don't know how glad I am to be rid of this grim place and away from these Navy doctors. The sorriest thing I ever did was join the Marines."

With that she was gone. I was so happy I had seen her. Truly, I would have gone through life wondering about her fate. Now I knew that she had a happy ending.

I returned to Barracks One to a welcome that was wonderful as it was unexpected. Once again I was home with all my bunkies, who were my dear friends, Gerry, Sherry, Fenton, and Lindsey and with my radio playing my favorite program, *ASSEMBLY*.

Gerry had gone to the Riverview Cafe in Quantico Town for hamburgers and returned loaded with French fries and Coca-Colas. We had a party right on my bunk. A box of chocolates had arrived from Spero and it was vacuumed up by everyone. A spirited exchange was carried on as some traded their half bitten pieces with those who preferred the soft centers over the caramels and nuts.

Other squadmates passed by and helped themselves to French fries and chocolates and they returned with snacks from their lockers to keep the party going. We danced and sang songs.

Blanche didn't join us which wasn't unusual but she did throw two bananas over to us. Those were the very first we had seen in a long time and it caused a great commotion. She watched us from her bunk and ignored us while we sat there shooting the breeze about life, loving and men.

I loved everyone in Barracks One. They were such a grand company of Women Marines. This was the kind of experience and sorority relationship I would have experienced had I been able to afford to go to college and live in a dormitory.

Here we were, in the middle of a war that was being fought on two oceans, the one the Marines and the Navy were fighting in the Pacific and the one the Army, Navy and the Air Corps were fighting in Europe and North Africa. Yet the war seemed far away.

We only knew what we read in the newspapers and saw on the newsreels in the movies or heard on the radio.

Marines had taken Eniwetok and Kwajalein in the Ellicells Islands and were landing at New Guinea. Thoughts that maybe this war would come to an end soon without my having freed a Marine to fight worried me.

Six months had passed since I had stepped into the Marine recruiting office in Buffalo on September 1943, to free a Marine to fight. I hadn't freed anybody yet.

So far I hadn't done anything but have a good time. Every now and then, a feeling of guilt and frustration came over me but it faded quickly as soon as I put on my Marine Uniform.

What a relief to be out of a hospital gown that didn't cover the buttocks.

A Seventy-Two Liberty–April 1944

I was given more good news when I reported to the duty officer. She too welcomed me back to the barracks and told me I was on the liberty list for a *seventy-two hour* pass. A 72-hour pass didn't count against the total thirty-day furlough time that was allotted to every Marine each year.

I had three whole days to go see Mama and Dad. They had not seen me in my Marine Corps uniform. It had been six weeks since I had graduated from Boot Camp. I couldn't wait one moment longer.

I took the hour long ride on the train from Quantico to Washington and the twelve hour ride from Washington D. C. to Buffalo.

Quantico in April had cherry blossoms on the trees and forsythia in bloom under a bright shining sun in a azure blue Virginia sky. The grass and shrubs were a bright green with their coats of new leaves. The occasional cloudbursts of rain were light, pleasant and refreshing. I saw colorful birds, robins, blue birds and cardinals, almost daily as they flew among the locust trees that had burst into new leaves full of promise to provide a canopy of wonderful shade during the warm months that were a few weeks away.

Warm mild spring breezes caressed me as I sat in my gym clothes or swim suit in the latticed fenced area that had been built to ensure our privacy behind our barracks

Virginia! What a beautiful state. One of the thirteen original colonies. I envied anyone who had been fortunate enough to have been born in Virginia.

Happy as I was to be going back home, I was torn between leaving this balmy state and my need to see my family and bask in their love and their pride.

My heart sank as I disembarked at Buffalo, New York, and stepped into dirty slushy snow still on the ground. More snow was falling steadily. A blast of zero cold air hit me hard and almost turned me around back on the train. How could I have forgotten that bone chilling Buffalo north wind that blew in across Lake Erie straight from the Arctic region.

The warm regulation trench coat with its wool lining and red muffler that I rarely wore in Quantico gave me welcome protection against the bitter chill. This was springtime in upper New York State. For the first time, I noticed how the cold climate made people unfriendly. As people got off the train they scrunched their heads into their coats, pulled up their collars and burrowed further into their layers of wool clothes.

As I passed them, no one lifted his head to greet me. Even in Washington D.C., where uniforms were a dime a dozen, a Woman Marine attracted attention, a smile or a greeting. Officers liked nothing better than looking an enlisted Woman Marine in the eye which meant a salute had to be rendered.

But Buffalo was either too insulated or too provincial. The cold weather monopolized all the attention. The people here were more conservative and they seem to be all wearing dark dismal colors, black, grey, brown and maroon clothes. Suddenly I had the answers

Top: The Cherry Blossoms are in bloom (author pictured).
Center: Bunkmate Gerry and Terry (author).
Bottom: Cotton stockings were a problem. They crept down,
          bagged and sagged. Pulling them up was a common sight.

Quantico Va. 1944
Top: Terry (author) dressed to go on liberty carrying one of the war dog puppies.
Center: Terry (author) and her kid sisters.
Bottom: Tonawanda N.Y.: author with proud Mama and Dad.

to many of the reasons I disliked the North and why I had fallen in love with the South. I had found a better place, a warmer climate, to live and spend my life.

An old song of World War One ran through my head, *"How you gonna keep them down on the farm after they've seen Paree?"*, and I hummed it to myself changing the last word to *Virginie.*

I knew this would be my last trip back home for a long time.

Soon I was enveloped into the arms of my Mama and Dad and little sisters. Their hugs, kisses and enthusiasm for my return were enough to make the nasty weather recede in importance.

After they admired my new tight muscles, my new figure, my healthy glow, my better posture, Mama showed me the star she had in the window which indicated to all who passed by that she was a mother who had a child in the Armed Forces. She had been invited to be a member of the American Legion Mothers Of Servicemen, Tonawanda Post which met every Monday over coffee to knit and crochet items to send across to our boys.

I had become a local celebrity of sorts.

All the letters I had written to Dad in which I described the discipline of Boot Camp and my observations of Marine Corps life, had been given by him to the editor of our weekly newspaper. They appeared regularly in the TONAWANDA EVENING NEWS with a little blurb about how I had been an employee there before the war, which made it sound as if I had been a war correspondent, instead of a clerk typist who also went for coffee.

The gang at the corner saloon bought Dad a round of drinks whenever one was printed. Now when he dropped in for his nightly beer they asked each and every time, "How's the Marine doing?"

I had to visit everyone we knew, even friends Mama didn't really care for, just so they could see her daughter, the Woman Marine. These same ladies had given Mama a difficult time right after I had departed on that troop train for the Marine Corps, asking her disturbing none-of-their-business questions of why she had let a nice girl such as me join the military and why didn't I marry Spero, that nice boy who went to the same church? Didn't her daughter know a good thing when she saw it? Didn't she know all the girls who went into the service were sluts or something worse and that I'd come home pregnant?

I was very happy to see her pride of me in my Marine Corps uniform. I really put on quite a show for her. I told tall tales to all these old ladies and exaggerated about my life in the Corps, telling them it was so strict that we had to be in bed by 10:00 P.M. and that we had to wear cotton stockings and a girdle even when we worked in the kitchen. They were most cordial after that. I elaborated that without the Women Marines, we couldn't win the war.

I hadn't freed one Marine to fight as yet. I didn't tell them that.

I squeezed a few minutes to visit my former co-workers at Remington Paper Box Company. I walked in the front door and went straight to the factory part. No more side doors for me!

I smiled a lot not only because I was glad to see some of the people I knew, but mostly because I never had to work there again.

I even slapped the old *Kardex Files* with affection. I'd never have to pull down one of those stupid drawers again. That felt so good.

I talked to the girl who got my old job and asked her to make sure she filled out all the requisitions first that were addressed to Marine Corps Depot of Supply, Philadelphia, even if they didn't have *URGENT* stickers on them. She promised as a favor to me personally, the only Woman Marine she would ever know, to fill out all the Navy and Marine Corps orders first.

It was a very satisfying happy visit.

Mama and Dad were so proud. When we walked they took my arm.

My little sisters were so thrilled. They stayed by my side during my whole liberty hanging on to me and ran errands even when I didn't need anything. We hugged and kissed a lot. We took pictures.

Mrs. Martin came over and we took more pictures so she could send one to Henry, old Squirtball who was on a ship somewhere in the Pacific.

I was so proud.

My friends were so proud.

The druggist at Rexall was so proud he treated me to a Tin Roof—that is a chocolate sundae with vanilla ice-cream, syrup and peanuts.

Mr. Krause was so overcome when I walked into his butcher shop, he gave me a knockwurst with the American flag on it.

Mr. and Mrs. Chang gave me *two* almond cookies with my tea.

When I visited the Sugar Bowl and saw my best friend's father and mother, they asked if I still wrote to Spero, their nephew. They beamed when I said I did and insisted on treating me to a banana split made with three scoops, vanilla, chocolate and strawberry ice-cream piled high with whipped cream, nuts and three marachino cherries.

Everybody at church was so proud. After Sunday Services all my friends clustered admiringly around me with whom I had been active in the Young People's Christian club. One of the girls lifted my left hand and asked, "Hasn't Spero given you a diamond ring yet?" I told her we Marines weren't allowed to wear jewelry with our uniforms. It was against regulations.

On the whole, it was a satisfying and happy visit. We were *all* so proud of me.

I think it was the Marine Corps Uniform that did it.

I hadn't changed at all.

Awaiting Assignment: To Free A Marine To Fight

Monday, upon my return from my seventy-two hour liberty I signed in and reported to the duty officer hoping my call to free a Marine to fight had finally been issued. Instead, she assigned me to more gold-bricking, to police duty. P.D. meant two hours of cleaning the lounge and being free the rest of the day to dope off.

I had missed the Corps and Quantico with an intensity that surprised me. My bunkmates and fellow Marines had become my real family. Tonawanda, my family and friends there, had receded into the back of my mind like old photos in a family album which I had stored in an unused chest.

I went to drill practice and did guard duty.

I went to the movies at Post Theater and saw a different movie each night. I stopped at the PX and shopped for gizmos, always having a Coca-Cola at the Tap Room or apple pie at Hostess House. If I sat alone, someone would join me, either another Woman Marine or a Marine.

Those who were fresh out of Boot Camp at Parris Island or Camp Legeune, could not hide how thrilled that they were to find themselves sitting with Woman Marines. We were still a novelty.

There were only few of us. We numbered only eighteen thousand or more in the whole United States. Many fighting Marines who had returned from overseas had never seen a Woman Marine. They had heard about us and their curiosity was a reason to start a conversation, in the restaurants in Quantico Town or in the line at the movies.

Theresa Karas Yianilos

A Quantico Marine was never alone for long. The uniform identified us as a member of the same family.

Each day I met somebody new. We would shoot the breeze about life, love and discuss our plans in a bright new future when the lights went on again all over the world. Conversations could become filled with intimate personal details of one's life on short acquaintance. Questions of home town, age, family, schooling and status of love life were answered immediately. Strangers revealed the tiniest details of their lives and aspirations as if talking about them would make them come true.

We were also one big sisterhood. If none of my bunkmates wanted to join me in a trip to town or for something else, it didn't matter. A call for accompaniment usually brought out two or three acceptances. There was always someone, one or another of my squadmates, always willing to break out with me for a trip to Quantico, a shopping trip to Washington D.C. an hour away on the train, a game of badminton at the gym, a swim at the pool or hamburgers at the Riverview Cafe. No one went to see a movie at Post Theater alone. While waiting in a line that extended around the corner past the PX door on the side, we would make new friends and become acquainted with those standing nearest to us. Sometimes a conversation and a discussion that began in the movie line ended up at the Tap Room or at one of the Slopschutes or the Women's Recreation Room. Many friendships and romances began this very way.

The number of women who had become engaged or married in a very short time was recounted endlessly like the score of a great football game which was tracked by all of us.

Any WR who became pregnant but was unmarried was not censured for her condition. If her Marine had been shipped out to battle before they could marry, everyone knew he would marry her as soon as he returned.

Getting pregnant was the only way to by-pass the Marine Corps rules and regulations in order for an enlisted Woman Marine to marry a Marine officer.

Similar to some of the marriage customs of natives in Samoa and other Pacific Islands, where a woman had to prove her fertility first before marriage, the rules of the Marine Corps made it necessary for a girl to choose the same route. Because of the Corps' alacrity in granting a medical discharge it was entirely possible to get pregnant, have a rabbit test and be discharged and married in six weeks. It didn't happen often on the Post between the Marines but when it did, the barracks buzzed for days about the Cinderella romance. It was everyone's favorite fairy tale.

We traveled in pairs or in groups and so did the men. But, the feeling that we were one big clan persisted throughout the Post.

Sometimes we were as many as four or six Marines walking abreast, walking in cadence, on the same left foot, often singing songs. Occasionally we'd meet our counterpart Marines at the Slopschute or at one of the dances given by the Women Marines in their Recreation Hall or by one of the different battalions and dance the night away until ten o'clock.

Or we would have an evening of telling sea stories at the Slopschutes, *beating our gums* about inconsequential things over schuppers of beer. They were basically all alike, the Privates' Club, the NCO Club, the Staff Sergeant's Club. I did not care what the Officer's Mess or BOQ was like, although Fenton's curiosity was still keen. I suspected beer and liquor flowed freely in all of them. I had heard the enlisted men complain that officers got whiskey, real beer and even champagne. That didn't bother me at all since Coca-Cola was my drink and I could get that anywhere.

Yet, permeating all this activity was a fog of loneliness, a blanket of longing for family and a very special love. Our average ages ranged from eighteen to twenty-four. Most of us were away from home, away from our villages and home states for the first time. The war time songs were full of this longing, this universal loneliness.

Everywhere jukeboxes and radios played sad songs with the same themes of love, fidelity, the agony of separation from loved ones, and the loneliness over and over. The titles and lyrics said it for everyone, even the most inarticulate of lovers.

I'll Walk Alone and if they ask me, I'll tell them I'd rather. I don't mind being lonely... I'll walk alone...

Missed the Saturday dance. Might have gone but what for, awfully lonesome without you, Don't Get Around Much Anymore...

Don't Sit Under The Apple Tree With Anyone Else But Me,... with anyone else but me... No, no, no, with anyone else but me...

Kiss me once and kiss me twice and kiss me once again, It's Been A Long Long Time...

I'm gonna buy a paper doll that I can call my own, a Paper Doll that no one else can steal...

I Hadn't Anyone Til You... I was a lonely one till you. I used to wonder if there could be. A someone in the world who could care for me, now I see...
I'm Making Believe that you're in my arms, though you may be so far away...
I'll be loving you, Always, with a love that's true, Always...

The Marines who had found someone to love, who were loved in return, talked about their romances openly. Those who were still looking were open for a relationship of any kind and were prone to make hurried proposals and propositions on very short acquaintance. War created an urgency that gave an edge of panic to these moments.

And those who had received *Dear John* letters of rejection, whose sweethearts or wives had replaced them with someone else took comfort when they were able to tell someone how miserable they were. It never ceased to surprise me how quickly our discussions became intimate with revelations and confessions of the most confidential personal kind.

No one was ashamed to admit his or her loneliness. Here we all were, living, sleeping and eating with a crowd of people, eighty to a squadroom, yet loneliness was a major topic.

It amazed me that with the percentage of men I met running so high in my favor that I see-sawed between being the girl next door and the understanding sister back home.

A few times I was viewed as a possible best girl and was asked to go "steady" which was a juvenile term I had left behind in high school. Going steady meant there was no diamond ring and no wedding date set.

This was not such an unusual request since so many of the Marines were young and had joined the Corps at seventeen and eighteen. They were here to do a man's job but basically they were still high school kids. Back home they would have been pumping gas, making deliveries or waiting on customers.

Hundreds of Marines all about me and I had yet to meet one who matched the shadow of the man in my heart for whom I searched. Oh yes! I knew what these Marines about to go overseas were talking about when they used my shoulders for a crying towel.

The Call To Duty

"Private Karas. You are to report to Post Service Battalion in H Barracks at 0900. You have been assigned as Post Courier. I know you will make us all proud."

I saluted the lieutenant and stood straight and tall.

Post Courier! Post Courier!

About six weeks after I had graduated from Boot Camp I received my long awaited call to report to the Commanding Officer and was given the news I had been waiting for all this time. It had taken almost nine months since the day I signed up. About as long as it takes to have a baby.

Finally, I was about "to free a Marine to fight!"

My hairs on my arms stood up just as they did when the bugler blew Colors and I held a salute until the flag was fully raised and the last musical note had died away.

I loved having to stop whatever I was doing every sunset and sunrise to renew my pledge to my flag and country. The stars and stripes, Old Glory, visually expressed all the emotions of patriotism that consumed me.

Gerry laughed cynically when I described my feelings to her.

"Terry, if you get that excited every time you face Mecca when the flag is raised and lowered, you are going to wear out all your batteries."

I could not stop grinning as I bounded into the barracks to announce, "I'm going to *Free a Marine To Fight!*"

I told everyone, even the girls sitting on the toilets in the *head* and the ones who were taking their showers.

Morning found me in full regulation in the uniform of the day: my forest greens pressed, my tie knotted correctly, my shirt crisp, my hat on straight, my matching lips painted with Montezuma Red lipstick, my girdle as high as it would go, my cotton stockings pulled up tight and seams straight, my gloves on, my insignias straight up, my shoes spit-shined to a mirror finish, my shoulder bag hanging straight down to my hip. My slip did not show and the warm humid morning air had made my hair so curly that not one strand touched my collar. I was G.I. and ready for duty.

I boarded one of the buses that lined up outside of the Mess Hall daily which transported Women Marines to their duty in command posts all over Quantico.

Post Services Battalion–April 1944

As carefully as if it were a marriage license, I held my assignment papers firmly in my gloved hand. They were to be presented to the commanding officer of Post Service Battalion, H barracks—Casual barracks.

I walked in a cadence step up to a set of wide stairs, towards the double doors of a very large brick two-story building. My cotton stockings had started to creep down to my ankles and they bagged at the knees. As I stepped on the first step, I propped my leg on the second step and lifted my skirt to pull them up.

Immediately I heard appreciative whistles.

I looked up and saw about thirty Marines wearing skivvies hanging out the many windows of the second floor watching me.

I plunged through the double door which slammed noisily and entered a hallway. Immediately to the left was an office with the door slightly ajar with the sign:

COLONEL K. I. BUSE.

Directly opposite across from this room was another office with the door fully opened. A huge map of the Pacific Ocean was on the wall on one side of the door and on the other side, there was a full length double mirror from floor to ceiling. I caught a glimpse of my flushed and blushing face in the reflection as I raised my knuckles to knock. I straightened my shoulders, pushed out my chest and took in a deep breath.

"Permission to enter, Sir."

A firm strong voice said, "Permission granted."

I stood at attention with the sharpest salute I could muster, ramrod straight. I held the salute. "Private Terry Karas, reporting for duty, Sir."

There before me stood a solidly built man of about fifty-five years of age with a goatee, round glasses and almost white hair cropped short in a military brush cut. His hands were akimbo and his stern eyes probed my face.

"Why are you in the Marine Corps?" He boomed the question at me and his voice vibrated out of the room.

Everyone in all the other offices down the hallway had to have heard him.

I looked him straight in the eye and told him. "Because it is the best outfit, Sir."

A moment later out of the depths of his rotund belly came a roar of a command. "Sergeant Queen!" He bellowed.

A handsome sergeant came bounding across the four feet of hallway and answered smartly, "Yes, Sir!"

"Pipe Private Terry aboard. She says this is the best outfit. What do you think of that?"

"Mighty fine, Sir," said Sergeant Queen. His eyes twinkled. He did a smart turn and escorted me across into the other office.

"Chick, this is your replacement as Post Courier. Welcome Private Terry aboard. Show her the ropes," he said to a very young Marine.

The smile on Private First Class Chick Young faded and was replaced with a look of dismay. "So soon? I just got here from Samoa!"

I met the Marine I was to replace. He could have been my blood twin brother. He was thin, sweet, with a pink baby face and younger than I by two years. We were both short and exactly the same height of five feet two. Even the brunette color of our hair was the curly same.

He showed me "our" desk and "our" files reluctantly and disconsolately. This was the Message Center.

Chick's disappointment was premature.

We were to share our "duty". He was staying.

I did *not* free a Marine to fight after all.

Post Service was a communications center and we were the message center responsible for the dispersal of all the latest information for the whole Quantico Post. It was our duty, as couriers, to keep a running communication with Post Headquarters by making *runs* between Post Headquarters and Post Service Battalion three times a day and whenever the courier was called for special deliveries and pick ups. Post Headquarters was also the building where General Torrey had his office. It was entirely possible I would bump into the fearful Commanding General of Quantico.

***Post Service Battalion,
H-barracks, Quantico 1944***
Top: Major Emery and
Col.. K. I. Buse, CO.
Bottom: Sgt. Major Jordan
reviewing the Women Marines
and drilling them in front of H-
barracks on the parade parapet.

Post Service Battalion 1944:

Top: The Marine Sergeants: Sergeant Queen is on the far right Sherry watching, on the far left.
Center: Chick Young and Terry visit Post Docks.
Bottom: Web, the Cary Grant look-alike, with author and the Colonel's car.

The offices here handled all the court martials, the deck courts, the transfers of all Marines, which outfit was shipping out or coming in, and all military matters, all of which were top secret.

First reports of all battles came through this message center. Movies of every battle and encounter with the enemy in the Pacific which were *Top Secret* were shown in the basement (or below deck) in a room that was restricted to all enlisted and unauthorized persons. They had been filmed by Marine Corps War photographers who were trained combat Marines and went into battle carrying their rifle and camera.

Correspondence between Post Headquarters and the Post Service was a continual stream of paper work.

That explained the careful instructions Sergeant Queen gave me.

"You are to go to Post Headquarters dressed in full uniform. Check yourself in the mirror in the hall."

He continued. "When you enter Post Headquarters, *request permission to speak*. Announce your mission and give the report to the officer.

Stand at *attention* until given permission to *stand at ease*. Sign for any return envelopes. Make an *about face* when leaving the room.

Return here immediately and deliver all packets stamped *Top Secret* to Colonel Buse upon return. Do not loiter. Any packets that are not stamped come directly into this office. Give them to Sergeant Major or distribute as marked to the other offices.

You shall not discuss any information you hear with anyone. Consider it all *classified*. Nothing leaves this battalion office."

I heard the words Top Secret and Classified. My heart swelled with the importance of my assignment. At last, I was in the thick of it all, practically in the combat zone.

"You have one more duty. I shall give you instructions for the battle map as soon as the information is declassified."

I was put in charge of the huge map of the Pacific Theater Of Operations on the wall in the hallway.

Chick listened as well to instructions he must have heard before. He and I had quite a bit of free time to become acquainted because, as couriers, our deliveries or "runs" were made at 9:30 A.M. [0930], 1:30 [1330] and 3:30 P.M.[1530]. Navy time had not become easier nor natural to me. I still thought in Eastern Standard Time. There was time between the filing of papers to drink cokes together and talk.

Chick had been with the 7th Marines of the 1st Division with the garrison in Western Samoa and had just returned stateside after a three month battle with a tropical fever he contracted while serving on that South Pacific island. He was still weak but capable of desk duties.

Fortunately his illness was not filariasis, the dreaded elephantiasis, which was one of the strange diseases a Marine could get in the South Pacific. That horrible affliction could affect a man's testicles and make them as big as cantaloupes which had to be carried in a wheelbarrow or make a man's leg grow as thick as an elephant's. He showed me his collection of pictures of people in advanced stages of various tropical diseases that he had taken on that island.

Many Marines had become afflicted with vicious unknown tropical diseases and practically every Marine in the First Division suffered from malaria which was nasty and debilitating, with its sudden attack of fevers and chills that could last a lifetime.

"I sure am lucky," Chick said. "Practically all of the First Division got malaria on Guadalcanal. The Japs have cornered all the quinine so it was very tough on my buddies. You never get rid of malaria once you've got it. It stays in your blood and flares up again and again."

As we talked, I sensed a lessening of his earlier resentment at my sudden appearance. By the end of the day, we were friends.

My other main duty was to place colored pins on a map of the Pacific Ocean to record where Marines were fighting. It covered the wall from ceiling to floor, from one office door to another and showed in detail the Pacific Ocean from Alaska to Australia, from the Dutch East Indies, Malay, the Philippines to the West Coast of the United States, 5000 miles from point to point in any direction.

I had to stick colored pins in it to indicate where the Marines were and where the Japs were at any given moment: green for the Marines, yellow for the Japs and blue for Allies. Red meant the island had been taken and had been won. Islands that were secured as our base with Marines on it had green and red pins.

Hundreds of yellow pins were already on the map, which meant the Japs were in control of most of the Pacific Ocean in May 1944. They dotted the map like a bad case of measles or chicken pox..

The Pacific Ocean was divided into four sections: Southwestern Pacific, South Pacific, Central Pacific and North Pacific.

The Southwestern Pacific, was south of the Equator, to the west of the Solomon Islands, Java and the Netherlands East Indies. This section included the whole continent of Australia, the island of New Guinea, the Admiralty Islands and the Bismarck Archipelago. The Japs had control of much of this area and yellow pins were stuck into the names of Rabaul, Cape Gloucester, Lae, Port Moresby, Biak, Hollandia, Emirau, Darwin, Timor, Amboina, Celebes, Borneo, Singapore, Java, Batavia, Andaman Islands, Mandalay.

The South Pacific Theater was all the territory south of the Equator and east of the Bismarck's. These islands were the lifeline to Australia and New Zealand and the reason the Marines were sent to Guadalcanal in the first offensive against the Japanese. The supply lanes had to be kept open or Australia and New Zealand would have been lost. This region held the Solomon Islands and the New Hebrides with names of Tulagi, Guadalcanal, Vella Lavella, Bougainville, Espiritu Santo, Efate, Noumea, Ellice, Fiji, Samoa. Yellow pins and red pins were there.

The Central Pacific Area was north of the Equator, west from Hawaii to the Philippines, to Japan itself, and included Micronesia, the Carolines which went from east to west and had Truk Island in the center, the Palau Islands, the Gilberts, the Ellicells. Strange names in a strange language identified these places: Tarawa, Makin, Kwajalein, Eniwetok, Guam, Peleliu, Saipan, Tinian, Iwo Jima, Okinawa, Formosa, Luzon, Mindanao, Bataan, Corregidor. The Japs were in control there and the map was filled with yellow pins.

A few red pins were already placed on the islands of Tarawa, Makin and Kwajalein in the Ellicells which had been won by the Marines.

The North Pacific was that vast region above the Hawaiians and included Midway and Johnson Islands all the way to Alaska and the Aleutian Islands. Yellow pin heads were on Kiska and Attu. The enormity of the ocean mileage was overwhelming to contemplate. It was over 5000 miles from point to point. Pick the direction. It didn't matter. I spent hours studying this map in contemplation of the enormous distances of the ocean mileage. The words of these far away places had their roots in Polynesian, Micronesian, Aboriginal, Philippine and Japanese languages. I had visited these exotic tropical islands in my imagination, in books and movies: Tahiti, Pago Pago, Samoa, Pitcairn Island, the Marquesas. In the South Seas adventure novels of Nordoff and Hall and Herman Melville, I could escape the reality of the cold city in which I lived.

I would dream of turquoise cobalt blue warm waters, swaying palm trees and soft caressing tropical breezes.

But death had come to these lovely coral islands in the South Pacific. These tiny dots on the battle map of the South Pacific had become the last resting place for many Marines. The palm studded beaches where Dorothy Lamour reigned in her sarong and hummed *The Moon Of Manakura* and sang *Jungle Drums* under the full tropical moon had been sullied with blood. I pushed away this horrifying image as I stuck in red pins for Marines, yellow pins for Japs. It became a job I didn't like to do although I felt pride and satisfaction when I picked off the yellow pins.

Pacific Theater of Operations
The combat map on the wall of Post Service Battalion.

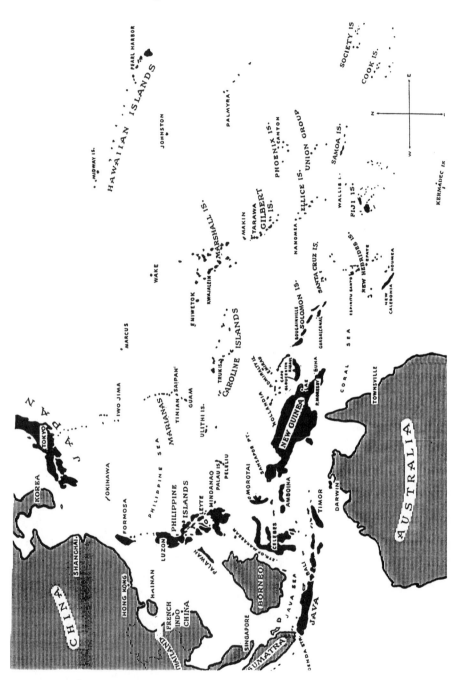

The Old Man of the office was Sergeant Major Jordan who smoked cigars which made the place stink. He was truly Old Marine Corps, a thirty year man who had extended his tour of duty for the duration of the war. He had served when the Marine Corps consisted of two regiments and a force of 18,000 men. Now he was serving in a Corps that had grown to four hundred and seventy-five thousand men, a Corps that included women Marines, all wearing shining new emblems and new uniforms. The zebra stripes on his arm gave him the status of an old bull elephant. He had earned the respect and homage that was paid to him when he spoke. I always jumped up to attention when he addressed me.

Major Emery who was the Adjutant was a *Retread*; he had returned to the Corps to give his services to his country although he too was overage. He had owned his own photography studio in Philadelphia before the war and was a professional man of great dignity of about forty-five years of age with salt and pepper hair. He had a quiet pleasant manner with a permanent half-smile on his face caused by the pipe he always held to the side of his mouth. He didn't seem to do any work because he would stay in his little office and refer everything to Sergeant Queen and to the Woman Marine at his side.

There was also a staff sergeant who had married an Australian girl while stationed in Melbourne for almost a year to recuperate after hitting the beaches in Guadalcanal. He spent most of the day leaning back in his office chair looking out the window whistling *WALTZING MATILDA,* an Australian tune the First Division Marines had brought back from Down Under. The only time he seemed to come to life was when a Coast Watcher who had been rescued by the Marines came into the office and they talked about Australia.

The other Woman Marine WR in my office was a blond haired sergeant named Ellice, who was secretary to both the Colonel and the Adjutant. She carried her rank and senority as if it were full combat pack.

Colonel Buse gave promotions to us WR's almost as soon as we started to work in his battalion and in the short time of four months here at Post Service, she had been promoted three times and married once. She had a very prim, cool manner and soft Georgia accent which was confusing because one way she was friendly and the other way she was forbidding.

Sergeant Ellice Stukey was attractive until she smiled—it seemed to hurt her to part her lips as if she had cold sores. She also had a peculiar way of laughing through her nose. I came to recognize it as her way of *ear-banging* whenever an officer reported for duty. She didn't use this laughing sound around the enlisted men nor me. It seemed to be something she did to officers, the Colonel, the Major and the Sergeant Major. Her southern voice also became softer and the Georgia accent thicker at these times also.

Her uniform hung on her and didn't fit very well. Probably her very small breasts and straight hips made it difficult for the Marine tailors to make the alterations right, which was a surprise because I remembered how particular the tailors were in Boot Camp.

I soon discovered Sergeant Ellice Stukey had one very great talent. She could remember name and rank and the proper salutation and regulation the very first time she heard it. An officer could come in once, be shipped out, and when he returned, she could call him by name. It made a very big impression on the officers and they deferred to her in everything because she was right there to remind them of things they had forgotten or had slipped up on.

Sergeant Ellice Stukey let me know from the outset that she was totally in charge. After Major Emery called me into his office alone and asked me if I could type or take dictation, which I couldn't, Sergeant Ellice came right out and told me not to foul-up her chances to be promoted to staff sergeant. I didn't know what triggered off that out-burst because it was before Sherry came to work in our office.

Colonel K. I. Buse–Commanding Officer–Post Service Battalion

I soon found out that the administration offices were only a small part of H-barracks. There was a Mess Hall for hundreds of men with separate entrances at the side of the building and a Recreation Room on the first deck—or first floor. Navy language was spoken here and it spilled out of the men's mouths naturally. We women did it for laughs. In this battalion, it was normal speech.

Hundreds of men were billeted on the second deck. This part of H-barracks was called the Casual Barracks because this was where Marines were billeted who were being transferred, who were returning or being shipped overseas, awaiting assignments or were out-patients at Post Hospital or awaiting office hours or court martials. Post Service Battalion was filled with transients.

Post Service Battalion also consisted of the Marines who did services for Quantico, the cooks, the bakers, the Motor Transport, the Military Police, the Field Music, the Police Duty, and a number of related categories that kept the Marine Corps in Quantico ship shape and ready. They were all combat able. Many of the Marines had returned from overseas, and those who hadn't been sent to combat knew they were here for a short while.

This was also the first post where officers reported before shipping out or transferred.

There were always a great many Marines hanging about, always respectful in manner and careful of language around us even when joking or exchanging pleasantries.

The two-story brick building had numerous windows and I soon learned that the men liked to hang out the second floor windows and watch the buses drop off the Women Marines.

Respect for the Women Marines started at the top.

Whenever a new recently arrived group of Marines who didn't know the Colonel's rules started the catcalls or name calling, the non-coms and the senior men in the command would stop it almost immediately. Our rough gruff Old Corps Commanding officer would not abide disrespect in any form to any Woman Marine by any of the one thousand six hundred men attached to his battalion under his command.

There was no loitering allowed around the Women Marines. This "Keep Moving" rule led to a few funny incidents. One smitten Marine circled the building over and over in order to say "Hello" "Hi" "Nice Day" to the same woman. She finally put a merciful stop to his marathon and invited him to the Saturday night dance at the Women's Recreation Hall which gave us all a good laugh and something to talk about.

Otherwise, persistent unwelcome attentions were not permitted. The men were allowed to talk and have interchanges with us but they were short, polite and respectful, not only during duty hours but off-duty as well.

Colonel Buse seemed to know what was going on throughout the whole Post just as General Torrey did. He had obviously laid down the law and given his Battalion the code of behavior he expected of his men.

The men behaved in two predictable ways when around us Women Marines.

If the men were recruits or newly returned combat Marines who had only heard scuttlebutt about the Women Marines but had never seen any real ones, they would stand in awe, sometimes shy, and skeptical, in the manner of someone meeting a "movie star," demanding assurances that we were really United States Marines. If the men had been stateside for any length of time, their approach was more direct and brazen with much bravado, especially when there were several of them in a group. They seemed to need the courage that came with numbers.

That is when you heard the call of *"BAM"* and the peculiar whistle or sing song chant that went with it particularly around the Slopschutes or outside the Post. Their manners changed when they had imbibed alcohol of some kind, even the three point two beer.

Colonel Buse would tolerate none of this kind of behavior. The word *BAM* was never even whispered within the perimeter of Casual Barracks.

He was a strict Commanding officer who ran a tight ship. He was Old Corps.

I asked him, "Sir, did you go to West Point?"

The Colonel laughed and said. "No, Terry. I attended "a trade school". He had been educated at The Citadel, which was a military college in Charlestown, South Carolina, his home town.

He had been a Marine for thirty years and would have been retired but the advent of this war gave him a reason to stay in his beloved Corps.

The men and officers snapped to his commands.

His eyes did not miss anything and he knew everything that went on in his command. Even little things.

If the Mess men were careless and threw precious cutlery into the garbage along with the left-overs, he would discover it and strike terror in the galley.

"Sergeant Queen, put that man on report. I found half a dozen forks and knives in the Mess cans."

He had not forgotten the decades when the Corps was starved for funds, where every item that was issued to a Marine had to be accounted for. The war had not changed his pattern of frugality. Decades of Quartermaster penury and working under six Presidents and a hostile Congress who was not kind nor generous to the Marine

Corps had made him treat every expenditure as if it came out of his own pension fund.

"Herbert Hoover was no military man. I would never say a word against my Commander in Chief but the Corps was lucky when he was booted out and Roosevelt got in. Hoover tried to cut the Corps down to a total of fifteen thousand men. There would be no Marine Corps today if he had succeeded. Our President Roosevelt was once Under Secretary of the Navy and he knows what it takes to make a Marine!"

He presided as a judge in the court martials that fell under his jurisdiction and he was reputed to be fair.

To the Women Marines, he was a teddy-bear, a wonderful grandfather figure to whom no problem was too petty or too small to consider; who was there for all of us posted to his command. The Colonel we came to know was a fun loving Dad, interested in our welfare, watching over each of us, helping us in many ways and was so openly proud of his contingency of Women Marines that we worked all the harder for him.

He owned a two-door 1936 Buick which he drove on the Post. He took a few of us to Washington D.C. on a tour of the Marine Corps Headquarters at Arlington Annex and Arlington Cemetary. On a separate occasion he arranged a trip for several of us and we rode in the Higgins Boats on the Potomac River to Indian Head Point with a detail going to the Rifle Range there. A squad of Marines accompanied us and the excitement of being actually in a real Higgins Boat, the one that made the assault on Guadalcanal, made our hearts swell with esprit de corps beyond any lecture in Boot Camp.

He established a room, a private lounge of our own, with a sign over it, that read *THE LAIR* for the lion cubs we symbolized to him. It even had a sign just like the ones throughout Quantico that read 'Out of Bounds' just as if it were officer's country. *THE LAIR* was the Women Marines' own exclusive private lounge, furnished with a couch, chairs and dressing table, with private stalls, shower and sinks. I think it must have belonged to the officers at one time but he had made it accessible to us. The room was just down the hall, past the other offices. The men passed it daily but not one lingered near it.

As Post Courier I was to walk on the double at fast pace to Post Headquarters, almost a mile away, three times a day and pick up and deliver restricted military correspondence in sealed envelopes. Much of it was top secret and I could not read it. To do so would have been a military offense despite the fact I'd be the one to file it away eventually in a locked cabinet.

Chick and I did the "runs" together. He carried the papers going and I carried them back.

I was about to make the afternoon run with Chick, when the Colonel stuck his head out the door and boomed,

"Sergeant Queen! It's raining. See that terrible Terry doesn't get wet!" He was wearing my havelock rain hat protector over his head that he had swiped off the coat rack. Once again I heard that distinctive laugh of the Colonel's at the pun he made out of my name. His laughter was catching and the whole office roared with humor.

As I checked my uniform at the mirror in the hallway and primped before going out, I heard a loud bang behind me and jumped a mile high. I heard another snort of laughter and realized The Colonel had popped a large paper bag at the door of his office behind me like a firecracker.

My Commanding Officer was a prankster! He loved wit and puns and poetry. He reveled in a good joke. He loved it more if you didn't fall for his pranks or gave as good as you got, providing, of course, you stayed within the rules of military courtesy.

Colonel Buse never forgot himself as an officer and a gentleman even while providing a boost to the morale of his men and women. Colonel Buse was also a romantic, a born matchmaker.

One of the first stories I heard was how he arranged the marriage of one of the WR's in his command when the man she loved, another Marine from another base, came to see her one last time before shipping overseas. He commandeered a jeep and drove her to the near-by town of Manassas for her license. The Colonel thought it hilarious when he, old and grizzled as he was, was mistaken by the clerk in the Town Hall for the bridegroom of the young Woman Marine he was escorting. Tears of laughter would fill his eyes as he enjoyed the memory every time he retold the tale.

That was my Colonel. My first Commanding Officer. His nature was romantic and he was a person who liked to laugh, who was sensitive, alert and respectful of Marine Corps property which in a way, we women were. He was a man of principle who commanded respect. Obeying him was easy because at the same time he gave orders he made you like and love him. That quality of leadership was what gave Marine Corps officers their commanding presence which ensured loyalty. Was that how they maintained esprit de corps in battle? I was so fortunate to have drawn Colonel Buse as my CO. I thought all commanding officers were like Colonel Buse.

Later, I learned that this was not so.

The sight of his Bobbsey Twins couriers, so alike in appearance, trotting off together several times a day, curly heads engrossed in conversation, amused him.

When Colonel Buse was told we had gone to a Post movie together, that secured it for him—he concluded he was seeing love in bloom. He teased us a lot, almost in the way we used to tease each other in high school when someone had a crush.

It may have looked like a romance but the Marine I released had become a good friend and co-worker. Chick told me interesting tales about his duty in Samoa. He had his problems finding romance and I could relate to his frustration. He wanted to marry and have two children. Every girl he dated treated him as a brother. I could see why. I also thought of him as a brother

I, in turn, carried on about Tonawanda, the terrible cold winters of Buffalo and of my difficulties finding someone to really love and marry too. I wanted to have two children, a boy and a girl and live happily ever after in California. I told him about *dumb* Spero and the *dumb* records I had been given when I was expecting a *dumb* ring.

Old maids and bachelors had to come from someplace. They weren't born—it happened along the way of life. No one actually made a conscious choice to be one. It was fate. It could happen to me.

Chick scoffed at my self-prediction. "You won't have any trouble finding the right one. It's easier for a cute short girl than a Marine that is only five foot two. The Marines wouldn't have taken me if it weren't for this war. The girls sure don't want me. I bet this Spero guy is the one you will end up marrying."

I said, "Now, Chick, that is really *dumb!*"

Our conversations often became philosophical and intense. Perhaps, we were destined to be Marines and never marry.

At least, Chick could be career Marine. Not I. My Marine career was only for the duration of the war and six months. I didn't know how much time remained for me to be a Woman Marine with the war in Europe going so well and the Marines pushing the Japs off one island after another in the Pacific Ocean. I had been putting a lot of red and green pins on the map.

Colonel Buse saw our two heads together and figured our "love" needed a push.

One morning, I found a two-line poem, signed 'Chick' in a folded piece of paper stuck in a roll of toilet paper with a pickle in it.

It was so naughty and such a bad parody of Dorothy Parker or Ogden Nash, whose limericks I always enjoyed, that I became suspicious immediately.

I knew shy sweet Chick would never have written a note that said, *"Candy is dandy but Chicker's quicker."*

How corny can you get? And a gift of a roll of toilet paper? Not his style.

"I think Our Colonel is having fun with us," I said.

"What can we do?" Poor Chick was so embarrassed.

I wrote a poem.

"Play along. Make a happy—no, better make it a sad face when you read this."

Your little gift I will accept
Because at love you are adept
I hope your present of a pickle
Does not mean that you are fickle
As I cherish you in my dreams
I'm glad you sent me reams and reams

Part of the Colonel's secret of knowing what everyone was doing and thinking in his command came from his observation of the expressions on his Marines as they primped in front of the huge mirror that dominated the hallway on their way in and out the front doors. That was one of the reasons he kept his door ajar.

I passed the note to Chick while standing in front of the mirror in the hallway. Chick read the note, couldn't remember if I had said a sad or happy face, so he smiled then frowned, and placed the note on the desk. We departed for the afternoon run immediately after.

Sergeant Queen or The Colonel, we didn't know who, picked it up as we anticipated and had replaced it on the message desk upside down.

The Colonel caught on immediately we were pulling his leg. He grinned in that knowing way of his as he called me into his office. He asked me point-blank a question that my father would have asked without bothering to shut the door.

"Private Terry, what's going on between you and the *lad?*"

"Sir, you have established this Marine on the wrong beachhead. This romance is *adrift* on a sinking ship. By your leave, Sir, I told Chick to *belay*".

I had boned up on my Navy language since coming to work at H-barracks. If he had been my Dad, I would have told The Colonel he had the wrong number, was barking up the wrong tree and to back off.

Here at Post Service you talked Navy but the message was the same.

Hearing Women Marines use sea-going language amused The Colonel immensely. To him, it was even funnier when the Navy word or phrase was used incorrectly or inappropriately—something I seemed to do quite often. In my attempt to be the best Marine adhering to strict military G.I. regulation and Navy language, somehow I would trigger off much of his merriment. Often I didn't know what I had said or done to tickle his funny bone but it made working here at Post Service Battalion fun and stimulating. Fun because of Colonel Buse.

The day that the Commanding General of the Post, General Torrey, himself, inquired about us was a red-letter day of triumph and one-upmanship for Colonel Buse. The relationship between the two commanding officers was not the best. A rivalry between them had existed for a long time, long before World War II, all the way back to the nineteen twenties at Culebra and Guantanamo Bay and the Fleet Marine Force amphibious exercises on the Potomac River at Quantico in the thirties.

Chick and I were on a morning run when General Torrey, striding out of his Post Headquarters, noticed us standing ramrod straight, staring straight ahead, as he walked past us.

He stopped suddenly and addressed us.

"Privates, are you two brother and sister?"

We stood frozen into position, saluting in the proper military manner. Chick had swallowed his tongue and his ears jiggled from his nervousness.

"Permission to speak, Sir. No, Sir! We belong to Colonel Buse, Post Service Battalion, Sir. By your leave, Sir!" I said.

Out of the blue, under some childhood instruction, I curtsied, while I still held my salute. It made General Torrey smile and he took another long look at us.

The General stood there eyeing us for what seemed an interminable agonizing long time. He turned to his aide and said, "How did the Corps do that? That is an amazing resemblance. I'd swear they were twins."

The result of that encounter was instant fame. We became recognized as Colonel Buse's "matched pair of Marines". The fact that we had attracted the attention of the Commanding General of Quantico made us a topic of conversation in Officer's Mess.

The QUANTICO SENTRY, our Post newspaper, took pictures and wrote about us.

We actually became one of the "sights" of Quantico. Drivers in jeeps would call to us and give us a lift on our "runs". Sometimes the officers themselves in the jeeps would stop the driver to pick us up and ask if we were the couriers assigned to Colonel Buse's Post Services Battalion.

General Torrey's singling me out from all the Women Marines on the Post tickled Colonel Buse no end.

I clearly became one of his "daughters" and was placed under his protection.

Within a short time, more Women Marines were assigned duties in Post Service Battalion at the Colonel's request. Now all the offices had Women Marines in them.

Sherry, my good friend and bunkie, was assigned to my office to assist Sergeant Ellice Stukey. Now I had someone to take the bus with, go to lunch and talk office shop. We hugged each other when we saw we had been assigned to the same office and were going to work together.

My celebrity status was noted one day by our new commanding officer, Captain Julia Hamblet, who had relieved our Captain Lloyd, sometime in June.

Captain Hamblet was by far the most attractive woman officer in the whole Women's Reserve, tall with dark curly hair and soft eyes that always held a smile, who could make heads turn even if she hadn't been in uniform. In her Marine uniform, she was magnificent. She also had a certain air about her of knowing who she was and where she was going and meant exactly what she said. I wanted to please her very much.

When she spoke to our group, she looked at me directly. Although she didn't mention my name, I knew she was talking to me.

"The actions of each Woman Marine affect each and every other Woman Marine," she said. "We are responsible for each other. The good reputation of one Woman Marine reflects upon each and every one of us directly. Keep up the good job you are doing."

It was the same message that Mama had given me over and over, "Don't ruin it for your sisters."

I basked in the cordiality of The Colonel's fatherly attention. Mrs. Buse, his wife of thirty years, was equally as lovely to me. She was motherly, quiet and serious, the opposite of Colonel Buse. She was a thin woman who spoke softly in the melodious tones of a well bred Southern lady, a real life Melanie.

I spent several evenings with them in their home on the Post which made me love the Marine Corps all the more.

"Your home is beautiful!" I exclaimed and noted her love for lace and embroidered linens which covered the chairs, couch and tables.

She corrected me immediately.

"Oh, this is not a home. These are quarters. Our real home is in Charleston."

She spoke of her longing to return to the family home in South Carolina. She held me enthralled with her tales of the South, the Confederacy, and her description of the house she had inherited from her Mama that was built before the war—the War Between The States, that is. I gave her some cut-work pillow cases that I embroidered with my own hands for that Hope Chest my Mama was always trying to get me to fill. I even made a Greek salad for them and changed the beef stew Mrs. Buse was cooking to a *Stifatho*, just by adding pickling spices, orange peel and a big glassful of port wine just like Mama did it. The Colonel loved it.

I had found a second family. My Marine Corps father and mother.

As things turned out, I would have need of his favoritism—not against the attentions of the men of Post Service Battalion—but against the petty officiousness of Sergeant Ellice Stukey who had consolidated her position and rank to grab power and secure the office as her private command post.

It soon became obvious, even to me, that she wanted to control everything and everyone that came into our little office. She was bucking for that promotion to staff sergeant as hard as she could. That was the highest rank to which she could aspire. There were no women Gunny Sergeants nor First Sergeants nor Sergeant Majors in the Women's Reserve. But with the rank of staff sergeant, she would have a room of her own and all kinds of privileges.

If an officer reporting to Post Service talked to me first, because I sat nearest the open door, she would jump up and take over before the officer had a chance to finish his introduction.

"Sir, Private Terry is *only* our courier. I'm Sergeant Ellice Joy Stukey," she said, her accent thick as grits, her name straight out of the Deep South.

That was not the only time we butted heads. Normally I didn't greet the officers nor billeted them.

But one day I incurred her wrath forever more.

An officer entered Post Service office whose name I recognized immediately.

Sergeant Ellice did not know who this officer was. She didn't read his kind of books. She realized something was different about him when I refused to be pushed aside and let her take over as she usually did.

"*The* John W. Thomason? " My voice went up two octaves and my eyes went wide. "FIX BAYONETS and A FEW MARINES? *That* Thomason?"

"Do Women Marines read military stories?"

My flabbergasted outburst had amused him.

I did not see standing before me a combat Marine officer which is what he was first and foremost. I saw only the writer—a real true live author who wrote books.

"Sir, I think you are greater than Ernest Hemingway or William Faulkner. Sir, I love your sketch of *Walking John*. He's a real Marine, isn't he?" His immortal illustration of the World War I Marine in leggings had been used as a recruiting poster for two decades.

"Yes! He was. Thank you, very much for your kind words."

Walking John
The sketch by Marine Corps author
and illustrator, John W. Thomason used on recruiting posters
since 1918. He was killed in the Pacific in 1944.

I fawned over him and knew I was acting star-struck as if Buster
Crabbe, Jon Hall, Clark Gable, Fred Astaire and John Wayne had
jumped out of the Silver Screen into Post Service Battalion.

I even asked for his autograph. My eyes followed him into The
Colonel's office. They were good friends and had served at many of
the same Marine Posts for the past two decades.

I had forgotten all about Sergeant Stukey until I turned around
and saw her glowering at me.

Other than that, I wasn't any kind of a threat to Sergeant Ellice
Stukey. Our work did not overlap. I was a courier. I didn't type nor
have any decisions to make. I was never invited to join the private
conferences with officers that took place behind closed doors as she
and her steno pad were.

Still, I did have access to some top secret information before she
received it. I was the first to know where our Marines were fighting
and when they had won their objective since I was in charge of the big
combat map. Once she and I had a few tense moments over a packet
I had picked up at headquarters when she tried to take it from me
before I had completed my run.

I was happy to be just the post courier. It allowed me to get out
of the office and gave me time to joke with the staff sergeants and
Sergeant Major Jordan and Sergeant Major Waldrop who headed the
other office and Colonel Buse. Adjutant Emery smiled a lot but he
and Sergeant Ellice never made jokes.

I continued to stick pins on the battle map of the Pacific which
certainly wasn't her cup of coffee or *joe* so I knew she didn't covet my
job.

It wasn't long before we all realized her focus was upon Sherry.
The WR who really had need of protection from Sergeant Ellice was
Sherry, our loving wife of the Submarine Service. Ellice Stukey did
not know that Sherry was married to a Navy officer. Her Boot Camp
buddies had kept this secret.

As the war deepened from 1942 to 1944, the Corps' rules
against fraternization were still strongly enforced: an enlisted Woman
Marine could not be married to an officer and remain in the Corps.
But, if she didn't tell and informed no one, the rule stayed on the
books and did not have to be enforced. It would have been dumb for
any enlisted Woman Marine to let anyone know her husband was an

officer. A euphemism for an officer husband was 4-F. The ultimate insult. But it worked.

We'd ask Sherry how her 4-F husband was and she'd smile and say, "He's a Shell back twice!" which meant his submarine had crossed the Equator again and again in pursuit of the Japanese Navy.

Had Ellice gotten wind of it, her problem of having to compete with Sherry whose competence made her so nervous would have been solved.

Sherry was a qualified secretary who was assigned to Post Service Battalion as the secretary to the Adjutant two weeks after I arrived. She knew shorthand and how to work all the office machines including the Dictaphone machine.

We each had a desk in the very same office. Mine was the smallest. Actually it was a Message Center with slots for envelopes more than a real desk such as hers.

Ellice had been up-graded to secretary to The Colonel and Adjutant but she had not been promoted in the last list as I had been. I was now a private first class and got sixty-six dollars a month pay and she was still a sergeant.

From the very beginning Ellice made it difficult for Sherry to do her work. Ellice treated every paper as if it were Top Secret and handled all duties personally herself, even when they were supposed to be performed by Sherry. She made certain that the Colonel and the Adjutant saw her as a hard-charger, a Marine who had the situation well in hand, who could be depended to take care of every little problem, who had her finger on every scrap of information and detail. She often pretended to check Sherry's work. Nevertheless, her lips got tighter and tighter every time Adjutant Major Emery asked Sherry to record his conferences because Sergeant Ellice was acting so busy and he didn't want to disturb what she was working on.

Her zealous bucking for promotion and obvious ear-banging every officer became very hard to live with and work by. The more determined she became in her quest for that next rank, the stronger my friendship and sympathy for Sherry grew. When she demanded that I hand over the packets I had picked up at Post Headquarters so she could be the one to deliver the Top Secret documents and make a show of how efficient she was, I reminded her of my orders and told her I would query Colonel Buse first. She backed off. We weren't enemies but somehow we weren't friends.

It was common knowledge I was treated with familial concern by Colonel and Mrs. Buse. They were my family so it was most natural to accept their protection. There was nothing ear-banging about our relationship. Ear-banging was when an enlisted tried to curry favor from an officer in order to ensure promotion or other self propelled motivation. I would do anything for Colonel and Mrs. Buse. I sincerely and truly loved them.

Otherwise, duty at Post Service Battalion became a way of life that made everything outside the Marine Corps irrelevant. I had this persistent feeling I was in a movie. Scenes changed daily, frame after frame. I'd arrive in the morning and there in front of the building was an officer calling cadence to a platoon of officer candidates, yelling: "ONE! UP TWO! COLUMN LEFT! MARCH!"

Next to the Coca-Cola machine were Marines in dungarees who would always say a few words, mostly flirty and funny.

Two prisoners, with the word "P" stenciled on their fatigues, stood facing the bulkhead next to an MP who guarded them with nonchalance.

The Sergeant Major watched from the doorway with a pipe in his mouth, having changed over from cigars because I had told him how distinguished he would look with one. Thank God! The office no longer stank of cigar smoke.

Curly, the bald-headed Old Corps corporal who was police duty officer barked instructions to several young recruits who were his whole clean-up crew.

"In the Marine Corps, we swab by the numbers: One, two, three four." He sang a cadence count to the ballet of swabbing mops.

An audience of Marines gathered to watch me put in new pins on the battle map. They had participated in the fighting on some of the Pacific Islands and they enjoyed pointing them out or correcting my pronunciations.

The Marines and our U.S. Forces had retaken some parts of the Pacific from the Japs. By the middle of June 1944, I was able to put red pins on Funafuti in the Ellice Island, as well as on Buka, Tulagi, Guadalcanal, Russell Islands, Makin and Tarawa, New Georgia, Attu, Finschhafen, Lae, Arawe, New Britain, Cape Gloucester, Saidor, New Guinea, Majuro Island in the Ellicells, Kwajalein Atoll, Roi-Namur and Kwajalein Island, Eniwetok Atoll, Talasea in New Britain, Bougainville, Emirau, Hollandia and Aitape.

I had yellow and green pins on Saipan. The fighting had begun there and the Japs were fighting back hard. There was no doubt the Marines would win, but the Japs weren't surrendering easily. This island was just too close to their homeland.

I was right in the middle of the war, but all I really knew was what I read in the newspapers. Occasionally I would catch snatches of conversation between the officers as I did when I heard them discussing Saipan but, I had to be told where to stick the pins by the officers after they had opened the envelopes I had brought to them from Post Headquarters.

Not until my duty as Courier took me into the secret filming room for a few minutes and I saw some of the slaughter of the Marines and Japs of The Battle of Tarawa did I have an inkling at what was really happening. The *March of Time* and the newsreels did not show close-ups of bodies that had been blown apart, with parts of bodies strewn here and there, heads and limbs decapitated. They didn't show Marines putting dead Marines in body bags. I was so shaken when I came out of that room that I had to lean against the wall and hold on to my lunch that wanted to come up.

One of the officers had spotted me and came out to warn me quietly and firmly that I had witnessed a top secret film and was not to discuss it outside that room.

The Corps had one bad experience with letting the public see the slaughter and they wanted no repetition of what had been a gross miscalculation. The Marines Corps had allowed the publication of dead Marines lying face down and some of the more grisly pictures that had been taken at Tarawa to give the home front an appreciation for the sacrifices the Marines made to win back the Pacific Islands from the savage inhuman Japs. Instead of praise, the Marine Corps, from Commandant Vandegrift down, was pilloried by mothers and fathers who called them butchers and murderers and other kinds of foul names. There had been such an outcry of protest and dismay from the American public that security was tightened up worse than before.

I also had put two blue pins on a small map of Europe that I had taped to the wall although we hadn't any Marines at either place. I knew too many boys who were over there, including my old high-school prom date who was in the 82nd Airborne Paratroopers. Strange, I hadn't heard from him since D Day, on June 6, when the Allied Forces and Americans landed at Normandy in France.

The Second Front that everyone had been expecting for over a year had finally been opened and our American troops were fighting through the villages of France.

I stuck in blue pins in Rome and parts of France which had been liberated by our Allies.

The war in the Pacific continued as more islands were secured.

Marines were being shipped out daily. New tired looking men with lined faces went in and out of Casual Barracks and replaced old familiar ones. A few stayed around long enough for me to know them, to learn a little of their family history, hear personal stories about who was in love, about to be married or had been married on his last liberty, or who had received a "Dear John" letter. Very few Marines were unattached. All were lonely. Their pleasure at being able to swap sea-stories with Women Marines was flattering and appreciated. We raised the morale in H-barracks for them and they did the same for us.

Post Service Battalion had become my second home and I had settled into my duties comfortably and routinely.

Chick introduced me to Webster, his handsome bunkmate, who had a romantic long scar on his cheek and was a double for Cary Grant, one of my favorite movie stars.

"Did you get that scar in a duel or in battle, Web?" I asked him full of curiosity and expectation of a heroic story. Errol Flynn had one just like it in CAPTAIN BLOOD or was it Douglas Fairbanks in THE THREE MUSKETEERS?

"Hell no! A coal miner came at me with a broken beer bottle in a bar fight in West Virginia where I worked before I joined the Marines."

"Oh!"

We three, Chick, I and six foot Web who towered above us both, often went on dates together on the Post, visiting Post Docks, walking on the grass alongside the Potomac River, watching the Higgins Boat in the water. Web tried to teach me how to shoot billiards in the Recreation Room at H-barracks but I was prejudiced against the game. Only bums and no-accounts hung around the pool hall in Tonawanda. Billiards sure looked like pool to me.

One Sunday we watched a rather dull baseball game between Post Service Battalion and Motor Transport Marines and I tried to hide my boredom. The Women Marines Quantico Trick Drill Team was practicing on the parade grounds at the same time and had drawn a small crowd. I suggested we go over and watch them too. They laughed at my silly suggestion.

Who in their right mind wanted to watch the women march?

Colonel Buse always knew whom I was dating. He no longer teased me about my triple dates nor of the Marines that took me to the dances on the Post or to the NCO clubs. He told Sergeant Major Jordan there was safety in numbers. I knew he kept track of me. Post Service Battalion was a tiny Tonawanda and gossip could be rampant here just as there. A girl had to be very circumspect even in Quantico.

On one of our quiet talks, I told Colonel Buse I had changed my mind about that white wedding dress with white roses that I had dreamed of since I was thirteen. I now thought the Marine dress whites with white pumps and gold insignias were ever so much more romantic.

I also confided in him that if I ever found *The One And Only* I would let him know and seek his blessing at the same time I sought my Dad's. The Colonel was so touched he put his arm around me and patted me on the head. He was so very understanding and never seemed to tire of his role of father figure to me and the other Women Marines.

Chick was transferred to the London Legation. He kissed me good-bye and departed happy with his new post. He wasn't going to fight but somehow that was fine with me.

I now made the Post runs alone hitching rides on jeeps whenever I could to shorten the time it took to make the message runs from H-barracks to Post Headquarters.

I had finally *freed* a Marine.

Without Chick, dating Web wasn't as much fun. Right in the middle of a movie, Web asked me to promise to wait for him until his return from the Pacific.

"Think you'd like to get engaged to me?" he said casually.

I realized his resemblance to Cary Grant wasn't enough for me to want to spend my life with him. I didn't want to promise fidelity and sit in a Marine Post surrounded by men and not be able to accept any invitations.

"I don't think that is such a good idea," I said and held my breath waiting for his explosion.

My refusal set him aback for a few minutes but he recovered within seconds. His nonchalance surprised me. He wasn't hurt one bit.

"That's okay. I got tired of having to worry about Colonel Buse every time I took you out anyway."

Soon Web was gone too, transferred to somewhere in the Pacific. He didn't ask me to write.

I was promoted to Private First Class and celebrated my new stripe at the Riverview Cafe in Quantico Town with milkshakes with Fenton, Sherry and Lindsey. The owners of the cafe were Greeks and when I told them my dad and mother were Greek, they wouldn't let any of us pay for our drinks. They were as proud of my new rank as I was.

Sergeant Ellice brought me down to earth when she walked by my desk later and said, "The Colonel promotes all the Women Marines. If you don't mess up the first six weeks he promotes you automatically."

When I was promoted to corporal along with twenty other Women Marines in Post Service Battalion and walked in the office with my two stripes sewn on my uniform, Ellice didn't take time from her busy schedule to congratulate me. She hadn't been promoted to staff sergeant as she had expected to be and she became more protective of her territory than ever.

The memories of Tonawanda retreated further and further. That was another time, another place as life there, my parents, my sisters, friends, Remington Box Company, snow and hail in April became hazier and figured less in my thoughts. I lived in a warm climate where flowers bloomed in March and April and red cardinals flew in the trees.

I had become a Marine, a Virginian, with eighty squadmates for sisters, and a Colonel and his Lady for my Dad and Mother.

I attended different churches.

One Sunday I went to Catholic Mass with Fenton. It was a lot like the Mass said in my church. I didn't understand the Latin spoken by the priest in Quantico anymore than I understood the Ancient Greek of the priest who conducted the Greek Orthodox service in Buffalo.

On Friday, I attended the Jewish services with another bunkmate and didn't understand one Hebrew word.

The next Sunday I went to the Protestant Service with Lindsey and found it was a lot like the Catholic Service but in this church the congregation spoke English and read from the King James version of the Bible and sang songs. Lindsey apologized because she was really Baptist and the services were Episcopalian, but it was all she could get in Quantico. She promised to take me to a real Protestant church.

I would never have been able to visit all these churches back home. I didn't know any Jewish girls in Tonawanda. Mama would have forbidden me to go with Lindsey because she maintained that all Protestants were heretics. Attending the Catholic service was also frowned upon. The Greek Orthodox Patriarch and the Roman Catholic Pope hadn't spoken to each other in a thousand years because of a fight.

At one time the Christian church was one united church with many patriarchs who could trace their authority directly to the original 12 Disciples of Christ. But, in 900 A.D., an argument broke out between the Pope in Rome and the Greek Patriarch in Constantinople. The Pope in Rome contended that while they were all equal in the eyes of the Lord, he was more equal than they. Because he had the power of Rome behind him, he insisted that he was higher in power and status than all the other Patriarchs. They argued for one hundred years over the chain of command. Since they couldn't settle it, they separated into what was called the Great Schism and one part of the original church became the Roman Catholic religion with a Pope in Rome and the other half became the Eastern Orthodox religion with Patriarchs in Russia, Syria and Constantinople.

I asked Lindsey if Baptists really immersed their bodies in the water, head and all. Lindsey was amazed I hadn't heard of the Baptists. But, she, on the other hand, had never heard of the Greek Orthodox religion in the small town in Texas where she came from so we were even in our ignorance.

I knew about the Greek and Roman schism and she knew all about the Protestant rebellions. She told me about Martin Luther and King Henry the Eighth starting his own church, John Calvin and the Puritans and John Wesley, and all the others that had set up their own shop.

"It seems to me, the Protestants didn't get along any better than the Catholics," I said. "I don't see much difference between the religions. They all use Greek words, *amen, hallelujah, Christos aneste.*"

Several of my bunkmates who were Quakers and Christian Scientists heard our discussion on religion and offered to take me to their meetings and I accepted.

Being a Marine had made me very tolerant of other people's beliefs.

I just didn't tell Mama that I attended all these services so she wouldn't worry about my turning into a heretic.

I had many brothers, all Marines, with whom I went to the Slopschute and an ever changing supply of beaus who were admiring and fun, always ready to go to the Post movie or dancing and still be back in the barracks by 11:00 P.M. before lights out.

Life in Quantico had become an adventure. It was a movie in which I was the heroine. Sometimes I felt like Dorothy in the Land of Oz.

A Visitor To Quantico

I had just returned from hanging my washed clothes over the rods in the dryer when I heard my name being paged in the squadroom. I was wearing a towel over my naked butt.

"TERRY!"

"Yoe!"

"There's a telegram at the Duty NCO's office for you!"

I ran to the office filled with apprehension. Who died? Telegrams usually meant bad news, in ten words or less.

"Arriving Quantico tomorrow. Will spend furlough with you. Love Spero."

The telegram dredged up certain suppressed feelings. This was an unexpected and unwelcome intrusion into my life. With a sharp thrust into reality, I was plunged back into the memories of my life before I had become a Marine. Thoughts flooded my mind as I remembered church socials where the girls outnumbered the boys, and dateless Saturday nights alone; food rationing and long lines waiting to buy scarce sundries that were available any day of the week at the PX in Quantico. I recalled lost years after high school that were aimless and purposeless, working at jobs I didn't enjoy, going out with boys to drive-in theaters who wanted to neck rather than look at the double feature. And all the while Mama nagging me to get married while she guarded my virginity as if I were Rapunzel.

Now, an old beau, a boy that Mama considered a good catch who never seemed to carry any money when he took me on dates was coming to be with me. I reread the telegram. Yes, it was ten words exactly. He had spent the minimum. How long was his furlough?

It's true, I had flirted with him and had kissed him and if push came to shove, you could say I had led him on. And if you wanted to be nasty, you could say I was a flirt. I did enjoy the attention and teasing I got at Mail Call from my squadmates when the Duty NCO called out my name several times over as she handed me letters from beaus who were scattered all over the globe. So now one of them was going to materialize right here in Quantico. The rich and handsome college boy from big city Buffalo who was six foot one and over two hundred pounds, a catch in anybody's book, was coming to be with me. I had qualms in my heart, indecision in my head and butterflies in my stomach.

Spero J. Yianilos
Photo taken in 1943 while an Army private at University of Chicago. Note the comfortable quarters that were provided to him. He was assigned to work for Drs. Enrico Fermi and Leo Szilard on a secret project.

Mama's voice floated in my ear, "You never know a good thing when you see it."

I was a Marine now. I loved my work and I enjoyed my brother Marines with whom I had so much fun, so much in common. I didn't want to share my new world with old boyfriends. My feelings were very ambivalent. It was a point of family honor and I had to be hospitable or I could never go back home again.

Spero's delayed letter of explanation was in the afternoon's mail call along with another photo of him, showing him smoking a pipe. I suspected that was a pose to impress me since he smoked cigarettes which I detested.

He had been yanked out of the lap of luxury as a student in ASTP and out of the University of Chicago and thrown into the infantry. The invasion of France and Europe had begun on June 6, D-Day and the Army needed every soldier it could get its hands on to replace the men they had lost in the landing at Normandy. The push was onward to Germany.

Spero had been transferred out of his soft duty at the University of Chicago into the 104th Army Division and was now on his way overseas to Europe to fight the Germans. He had a few days furlough before he reported to his ship in New York City and he was all mine.

I made reservations at the Hostess House in the PX Building, where a little guest house had been set up. Only a few rooms were available for visitors to Quantico but he had the luck of the Irish, sorry, luck of the Greeks. He could have a room for two nights.

Two nights! You can see all of Quantico in two hours! Let's see, what to do in Quantico? The Post Theater, a walk on Post Docks, the Marine Corps museum? My mind searched for a list of activities that would fill every minute of his visit.

No use taking Spero to any of the Slopschutes. He couldn't dance and he didn't like to drink beer. His drink was Coca-Cola, one of the things we had in common. Besides, I didn't want to introduce him to all the Marines with whom I had gone to the Post Movies and had jumped and jived to the juke box at the NCO Club. He might have gotten the wrong idea that I had become one of those military "sluts" we women were accused of being.

I could take him to Washington D.C., the zoo and the museums. We could climb those eight hundred and seventy-five steps inside the Washington's Monument to the top. Walk around the Basin. Rent a canoe and bicycles. It would mean spending the night there if we could find rooms. We would have to take that chance.

News of his arrival spread through Barracks A as if it were juicy scuttlebutt.

"Terry's boyfriend is coming. Right. The one with the chocolate store."

The whole squadroom had partaken of his candy since one piece of chocolate had always filled me up and I had always thrown the five-pound boxes at my bunkies unopened so they all got first crack at it.

I hastened to dispel any such notion.

"He's not my boyfriend. He's just the boy back home. I'm going to show him the sights in Washington D.C."

"C'mon, Terry. Don't give us that snow job. Don't tell us you didn't neck hot and heavy. He wouldn't be spending his last furlough with you if you hadn't promised something."

"A little necking at Mayor's Park doesn't count."

I wasn't about to tell my bunkies that I had never gone any further than that. I would have lost credibility in the eyes of the more experienced women who had shared their stories of sexual exploits with me, the ones who were or had been married, the ones who took lovers and had sizzling hot romances, who knew all about condoms and other sexual matters.

My bunkies insisted upon imagining romance where none existed. Some of the girls made suggestive clicking sounds with their tongues as if I had announced we going to shack-up.

"Spero wouldn't dare try anything with me. He's not like that! Besides, my mother knows his mother."

"All men are like *that*! Does your mother carry the shotgun?"

"No! But his mother does. And she'd aim it straight at me. I'm a fallen woman since I joined the Corps. I don't think I would be her first choice for a daughter-in law," I said.

My bunkies knew exactly what I was saying. They came from small towns too. Despite the raging World War and the need for the participation of women to help win it, we who had joined hadn't achieved respectability in all social circles. The reputation of "camp followers" remained in the historical prejudices that people had towards women in the Armed Forces, whether Marines, Army or Navy. Even the nurses and officers weren't spared the snide remarks. We all knew the prejudice was there.

"He's come all across the country just to see you, Terry. That means something," said Fenton with some envy in her voice. Her beau was supposedly still taking catechism lessons to turn Catholic for her yet he hadn't made the short trip from Boston to visit her..

"Spero is on his way overseas. From New York, Quantico is only two hours away by train. He's not going out of his way at all," I said.

"He's missed D-day in Normandy. But the fighting is still fierce. He'll be right in the middle of the push towards Germany. You had better be nice to him," said Sherry who could eat half a box of chocolates all by herself and didn't want to be cut off from the supplier.

Spero lumbered off the train. He was still clumsy in his gait but the smile on his face at the sight of me beamed a light as bright as the lamp on the front of the engine. When I kissed him right there at the station platform, he was embarrassed at the public demonstration. When he kissed me back, I knew right off he hadn't met any girls while training for combat at Camp Carson, Colorado since he still hadn't learned how to do it any better. Some of his weight had been lost, but he was still big and tall if no longer fat. He filled out his Army khakis in a more muscular way but he towered over me. He no longer slouched. His face was round and full and his eyes were the best part of him, bright blue, kind and shy, shining with the joy of seeing me there. His hair was a blond brown and curly around his Army overseas cap and his bushy eyebrows on his large head made him look like a friendly St. Bernard.

I was amazed at the depth of my happiness and the emotion that welled up when I caught sight of him. Tears came to my eyes unbidden. He was a face from Sunday morning services in church. He was bumpy moonlight rides in an ice-cream truck to the drive-in movies and hot dogs afterwards. He was the boy who had chased me at the church picnic when I was only fifteen and not allowed to date. He was home. He was family.

I held his hand and his arm, delighted to be able to touch him and be with him. I kissed him again very warmly on the lips bringing his head down to mine. He responded and then turned around embarrassed to see if anyone had observed my impulsive gesture.

After all, we were on a Marine Post and my behavior was unmilitary. Even the Army had rules.

I had forgotten how he was naturally reticent and had a certain reserved manner of formality. He always observed the rules of politeness, never forgetting to say "thank you" and "please". Sometimes he would chide me because I was quite careless in these niceties thinking a smile said them for me.

I took him immediately to the Hostess House where he wanted to change his shirt and pants from the dusty coal of the Quantico train ride out of New York.

I no sooner closed the door and sat at the bed while Spero changed in the bathroom that I heard a knock on the door. I opened it and there was the Marine corporal, the desk-clerk, with strong disapproval on his face.

"You can't close the doors when visiting a male guest. You have to keep it wide open. Unmarried guests of opposite sexes must keep their doors open as long as they are guests of the Hostess House."

He pushed the door as wide as it could go and just stood there to make sure it stayed open.

I felt my face turn warm, yet I stifled a laugh overcome with the humor of the ridiculous assumption he had made. Me and Spero? I was so safe with him that I could have been sitting there naked and I wouldn't have a thing to worry about. He was just too much of a gentleman.

Spero knew my mother would have killed him if his didn't do it first. Worse, he'd have to buy me a diamond ring. A ring *and* a record player? He'd have to marry me for sure if he spent *that* much money on me. I giggled at the thought.

Besides, I wasn't about to get pregnant and leave the Marine Corps for nobody, least of all a boy back home who would wait for me anyhow until the cows came home or the war was won.

The corporal was not amused. He eyed me suspiciously.

"We're just friends. He's a friend from back home." I didn't know why I had to explain anything to this desk-clerk. It's not as if he had actually caught us in the middle of a fervent embrace.

"It's the rules. The doors have to remain open at all time when there is a Woman Marine with a male guest. General Torrey's orders."

I was about to say "This isn't the boondocks," but I thought better of it.

My bunkies loved Spero immediately. More than that. They liked him. The visitor's lounge filled up with the whole squadroom while he waited for me. Some of the girls actually went to the trouble to put on their uniforms and get dressed since no one could be in the downstairs lounge during visiting hours unless they were fully dressed. Everyone wanted to get a good look at him. They oohed and ahhed over his classic Greek features and curly hair and hung around after I had made the introductions. They insisted on thanking him for the chocolates over and over.

Spero was very polite, attentive and I must admit, charming. I found my irritation at my squadmates' persistence in hanging around growing with every passing hour as they continued to make small talk monopolizing all of Spero's attention. Here it was his first night and we weren't alone a minute. This was as bad as the open door at the Hostess House. My bunkmates had believed me when I told them he was just an old friend.

Colonel Buse liked Spero immediately and he took me aside and said, "Terry, if you and the Lad want to get married, I'll be here to assist. I know the time is short but I can pull it off. He's a fine boy."

"Thank you, Colonel. But I don't know about this one. Since I joined the Corps I don't think I would be his parents' first choice for a daughter-in-law." I confided in him some of my doubts.

My beloved Colonel smiled at my protestations and patted my shoulders. "In this case, I think his parents have made a serious misjudgment. I'm here if you decide anything, Terry. You make a fine pair."

My Colonel wasn't convinced that there were no marriage plans being discussed between us. "That lad really cares, Terry. I can see it in his face when he looks at you."

The Marines in H-barracks who were billeted on the second deck liked him immediately as well. The men with whom I had joked and gone to the Post Movies or dancing at the Slopschutes took charge of him and gave him a tour of the barracks top-side where the men were billeted. They offered him an empty bunk, and played pool with him in the recreation room while I prepared for my runs.

They told me how much they admired him several times, as if their approval was all I needed to make our relationship official.

I don't know what they saw in him.

Spero said very little, didn't tell funny stories and didn't play pool that great since he had lost several dollars to them. They still liked him even when he won it all back in one of their poker games.

They all had become big brothers passing approval on little sister's beau. I had expected some evidence of jealousy from the Marines with whom I had gone on dates but there was none.

They made Spero an honorary Marine and gave him a Globe and Anchor to wear on his collar which he never took off.

Spero walked with me on all of my runs to the Post Headquarters. It was very pleasant having him next to me. I enjoyed seeing the surprised looks that passing Marines gave the "Dogface" walking their Post with a WR in the middle of the day. It was indeed an unusual sight and made heads turn. A courier from Post Headquarters from General Torrey's office who drove a jeep for his long runs always gave me a ride on my short runs. He saw me holding the usual packet, and he stopped and picked us up. The two men talked about the problems of cleaning rifles which left me out of the conversation all the way there and back.

Spero and I seemed to have a lot to say to each other. Yet, he didn't really say very much, come to think of it. I always did most of the talking.

At least, I didn't have to ask him where he was from as I always had to do with my Marine dates which would turn any conversation into a geography lesson. I knew Buffalo very well, the city from where Spero originated. And it was a city I didn't want to ever see again. This basic conflict between us led to one of our most serious conversations over apple pie and coffee at the Hostess House.

One minute we were laughing and I thought Spero was leading to a proposal and the next minute we were on the edge of an argument except for the fact that Spero never argued. We had been talking about the future just as if he were going on a trip and not 'in harm's way'.

"What are you going to do after the war, Spero? Finish college?"

"I guess so. But I flunked German two times so chemistry is out for me. I probably will end up running the chocolate business. My dad's not well and the family needs me."

"In Buffalo?"

"Of course in Buffalo. That is where the factory is."

"Do you really like Buffalo? Since you've seen the rest of the United States, didn't you find someplace else you'd rather live in than in Buffalo? There are better places to live than that ice-box! Like here in Virginia or California," I said, testing the waters.

"I grew up there and so did you," he said calmly. Spero had a habit of turning very quiet when he didn't concur with something I said. He considered arguing bad manners and arguing in a loud voice in public was about as rude as anyone could get.

His obtuse insensitivity and silence irritated me immensely.

I plunged on. "When this war is over, I will go as far away from Buffalo and the cold as I can get. Probably California. To Hollywood. I plan to be a writer."

My voice had become a little shrill and perhaps had too much vehemence. I had embarrassed him. He looked around but the clatter in the restaurant had drowned out my voice.

By mutual unspoken consent we dropped the subject. I didn't pursue the discussion. Spero was comfortable like a pair of old sneakers that you kept in the back of the closet. I didn't want to throw him away.

I had my dreams for the future and he had his.

My dream man would probably come from California and I would marry this romantic stranger and live happily ever after under the palm trees in that golden State.

Spero would probably marry a girl of his mother's choice and he would feed her chocolates and she would end up getting fat in Buffalo. How dull! The vision was most dismal.

In the meantime, Spero was mine to entertain and enjoy. After all he had come to see me just before he went overseas. That meant something. After walks on the Post Docks, a trip to the PX and an early show, there was nothing left to do but go to the Capitol.

We took the train to Washington D.C., visited the Thomas Jefferson and Lincoln memorials, which were always first on any list. We held hands and linked arms because it seemed so natural and friendly. We kissed and found a bench near the Spanish consulate and did a little necking just as if we were back in Tonawanda at Mayor's Park. Practice improved his technique. I enjoyed the shy almost embarrassed way he had of looking around to make sure no one saw us as if anyone in Washington D.C. cared who was kissing whom. After all this was war time; public demonstrations of affection were common spectacles. Passionate kissing was seen everywhere, on the park benches, at bus benches, railroad benches and airports. Maybe the couples were saying hello or saying good-bye or just passing the time of day. One thing was sure, no one thought it unusual nor cared. We made records at the Free Pepsi-cola Center where they let you talk into a machine that recorded your voice and afterwards you had a plastic disk to take home and play on a record player. We now had our voices on record and the moment became sentimental.

"Now you really have to buy that record player," I said playfully.

"As soon as they are made available," he promised seriously. I really didn't care. I was only teasing.

We asked one of the Pepsi volunteers to find us a place to stay for the night since Spero had to leave the next day for New York to join his 104th Division and board the troop ship. Spero asked her for two rooms. She handed him a slip of paper with an address on it for the $4.00 deposit Spero gave her.

"That is the last one I have. You servicemen are lucky. It's really a good address." She hadn't noticed I was a girl.

He also paid for our dinners of $1.99 for a bucket of fried chicken at Chicken In The Rough. I reminded him it was his treat. I had to pay for our movie and hot dogs the last time we had gone out. We walked around and visited the shops and because my birthday was a week away, Spero bought me a ruby birthstone ring that cost him twenty five dollars which was practically all the money he had left. I lent him five dollars to see him to New York.

The hour grew later and later but the evening was so pleasant and lovely, we hated to see it end. July nights in Washington D. C. are so delightful. We finally found the two-story house we had been sent to in a section called Georgetown. It was past twelve o'clock.

The front door was open; no one was there to greet us, and a guest book was on the table for us to sign. What a relief we did not have to meet anyone and explain our relationship. I had been prepared to lie and say Spero was my brother. We entered a simple room at the top of the stairs that was furnished with one double bed, one chest and one chair. This would never have met with his mother's or mine's approval although it was clean enough.

The window was open and we heard a woman's voice rattle off some words in a foreign language. It was Greek which Spero understood and spoke. He could also speak high school French and college German, and neighborhood Yiddish and Italian, and even a few words of Polish, but Greek was the language of his mother and father.

He stiffened and the situation became very uncomfortable and awkward. We were both embarrassed, especially with the family language coming through the window.

I studied the one double bed, looked at Spero's stricken face and said as casually as I could, "I sleep on the left side of the bed, okay with you?"

I giggled and then I couldn't stop laughing. The image of the shocked expressions that would have been frozen on the faces of both our mothers, his and mine, swam in front of me.

Spero sat down in the chair by the window, looked at me puzzled and waited patiently for me to explain what was so funny.

I couldn't help it. He and I alone in a room. Overnight! Too scandalous for words.

His mother was the dragon of Buffalo, while mine was the tigress of Tonawanda.

My mother was short and fat and her only goal in life was to protect my virginity which was my most valuable asset.

His mother was tall and thin and rarely smiled because her dignity didn't allow it. She had made it known that the wife of her first-born son would have to be someone of good breeding, preferably with money, who could take her place and inherit her mantle in Buffalo society.

I didn't have money but I had virginity. Maybe I qualified and maybe I didn't. If she heard about tonight, she'd never find me acceptable.

What I was about to do, sleep in the same room alone with him and spend the night with him, before marriage, would ruin whatever chances I would ever have. How could he respect me in the morning? My reputation would be shattered. I would have ruined myself and whether my virginity was intact would be immaterial.

The thought of their wild anxieties sent both of us into spasms of laughter. I made fun of both our mothers and imitated them in a pantomime as if they had just entered the room. My knack for mimicry lightened up the tense moment and we started to enjoy ourselves and relax.

Spero couldn't resist the joking and we chatted far in the night, me in my pink pajamas and Spero in his shorts, shocking but decent. We had not broken any code of honor we had been taught from childhood but it certainly didn't look that way. The thought kept us laughing most of the time.

At dawn I found I had fallen asleep in Spero's arms. We had hugged and kissed like two kids lost in a Grimm's fairy-tale forest who had staved off the cold by cuddling up. I knew he was chasing away the gods of war, the loneliness, the unknown future, the fears and terrors, the memories of dead friends who had been killed already by the bullets and bombs of the enemy. The familiarity we had with each other from years of friendship and being together at church socials made laying together the most natural thing in the world. I felt no guilt whatsoever.

Yet I woke still a virgin. He had respected me and I had discovered a new depth to my feeling for him.

I had come to appreciate his gentleness, his dislike for confrontations and conflicts. He was the last person on earth that should be going to war to kill other human beings. That was the obscenity of war. I felt a wave of fear and anxiety for my gentle giant. He was going into harm's way where they did not say "Please" or "Thank you" before they pulled the triggers of rifles and killed you dead.

When I kissed him one last time and held him in my arms at the Washington D.C. station, I didn't know if I would ever see him again. He told me not to take my ring off. Whether that was a proposal and a promise to replace it with something larger I didn't hear. The train made too much noise. Somehow, during his short liberty, he had gotten the idea that because we shared a room and a bed I was "his girl".

Colonel Buse began to ask me questions frequently along the lines of: "What do you hear from that nice soldier boy from your home town?" and "Have you decided anything about that Lad who is in Germany?"

I had returned to a barrage of questions because I was wearing the ruby gold ring that Spero had bought for my birthday.

The Marines of Casual H-barracks treated me as if I were engaged. They didn't ask me out any more, not even to the early movie. The men had a code of honor. If they knew a woman Marine was engaged or married, they kept hands off. Fidelity was sacred. That was one of the things they were fighting for. Democracy, Mom, apple pie and the girl next door. I was the girl next door. Had I truly been engaged or married I would have followed the same code of fidelity but since I was neither I didn't like being treated as a married woman.

After a while I began to resent the fact that Spero had visited me and still later, I became upset that I had been dumb enough to introduce him to the whole of H-barracks.

I took off the birthday ring, pretty and sentimental as it was.

By The Grace Of God And A Few Marines, MacArthur's Back In The Philippines–Autumn 1944

But this was wartime and nothing stayed the same very long. Great changes had taken place at Post Service Battalion. The next shipping out orders cleaned out the offices of all combat able Marines.

The staff sergeant who dreamed of returning to Australia was transferred.

Capable Sergeant Queen who kept the office ship-shape and everything under control was shipped out to the Pacific along with all the Staff, First and Gunny sergeants from all the other offices.

We never knew where our Marines were shipped after they left Quantico so the pins on my Battle Map of the Pacific didn't have any names nor faces on them. I did not know where any of our six Marine Divisions were fighting until after they had fought and won the objectives. All my information was classified and second-hand.

In July, I stuck red pins on the Marianas, on the islands of Saipan, Guam and Tinian and on a little dot in the ocean named Biak next to New Guinea. Our Marines had secured more islands but the costs in Marine deaths and casualties had escalated with each step and numbered in the thousands.

A miasma of sadness prevailed over Post Service Battalion. We wondered if the men we had dated and worked with, our Sergeant Queen and all the boys we had joked and drank with, were among these numbers. It was worse not knowing. There was no way to find out. The War Department only notified next of kin, not friends. Our victories came at a very high price.

Summer in Virginia was beautiful. August was hot but wonderful and the weather held into September. Several of us from post battalion offices and bunkies from Barracks A swam in the post pool on a regular basis. My two piece leopard bathing suit which did not reveal my scar after all caused several comments and there were many photos taken as we posed.

While we women relaxed after the hard day's office work, the fighting Marines were winning the war.

The beautiful Indian summer, with its warm lazy days and cool nights, brought news of the landings on another island. The First Division, the 7th and 5th Marines, was fighting in Peleliu in the Palau Islands along with soldiers from the U.S. Army, 321 Infantry Regiment and the 81 Infantry Division. I added green pin heads next to the yellow ones. The Marines had landed on Peleliu in the middle of the month, and rumors filtered back to Quantico that it was a very bad scene. Many Marines had been killed and the casualties were high. Once again the numbers had escalated into the thousands.

October was warm, a few of the trees had turned into colors of gold and red and many other species remained evergreen. Late blooming roses and fall flowers of marigolds and chrysanthemums dispelled the sense of impending doom of winter. So many of the shrubs and trees retained their greenery in Virginia that death seemed far away. It was sometimes very difficult to remember that death and war was the reason I was in this beautiful Marine Post.

Peleliu was ours but that news was on the inside pages of the newspapers. The war in Europe had been given more coverage by the press. Our newspapers and magazines were full of the exploits of the Armies in Germany, France, North Africa and England.

The front pages had pictures of the lst Army in Germany taking Aachen, the first city inside Germany to fall to U.S. troops, and soldiers of the 104th Division marching onto Cologne. I knew that Spero's company was part of that push and I searched the faces in the photos and in the newsreels.

I received a photo that Spero had taken in Brussels and he looked gaunt, tired, very thin and mean. I didn't like it at all.

Then in late October 1944, General MacArthur landed at Leyte, returning to the Philippines as he had promised. He had with him two battalions of Marines who were attached with the 6th Army.

The photograph of him walking in knee-deep water towards the beach with a few of his men crowded all the other news to the back pages but it gave the whole Marine post a hearty laugh. Behind the famous general there stood a Marine in the background holding up a sign that said *"By the Grace of God and a few Marines—MacArthur's back in the Philippines!"* In later publications of the photograph, the Marine and his sign had been air-brushed out and the first photo became a collector's item.

I now had a map of the European Theater of War on the wall in the hallway and I followed the 104th Division across Europe, from Cherbourg to Holland, to Aachen into Germany.

A letter from Spero told me he had fallen asleep in a fox-hole and he never heard the artillery bombardment that had come in the night. When he awoke late the next morning he was all alone in an empty field. Shell hole craters were all around him that miraculously had missed him. There wasn't a soul around. His division had moved on without him. He retraced his steps and found the British. Field Marshall Montgomery's troops were moving fast into Germany and he spent a week with the Brits. He was in shock, not about the shells that had narrowly missed him, but about the cold mutton stew he had to eat three times a day. The British mess cooks did not make a new hot batch of food until the old one was all gone. His letter was full of how good the American Army had it with cans of SPAM and K-Rations and chocolate bars and he couldn't wait until he found his outfit again. He was so thirsty for a Coca-Cola, he'd give a month's pay for one.

I wrapped up two bottles and mailed it to his APO number hoping they would arrive safely.

I read parts of his letter aloud to Colonel Buse and to the few remaining Marines of Casual Barracks who had known him. This triggered the Marines of Casual Barracks, those who had survived and had returned from overseas, to relate their battle stories.

There were two types of Marines. Those Marines who wanted to forget the trauma they had experienced in fighting the Japs acted as if they didn't have a care in the world, as if there was no war. They said nothing about what they had gone through. If you asked them about the battles they fought, they would clam up and become silent. I learned to flirt and joke with them and made small talk about the wonderful Quantico weather, the latest movie that was playing at the Post Theater, the score the Quantico team had made in the last baseball game and chided them on what heart breakers they were leading a girl on like that as if their extravagant compliments had turned my head.

Then there were those Marines who wanted to disclose every detail of their deprivations and hardships in the battles of Guadalcanal, Tarawa, and the battles for New Britain Islands and other obscure dots in the Pacific Ocean. These men relived the battles and remembered the bitterness they felt about the lack of support they had received from Army and Navy. They scoffed at the Army's fighting men who were untrained in amphibious assault. Their talk became political as long as there were no officers around to hear them gripe. I learned from them about the political war and inter-service rivalry that was being fought right here in Washington.

Once the Marines got started on their bull sessions, they even forgot I was there.

"The Joint Chiefs of Staff control this war. It's those two Army generals and two Admirals who run this show. They tell us what to do, where the Marines are going to fight and how many of us are going to do the fighting. Our Commandant is the last to know. Just like us grunts. After we Marines have secured the beachhead, they bring in the Army and who gets the credit? You guessed it. The Army."

"The Corps is supposed to have air and naval support during the assault of the beachheads and look what they did to us at Guadalcanal. The ships sailed off after forty-eight hours and left us without enough supplies to fight the Jap bastards. But we showed them and took the damn island anyhow."

Frankly, it seemed to me that to complain about the famous generals and admirals who were in charge of conducting this war was as ineffective and useless as griping about God and acts of nature.

"The Joints have put everything we've got in Europe for the big push in Germany. The Army and Air Corps is backing the Allied Forces all the way. Our Air Force bombs the cities of Germany daily. If we had that kind of support, we would have won the whole Pacific in months instead of slugging from island to island."

The combat Marines were not impressed with the Army soldiers that had been sent to support them either.

The Marines who had returned from the most recent campaigns were particularly bitter. They compared the kind of massive commitment the Army received in Europe and North Africa to the skimpy support they had received in the Pacific which made the fighting on Guadalcanal, Tarawa, Saipan, Iwo Jima and Peleliu Palau so bad. They had experienced the disparity first hand. The inter-service rivalry at the top filtered down and became more vocal at the bottom of the rank. Their disparagement about the lack of ability of Army men to hold the assault in the island wars and the inability of Army training to train amphibious soldiers as the Corps was able to do was a recurrent theme.

What it really boiled down to was this: unless a Marine had a Marine to back him up and fight beside him, he did not trust any other branch of the service.

When the Allied Forces made an assault landing in Normandy, Army soldiers used techniques that had been perfected by the Marine Corps. As they landed on the beaches these Army divisions had tremendous support and were backed up by an Armada that was larger than anything the world had seen.

The Marines who had stormed the Pacific Islands with considerable less support and had fought with fewer men covered their disgust with a sort of esprit de corps nonchalance. "Nothing was bad enough for the First Division," said one of the H-barracks gyrenes.

"If we had anywhere near that kind of support we would have taken Guadalcanal in a week. We wouldn't have had such a hard time on Peleliu. That hell hole should have been a piece of cake. A lot of buddies died there that shouldn't of."

They fell silent as memories flowed over them.

There was still more fighting to come, both in Europe and in the Pacific and everyone knew it. No one was going to stay in Quantico for long.

Colonel Buse, Major Emery, Sergeant Major Jordan and some of the Old Corps who would have been mustered out if it hadn't been wartime, stayed with us, but there was a new look of younger men and more women.

As the war continued, Marines went in and out of our office so fast that even Sergeant Ellice had trouble keeping up and depended on Sherry a little more which lessened the tension that had developed. In each office, all the work was done by the old sergeant majors and Women Marines. All non-commissioned and staff sergeants had gone to battle. In our office, there was only The Colonel, the Adjutant, Ellice, Sherry and myself. We awaited a new lieutenant as replacement.

Sergeant Ellice Stukey

Then one day First Lieutenant Slater reported to duty.

He was a *mustang* which meant he had been promoted from the ranks. He made it in the battlefield when just about everyone in his company was killed or hurt on Saipan. He did not wear the bars very comfortably.

He tried to join the camaraderie in the office but his sense of humor was mean and his jokes suggestive with double meanings, some of which Gerry or Smoky would elaborate upon when I repeated them in the barracks at night.

I never liked having to pretend laughter which is one way I sought to handle the uncomfortable moments when I didn't really catch on or quite understand one of the lieutenant's riddles or jokes that passed over my head. Once he handed me a cartoon which was crudely drawn and suggestive. I returned it to him with a half-smile and said, "I don't get the point."

My reply only encouraged him more. He didn't believe me. He said, "I bet you're a wild one. I bet you're hot when you're hot."

I didn't like his leer nor his hand ruffling through my curly short hair.

I heard him say the same thing to Sergeant Ellice the very next day only she didn't have the kind of hair that ruffled. Within one week, the cozy manner in which he and Ellice worked together aroused gossip.

Sherry and I avoided the lieutenant while she welcomed him and basked in his attention. We acted with strict military courtesy in order to fend off his familiarity and wandering hands.

Ellice treated him with an intimacy that transcended military rules. He took unwarranted liberties, patting her hips and standing much too close to her when they conferred over the same documents, while she looked up at him and brayed through her nose making sure that only enlisted personnel were in the office at the time. Her actions made every Woman Marine in the H-barracks offices who saw what was happening very uncomfortable.

Sherry, feeling the brunt of it, became more and more distressed with each passing day. A small group assembled around Sherry and me in the WR's Lair. Advice was freely offered but what we really needed was a plan of strategy. Ellice's behavior jeopardized the strides we had made in being accepted as gender neuter Marine equals.

There was nothing in the Women's Marine manual that dealt with this sort of problem. Techniques of survival that were fine for assaulting the beach were not applicable for the battle of the sexes.

No courses in Boot Camp had ever been offered on how to deal with the bucking ambitions of a Woman Marine who would stoop to lying on her back to make the next rank.

But on the other hand, we had never received any instructions nor lectures of what to do with men like the lieutenant who was just "fresh," just " kidding," who told off-color jokes, touched and patted, and asked questions that were personal. He bumped against me deliberately and he brushed against Ellice quite frequently. When he laid a hand on Sherry, she stood up straight and tall with full dignity and stared him down. The military rules against fraternization were supposed to make all of these problems that were so common in the civilian work world non-existent. The fact that we had not experienced any of these offensive indignities from the men in Post Service Battalion up to now, made the lieutenant's actions all the more abhorrent, and Ellice's encouragement all the more repugnant.

"Should we report what's going on to The Colonel?"

That was vetoed. No one wanted to get involved in the chain of command. I knew my Colonel to be a fair man, but the other WRs said that a formal report should be a last resort and we'd have to make sure of our ground. Right now we had nothing but a couple of incidents that had made a few of us uncomfortable.

"I thought it was the men we had to worry about. Not the rank-happy *BAMS!*"

"Our survival as Women Marines depends on the men accepting us as equals and respecting our work. When a woman uses her sex to get promotions she threatens all of us."

"She ruins it for all of us Women Marines," I said. It was my mother's voice that came out of me but it was Major Towle's ethics.

The air in the office became so thick with tension, that had it been gas, one match would have been blown the whole barracks to kingdom come.

The Colonel, the Adjutant and Sergeant Major Jordan saw nothing. They would not have needed a topographical map to read the lay of the land had it been a male Marine on the prowl. T h e y had no inkling the Women Marines were tense, watchful and wary and were having problems with one of their own. Had this been the jungle they would have been alert to snipers. But no one expected a sniper in an office full of women so Sergeant Ellice picked us off one by one. She didn't bother me but others felt the brunt of her attention.

Sherry was beside herself with frustration. "I'm not a threat to her. She outranks me," she said.

We were puzzled and spent many hours wondering why Sergeant Ellice had turned her guns on Sherry.

"She's afraid of you. You do good work and it shows her up."

Sherry and I went to work together and returned on the same bus at 4:30 P.M. Our friendship thickened. After a few days, all our conversation centered about Sergeant Ellice and Lieutenant Slater and little else. More and more of our co-workers in Post Service Battalion entered the fray.

The Lair became a message center of its own as the latest scuttlebutt about the two was bandied about from WR to WR.

"She is his shack-job! It's not love. She doesn't care one bit for him. It's all *ear-banging*. She wants to make staff sergeant that bad and thinks Lieutenant Slater will get it for her."

"I thought Sergeant Ellice was married."

"She is! To a Marine sergeant. He was shipped overseas two weeks after the ceremony!"

"But, Slater's an officer."

"Not a real one. He was a sergeant and got his commission when there was no one left. It's not as if he's gone through OCS. You can tell, he is no gentleman."

"How do you know she's shacking up with Slater? He just arrived two weeks ago."

"Doc in Post Dispensary saw them in D.C. last week-end. She looked up his service record file. Doc says he had syphilis."

"That can be cured now."

"Sure. But who knows when he'll get it again? That's the type of Marine to stay away from. He's bad news!"

Everyone grinned knowingly. Sherry who was true to her husband, the lieutenant in the submarines, just smiled along with the rest of us.

No one was about to warn Sergeant Ellice of the dangers of infidelity nor would anyone tell her this latest bit of information on the slimy Lieutenant Slater.

Lorena, A Buddy Lost

About that time, Lorena came to work at H Barracks.

I had gone into the Lair after I had been caught in the warm rain on one of my runs. I took off my hat and looked in the mirror and screamed at my reflection.

Lorry, fresh out of Boot Camp, who had just walked in and was on her first day on the job heard my scream and rushed to my aid. I didn't realize at that time that she was easily startled and that instantaneous compassion for every living thing flowed in her blood like a beer bust at the Slopschute.

"What's wrong? Are you hurt?" She asked with so much concern in her voice that I laughed at her.

"My hair. The humidity has made the curls so tight, I can't comb it. It's a mess," I explained.

She giggled with such delight at her own silly reaction that we became fast friends immediately.

She lived in the same squadroom in the middle of the room but I had never noticed her before. There was a good reason. She was so self effacing and so quiet she melted in the background even when she was part of a group.

Lorry was a sweet shy young French-Canadian country girl from Maine. She never had to fend off any persistent Marines. She would cast her eyes downward and contemplate the deck whenever any male approached her. She even stepped off the sidewalk to let the men pass by.

She reminded me of my kid sisters in two ways.

First, she seemed to depend on my advice and needed my help desperately. Secondly, she admired me as if I were a glamorous movie star. Whenever I gave her little lectures, I took her hand as I would have done to my sisters. Her inexperience with life showed in every movement. I feared that Lorry would never find a husband if she were afraid of strangers. As Mama said time and time again, "A man is a stranger until you marry him." I tried to tell her a few facts about life, men and the ways of the world. I tried to teach her things that she should have learned by observation, naturally and automatically, after the age of thirteen.

"You must stand straight. Don't slump and act embarrassed when a Marine asks you to dance. Look him straight in the eye. Give him a date. It's okay to hold hands in the movies, but just don't go off the Post. Don't go in the boondocks!" Advice rolled off my tongue with ease.

Gerry passed my bunk and added "Kiss him with your mouth closed. Hey, bunkie, is it okay if I borrow your radio? Me and my shack-job have got a room for the night." Gerry was referring to her husband, the Marine from Post Stables with whom she fought constantly now that they were married.

Lorry loved being part of our group of "Old Salts" as we were known to the newer WR recruits who were arriving weekly. Several times, I arranged double dates, not because I was attracted to the Marines, but because I wanted Lorry to learn and be more comfortable about flirting and how to shoot the breeze with men about to be shipped into combat or having returned from combat. Their offers of love and clumsy passes were not to be taken so seriously to such an extent as to spoil a good evening of fun and dancing.

Lorry never got the hang of it and soon, I did not chide her when she preferred to stay in the barracks rather than go out. Lorry reacted with gratitude and gave me her total friendship. She appreciated my motherly concern and my sisterly solicitude.

It was selfish of me, but I enjoyed having someone who wanted to run errands, iron my uniform, and wait up for me when I returned from my dates on the Post. Just the way I had fun with my baby sisters, I enjoyed recounting to her the tales of my adventures and embellished them with funny quips. I even brought her bags of potato chips from the NCO Club or *pogie bait* as I used to bring snacks and candy to my kid sisters. These were the times I missed my family and baby sisters the most. Having someone like Lorry for a friend in true sisterhood eased the ache.

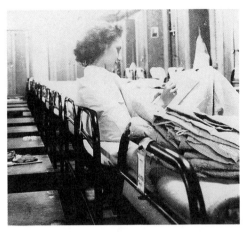

Women's barracks, Quantico 1944

Top: Lorry, alone in the barracks, writing a letter.
Center: Terry (author) and Lorry, sunning in the area behind the barracks which was built just for the women Marines.
Bottom: The Chow line: L to R: Lorry, Stretch (Motor Transport), Josie, Lindsay, and Belle.

But a fear stalked the barracks and I never sensed it until it destroyed our friendship and left me wary and careful of whatever I did in the Corps thereafter.

The beginning of the end of my innocent life at Quantico began with a sisterly kiss, the kind I always gave my kid sisters.

I had returned from one of my evenings at the NCO Club where I had danced to the juke box music with a sergeant from New York who really knew how to jitterbug, rhumba and swing. I limped back to the barracks with a blister on my heel, tired but having enjoyed myself immensely.

Lorry waited up for me. She had washed and ironed my whole uniform, including the dungarees. She followed me from the bunk bed where I threw my uniform and all my clothes, to the shower room where I had dashed with a towel around me in order to wash up and crawl into bed before lights out at 10:00 P.M.

"You shouldn't have done all that for me, Lorry. I'll tell you all about my date tomorrow," I said.

Lorry's face was crestfallen. We could have gone to the WR lounge which had lights for one hour longer, but I really was exhausted.

I hugged her and gave her a kiss as I did my sisters when I didn't want to tell them another bedtime story. I shuffled off to my bunk oblivious to who was in the *head.*

Fear Stalks The Barracks

Within a few weeks, I had noticed a definite cooling off toward me by some of my squadmates. If I sat alone in the mess hall, or the Hostess House, or at the Tap Room at the Post Exchange, none of the WRs from my barracks joined me as was the common custom. No one walking behind me asked me to wait up to join me as I went from one WR building to another. Small clusters of women in the barracks or at the bulletin board broke up soon after I had joined them.

Finally, after a few such incidents and with the passing of time, I mentioned to Lorry that something was happening that I didn't understand. Had I said something wrong to someone? Had I disgraced the Marine Corps in some way? Where had I fouled up? Whom had I insulted?

Lorry said nothing. She shuffled her feet in a way I had to come to recognize as extreme discomfort and embarrassment as she studied the concrete floor intently.

Gerry had just walked in and heard the tail end of my interrogation. "It's all female crap, Terry! These crummy foul-ups are nasty gossiping bitches!"

"What are you talking about?"

"About you and Lorry! I told them all to shove off. They're looking under the beds for queers like a bunch of old maids."

"Who? Who? Who?" I looked about. There was hardly anyone in the eighty man squadroom.

Lorry said in a timid voice, "Remember that night you hugged me and kissed me when I ironed your clothes? I was asked about us the next day."

"Asked what?" I still didn't have a clue to what she was talking about but I knew I had been excluded from something important and I was in danger. I now recognized I was being rejected by my squadroom on purpose and it hurt all the more.

"That you and me are-are...."

"Are what? Lorry—spit it out!" My patience was snapping.

"They think I am lesbian and you're one too because we're friends." She blurted it out in one choking sentence.

"I didn't know you were Lebanese. I thought you were French-Canadian," I said.

Gerry's cynical laugh didn't help the situation at all. "No, no, Terry. A lesbian is a homosexual."

She used a word I had never heard before.

"Don't you remember when you filled out the psychology questionnaire with four hundred questions when you enlisted? How did you answer the one where they asked you whether you preferred men or women?"

No, I hadn't remembered that question.

"Homosexual. Sounds medical. Or scientific. Are you born with it or is it catching?" I asked.

Just as Gerry had deciphered some of Lieutenant Slater's jokes, she now explained what being a lesbian meant.

She told me anyone could be a homosexual, male or a female. No one could tell who was a homosexual. They looked like normal people but they weren't. They did nasty dirty things to each other. It was a criminal act in the Marine Corps. A dishonorable undesirable discharge was issued as soon as a person was found to be a homosexual.

No wonder my squadmates had avoided me. They had acted as if I had something contagious. My stomach hit me with cramps just then. Anger welled up in my chest.

I turned to Lorry with all my fury. "And you didn't shut them up? That's what this squadroom thinks of me? Of us?"

She didn't answer me, just stared with enlarged black pupils.

"Why didn't you tell me so we could fight back?" I confronted Lorry with disbelief at her cowering stance.

"I knew it would upset you," Lorry cried in a whimper.

"Well, it has. It has upset me that you have kept it from me. Three weeks! You have known all this for three weeks?"

I lashed out in tremendous fury. It was as bad as not reporting a fire and letting the place burn up. Lorry's timidity, anxieties, fears and inexperience no longer were of any importance to me.

Never in my wildest dreams did I ever anticipate this kind of gossip. I knew how men and women made love but to tell the truth, I was puzzled how women did it. I never thought about it before this. Wasn't there a physiological problem between two women who had the same privates?

And to be accused of liking women better than men? I didn't join the Marine Corps to be without men. I joined it to be with men.

Confusion, anger, frustration and fear, pure strong terror, swirled within me.

Of course, I liked women. I loved some of them too. I adored Barbara Stanwyck and Vivian Leigh.

I admired a great many women too; women who had accomplished a lot in life: Eleanor Roosevelt, Fleur Cowles, Amelia Earhart. There were the women I respected, looked up to and wanted to emulate: my commanding officers, starting with our WR Director Colonel Ruth Streeter, Major Towle from Camp Lejeune, Captain Lloyd and now Captain Julia Hamblet of Quantico.

I remembered my third grade teacher. I had such a crush on her when I was seven or eight. She had red hair and wore high heels.

My list got longer and longer.

I would love to be Ginger Rogers, Ruby Keeler or Rita Hayworth, or at least in their dancing shoes. My mind ran down a list of women, picking their names off like the petals in daisies: like her, love her, like her, love her.

How could my squadmates even start such a rumor? I had never met a lesbian so how could I be one? I thought that each and every one in the squadroom was my friend and they liked me. I wasn't wrong about that. They did like me. How could they all turn so quickly against me?

Mother never warned me about this kind of problem. This was as bad as having to prove you were still a virgin after you had lost your reputation in Tonawanda. I take that back. This accusation was much worse. There was no way to defend it.

The Women Marines may be a sisterhood but we weren't real sisters. No kissing nor hugging was allowed in the Corps. Of course! How dumb of me!

General Torrey's order had said, *"There will be no hand holding between Marines."*

I thought he meant between girl and boy Marines. I didn't know there was another kind of hand holding.

I had been kissing and hugging my girl friends since grade school. We hugged and jumped up and down together after we won a game. No one ever said anything then. We slept together at slumber parties. No one ever said anything then either. We kissed each other hello and good-bye and when we had happy news or sad news, when the boys we had a crush on didn't call or when they did.

When our menstrual began, all our mothers warned, "Stay away from boys!"

If you have to stay away from your own sex what was there left?

I was afraid. I had felt the cold breezes of withdrawn friendship and it left me in terror. The hostility and enmity I encountered had been painful beyond belief. I questioned my own actions and my confidence was shattered.

A fear stalked this barracks. Anyone who was suspected of sexual perversity was ostracized without a hearing. What was sexual perversity? At what age did it start? Could it be cured? No one explained. No one had ever uttered the word, homosexual.

At least Lorry knew what the word meant. It shocked me to discover, I was more naive than she. I had been so smug in my role as her mentor and teacher only to discover that I needed one myself.

I ranted and raved and talked to myself and anyone else I could find in the *head* and lounge. I didn't care who in the barracks heard me.

Lorry hid under her blanket.

No one came near me as I threw gear into my locker storming in and out of the squadroom, going from lounge to *head* to bunk. I even swore! I yelled to no one in particular but to everyone who could hear. I could only hope that if I brought out into the open the horrible accusation that its poison would shrivel up in the light of righteousness. Such malice could only flower in the shadows of innuendoes and whispers. I shouted a challenge for anyone to prove these lies.

Whoever had started this malicious rumor never stepped forward to admit it. I was alone until, one by one, my dearest bunkies approached me.

Fenton came in and her words didn't help matters as she tried to ease my distress.

"Lesbianism is a sin, Terry. The Catholics are very specific on this sin. A pervert goes against God's Commandment."

"Did you think I was one?" She hadn't been unfriendly, but she hadn't been around much, so I couldn't remember if she had snubbed me as well.

"Perverts hide it. So you never know who's one or isn't." She hastened to comfort me. "Of course, I don't think you're one. Have you thought of changing your religion to Catholic? Would you like to come to chapel with me tonight? Father Bob is so good at giving advice."

The Duty NCO came by to check up on the commotion I had been making but no one else came near me. I was in my bunk in tears.

What does a person have to do to prove she wasn't a lesbian? Get married?

There was only one person who could help and tell me what to do.

The next morning, I approached Colonel Buse and asked permission to speak to him, privately.

It took several false starts for me to find the right words. Colonel Buse could see by the expression and color of my face that it was serious. He drew himself to full height and became very grave as I asked for his help. Very quietly, in his office, behind closed doors, I explained.

True to his word, he did take care of it. He had a conference with the new Women's Reserve Commanding officer who called in each girl in the squadroom for a talk. It was done so quietly that I never knew how the problem had been taken care of for me. I only realized that it had been resolved because life resumed as before. Well, not quite. Lorry and I no longer were close friends. Her eyes were sad when I greeted her as I passed her by but I didn't enjoy her company anymore. I went back to ironing my own uniforms.

While I was fighting to save my reputation in Barracks One, the same accusation had been made against two women in Barracks Two.

Over in Barracks Two, the whole squadroom was involved in a court trial over the charges of lesbianism they had made against two women. We, in Barracks One, had not caught wind of it because the trial had been conducted behind closed doors under a code of silence.

One of the judges, I later found out, was Colonel Buse.

The consequences to what had happened to me splashed over and ended up affecting the outcome of that trial because I took my problem to Colonel Buse when he was right in the middle of deliberations.

One morning, Colonel Buse called me into his office to tell me of the decision that he just handed down as a judge in a Court Martial: The results were still top secret but he wanted me to know that he had been working on a case of two other Women Marines who had been brought before him accused as I had been of being lesbians. It was a military crime that carried a Bad Conduct Discharge.

The Colonel had been in a serious quandary. He admitted to me that until that crucial moment in his deliberations when I approached him with my problem, he had been having difficulty arriving at a fair verdict.

The accused were the first women he had to pass judgment upon for such a crime. From the depths of his Southern upbringing and South Carolina background he knew that women were different from men. Ladies were to be treated as ladies always, to be protected from harm. That was how he treated all the Women Marines in his command.

Had these accused Marines been males, he would have had no problem reaching a verdict sooner. With men, there was usually a specific pornographic act that could substantiate any charges brought against them. Even circumstantial extenuating circumstances, such as duty aboard ship or at a lonely station where women were absent for long periods of time, could influence a decision and brought to bear against them. An open and shut case of perversity would be easier to prove against such men who invariably were often found "guilty". For *the good of the Service* they were dispatched with alacrity with an *Undesirable Discharge* before their bunkmates would execute their own sentence upon them.

It was common knowledge that Marines would beat up any suspected perverts in their midst. The Corps was a very hostile environment for any homosexual.

He concluded that hysterical fear was rampant in the women's barracks, that mass hysteria had spread like a common cold. To this gracious man, women were fragile creatures, prone to hysteria and fainting and could make accusations out of nothing. He had been married for over thirty years and he knew women had bad times of the month where it didn't take much to make them upset and they said and did strange things. He wasn't going to let this nonsense go on any longer. These two women needed his protection as I had.

Besides, lesbianism didn't make sense to this Southern gentleman.

Why would a woman turn to another woman when there were so many hungry men on the Post willing to be of service and demonstrate their masculinity?

"So, Terry. I have come to the conclusions that these accused women must be innocent and were victims of malicious female gossip as you have been."

The following week, the verdict of "innocent" was telegraphed from squadroom to squadroom until the news spread throughout all four barracks and the one thousand women. There was general outrage at the verdict which exonerated the two women.

I soon found out that there was a difference between their case and mine with perhaps some real smoke to that fire.

The accusation against me was based on a malicious remark made by a half-asleep person who had voiced her own dirty thoughts aloud.

The other case was based on the conduct of the two women which had been observed by many in the squadroom over a period of several months.

In the beginning, Barracks Two tried to deal with the situation themselves but the lovers had become arrogant. The two infatuated lovers had become unguarded and carried on overtly and flagrantly in the barracks, shocking many and disgusting others. Their squadmates told of witnessing sexual acts, the coupling in the bunks and fondling in the showers over a period of months. The squadroom had used scorn, disgust, ostracizing and overt nasty remarks to stop it.

One of the accused women boasted foolishly that she had a brother who was a general in Washington D.C., and any complaint against her would be stopped along the chain of command. The lovers maintained what they did was nobody else's business.

Homosexual behavior was an affront to every heterosexual Woman Marine in the barracks and they banded together and followed democratic procedure. They signed and presented a formal complaint and petition and sent it up the chain of command.

I kept still and did not contribute any comments to the discussion as the facts of the case was brought out into the open now that it no longer was on the court docket. I ventured no opinions of my own either way and I certainly never told anyone what part I had played in bringing about that verdict.

The two accused women, when set free, were transferred. They never returned to the same barracks. So were the Women Marines who had signed the complaint.

Colonel Buse was pleased he had averted what he perceived as a great injustice.

My sympathies had gone to the women of the Barracks Two who never knew why the verdict had gone against them. To them, it was more proof that the chain of command was stacked against the enlisted and it made everyone leery of signing formal complaints.

I never said a word to Colonel Buse about this affair ever again.

The barracks still talked about the lesbian incident but I only listened and said nothing. My bunkmates in the squadroom who had been less than supportive of me during my twilight time, went out of their way to show me that they knew all along that Lorry and I weren't one of *"them"*.

They never said so in so many words but they made amends in many ways for their abandonment and lack of *Semper Fidelis.* Once again I was welcomed by everyone and any group. I wasn't alone for long when I was alone. Someone always joined me.

Soon I put the incident aside in my mind, chalking it up to life in the military, content that I was being treated as a buddy who was a normal human being. I noticed that the squadroom also made the extra effort and included Lorry in their trips to the PX or Quantico Town which brought roses back into her cheeks and grins on her face. She now waved at me blithely as she walked by in cliques of threes and fours, her growing self-esteem quite evident.

I wondered what the verdict would have been had I not confided to my Colonel and inadvertently brought him to their defense. I wondered if the women of Barracks Two were really innocent and had been accused falsely.

I didn't care either way about who did what to whom and it worried me that I felt this way. To be a homosexual was considered a crime by the Marine Corps, the State and GOD. That was enough to frighten me to the core of my soul. I didn't understand why anyone would take on the big three powers in all the earth, yet here I was, questioning the wisdom of thousands of years. I not only worried about the Corps but I had to worry about God reading my thoughts about the unfairness of it all, not only to me but to anyone who was a homosexual. Too much pain had been inflicted on too many people.

I hadn't liked what had happened to me. I now knew I could lose very easily my Marine Corps family that I had come to love. A malicious whisper could bring all this friendly rapport to a sudden halt. I did not want to experience that kind of hostility ever again. I became very careful about what I said or did.

Somehow, a personal freedom was involved here, but I didn't know which one it was. Seems what you did with your body should be your own business. The Corps had many rules against some basic personal liberties that I had taken for granted in civilian life. Yet once I gave my oath and became a Marine I handed my basic American rights over to the Corps as if I didn't need them any longer and traded them for a vow of obedience.

I had never given a moment's thought to whatever liberties and rights I had as an American when I pledged my vow of allegiance to the Corps. It wouldn't have mattered if I had. There was no choice. You did it the Marine Corps way. By the numbers. The Marine Corps had issued a red book of rules and regulations called the Marine Corps Manual for each and every Marine to memorize and follow.

But who made those regulations? Men, that's who.

Men had written the Bible too. Men who spoke Greek, Latin and Hebrew.

Where were the women's contributions?

I never had that thought before. Once it started, other ideas rolled in.

You couldn't have a baby in the Marine Corps, take hormones or marry anyone you wanted. It seems there were special rules written just for females. Did it matter if there was one more rule that said you couldn't love another woman? What difference did it make? It was simply one more rule.

As for women wanting to be with women, I didn't know. Maybe it was a natural thing. I remembered a love I had for my teacher when I was twelve years old. I would have been thrilled out of my mind if she had held me and hugged me. Could love of any kind be worse than the hate I had seen? No, I would prefer the hugs and kisses.

Could that kind of love hurt the Corps? That took some thought.

I had never met or known anyone who said she was a lesbian. I only knew I had never seen such hate, anger and fear as I had experienced in my squadroom. To get a taste of it was frightening. I knew one thing, a squad, platoon or company couldn't function if there was that kind of hostility in the ranks. The Corps was right on that point. There was damage to the esprit de corps and it did tear the barracks apart. I had seen it and felt it.

On the other hand, if I had been a real lesbian, I wouldn't be dumb enough to let anyone know about it, especially anybody in the Marine Corps. I would have kept it a deep dark secret. I would have been very careful of my conduct and controlled my tongue and watched what I said. I wouldn't have been as dumb as those two girls in Barracks Two. In my opinion, they were really *dumb.* Since they were breaking known and published rules and regulations so flagrantly, their common sense should have told them to go to Washington D.C. or Baltimore like the enlisted Women Marines who were dating officers did.

The consequences of being recognized as homosexual were simply too harsh otherwise.

My thoughts were heresy but I could not stop them from wandering to the final conclusion. It seemed to me that the Corps had a lot of rules that applied only to women and didn't affect the men.

If the Marine Corps changed the rule on pregnancy and allowed a Marine to have a baby and remain in the Corps, (providing she had a good baby sitter) would the Marine Corps lose its strength? They had gone to the expense of training all of us, why not use us? Our labor was cheap enough. A good secretary could always earn more outside the Corps. So, after going to the expense of training us, why let us go? That didn't make much business sense to me. Couldn't the Corps see that?

If the Corps allowed women Marines to take hormones, would it harm the men? Each month there was proof women were different from men. Why did the Corps refuse to acknowledge this when it was plain as the noses on their faces?

Would the Marine Corps be more compromised if the Corps somehow allowed enlisted to marry the officers they were shacking up with? They were fraternizing already. Did the Corps actually think that they could stop what was the most natural thing in the world by declaring one of the sacraments of the church an act that could be subject to discharge?

What was behind all those 'Out of Bound' signs that kept some of us beyond the pale that lowly enlisted should not see? Were there private realms and fiefdoms, private park like grounds for recreation and plush clubs not to be shared? Were the rules of fraternization archaic, there to perpetuate a class system that benefited a few? If we enlisted saw how the officers lived would there be an uprising and anarchy?

If women Marines were allowed to volunteer to go overseas into combat areas with the men would it really jeopardize the Corps?

The Russian women had manned guns and protected their land from the Germans. They had stopped them at Stalingrad.
The English, Canadians and Australian women were fighting along side their men.

The Free French and the Chinese women had shouldered arms.

Were we Women Marines made of lesser material? I didn't think so. If the Japanese hordes were at Washington's gates, I bet we'd be given rifles. At least our President Roosevelt and some of our

Congressmen recognized we women were needed, otherwise we wouldn't be in the Army, Navy and the Marine Corps.

It was our country too. Maybe it was a matter of timing and expedience. It was true, I didn't want to go into combat and fight on some God-forsaken tropical island filled with malaria mosquitoes, leeches, and snakes, but to protect my country I would carry a rifle. I couldn't speak for everyone but many of us had the same attitude.

On the other hand, I wouldn't mind going overseas as the WAACS did who were posted overseas, in London, North Africa and Paris, who intermingled with the women of our Allied Nations who were also in uniform; women who represented England, Free France, Australia, Canada and others.

I didn't waste any more time thinking about a subject that made me a little sad and very uncomfortable. Instead I thought about the coming Presidential election. I was glad I was able to cast my first vote following my twenty-first birthday for President Franklin Delano Roosevelt, a Democrat, who was running for his fourth term on a slogan that we shouldn't switch horses in the middle of the road. He was leading us to victory and he was my Commander-in-Chief.

Good-Bye To Colonel Buse

Another bombshell hit Post Service Battalion.

My beloved Colonel Buse retired from the Marine Corps. His departure was sudden, expedited by General Torrey.

I helped Mrs. Buse pack. She fought back the tears despite the fact she was happy to be going home, at last to her ante-bellum home on Moultrie Street in Charleston, South Carolina. There was an element of disgrace in their departure.

"You know how The Colonel loves to joke," she sighed.

Oh, yes, I knew! That was why we loved him.

"He was joking at the reception for the general and he made a remark which the wife of the newer officers took as an insult. General Torrey was just looking for an excuse to force him to retire and The Colonel gave it to him. They've known each other for over thirty years."

The rivalry had come to an end.

Theresa Karas Yianilos

Tears ran down my cheeks. The parting was a wrenching of the heart. They comforted me and went about the task at hand with calm resignation. The Colonel and his Lady had experienced many moves while serving the Marine Corps for thirty years. It was all in the line of duty.

"When you are ready to put on that white dress you told me about, I want to be the first to know. That is an order, Corporal Terry."

"Yes, Sir. I promise. May I call you in Charleston if that day ever comes?"

"I shall expect it."

I kissed my Quantico father and mother good-bye.

The whole Post Service Battalion stood at the steps with heavy hearts and watched their departure. We all held our salute until they were gone and couldn't be seen anymore.

As we all turned to go back into our offices, I saw the smiling smirk on the face of Sergeant Ellice who hadn't gone to any lengths to hide her satisfaction at the departure of our Colonel. I never liked her before, but now at that moment, I felt hate.

Good-Bye To Post Service Battalion

Quantico was changing in so many ways.

Adjutant Major Emery, became the commanding officer. A new name plate was on the Colonel's door which remained closed all the time. The Major didn't care who went in and out of the battalion and he wasn't interested in facial expressions in the mirror to keep track of the mood of his men.

He handled his command as a corporate executive. He did not know what went on beyond the papers that were placed on his desk. He never questioned the Marines, never looked at the mess hall nor inspected the chow. He didn't stick his head in any garbage cans in the Mess Hall looking for discarded precious cutlery.

He didn't joke with the WR's and didn't commandeer jeeps or boats to take us on trips to near-by battlefields or Washington D. C.

Post Service Battalion was run as a business, with the office personnel staying in the office, and the officers doing what executives did.

He liked the status quo, which in wartime Quantico was not possible, with outfits shipping in and shipping out weekly.

Sergeant Ellice was promoted to staff sergeant and she was the only one who had access to the Major, going in and out of his office, her steno pad in hand, with an air of officious importance. She always smiled as she came out, closing the door behind her, as if she alone were privy to the top secrets in the Post. She parceled out the duties as she saw fit.

Ellice had filed for an annulment and now she was quite open about her love affairs. Obviously, Slater had no monopoly on her favors. The whole H-barracks became her personal pool from which to draw her conquests. She dated only officers and her braying nasal laugh was heard often.

Supposedly Sherry was secretary to First Lieutenant Slater but, he preferred to consult with Sergeant Ellice at every turn and left Sherry with no work to do. At least, I was able to get away on my runs and cork off at the PX and hitch rides on the jeeps.

The atmosphere at Post Service Battalion had changed completely.

The Marines who came to Quantico returned tattered and torn from the battles that had stretched the First, Second, Third, Fourth and Fifth Marine Divisions from The Solomons to the caves of Peleliu's coral limestone ridges. A few had that *thousand yard stare* and they needed time to adjust to the trauma of their experiences in battles of the Pacific islands.

Many were disillusioned and were anxious to be out of the Corps. They had been inducted, had served and had fought valiantly. They considered their survival a miracle and almost all of them had a fatalistic fear that if they were sent back to combat, they would not return a second time, that their luck had run out. Their main concern was centered around their buddies, the ones that were killed and those left behind.

Any excuse would be fine that would get them mustered out. Many of this new batch of Marines who were billeted to Casual Barracks were posted to the Post Hospital as out-patients. Each day they made the trek to get more atabrine or medicine for what ever had been the reason for their return.

As these combat weary Marines returned from overseas and filled the Post, they carried their own interpretation of *esprit de corps* and had their way of following orders. Nobody messed with them. If their drill formations were not Boot Camp sharp, there was no shavetail officer nor NCO who was dumb enough to discipline them into line.

Often, as I arrived to work, they would be standing in formation outside H-barracks. I would accept their appreciative whistles with a big smile. Once I waved and they all waved back while still in formation. They were *Old Salts*, brave men who had survived the hell of battle in the Pacific and were happy to be alive and able to wave at a pretty girl again.

Sherry's Story

Sherry's distress with her situation increased daily. She pleaded with me to help bring about a change in the office.

"Terry, you have been here the longest. The Major trusts you. You are the one to tell him what Sergeant Ellice is up to. Since The Colonel has gone, she's gotten much worse. Tell him what really is going on. If you let him know he'll believe you. You have got to give him the word."

"How about telling Captain Hamblet, our CO? She's strong and firm. She'll put a halt to these shenanigans on the double!" Lorry said.

Lorry had come into The Lair and it was her suggestion. As usual, I found it not a viable solution. Had she forgotten the incident in Barracks Two? Written complaints had a way of boomeranging.

"Sherry, I don't think petitions work in the Marine Corps. And I don't want to send anything up the chain of command. That's asking for trouble!" I begged off.

Not going to a buddy's rescue when you heard the call "help" was about the worst thing a Marine could do. It wasn't *Semper Fi* and I knew it.

The Women Marines from the other offices in Post Service often came together in the women's lounge, The Lair, that had been given to us by our beloved Colonel. They knew what was going on in our little office and they looked forward to the latest gossip about Sergeant Ellice's most recent peccadillo or conquest and were always appropriately shocked at her newest outrage.

They reinforced Sherry's pleas.

"Something must be done about that ear-banger! Terry is the one who should tell him."

"You've been here the longest, Terry!"

One of the women from the other office named Margaret upheld my reluctance and disagreed with the others.

"If she does tell The Major, the bajahooma will hit the fan!" Margaret said.

"What is bajahooma?"

"It's cow manure!" Margaret came from the dairy state of Wisconsin.

They finally pushed all my buttons, my righteousness, my vanity, my moral outrage and pure hate for the smirk on Ellice's face when my Colonel departed.

I joined the battle to put Sergeant Ellice in her place.

I asked Major Emery for a conference. I did not type up a formal request nor did I send anything up the chain of command. It was all verbal. I just did it with a request for *Permission to Speak.*

The Major opened his door to Sherry and me at the appointed hour for our conference. He sat there in The Colonel's chair, a half-smile on his face with the pipe in his mouth.

Staff Sergeant Ellice Stukey was there also. My heart sank. There was that cold-sore smile on her long face and the tight rolls on top of her head in last year's hair style.

I waited for Sherry to speak. She didn't say a word. She seemed to be hypnotized by the serpentine smile on Sergeant Ellice's face.

"Sir, there is a situation in the office that needs to be corrected." I began.

I waited for Sherry to pick up the rest of my sentence. She said nothing and stared straight ahead, her face as stiff as her back.

"Sir, we have a problem of morale in our office, Sir."

I turned to Sherry who gave me a look of pure distress.

I continued recklessly, "Sir, Ellice, Sir, I mean Sergeant Stukey, Sir, is using her—her—sex to control the office, Sir. It is making it difficult for Sherry and me to continue our duties efficiently, Sir," I continued.

I turned to Sherry since it was her problem as well.

Sherry opened her mouth. For a minute nothing came out. She had become tongue tied and stood there frozen at attention.

I tried to explain. My prepared speech had fled from my memory. I tried to recall exactly what I planned to say. Why didn't I bring my notes? I hadn't expected to be this nervous.

Theresa Karas Yianilos

"She, I mean, Sergeant Ellice, doesn't let Sherry do her work. She, I mean, Sergeant, keeps all the assignments to herself. Uh, uh— she makes a play for all the officers—uh." Our case sounded very weak even to my own ears. I made a very poor lawyer.

The Major puffed on his pipe and regarded me with a penetrating Sphinx like expression. I knew I hadn't gotten through to him.

I suddenly realized I couldn't prove a thing I said. Ellice had dated off the Post and I had never actually seen her do any of the things we had accused her of. So she grabbed all the work. That meant she was diligent and industrious. So she shacked up with officers. If you weren't caught and you didn't do it on the Post, so what!

I was all tangled up in a bowl of spaghetti of accusations.

I turned to Sherry in sheer frustration. What were we complaining about anyway?

I said, "You tell The Major, Sherry, what's going on."

Sherry opened her mouth.

A short croak came out and she said, "I request a transfer, Sir."

The Major smoking his unlit pipe, just listened and watched our faces.

Sergeant Ellice never stopped smiling her tight lip grimace.

"That includes me too, Sir," I blurted out, finding my *Semper Fidelis* at last and shocking myself.

I never intended to say that at all. If this had been a combat situation, I would have been the buddy that went up the hill after my buddy only to get shot and end up just as dead as he. That is exactly what happened to me standing at Sherry's side.

"Not you too, Terry?" The Major's eyebrows went up. He was really surprised and hurt.

So was I. I wanted to retract my statement as soon as I had made it.

I think the same sort of reflex overcame me that triggers off a Marine when he braves a hail of gunfire to rescue a buddy that had been shot. When asked why he went beyond the call of duty, he answers that he couldn't let a buddy down. And he gets a medal.

Major Emery stood up and thanked us in a military fashion. We did an about face and were dismissed.

Staff Sergeant Ellice typed up our transfer orders.

I was replaced by a male Marine, a PFC, who had returned from fighting overseas. I, a WR had been freed by a fighting Marine. The irony of it all was not lost upon both of us.

We reported to our Women's Reserve Commanding Officer. Sherry went to Mess Duty.

I was put on Police Puty, P.D. Police duty had nothing to do with police work. It meant cleaning up, picking up and washing toilets. It was military housework.

Reassignment, Quantico–June, 1944

I, a line warrant corporal, awaited reassignment and returned to filling my time with police duty, guard duty, duty NCO (since I was a corporal) and drilling.

I missed my life at Post Service. I longed to see Colonel Buse again. I missed him fiercely. I missed Sergeant Major Jordan and the men of H-barracks. I ached all over.

I kicked myself over and over for our folly. Sherry and I had accomplished nothing. We ranted and raved over the injustice and the unfairness but there was little comfort in our conversations. We weren't fooling ourselves.

Even the women's compound had major changes in personnel. Familiar faces had departed.

It seemed I was always saying "good-bye" to someone I had learned to care for.

There were so many people I'd never see again; Colonel Buse, Sergeant Queen, Chick, Web, Sergeant Major Jordan, Major Emery, and the Marines of Casual Barracks. I missed my office co-workers in Post Service Battalion and I missed my runs and the people I met on my runs.

I had lost "my family".

Secretly, all by myself, I sat on the *"john"* in the *head* and let the tears flow.

For a week I moped and tried to find a new niche for me in the Corps. There were exciting things to do in Quantico. I simply had to search for them and volunteer.

The Women's Reserve Quantico Trick Drill Platoon marched at the Marine Corps' birthday celebration on November 10, to the applause of many dignitaries who had come from Washington D.C. to watch them. They were admired and so much in demand that I wanted to be part of them. But they had become a tight group with a waiting list as long as a flag pole. Their fame had spread from coast to coast.

I signed up for tennis, horseback riding, bowling and started two classes in the correspondence courses under the Marine Corps Correspondence Institute for college credit. Spero wasn't the only one who could go to college. I could be a Marine and a student.

I tried to join the Women's Reserve Basketball Team. They traveled to other Marine Posts for games. My being so short made their refusal of me a foregone conclusion.

A notice on the bulletin board caused a great commotion. What had been rumor for months had finally become a fact.

Women Marines were going to be sent overseas at last: to Oahu, Hawaii. What had been a sore point between the women's military services for over a year was being corrected. Women Marines were finally going to go overseas just as the WAACS and WAVES were. Not to London or Paris, and certainly not to Europe, but to Hawaii.

I was among the thousands of volunteer Women Marines who wanted to serve in a combat zone although there was little fear or likelihood that the Japs would come back to bomb Pearl Harbor again.

I wanted to be part of the first two detachments of Women Marines going in January 1945 to be sent to Oahu, Hawaii.

Visions of palm trees waving in warm tropical breezes did the hula in my head. But my application was turned down. I had not done myself a favor by resigning my last duty.

The lieutenant in charge was overwhelmed with the response. She explained carefully why she had turned me down.

"Hawaii will not be the glamorous adventurous duty which is what you list as your main reason for volunteering," she said.

"It will be hard work, with more restrictions than you have right here. The living and working conditions may not be good. You will meet men who have been recently in combat. Our greatest need right now is for job categories that will release men for combat, communications, quartermaster, telephone operators, mechanical motor transport and radio operators. We have enough clerical," she explained.

"Do you have any brother killed in action or is a prisoner of war? Do you have any relatives on the fighting front?" She asked each of us who had expressed the desire to go.

My answer was No, no, no. I didn't fit the Corps requirements for duty under the coconuts.

"We will find the right duty for you here in Quantico," she consoled.

She was right. Within days, they did find something for which I was qualified

I cherished the friendship of my bunkies and squadmates in Barrack-A more than ever. Since I had lost my Post Service Battalion family, my need for their camaraderie and good-will had increased. I wasn't too unhappy that I wasn't posted to Hawaii. After all, I had my good bunkmates and mail call was particularly bountiful. I carried Spero's latest five pound box of chocolates to my bunk and a small crowd gathered around me. Although Spero was overseas, he had left instructions with his cousins to make sure I had a regular reminder of his affection.

We had an impromptu scuttlebutt party on my bunk which everyone had to pass since it was next to the door. Sherry, now on mess duty, contributed a cherry pie from the galley which we had to eat without forks.

In the middle of all this frivolity I was summoned by the Duty NCO.

"Don't go away," I said, "It's probably more police duty. I'll be right back. And save some pie for me."

I didn't want to miss a minute of the fun.

My bunkies were still there eating the last of the chocolates when I returned from my interview with the classification officer.

"What is the word, Terry? You've got a gooney bird stare!"

I was trying to understand the full impact of the instructions the duty non-com had relayed to me.

"I've been transferred! To Motor Transport! I have to move my gear tonight to Barracks Three! Right now!"

"You're going to drive a six by six truck? Isn't that what they do at Motor Transport?"

"I can't drive."

"Maybe you are going to be a grease monkey."

"I know nothing about automobiles. I can't tell a Packard from a Ford!"

"We'll bear a hand with the moving."

"The worst part is having to leave all of you."

"Hey, Bunkie, it's not so bad. You are only two barracks away."

Tears brimmed in my eyes. The thought of leaving my buddies, of starting all over again to make new friends and living with strangers after a year of what we had gone through together was so devastating that I flopped on my bunk in utter desolation.

I saw red stain oozing from my chest.

It was the last piece of the cherry pie but it might as well have been my bleeding heart.

Transferred To Motor Transport

Six buddies from Barracks One helped me move into Barracks Three.

The Motor Transport squadroom was empty of women except for two WRs off at one end who had hill-billy music on their radios and another pair standing next to my bunk, one a six-foot woman who was talking to another Marine dressed in heavy dungarees, a sheep-skin jacket from the men's issue, and the usual men's boondocker high top boots. They took one look at us and moved three bunks down and continued their conversation.

Fenton, Sherry, Gerry, Lorry, Lindsey, and Moonbeam tried to be cheerful but their joking only made the separation more painful.

"Write when you get work, Terry."

"Just give us your radio and we'll keep it on your favorite program, ASSEMBLY, and no one will even notice you are gone."

"You're moving away from us so you can eat Spero's chocolates all by yourself."

The jokes fell flat. I looked around me but all the barracks looked alike. The only difference here were the bunks. They were doubled.

I complained, bitched and griped, forgetting that you never said anything in a squadroom you didn't want repeated or you didn't want heard.

"I'm not going to like it here. I just know it. These aren't my kind of girls." I moaned not lowering my voice. My words echoed in the near empty squadroom.

I was so morose that I just lay there staring at the overhead after my bunkies left. I was sleeping topside again. I hated the top bunk. I wasn't even near a window. I wasn't next to the door.

I didn't stow away my gear nor did I arrange my locker. That is how depressed I was. I didn't feel like picking up the threads to knit new friendships, nor took notice that no one greeted me neither.

The squadroom filled up with the women of Motor Transport. I had noticed them in the mess hall at various times so their faces were not unfamiliar. They were always easy to spot as garage mechanics and drivers because of the uniforms they wore—usually dungarees, heavy sheepskin lined men's jackets and clunky men's boondocker boots which laced up to the ankles with several pairs of socks to make them fit better. They had hearty boisterous manners and ate together, drank beer at the Slopschute as one big clan and stuck together.

Seeing them all at once, in one squadroom made a greater impact than they did individually.

They were big women. Well, bigger than our group in Barracks-A. Not that the Corps took really big women. Fat and massive was fine for the men but not the women. Their average dress size was twelve, fourteen, easy...maybe a few were size sixteen. Were big hips a requirement for truck driving? Or was it the baggy heavier fabric of the men's dungarees and belts they wore that made them look bigger?

These Women Marines were the mechanics and drivers of all the tactical vehicles on the Post. They drove the hundreds of men to bivouac early in the mornings and to the rifle ranges for field practice and waited until late in the afternoon to drive the troops back. Their work days were long and hard. Many times they didn't return until the long day had turned into night.

These women were as strong as the men. I was a small short girl who weighed one hundred and eight pounds. What was I doing here? I was Class III 9d and a clerk-typist. That meant *I would be doing a job where a woman was not as good as a man but could be used effectively in wartime.* What could that be? What did I know about trucks and jeeps and tactical vehicles?

There was no other non-commissioned rank in the room, not another corporal nor sergeant. Everyone was a private. That in itself was strange. I had come from a squadroom where everyone had a rating from sergeant to private first class. No one was a buck private there.

I heard someone say, "Lucky you. You've got a corporal for a bunkie."

"She better not try pulling rank on me!" said the tall six-footer. She turned out to be my bunk-mate. I smiled at her but she stuck her head in her locker and never greeted me.

More hillbilly music came on. This was obviously the Grand Old Opry bunch. Two big and burly girls with pajama tops tied across their midriff and their pant legs rolled up above their knees put on roller skates and actually rolled down the aisles between the long rows of bunks with great exuberance. The noise was gross. I couldn't believe my eyes they were allowed to do this.

I went to sleep without brushing my teeth. I just didn't want to confront any of these women in the *head*.

The women of Motor Transport had to stand reveille at 5:15 A.M.

Hearing the bugler blow at that hour was another shock. I was the only one in a squadroom of one hundred and twenty girls who didn't have to report to work until 7:30 A.M. Groggily I stood for roll call. I crawled back into my sack but there was to be no further sleep.

The heavy boondocker boots against the wood decks and the swish swish of the sheep skin jackets the girls wore over their dungarees against the cold of a Virginia dawn made an incredible amount of racket.

They yelled across the bunks to each other.

"Would you rather be a lieutenant or a corporal?"

"Hell! It's the corporal's life for me!"

"I'd rather see one than be one!"

"Buck up! If she bangs the Captain she'll rate her own room!"

"Oh, she'll get more than that!"

There was much raucous laughter.

I knew they were talking about me. I hid under the blanket.

My new bunkie did not say a word to me. She had a pleasant face and I could see she had laugh lines on her face, but she didn't smile at me.

I boarded the women's bus at seven-thirty and was overjoyed to see my old bunkmates from Barracks-A aboard who were going to their administrative posts. Their quiet lady like manner was a contrast to the free-wheeling boisterous almost masculine behavior of my new Motor Transport squadroom mates.

I reread the orders I was carrying that I had to present to my new commanding officer and checked them for the third time. Yes,

I was a line warrant Marine with the same rating as a combat Marine. By the time I walked into Post Garage, the Old Glory was waving brightly inside my heart once more. My Corps and Country called. I was prepared to do my duty.

Post Garage

I squared my shoulders, marched briskly into Post Garage and presented myself and my papers to a First Lieutenant, sounding off in the proper military manner.

He stopped me half way through my speech.

It was only 7:30 (07:30) in the morning, barely light outside, but I'd swear he was three sheets to the wind smelling of stale and freshly poured liquor.

He sat astride a chair and pointed to a door. "Give your report to Captain Bungle there," he said.

Another Woman Reserve sitting on the only other chair in the office, watched me with a glum expression.

I smiled. She didn't smile in return.

I looked around the room. And froze in horror.

There, taking up one wall was the one sight I hoped never to see again.

The *REMINGTON KARDEX FILES SYSTEM* filled the whole end of the room from window to door way. There stood a whole row of the dreaded old familiar metal file cabinets painted in Marine Green.

I could barely choke out the words, "Corporal Terry Karas, reporting for duty, Sir!"

I snapped to the sharpest salute I could muster and stared straight ahead into the Captain's eyes as was military courtesy.

We were almost the same height. He was short, round and old, definitely over forty—maybe forty-five—with thinning hair, old fashioned wire eye-glasses and no neck.

"Welcome aboard!" He said in a gravelly voice filled with cigarette smoke. He shook my hand and held on to it as he asked questions of me. "Can you set up those files out there?"

My heart sank. Those files were for me after all.

"Yes, Sir!" I said as I fought off the irresistible urge to run out the door.

"Depot Philadelphia dumped this whole new system on me and those damn things have been sitting there. You actually know how to handle those files?"

"Yes, Sir! I did this kind of work as a civilian in a defense plant! My job classification was *Remington Kardex Running Inventory Supervisor Clerk.*"

I tried to hide my panic and put more enthusiasm than I felt into my voice. What I wanted to do was make an about-face out of there back to Post Service Battalion and beg for my old job back on bent knees. It was a useless thought. I tried to focus on what the captain was saying.

"You willing to work days and nights to put this together?"

"Aye, Aye, Sir." I looked around but there was no way out of this. I felt the beads of water forming on my temples, felt moisture under my armpits and between my breasts. My new duty assignment was a nasty surprise.

"I am glad they sent you." He shook my hand and held both of them to let me know how grateful he was I had come to him. He put an arm around my shoulder and shepherded me out of his office.

The First Lieutenant burped and the WR turned around and doubled over as if she had a cramp in her stomach when the captain personally escorted me into the office where I was to work.

Neither of them stood up when the Captain spoke to them as the people in my old office had done every time Colonel Buse came into the room.

Captain Bungle said smugly, "We have an expert here. The corporal here is a classified *Running Inventory Supervisor Clerk for the Kardex File System.* Now we will see some action. She's going to square away this fouled up mess. She will keep track of our seventy-seven thousand automotive parts."

He smiled at me again, as if I had just pulled him out of a big hole that he had fallen into.

I stood at attention again and said, "Aye Aye, Sir!"

It was mighty fine that Captain Bungle had taken a personal interest and liking to me but I wish he hadn't bragged like that. It made for hard feelings right off the left foot. Did he say seventy-seven thousand automobile parts?

The sour expression on the WR's face hadn't changed and the lieutenant's bleary eyes glistened as if he had swallowed a bottle of rum with his atabrine and didn't need another thing in life.

I was left alone in the middle of the room to face a whole row of these familiar ugly cabinets, now painted in the same colors as the Marine Corps trucks and buses. In their file drawers were seventy-seven thousand cards, one for each automotive part, each with an item number, the name of the part, and the code number for the bin or section of the warehouse or garage where the item was stored and could be found.

It was up to me to keep track and locate the parts and make sure the bins were filled. If the parts were not where they were supposed to be according to the little cards, it was up to me to write the orders or requisitions and make sure they got filled.

The wheels of Quantico revolved on my shoulders.

These files might as well have been written in Egyptian hiero-glyphics.

I didn't know a screw from a bolt. I didn't know how to drive. I couldn't recognize a Ford from a Chevy from a Hudson or a Studebaker from a Packard. How was I going to recognize the different parts that went into all the military vehicles?

I couldn't even find a chair to sit on. She didn't offer hers.

The other WR did not say a word. Just watched me. She was waiting for me to give an order since I was the corporal and she was a private, waiting for me to pull rank. I wasn't going to do neither.

"I'll need your help," I said.

"Aye, Aye, Corporal," she said using the response reserved for officers only. She was not a Boot so I knew right away her salutation was a sarcastic answer.

"Call me Terry," I said, trying to make sense of this animosity.

"Aye Aye, Corporal. You're the only non-commissioned WR officer in the whole Motor Transport. I'm sure you've earned your rank."

The way she said it was full of more sarcasm. It was as if she said, "You made your bed, now you lie in it."

.   "Is there anyone else in this office to help?"

"No, sir. You're in charge. Ten girls have been transferred when they signed a complaint against the captain. You are the whole squad."

She left the room and walked into the garage to shoot the breeze with a few of the garage mechanics working on jeeps and trucks.

Complaint against the captain? He seemed like such a nice old gentleman. What was that all about?

The captain called me into his office several times. "How are you getting along?"

"Yes, Sir!"

"The men treating you fine? They can be uncooperative and hard nosed."

"Yes, Sir!"

Actually, they were not treating me fine. They were rather strange and unfriendly. They did not return my smiles of friendliness. All day long the men of Motor Transport in their fatigues and boondockers trickled into the office, strolled past the office or lounged in groups outside the office, checking me out. They walked away almost to a man without introducing themselves. Not a single pass was made at me. Not one joke. Oh well! Practically all of them were wearing wedding rings anyhow.

I remembered my first day at H-barracks and the warm welcome I had received. How I missed the joking and affection from the Marines at H-Barracks. Waves of nostalgia for my old job, my old duty, my Post Service Battalion hit me in the pit of my stomach. If my head wasn't in such a revolving spin over the seventy-seven thousand automotive parts I had to memorize, I would have gone to the *head* and thrown up or cried or banged my head against the *bulkhead*.

Instead, I stared at the Remington Kardex files and resisted the strong impulse to grab them and push them over. I kept calm and hoped anyone who observed me saw a military person in command of the situation. I knew every movement was being watched. I went into a little play acting as if I knew what I was doing.

I took a few cards out of their file jackets. I walked into the garage storeroom authoritatively. I ran smack into a jumble of various sizes of bins, open shelves, platforms, large parts of vehicles and broken down vehicles of all kinds of military wheels. The men watched me carefully as I touched an engine here, a bin filled with ugly metal things there.

I retreated quickly back to the office. My first attempt to count the balance of stock had got me nowhere.

"It's going to take me a few days to get used to the way things are done here," I said to Private Olga hoping she hadn't observed my panic. "I hope you will show me the ropes until I can become familiar with automobile parts."

She said with visible hostility. "You're taking over. Let's see how good you are. I don't have to do a damn thing. This is my last day. I've been transferred. To P. I." She let that sink in.

Parris Island. P. I. was an outpost in the boondocks of South Carolina. That was the Siberia of the Marine Corps when compared to Quantico, which was near wonderful liberty cities such as Washington D.C., Fredricksburg, Richmond, New York.

"Did you say ten women have been transferred out of Motor Transport?"

"Don't pretend you didn't know all about it." She said it in a challenging tone as if about to call me a liar. I believe the two stripes on my sleeves kept her civil but no more than the minimum. She refused to talk to me other than in short cryptic sentences. I didn't see her until I took the bus to return to the women's barracks at 3:45 P.M., 1545 Navy time.

The Women Marines of Motor Transport
Women Marines drove buses, trucks, and autos and were capable of repairing all Marine Corps vehicles.

The Women Marines of Motor Transport

Top: The waiting buses to transport WRs to their duty stations.
Center: A Woman Marine bus driver shifts into gear.
Bottom: A heavy engine is tackled with expertise by two WRs.
R. A smiling WR waits for Marines to board her truck.

The next day I was alone in the office, the only Woman Marine assigned to this *Kardex Inventory System.* The captain didn't have a secretary. I was to do all the work, type up the orders and requisitions, find the parts in the garage, count them and post them, check the balances and write any letters he needed. The work load was staggering. Too bad this duty hadn't been assigned to Sergeant Ellice Stukey. She would have loved having a whole office and its CO all to herself. As it was, I hated being alone. I didn't want the full responsibility of keeping the wheels of Motor Transport rolling.

I looked around the office and thought, "Where is everybody? Where is my staff? Where is someone to help me?"

I wandered alone in the Post Garage warehouse to search for the parts again that would keep all the Motor Transport trucks, jeeps and vehicles running. I didn't know the names of anything. I had to learn a completely new automotive language. With a little help from the mechanics, I could probably do it but that help was not forthcoming.

It was my responsibility to order any items that were low in supply and write requisitions slips for the Captain to sign. I ended up talking to myself. How much was low? How much was just right?

Let's see what we've got here. Carburetors. Okay, I found the carburetors. This isn't so bad. The bin was labeled. One part found. Only seventy-six thousand nine-hundred and ninety-nine to go.

Here was a card for two generators. Okay! Two items should be a cinch to find and count. Where were they? What did generators look like? What were they used for?

I asked anybody and everybody in earshot. Nobody answered. No one helped me.

The men, who were all privates and only a few private first class rank, walked away as I approached.

I chased after them and asked as prettily as I could, "Where are bins six, ten and twelve? The bin for *two generators*? Can you point out where I can find *generators*? There should be only two. How small are they?"

They shrugged their shoulders.

"Can you show me some condensers? How about grease seals and cotters? Seen any distributors? A wheel-bearing maybe? Some screws? Nuts? Axles? Spark plugs? *Two Generators?*"

They didn't react. They said nothing as if I had lost my voice and they hadn't heard a thing. They kept on moving away, their backs to me. How could I count something if I couldn't identify it? There were seventy-seven thousand different items I couldn't recognize when I was staring right at them.

"Can anyone show me what a *generator* is? Just point to the bin. I have no idea of what a *generator* looks like! The number is *GE 15*. Has anyone seen bin *GE 15*? Maybe it's section *GE 15*. There's supposed to be *two* of them. *Two generators*. That should be easy to find. You don't have to take me there. Just point," I pleaded.

The men ignored me without even making an attempt to look busy.

Post Garage was not in ship-shape G.I. condition. There were broken down vehicles sitting around. Anyone could see, this Commanding Officer, Captain Bungle, was having great problems in controlling the Battalion. This was not a tight ship, run with a firm hand as Colonel Buse had done. Something was not secured here and greatly amiss.

The men and the Women Marines barely gave him the military courtesies due an officer of his rank. After he issued an order they would make the *V-for-victory* sign behind his back, but the middle finger would stick up higher than the other so it had a different meaning altogether.

My squadmates in Motor Transport barracks treated me with cool disdain as if I were a civilian guest who wore too much make-up and heavy perfume.

I avoided my bunk, returning only after lights out. I spared myself having to hear the constant hillbilly-Grand Old Opry-music that never stopped floating from squadroom, to *head* to lounge.

I dashed over to my old Barracks-A every night and took evening chow with my former bunkies. I waited in the chow line with them and sat with them at their table while my Motor Transport squadmates sat at another table. I hadn't endeared myself to them by showing my preference for my old bunkies. I noticed several of the girls including my six foot bunkmate glanced over at our table several times.

I spent the evening hovering over my old squadroom, sitting on different empty bunks to chat with my old buddies. I usually returned to my own bunk just before lights out.

I continued to write love letters for Moonbeam so she could copy them in her own hand-writing to mail to her Marine beau who was stationed in Washington D.C.

I talked with Fenton when she wasn't at evening Mass and I interrupted Sherry as she wrote letters to her husband in the submarine service.

Gerry was shacking up with her husband at Post Stables where he, as Duty NCO, had his own little room where they enjoyed some privacy which was a rare commodity on this Post.

Even Lorry who had always been available for a few minutes of conversation now that our friendship was on a straight course had a stream of steady beaus and she went to the movies every night. She now barely had time to iron her own uniforms.

I was being worked to a frazzle in a schedule that included having to work late hours at night and on week-ends just to finish up on my posting. Sometimes, I worked alone in the Post Garage office until nine at night to catch up just as I did for Remington.

The mechanics worked in the garage all night long repairing vehicles and the lights were always on. They were friendlier to me at night and occasionally one would poke his head to see if I was okay. I thought that I was making some progress in winning them over until Captain Bungle started to work late too. He'd interrupt me, call me into his office and talk to me which put me behind that much more.

Old roly poly Captain Bungle kept close tabs on me and sprang out of his office almost hourly like the wooden bird in a Black Forest cuckoo clock to ask how I was doing on these nights when we were alone.

"Keep me posted, Corporal Terry, on what you are posting and ordering, " said Captain Bungle chuckling at his own pun. "The Navy scrutinizes and passes or rejects all recommendations. All Marine Corps procurement comes from the Navy. Make sure you tell me what we are ordering. How are you doing?"

"Yes, Sir. Fine, Sir!"

I always stood up with correct military courtesy as I had done for Colonel Buse, but I wasn't fine at all. I didn't know what I was doing yet I wouldn't let anyone in that office or garage know it. I wasn't among friends. I was among the Philistines.

When we were alone, the old Captain would look over my head as I was posting, and rest his arm on my shoulder which reminded me of the foreman with false teeth at Remington back in Tonawanda. It was unpleasant but I figured he didn't mean anything by it. Colonel Buse would never have done anything like that. Captain Bungle was more like an obnoxious relative that you couldn't wait to get away from who pinched you on the cheeks or squeezed you too hard in all the wrong places.

I wandered the garage warehouse like a lost ghost in a haunted castle.

"Can you help me find *GE 15*? It's something called a *generator*. Is it like a carburetor? *GE 15*? *Generator*, anybody?"

I prowled the Post Garage and warehouse searching like Kathy on the Moors for her Heathcliff.

I had managed to recognize a few parts but not *generators*.

The Lieutenant wasn't much help. He rode his chair side-saddle and sang off-key most of the day when he wasn't muttering about getting back into combat. He had been shot up very badly at Tarawa last November. I could tell he was in pain because he kept swigging from a medicine bottle. At 11:00 A. M. he secured for the day, staggering out as soon as he could.

He didn't give a wooden nickel for the requisitions, orders or all the inventory sheets that were piled up in front of his eyes. He was supposed to look my work over and check them off before I took them in to the captain. I would put the papers in front of him and the next day I would take them away and replace them with new orders, knowing full well he had never looked at any of them.

No order left my desk to Marine Corps Supply Depot in Philadelphia without Captain Bungle's signature of approval. All supplies, merchandise and equipment that was shipped to Marine Base Quantico was distributed from Navy because the Marine Corps was part of the Navy.

The Navy was noted for its penury especially where the Corps was concerned.

Every day I was reminded of my job at Remington where I filled orders that had come from Marine Corps Supply Depot in Philadelphia requesting paper goods and aluminum clips. Now I was at the other end, sending those orders.

Back in Tonawanda, I was at the filling end of orders and requisitions. Now, here in Quantico, in the Motor Transport office, I was at the receiving end.

I had made a full circle. I was in the combat zone.

The circle of supply and demand was complete and I found myself serving the Corps at both ends.

Fate had determined my role in this great war. Fate had taken charge of my life. I believed in fate. Oh, yes. Fate was the reason things happened to a person. Everyone's future was written in a big Kardex file in the sky. There was a reason why I was dropped in the middle of Motor Transport in Quantico, Virginia, with a whole wall of Kardex File Cabinets to call my own.

I might as well make the best of it.

I really didn't like going into the warehouse looking for parts. The place smelled of oil and gasoline and diesel. Sometimes I got scratched up if I weren't very careful. I banged my shin several times against this one thousand pound machine sitting on a pallet. I learned to walk around it as I searched and poked around the garage.

I gave the monster a pat, leaned against it gingerly and announced nervously, "Hi, Boys. Here I am again. I'm still looking for those *generators.*"

The men looked up from the engine they were working on and grinned as if I had done something that had amused them. All I had done was sit down on the palette of this huge machine. I hadn't spread my legs apart so what they were grinning at, I didn't know.

"I really need some help here. What's a *generator*? There's supposed to be two of them in bin *GE 15*. I can't find even one. "

I was exhausted with all the expended effort and stretched my arm against the huge machine in a half hearted embrace.

"Is Post Garage out of *generators*?" I asked.

The mechanics let out a roar of laughter as if I had pulled a Bob Hope or Jack Benny and had done something very comical.

At least I had gotten some kind of a response out of them. I stood up, dusted off my uniform skirt, and left in disgust.

It didn't take me long to see that Post Garage Quantico, was as fouled-up as the Remington Paper Box defense factory. The balance on the cards had nothing in common with what was in the stock room. I discovered that no substitution would do. A five/eighths screw would not work instead of one/half, and so on.

The disabled jeeps or trucks would have to sit there until I found the right parts. If it weren't in stock, I had to send a purchase order right away to Supply Depot in Philadelphia.

Sometimes, after looking for an hour, I'd become so frustrated that I'd write up a requisition, and add it to the list for the captain's approval and signature. So what if the stuff turned up later and it meant a double supply? What was a few more nuts and screws in the Marine Corps?

"Look, boys. Just point to what a *generator* is. I can't find either of the two we have listed on the files. I can't even find the bin number! It's *GE 15*. Do I need to order more *generators*?" I asked.

"Why don't you do just that?" they said. They grinned at me and at each other. At last they were a little more friendly.

So that is what I decided to do. Order two more *generators*.

I wrote the requisition for them and put the order with the pile that was waiting for the Captain's signature. In the meantime, if I ever located the first two *generators*, I would add the new ones to the stockroom and Captain Bungle would never know the difference. Motor Transport could probably use four *generators*. What could two more *generators* cost anyhow?

I had gotten away with ordering extras before. Nevertheless, I was nervous when I did something like this because Captain Bungle had been very clear in his instructions.

"Now, spread the orders out. Let's not hit Depot Supply all at once, Corporal Terry. The Navy hates to see us spend government money. I want to see every requisition you write out, personally. I shall go over every item."

He was touchy about the requisitions that went to Depot Supply, Philadelphia, to the point of being sticky picky. At times, I had the feeling he was afraid I would order something that wasn't necessary and he'd be accused of wasting Marine Corps money. I had to write down the description of every little item, some of which we had ordered so often that I had memorized their code numbers.

The stack of orders grew into a little pile and still I was posting and writing furiously. Everyone had secured for the day in Post Garage except me and Captain Bungle. I had been particularly anxious to make that four o'clock WR bus. It was the wrong time of the month for me and my body cried out for a stinging shower, early chow and sleep.

So I did something that I never did. I slacked off. I cheated. I did exactly what the Captain had ordered me never to do.

I did not write down the descriptions of what was being ordered. I wrote down only the code numbers, that was all.

Another clerk at Depot Supply in Philadelphia would have to look them up. I know it was a mean trick but I was just too tired to do it and these orders had to go out today. I was working overtime without extra pay anyway. It's not as if I wasn't doing my duty.

I took in the sheaf of orders on which I had left the spaces blank where the descriptions were supposed to be and placed the pile on his desk. I waited while he glanced through them.

Captain Bungle spotted my omissions right away.

He asked, "What are all these items we are asking Depot Philadelphia to send us? There are no descriptions, Corporal Terry."

I rushed over to his side of the desk flustered at being caught delinquent in my duty so quickly.

"Sorry, Sir," I said. "I took it for granted you knew all these numbers by heart. 463856's are fan belts and 2780X are oil filters and F813 is water proofing compound for amphibs and *GE15* is *Geeeee-*"

But the Captain wasn't paying attention. His nose was on the shelf of my chest right between the crevice of my breasts.

I had leaned over his shoulder to fill in the empty spaces on the forms just as his chair swiveled. His nose and metal glasses hit several buttons on my khaki shirt and I heard something hit the floor. My shirt popped open like a bursting balloon.

I dropped the papers in a jumble on his desk.

A strong whiff of my Blue Bonnet cologne and Capri bath powder wafted out from the warmth of my chest and I hurried to cover myself feeling the blush start up from my neck to my forehead.

My bra straps fell down my shoulders at that moment and the shirt no longer fit across me. The tiny buttons refused to go back into the little button holes. My fingers had frozen in embarrassment. A nervous giggle came out of me.

Captain Bungle watched my struggles with a smile and a sympathetic amused glint in his eyes.

"Uh—do you need any help there?" he offered.

"These buttons are so difficult sometimes!" I held my head down, unable to face him.

He shuffled the papers and signed them without reading them as he eyed my efforts to pull myself together.

"I'm sure your orders are all uh-ship shape!" he said, offering the papers to me without letting go of them, playing a little game of tug-of-war.

I grabbed the papers almost rudely and held them in front of my chest. My shirt was still opened behind them. All I wanted to do was to take the signed orders, be dismissed and get out of there, but Captain Bungle wanted to talk.

"I bet you have lots of boy-friends," he said. "A pretty girl like you. You must have better places to spend your liberty than here at Post Garage with me."

"No, Sir! No one special. I'm still looking."

"I'm looking too. Made two mistakes. But now I'm available."

I didn't have the heart to tell him I hoped I had better luck than he by the time I reached his age. He didn't realize it was too late for him. When a person reached his age and was over forty, he should be having grandchildren, and not still be looking for someone to share his life when it was practically over.

"Sure you don't need help with those buttons?"

"Thank you, Sir. I'm fine." I straightened myself and clutched my papers to my bosom. I didn't trust those stupid buttons.

"What's a beautiful young lady like you doing in the Marine Corps?"

"To free a Marine to fight, Sir! Have you been in it thirty years, Sir?"

I remembered the dedication of my Colonel Buse who was Old Corps and Sergeant Major Jordan who was a China Marine, men who had given their lives to the Corps.

He snorted at my suggestion. "I'm what you call a Volunteer Specialist. They gave me my commission as soon as I joined. I never had to go through OCS or that Boot Camp nonsense. You never get rich in the military. I own my own garage in Fredricksburg, a fleet of trucks and taxi cabs—all running. As soon as this war is over, I'm taking my nuts and going home."

No wonder the Captain had troubles in his Motor Transport battalion. The esprit de corps was lacking in his command.

"Have you ever been to Fredricksburg, Terry? It's only twenty miles from here," he said.

"No, Sir. Virginia is very lovely." I said politely.

Not all my buttons were in place and I needed to get away. The only way I could get comfortable again was to bend over and let my bosoms fall back into the C cups of my bra naturally. I wasn't about to do that in front of the captain but I could not help fidgeting, twisting my shoulder this way and that.

Captain Bungle noted my squirming and offered to ease the situation. He said, "You need a rest. Tell you, what I'll do. Next week-end we'll go down to Fredricksburg and I'll show you my garage. I have some etchings in my apartment you might want to see."

"Yes, Sir!" I said.

He took it as affirmative which was a *snow-job* on my part and as close to *ear-banging* as I'd ever get. I wasn't thrilled at all with the idea of spending a week-end looking at trucks and jeeps in a garage in Fredricksburg. What were etchings?

After that Captain Bungle began to display a special friendliness to me and would stand too close when I gave him orders to sign. I began to feel very uncomfortable and uneasy being with him. The captain had become a little problem.

Each day, he was a little more familiar and called me Terry, instead of Corporal Terry, and several times he slipped and called me "Honey". He mentioned our trip to Fredricksburg several times. I became more and more nervous in his presence although he was about the only one nice to me in Motor Transport Battalion. The more I smiled and tried to hide my nervousness, the more frequently I was called into his office to discuss one or more automotive parts. It had become a round robin. The other Marines could see us talking through the windows of his office. They could see how hard I was working on the crummy files yet no one offered help.

I no longer went around asking the garage mechanics to help me find *generators* or tell me what they were or what they looked like.

"Still looking for those *generators*?" asked one of the Motor Transport mechanics, when I went through the warehouse without my usual solicitation for their help.

Now it was my turn to smile. I had the situation well in hand and the ordered *two new generators* should be on their way to Quantico in a few weeks.

Captain Bungle had signed his name on the requisitions the night my buttons had popped open and I never did have a chance to write down the descriptions. I sent the documents post haste to Supply Depot Philadelphia and felt good about my own initiative.

That week, I even worked harder. I was due for a ten day furlough and I wanted no *Irish pennants* in my files, with all loose ends hanging everywhere. Never had I needed a furlough more.

The men and women Marines at Motor Transport still hadn't taken a liking to me. I didn't hold it against them.

They had formed their own groups and I was a stranger. Even those who were non rated, privates and private first class ranks can be snobbish, clannish, and suspicious of any outsider, especially one with rank. The chain of command had been instilled in all of us very firmly in Boot Camp. To them, I was a corporal. I had rank. They didn't. Rank got more pay. That was probably the real reason for the animosity I always seemed to stir up.

It was the same with the Women Marines. They should have been given better ratings but promotions were dependent upon the commanding officer. Captain Bungle was not like Colonel Buse who was generous with his recognition of good hard work and had shown his appreciation of the dedication of his Women Marines.

The girls of Motor Transport who drove all those huge trucks and transported the battalions of Marines in the early dawn to bivouac in the boondocks for maneuvers worked hard. Many of them could take an engine apart and put it together and had to endure grease on their faces, hands and clothes. They had achieved a camaraderie with the male Marines of Motor Transport and many of them had married their buddies. It was one big family, except they didn't consider the commanding officer, Captain Bungle as the father.

One didn't have to have a high I.Q. to realize that when a commanding officer showed appreciation in tangible form for dedication to duty, respect flowed in two directions between enlisted and officer. The commanding officer set the pace for the morale and esprit de corps his men or women had. It came down to ratings and promotions.

I tried to ignore the brick wall of hostility I found at Barracks Three that I could not break through. Fortunately I had my buddies over at Barracks One with whom I was most comfortable to shoot the breeze with. They were always happy to see me.

Almost all the women in Barracks-One had ratings; morale was high and competition at a minimum. Barracks A was filled with corporals, sergeants and a few staff sergeants. Here, the Women Marines of Barracks-One were part of Company-A and carried classifications as clerks, secretaries, and administrator assistants. They did office work in Post Service Battalion, Equipment Board, Post Headquarters and Post Exchange. The commanders of these battalions were more generous with the promotions than Captain Bungle was to the WR's in his command. And it made a difference. The women in Barracks-A considered themselves to be elite and they carried themselves with a military formality that showed in their stance, their dignity, their walk, weekly drills and performance of duty.

Liberty In Washington D. C. With Blanche

The news from Germany was not good. The Germans had begun a counter offensive.

Letters from Spero had stopped and I feared for him. I was not alone. Anxiety for loved ones overseas across the Atlantic and in the Pacific permeated the women's barracks.

The Army had begun to fight in the Philippines.

Air Force B-29's had bombed Tokyo.

Newspaper headlines alternated between good news and bad news while Bing Crosby's voice singing *WHITE CHRISTMAS* and *I'LL BE HOME FOR CHRISTMAS* floated out of every Wurlitzer juke box and every radio, and every loud speaker, at the PX, the Hostess House and in every shop.

I was the only person in the United States military who did not like those songs.

"I'm dreaming of a White Christmas. Just like the ones I used to know..."

No, I wasn't!

I'll be home for Christmas
You can count on me
Christmas bells and mistletoe
And presents on the tree

I didn't want to go home for Christmas.

I didn't want a White Christmas.

Spero's Christmas present of the year before, his album of *HOLIDAY INN* music could stay in the bottom of my cedar Hope Chest forever. Even if I owned a record player, I wouldn't play it.

I didn't want to see snow again ever in my life. Of course, snow fell in Virginia, but the flurries that floated gently like feathers which melted immediately didn't deserve to be called snow just as the fine misty Southern rain wasn't in the same classification as the mean punishing storms of Western New York.

When I requested a ten day furlough, Captain Bungle assumed I was going home for Christmas.

He hemmed and hawed. "I had planned to show you my etchings in Fredricksburg this week-end, Terry. I hope you change your mind."

"Sorry, Sir. My plans are all made. According to my records, I am due for a furlough."

Captain Bungle could hold up promotions but he couldn't deny a Woman Marine her furlough. The best part of being in the Women's Reserve were the liberties and the furloughs. If a Marine had free time coming, she could take it.

My work was all caught up, all posted and all the orders had been sent to Philadelphia. Motor Transport should be getting those *generators* any day. My duty work was *secured*, and my *hatches were battened down*, as we say in the Navy.

The bus to Washington D.C. broke down. That was such a common occurrence I didn't think of it as an omen, especially since light snow flurries had started up again. You couldn't blame the bus company. Automotive parts to keep buses and autos running were scarce and hard to find. I didn't know how Captain Bungle could keep all his wheels rolling when city and inter-state buses couldn't do it.

There were no new autos nor buses being manufactured during the duration. Detroit had tooled up for war and was going full blast putting wheels under the military. Tanks and military vehicles had priority. Who knew how long we'd have to wait by the side of the road? We prepared for a long stand in the cold.

A taxi cruised by filled with Marines and I accepted the offer to sit on a Marine's lap. I heard a familiar laugh and saw Blanche from my old Company A sitting up front on a Marine's lap also. Her hat was on his head and his hat was on her head.

I was filled with joy at seeing someone from my own old Barracks-One for which I now had so much affection. Everyone had been my friend there. I remembered her gift of bananas.

Blanche and I were now Old Corps bunkmates. Never mind that I had not said more than two words to her all the time I slept six bunks away from her and she had been such a loner that even her own bunkmate hardly knew her. She was now my buddy and we called each other bunkie.

The Marines on whose laps we sat made all kinds of jokes. My seat said, "If I have to carry another *gyrene* this is the way to do it. By the numbers." We laughed at everything that was said.

When the taxi dumped us off without taking us to our designation, you'd think I would have sense enough to recognize the signs of how my liberty was going to go.

The driver was anxious to return and pick up ten more people to put in his six passenger car. He didn't even bother to ask if that was where we wanted to get off.

We were laughing too hard and I was having too much fun to worry about portents.

Blanche pulled out a roll of money which was surprising since as a private first class, she got less than I did as a corporal. I tried to pay my share but she waved my one dollar and fifty cents aside.

We had the same errands to do. So without so many words to that effect, we buddied up for our day in Washington.

We went straight to Jellep's department store at the little WR uniform counter there for our regulation items, pumps, purses and gloves

Washington was worse than Quantico for having officers to salute. Every two seconds my hand went up until finally I was utterly exhausted and would look away or up in the sky when I saw an officer approach to avoid eye contact. Several of them actually turned around and followed us. I had the devil of a time discouraging them. They knew the rules about fraternization. What was wrong with them? Blanche thought I was cute and funny, the way I sent the men adrift. She wasn't the least bit sad when the Smithsonian closed its doors and we didn't get to see the Spirit Of St. Louis which I had raved about.

"I need some spirits myself," Blanche moaned.

My new dress pumps pinched and I was dying to sit but there was no room in the Hotel Statler Bar. Blanche was crushed behind a mixture of uniforms trying to get beverages for both of us. We could have gone to the free Pepsi-Cola Center for the enlisted which was closer but she had insisted on coming to this crowded place.

She returned with two drinks and one drunk.

That was no snap judgment on my part. Anyone who has been to an American Legion picnic can spot an Army man who has had too much to drink.

This Warrant Officer was wearing a tanker's jacket like Patton's with a quartermaster patch on the sleeve.

"Meet an old pal," she said. "Dumplins."

Dumplins couldn't have been a very old friend. He was much younger than Blanche, but he had an arm around her and was giving her a squeeze now and then, here and there.

"He has a suite. He's going to share it." Blanche said, coyly, in a high trilly pitch that was kind of hard on the ears.

"I don't want anything sweet." I had missed noon chow of frankfurters and beans thinking I'd do better in Washington at Chicken In The Rough. My stomach growled from hunger. No one heard it in that noisy bar.

Blanche danced into the elevator. I followed her and Dumplins. Where was she going now?

The door opened to the suite and another Army man stood there, a lieutenant wearing an Eisenhower jacket with a quartermaster patch on it. He was medium height and very unattractive, the runt of the litter that always ends up at the pound. He had Clark Gable's ears, Jimmy Durante's nose and Groucho Marx's leer and he was hanging on to a short squat glass with ice in it. His eyes widened a little when he saw me.

"The Marines have landed," he said stealing the words right out of the mouth of Richard Harding Davis who said it first at Panama City after the Marines scared off the Colombian rebels.

"We're not a Marine Brigade. Just two WR's," I said.

"Willie, meet Terry."

We, Marines, don't salute indoors but I knew Army regulations required it. I snapped to attention and brought my right hand up to my forehead in a snappy salute.

His eyes slithered up and down me and through me as if I were standing there stark naked, completely out of uniform.

Theresa Karas Yianilos

I held my salute, waited for him to return my military courtesy before I made an about face and a retreat out of there on the double.

He planted a wet whiskey kiss on me which landed on my hand as I was removing it from my forehead. My little finger went directly into his left eye and jabbed it hard. "I'm so sorry," I started to apologize.

"What the hell! A shrimp like you can't hurt me. Eyes as big as a cow and stacked like pancakes." He rubbed his eye.

My stomach heard the words 'shrimp and a stack of pancakes' and growled with hunger. This time I blushed.

Willie put his arm around me and still rubbing his eye said, "What's a cute little trick like you doing in a chicken-shit outfit like the Marines?"

I didn't think him witty. Marines never cussed nor used obscenities nor any such salty sea-going language in front of us Women Marines. Sure, some of the Women Marines were salty in the barracks but not in front of the men. We respected our male counterparts and they gave us the same courtesy. Besides, Commandant Archibald Henderson had outlawed swearing in the Corps way back in 1836, that is the kind of men we had in the Corps.

I began to have a clear understanding of why the Marines did not get along with the Army.

Frankly, Blanche had me kind of worried. For an older woman who supposed to be experienced with men, if what Gerry said was true, she seemed to be unaware that these two Army dog-faces were not of the highest caliber. No wonder she wasn't married at thirty-whatever odd years she was if she wasted her time with men who were not looking for wives.

I tried to catch her attention but she had headed straight for the bar that was set up in the suite and was busy mixing her fourth drink.

So this was what is called 'a suite'— a hotel room with two rooms— one that had a bed in it and one that had a bar and a couch that opened up into a bed!

I did not like the lay of the land one bit.

I made a grab for Blanche's arm and the expression on my face should have let her know that I was anxious to leave right there and then. Willie didn't appeal to me one bit. I didn't want to waste one more minute of my furlough here in this suite.

She ignored my facial Morse Code and semaphores.

"Blanche, drinking without eating is bad for you. It will make a hole in your stomach. Let's go out to eat," I suggested.

She waved her little fingers at me and wiggled her body into the bedroom and left me standing there alone with Groucho.

I really didn't worry about Blanche. I knew she wore this black corset which was a great Maginot Line. It would take a blitzkrieg to by-pass that gear. She wouldn't need any hat pins to ward off groping male hands. That was a trick we had been told that some of the Women Marines in Camp Pendleton and Parris Island used when they were crowded like cattle with the men in the make-shift buses of four by four trucks that took them into town for liberty.

The smoke from Dumplins' forgotten cigar in the ashtray was making me sick to my stomach, although moving from chair to chair and to the bar to avoid the octopus tentacles of Willie was helping the air movement in the room.

Everything I said amused Willie. Even drinking my Coca-Cola from a bottle. I hadn't forgotten Henry's advice about the *Spanish Fly*.

The lieutenant lunged at me again as I offered him some more ice for his drink. His arms went around the frosted bucket hard and the ice cubes bounced out of it over his chest.

I passed the bedroom door and called out to Blanche, "Lieutenant Willie and I are going out for some chow."

He had said no such thing but I was hungry and let him know it. I took his arm and I slid mine in the crook of his elbow in the proper way of an escorted lady.

He was so happy he finally got a hold of me, he hollered at our buddies, "The Marinette is right. We eat first."

I winced. He didn't even have our name right. Or the right war. That was what the three hundred and five women who served in the Marine Corps 1918 were called, not us. "We are Marines. Just plain Marines," I said.

"Nothing plain about you broads," he flattered.

Free as he was with his compliments, I knew this officer was not going to have any part of my future. What a wasted liberty this was turning out to be. I was caught in a hotel room with two soldiers. My God! How stupid could I get? Blanche and I had to get out of this situation fast.

Just then, Blanche and Dumplins came out of the room grinning. She seemed to be so thrilled over him. He had Montezuma Red lipstick over his forehead. Some women were so easily pleased.

I remembered another one of Mama's warnings that if I continued to be so picky I would have the same fate that had overtaken a neighbor's twenty- five year old daughter.

"Oh, she had her chances but 'one smelled and the other stank to her'. So now she is an old maid. That's what happens when a girl is too particular." It seemed that twenty-five was the cut off point for being left on the shelf. There were few takers after that.

These two Army men were stinkers and really smelled and they needed to be thrown back into the sea. Blanche wasn't about to throw her fish back in the sea.

Willie hung on to me as he hailed a cab which was about to drive away. A light mist had begun to fall and Bing Crosby's voice singing WHITE CHRISTMAS followed us out from beyond the lobby.

I tried to pull Blanche aside to tell her that if we didn't throw these two sad sacks overboard I would take the last train back to Quantico alone but she had plopped herself in the cab, bubbling all over young Dumplins.

The nippy air of Washington felt wonderfully refreshing, carbonating me so much, charging me full of pep, that I began to bubble a little too. The situation seemed to be less menacing down in the lobby filled with people than alone in that suite.

Two other people were in the cab already, a man with a large white hat, the kind Senator Truman had and an elegantly dressed woman in an evening gown.

The cab driver told them, "You have to share. There's a war on."

"We don't mind," the couple said.

Blanche and Dumplins squeezed in next to the driver. It was one of those larger automobiles with two seats that folded down in the middle. Willie sat on one. He had stopped laughing.

I sat facing the charming woman in her magnificent ball gown with the diagonal ribbon across her chest.

"You are so beautiful. Are you royalty or dignitaries?" I couldn't help being impressed.

"Yes, my dear. I'm the chairman of the ball in honor of the State of Oklahoma being held at the Hotel Washington. You are welcome to come." She smiled at me and ignored Willie.

The cab dropped off the beautiful people at Hotel Washington first. It was quite swank with a doorman that opened car doors and had a carpet that extended beyond the front doors into the street. It looked so inviting. I knew I'd rather be going there than any place else and had an irresistible impulse to jump out.

Instead we went to a Chinese restaurant that was fancier than the one my classmate, Jennie Lee Chang's father owned on Young Street in Tonawanda, where she had to help wait on tables after school. But the food was almost the same. The room was dim and dark with lanterns. It had red walls and shiny black lacquered chairs with gold upholstery and the menu was on cards instead of a blackboard. Many people were eating there in chairs and tables but we were led to some private rooms with booths that forced me to sit closer to Willie.

"The prices are higher here," I observed.

"Nothing's too good for the United States Marines." He turned to the Chinese boy. "Bring some good red wine too. No weak tea. Chop. Chop."

"Our Dragon Well no longer comes with the Family Dinner #8 unless specially ordered. It's five dollars a pot," said our Chinese waiter in excellent English. "There is very little of it left."

"Bring the tea too," Willie said.

He turned to me and boasted. "That Chink thought he had me. I didn't get this commission for taking any crap from anybody. I'm Quartermaster. Best spot to be in. We get everything first. That's how I got this Eisenhower jacket." He nudged me again.

Dumplins pinched me between the Egg Roll and Barbecued Ribs and said to Blanche, "Aw, Blanche you don't mind?"

Why he needed her permission to pinch me didn't make sense.

I scolded, "Dumplins, Sir. You can pinch Blanche and she can't feel it. But I'm not wearing anything to keep you from coming through."

Blanche thought that was so funny she choked on her wine and a spray of red spittle hit him in the face.

Lieutenant Willie put his lips next to my ear and said, "How about sharing what you got with me, Baby Marine?"

So I did. I popped a piece of my seven spices pork covered with a big glob of delicious authentic hot Chinese mustard sauce right into his mouth. It slid down his gullet before he realized what it was. Willie's Adam's apple bobbed up and down, stayed in one spot for a moment and slowly receded like that of a boa constrictor eating its monthly meal.

His friend laughed heartily at his buddy's discomfort and made no effort to hand him a glass of water. No esprit among the Army men, that was plain to see.

I hit him on the back and hurriedly poured some tea for him quickly.

He gulped it down. Unfortunately, I hadn't noticed the steam from the spout and his eyes began to bulge as his face turned purple pink and he got a coughing spell.

Finally, Dumplins offered a helping hand. "I can take care of your piece if you aren't up to it, ole buddy."

Willie made a grab for him but Blanche had chosen that same moment to jump up, upset with Dumplins' attention to me. Her tall wine glass which she had just refilled with more red wine tumbled right on to Dumplins' trousers and all over her skirt.

I took her arm and rushed her to the toilet. "Don't worry. It's only grape juice. You've just got to get some cool water on your stains right away."

I knew all about wine stains. Mother always served home made wine at the table, all through the Depression. Dad had a friend who made his own muscatel in his cellar and kept our family well supplied because he had always been grateful to Dad for lending him his rowboat during Prohibition to make trips across the Niagara River to Canada.

Obviously Blanche was not used to mixing wine with tea and whiskey. She staggered a bit and bumped into the wall as she walked to the ladies room.

"Take off your skirt. I'll fix it." I stretched her skirt over the basin and turned on the water tap. Hot water steamed out all over her wool skirt.

"You're a sweet kid," she said, only too happy to sit on the toilet seat.

The thoughts in my head weren't sweet. I was thinking of going over the hill, ducking out the back door and shoving off without her, but that wouldn't have been the Corps way. It wasn't *Semper Fi*. Besides, the last train to Quantico was probably gone.

Lieutenant Willie had quieted down when I returned alone. He was watching Dumplins wipe the spray of stain off his trousers. The green color of the embroidered round Chinese figures spelling out 'Good Luck' was not color fast and it had left streaks on his light tan pants.

My appetite hadn't been touched at all, so I sat down to finish the sweet and sour pork and Chinese vegetables which were delicious with scallions, mushrooms, water chestnuts and chili oil.

"Where's Blanche? Willie popped some pills in his mouth. "Sonafabitch mustard," he muttered.

"Out of uniform. She'll be here." I helped myself to the remainder of the egg rolls.

I could tell Dumplins was feeling a little better because he was playing footsies under the table. He leaned across and picked up my hand—the one without the chopsticks.

"If you're not going to be able to handle your gal, I'll be glad to, ole' buddy," he said.

"To hell with you. You got the other broad." Willie tried to put his arm around me, but I reached across the table for more food.

Blanche returned, with a partially wet shirt and skirt which seemed to have shrunk a little. A few of her hair-pins had fallen out of her bun making her dyed black hair droop.

She should cut it to Marine Corps regulations and then she wouldn't have all those demerits for having her hair touch her collar.

Dumplins moved over rather than stand up to let her in the booth.

"Blanche, let's cast off. This is no place for us." I whispered to her. "We can go over to Henderson Hall and bunk at the WR barracks there. There are always empty bunks."

"You are abshoulutely right, bunkie," she said. "Let's go to Lanie's. I used to work with her in the Windy City. We can shack up at her place."

Rooms were impossible to get. How fortunate that Blanche had a friend in Washington D.C.

"What did you do there?" Blanche never told on herself, not like the other girls did. This is the first I knew she came from Chicago.

"I waited on men."

So Blanche had been a waitress. I had been one too when I worked at the Sugar Bowl to help out Spero's aunt and uncle on week-ends when their waitresses all quit and went to work in defense plants. But this was no time to play 'Where's your home-town" geography. It really was time to roll Blanche into the sack.

I had hoped we could scuttle these sad sacks, these doggies, but Blanche was as much of a problem as they were. She had loose lips and didn't know how to keep her mouth shut. There was no way to abandon this ship.

"Lanie's place is great," they said to Blanche's invitation.

I no longer wondered about the reasons there was strict enforcement of the non-fraternization rules. Some officers simply weren't gentlemen and were only too ready to take advantage of an unprotected enlisted girl.

The cab drove to the heart of the entertainment district of Washington D.C. Washington was wide awake.

A light chilly drizzle fell. Many lonely soldiers, sailors and Marines milled about by themselves, although plenty of girls were walking the streets.

The marquees of movie houses, penny arcades and tattoo parlors still had their lights flashing at this hour despite the partial blackout. I had never been in this part of Washington D.C. A few shops had jewelry stores and pawn shops with iron gates across them. The smell of hot dogs, hamburgers, frying onions from all the snack canteens and bars, one after the other, left a tantalizing appetizing taste in the mouth. I could go for a hamburger with onions. You know how Chinese food is—one hour later, you're hungry again.

We stood in front of a small bar. It seemed closed because it had blackout curtains draped across. At least, Lanie was patriotic and obeyed the laws. An artist had painted swaying palm trees and hula girls in grass skirts which filled the window with the bright poster paint colors of a tropical sunset.

Blanche was impressed. "Lanie's doing great. She's got her own place now. She was always lucky. Her Johns always gave her big bucks."

Lanie was certainly surprised. Lanie was a much older version of Blanche. She broke into a whooping guffaw at Blanche's uniform and laughed until tears rolled off her cheeks splashing big drops of wet spots on her black beaded green satin bodice. "You! A Lady Marine! How did that happen?"

Blanche and Lanie then went into a patty-cake routine and broke into a duet simultaneously in high pitched voices:

Oh, the doors swing in and the doors swing out
The men fall in and the men fall out
Oh, how the money rolls in
And the money falls out

I looked around in the dim red light of the bar. A mirrored ball twirled around tossing quick flashes of light into the corners.

The place was filled with uniformed men and females in clinging and revealing rayon cocktail dresses who went from table to table. Everybody seemed to know everybody else and there was a lot of hugging, kissing and touching between these old friends.

The light picked out a Marine sitting in a corner alone at a table with four chairs. His back was to the wall and his arms straddled two chairs.

Lanie put a motherly arm around me. Willie picked her arm off and put his proprietary arm around me instead. I wiggled away from both of them.

We sat at silly little tables on rickety chairs that balanced precariously. Willie kept his hand on mine. I held on to his other one. That way it stayed in one place.

A few Petty Officers and sailors were grouped around two tables and the revolving red light changed their whites into pinks. They must have come from southern latitudes. We weren't scheduled to go into summer uniforms for some time.

A Marine and a girl came downstairs and separated, she to the bar and he joined the lonely Marine who had been waiting for him in the corner.

Lanie returned with a tray of glasses and a bottle.

"I've been saving this Johnny Walker special," she said and collected a fifty dollar bill from Dumplins.

A Marine passed our table and the revolving bits of mirror caught the reflected light of a lieutenant's bar on his rumpled khaki shirt collar.

Lanie's hand delayed him. "Slushee, remember Blanche? From Chi?"

Lanie introduced him to us. "Slushee celebrated the *red lead* on his britches when he made corporal with me. Broke the place apart. Now he's celebrating with me again. He's a battle field *Mustang*."

The Marine squinted his bloodshot eyes, probably from combat fatigue and focused on me. He steadied himself on my shoulder.

"You're the prettiest *BAM* I've seen!"

Willie didn't like that one bit.

"Get your webbed palms off my *BAM! You Island Commando!*"

Friends of Blanche or not. I had enough. I stood up.

"I'm not your *BAM!* I'm a United States Marine!"

My flimsy chair cluttered to the floor loudly as if it had been thrown.

Willie rose from his chair probably to pick it up.

Theresa Karas Yianilos

The combat Marine said, "No chicken-shit Dogface is going call a Lady Marine a *BAM!* You apologize and show respect to the Marine Corps."

The soldiers, sailors and Petty Officers at the next tables stood up.

Who threw the first punch, I don't really know.

Suddenly the chairs started flying. Lanie's precious bottle of whiskey went sailing through the blackout curtains and the palm trees came crashing down, coconuts and all.

The Marine ducked and sent Willie flying over his shoulder in a judo twist.

Willie landed under the twirling mirrored ball.

Someone yelled, "This way Marines!"

A couple of males dashed in as a few females ran out the door.

Blanche gathered our hats and new purses and pulled me towards the ladies room.

"Move it! On the double. If the MP's find us, it's the brig and bread and water for thirty days." She had sobered up very fast.

"Oh, no, that's not true. WRs don't get brig. If we explain-"

"*Knock it off,*" she ordered and shoved me up and through the small bathroom window above the toilet and didn't let me finish.

PART FIVE

City Of Love–Washington D.C.–December 1944

The window was several feet above the asphalt pavement and my toes reached for the ground frantically. My stomach had balanced as a fulcrum on the window sill and I was frightened. I hated high places. Blanche gave me a shove and I felt two arms catch me as I fell. I landed hard on wet concrete but the strong hold kept me from sprawling all over the pavement and I was grateful. I could not see the man who had come to my rescue too clearly.

The alley was dark. The lights flickered from the kitchen of another cafe on one side and from dimly lit rooms that had unmade beds in them. Weird shadows had formed on the buildings that filled the narrow alley.

I hesitated and waited to see if Blanche made it through the window behind me. Just then the urgent whistles of the MPs came piercing through the air.

He grabbed my hand and pulled me along with him. I went flying down the alley. I hung on tight and had to run to keep up with his long quick steps. Out on 9th Street we slowed down to a walk, still holding hands, while MPs jumped out of a jeep and sprinted into Lanie's bar.

I looked up to thank him and froze at the sight of the railroad tracks on his shoulders. A Marine Captain. Oh! God! Not another officer and gentleman!

I let go of his hand and saluted nervously.

He grabbed my hand, almost as tightly as before. "Don't do that!" He said it sharply, with irritation in his voice.

"No, Sir," I said angrily. Angry at myself for getting so fouled-up and at finding myself in such dangerous situations. I could have been in serious trouble with those dogface soldiers. I instinctively recognized they weren't respectful, that they were a different breed of men and wouldn't be considerate of a woman's wishes.

They weren't safe like Spero where we could laugh about being in one bed. Being in a hotel room with a couple of soldiers meant one thing and I knew I had a close call there. Thank God! I was out of that danger.

As I peeked at those Captain's bars, I knew things had gone from bad to worse. I could lose my corporal stripes if I kept this up, being with another officer and a Marine at that. What if an MP came by? And where was I going to sleep tonight? How stupid of me. I was breaking every regulation in the book. Out of the frying pan into the fire.

He said, "Now, what are you doing?"

I had dashed quickly around his back to the street side of the sidewalk.

"I'm walking on your left, Sir. In case an MP comes by," I said, reminding him of the rule that a subordinate always walks on the left side of an officer.

"I see. You don't have to worry about any Army MP or Navy Shore Patrol. You are with me."

He replaced his arm around my waist. He had noticed I was still shaky from the fall.

"What the hell were you doing in Lanie's Puka Bar?"

Now I remembered him. He had been sitting in the corner by himself.

"My squadroom bunkmate knows Lanie from a place called the Tenderloin in Chi and thought we might bunk with her."

He peered into my face and said, "How long have you known this bunkmate?"

"I am not showing her much *Semper Fidelis* leaving her back there alone, *shoving off* without making sure she was *secured*,'" I said.

"This is the *Semper Fi* thing to do in this case, Mac." He had smiled just like Colonel Buse did when I had used Marine Corps language. "Sometimes the better part of valor is to *pull up the ladder* after you. Slusher thinks a good *wetting down* always ends up with breaking up the place."

Was he laughing at me? I looked at him again, this time more boldly.

Then he chuckled and said, "We heard all about you Women Marines coming in when I was in the Pacific. Now I've got one all to myself. If this isn't a piece of luck."

I wasn't sure what he meant by that statement. He smiled when he said it which made the lines in his face disappear but he still looked older than what I pegged his age to be, twenty-eight, perhaps.

We passed a movie house. The pictures on the side walls were bare-breasted women being threatened by villainous Nazi and buck-toothed Japanese soldiers.

I averted my eyes and tried to think of something to say. The silence was embarrassing. I guess I'd have to tell him my name and station. He must have had the same thought.

"I'm Walker. John. John Walker," he said.

At first I thought my ears had played tricks on me.

"Walking John? The Marine in the recruiting poster?" I asked in disbelief, stunned at the fateful coincidence. He was handsome enough to be that poster Marine.

"That's who I am. Walking John. You got that right. And I've come straight out of the jungle to rescue you," he said playfully.

I didn't believe him for a minute but his sense of humor was infectious and his joking introduction amusing.

"I'm Lady Jane Greystoke," I said and entered the game with relish. My captain looked a little like Buster Crabbe who had replaced Johnny Weismuller in the new and latest Tarzan of the Apes movie, *Son Of Tarzan.*

"What tree did you fall out of, Jane?" he asked with exaggerated gallantry.

He was quick. He had caught my literary reference. This was fun. Much better than those stupid old Knock-Knock jokes.

"Henderson Hall, Arlington Annex." I lied. I just didn't want the game to end and to spoil the flirtation. To tell him I worked in Motor Transport and had lost a warehouse of automotive parts and generators and furthermore I had been replaced by a combat marine, would make me sound stupid.

A subtle spark had sizzled between us and it lay there as fragile as the fire that was made from two sticks being rubbed together.

His bars had intimidated me at first which had made me forget my manners. Belatedly I said, "How can I thank you, for rescuing me? High places scare me."

"I'm happy I was able to help you pull the cord and parachute out of Lanie's," he said with a mischievous grin on his face that made him look adorable and younger. I could tell I had intrigued him and had stirred his interest. It made me bold enough to ask him a question.

"Are you stationed in Washington?"

"Not exactly. I'm on temporary assignment. The paratroops are all Marine Infantry now." There was a touch of irony in his voice and I didn't understand what he meant but it was obvious that was all the information he was going to give me.

He was one of those Marines who was either going or coming. He was also one of those Marines who didn't want to talk about his battles.

He did not want to explain the *fruit salad* on his chest which had a few ribbons I didn't recognize immediately. Most Marines that I had asked enjoyed boasting about them. Nor did he talk about his campaigns as most of the Marines liked to do who had returned from combat. He didn't even mention his home town. I didn't mention mine. No geography patty-cake conversation was necessary. We said nothing more.

I glanced sideways at him to make a closer appraisal and I caught him doing the same to me. We looked away at the same time. There was that sizzle again.

His face had a serious sad expression all the time, yet I could tell he laughed a lot. If he were a dog, he'd be a Labrador. Still, those weren't laugh lines on his face. His complexion was ruddy yet there was a yellow cast. Could be the yellow lights. Or malaria. Practically all returning Marines had malaria. Dengue fever or fungus. Or filariasis. I peeked. No! He didn't have that. He looked rugged and right. There was nothing wrong with him.

He dropped his arm from my waist. I found myself wishing he hadn't. Also wishing I hadn't lied. I wondered how I could gracefully retract my statements without sounding like the liar I was. I framed words in my head but didn't say them. *How should I say it. Ha! Ha! My name is Terry and I'm a clerk at Motor...no, that sounds like a jerk. I'm not really Jane Greystoke who was Mrs. Tarzan! Was she really his wife...no, that doesn't sound right...where would Tarzan and Jane find a minister in the jungle? How do I get out of this...oh, nuts, I'll just keep playing. I probably will never see him after tonight. He's an officer, for God's sake!*

I didn't realize I held my hat in my hand until I felt the ripple of his hand through my hair.

He apologized. "I couldn't resist it."

His arm went around me and one hand held mine. I squeezed back. It felt wonderful and secure.

An Army MP walked by conspicuous in white helmet, white belt, gun in holster, club in hand.

I froze.

"Put your hat on, Marine Corporal," the MP said.

I did as I had been told immediately.

He saluted the captain. I watched the MP stroll by us with no further admonitions.

Was that it?

I didn't dare turn around to check if he were actually walking away from us without further arrest. Army MPs loved reading off Marines every chance they got. Even the Navy SPs, the Shore Patrol, loved to slap the Marines they caught breaking the smallest rules in the brig. The Army and the Navy had cross-jurisdiction over the Marines and both services had the authority to arrest Marine personnel. They often did it with great gusto.

I had heard that the rules of fraternization were ignored or just weren't enforced in Washington D. C. I knew this was where many of the WR's who dated officers met in the week-ends. I had never heard of a Woman Marine being picked up for walking with an officer here.

In Quantico, if caught holding hands with a Marine, General Torrey would personally see to it that a deck court would be recorded in his SRO and *office hours* would go to the woman.

The general was notorious for patrolling the street and beating the boondocks for just such fraternization.

So my being jumpy and cautious was understandable.

The captain said, "Let's get off this crummy street."

I obeyed his command with relief.

A street car clanged to a stop at the corner. He made a dash and propelled me on to it, his arm once again around my waist to steady me as he dropped the money in the slot. He didn't ask me whether I had wanted to go along.

He finally spoke.

"I'm staying at the Hotel Washington. Anywhere you'd like to go?"

I remembered the elegant couple who were on their way to the Oklahoma State Ball at the Hotel Washington. The lady in the beautiful ball gown had given me an invitation and I had just enough time to spend an hour at the ball. If I left before midnight, I could make the last train back to Quantico. Meeting the captain was fate.

"If it doesn't take too long, I'd love to go to your hotel with you," I said eagerly.

He didn't say anything for a long minute. Then I felt the pressure increase around my waist. "If that's the way you want it, Little Lady," he said.

"Oh yes! I have an invitation to—"

"You sure do! This is my lucky night!"

I thought so too. Even though I had lost Blanche, I hadn't been picked up by the MPs and I had found this captain who could take me into the Hotel Washington to that ball I ached to attend.

"There's an Oklahoma State dance there and I know the chairman and—."

He shrugged. "Why not? We can find time for that as well. The night is young," he said.

"Do you dance?" Of course, he must. I felt silly asking what was obvious of someone who looked so compact and had jumped onto the street-car with such agility.

"I'm a real Fred Astaire. I've got rhythm!" he boasted. "You got rhythm?"

"I'm a Ginger Rogers," I said happliy.

I had found a dancing man.

I changed sides again and put my arm through his. This time I walked on the proper side where a lady should walk, away from the street, and strolled on the carpet into the lobby.

Navy officers were standing in the lobby, deep in conversation. They were absolutely the most magnificent sight I had ever seen—all dressed in white short-waist jackets, gold cummerbunds and black shoulder boards with stripes of gold braid everywhere, on the sleeves, the shoulders, the hats. I was completely awed by their splendor. Their women companions came out of the Powder Room, and they all walked away, the men following behind the women, still talking to each other.

My Captain's manner became more formal. He no longer held my hand and his long legs carried him six steps ahead of me.

"I didn't realize Navy men could be so magnificent," I said, catching up to him after they had gone down the hallway.

"Haven't you ever seen a Marine officer in his Mess Dress with his scarlet cummerbund and Mameluke sword? Now that is something to see!"

I closed my eyes for a second. Yes! I could see him in his whites. He'd look downright dazzling, gorgeous. "Mameluke sword? No. I have never seen one. Do you use it in combat?"

I remembered the bayonet demonstrations of Boot Camp and shuddered at the thought of my Captain in hand to hand combat with a Jap.

"It's a Marine tradition. We wear them when surrendering to an enemy—or a woman. It's used to cut the wedding cake. A few Marine officers have contributed their swords to the scrap metal drive that Navy ordered a couple of years ago but I'm saving mine."

I was so relieved to hear that. "You haven't cut a wedding cake with yours yet?" I asked. I bet he could have any girl he wanted. "You must have an island full of girl friends."

He wasn't fooled by my question for a minute. "My men say the native gooks got whiter each day but I didn't see any beautiful enough on New Britain to qualify for my harem."

Marines called the natives "gooks" and "fuzzies wuzzies". I had heard some of the men boasting about the cordiality and hospitality of the native women especially in Samoa. I was so happy my Captain *(there I said it again)* had been made of sterner character, I practically melted in his arms right there.

He ruffled my short feather hair-cut with his large hand unconsciously. A tingle went through me like the whistle being piped for an admiral aboard ship.

The ballroom where the Oklahoma dance was being held was very large, very grand and very crowded. Women in evening gowns and men in dignified business suits with string ties or in uniforms were dancing and mingling, creating a rainbow collage of humanity that filled the room to bursting.

Music from the orchestra reverberated into the foyer.

The committee-person at a ticket table wouldn't accept the Captain's money.

"We are delighted to have our fighting men and women here to honor our fine State of Oklahoma. We are so pleased to have a Woman Marine."

"You are a bargain. You are cheap at half the price," he said amused at the look of admiration I had received. "I'm going to hang on to you. How do you feel about that?"

I loved the idea. I loved hearing it. I loved his saying it. How had he guessed I would say "yes" so fast?

My friends from the taxi cab were in the receiving line at the door. She recognized me immediately and appraised my new escort. Her face crinkled in an approving welcoming smile which really pleased me. We chatted for a few seconds.

I took one step forward and Captain John Walker grabbed me and kissed me, right there in front of the whole committee, catching me by surprise. People around us laughed in unison pleased with his gesture.

Over my head was a bunch of mistletoe. The whole ballroom was completely covered with Oklahoma's State flower.

I kissed him back very hard. I wanted more. His kiss was different and thrilling; his lips sure and strong that spoke of experience and knowledge. What a difference to the boys from back home, who pressed lips and thought that was all there was to it.

He knew how to do it right. A sizzle went straight up from my ankles to the top of my head. It was better than having a foot massage.

Now I was the one that felt I didn't know how to kiss.

He gave me a strange surprised look and there was a glint in his eyes.

The music was playing and we glided on the floor. I was in his arms swaying to Glenn Miller's *Moonlight Serenade.* I closed my eyes and floated away in this new emotion I had never experienced before. It lasted about three minutes, long enough to imprint into my mind, the feel, warmth and emanation of his body.

Suddenly he was gone from me, torn away from me by a dancing line of Oklahoma natives. My Captain John Walker was on the other side of the room in a serpentine dancing line. He was a good dancer and he wasn't dancing with me.

An announcer broke into the music and started calling all kinds of dosie-do-grab-your-partner instructions. A hand latched on to me and I was yanked into another line of people all holding hands in Ring-a-round-a-rosie which broke off into couples almost immediately.

"May I have this dance, little Lady?" I went whirling off with a man who was wearing one of the string ties.

"Ahm aide to the Gov'ner," he said by way of introduction. "What paht of Oklahoma are yoh from?" He asked.

I said truthfully, "No part."

"Bes' paht of the state." He wasn't paying the least bit of attention to my reply. His head swiveled while he danced as he greeted constituents. My eyes twirled around looking past him searching for my captain. *My Captain. Where had that phrase come from?*

I finally caught a glimpse of him waltzing by with a very pretty girl in an apricot strapless gown with a necklace around her neck and the mounds of her breasts showing. He was looking down at her and her animated face was turned up toward him.

The wool fabric of my Marine green uniform suddenly felt sticky, and woolly and my tie around my neck seemed too tight. My brown new pumps looked clunky. My khaki shirt and uniform blouse hid the truth of me. I could have really done justice to that strapless gown if I were in it. Pangs of jealousy jabbed at me. I regretted ever suggesting this dance.

The minute the music stopped I was surrounded by a group of middle aged people who asked me all sorts of friendly questions. The people of Oklahoma were so hospitable. "We don't see many Woman Marines. We are so thrilled you came to our dance." "How brave of you, my dear—to free a Marine." "What paht of Oklahoma are you all from?"

Through a corridor between the bodies, I could see my Captain getting the same treatment from the beautiful butterflies in colorful net dresses. Every time he started to walk across the room towards me, the caller would announce another of those get-acquainted dances where the girls are in a circle and the men are in another circle facing them and when the music stops you have to dance with whoever lands in front of you. My Captain ended up on the opposite side of the room again.

We recognized at the same time that our desire to be with each other was mutual and we didn't let any more dancing games or happy Oklahoma natives tear us apart. We finally found each other when the strains of the song *My Ideal* was playing.

Will I ever find
the boy on my mind,
the boy that is my ideal?

I melted in his arms. It felt so natural. He began to play with my hair and there was no MP to stop him. His fingers massaged the back of my neck sending a current straight through me to the top of my head. I felt his lips touch my hair.

"I feel the rhythm of your body when you dance. I can tell you love to dance," he said, holding me closer.

"This dance is so elegant."

"This is nothing compared to the pomp and ceremony at the Marine Corps Birthday Ball every November the tenth. Wait until we celebrate the ball. It's an exciting event."

His words changed me back into the pumpkin of a Marine enlisted personnel. I couldn't go with him to the Marine Corps Birthday Ball with officers and their wives and champagne and Mameluke swords at any Officers' Club on any Post in the U.S., even if I took off this uniform and put on a ball gown of apricot net. I could only go to the party for the enlisted with cake and beer.

The end of the dance was announced with the strains of *"Goodnight Ladies"* and *"Old Lange Syne"*.

He danced me next to the potted palms behind the large banner that read *'Labor Omia Vincit—Hail Oklahoma!'*

Labor Conquers All.

I remembered my high school Latin. It seemed to be an omen. Yes! It was a portent. The motto cheered me up. I always believed if you worked hard at something it will come to you.

There was no mistletoe where we had stopped. It didn't matter. He nibbled my ears and slowly kissed his way across to my lips. I was ready to swing through the potted palms at his touch. He held me in a hug so strong and tight I could barely move my head to return his kiss.

It certainly wasn't anything I had experienced before. I said I would recognize it when I felt it. Yes! Yes! This was the feeling I had been waiting for.

His lips were full yet they lay on mine lightly. His tongue brushed my lips and then tickled mine on the tip sending a Morse code of hot dots and dashes. He kissed my hair and ear and then back to my lips. A kaleidoscope of colors, mostly peacock feathers of iridescent blues, greens and violets swam inside my head as I returned kiss for kiss.

"I'm hanging on to you, Little Lady. We are going to make music together. I'm never going to let you go," he said.

He held my hand tightly as he led me down a hallway out of there. I held on just as firmly. I wasn't about to let him get away either. Two people with one mind. Fate. That's what it was.

He was what I had been waiting for. I knew it right there and then. His arm was firm around my waist as he guided me through the horde of people leaving the dance and we went down the hotel corridor to an elevator. He was breathing hard. Probably from all that dancing. But so was I. I was willing to go anywhere with him. Away from this crowd, alone together.

I said, "Where are you from?" I didn't mean what State. I meant it like "where have you been all my life?"

He said, "California."

That cinched it. Fate had predestined our meeting. I always believed that some day my prince would come. And from the right State too. Just as he was going to hang on to me, I wasn't going to let go of him.

The happy people of Oklahoma moved to the rear of the crowded elevator making room for two more people.

"Where are we going," I said dreamily, not caring.

"To my suite," my Captain said.

"Your suite?" I cried, my voice louder than anyone else's in the elevator. My reflexes responded to the word "suite" and I jerked involuntarily, pulling my hands from him at the same time he let go. The unexpected force sent me outside.

The doors closed automatically with a clang and he was gone. I stared at the rising cage, the closed grill and the moving pointer of the numbers of the floors.

What happened? I backed away, still staring at the blank wall. I walked backwards, stunned and worried. Something hit the hinges of my knees and I sat down suddenly—right on top of somebody's lap.

A wrinkled hand with diamond bracelets up to the elbow and rings on every finger hugged me instead. There I was rolling down the lobby in a wheel chair. A little old man in livery pants, the kind that stick out at the thighs, helped me up out of the chair.

I turned to see a very old lady half the size of me with powder blue hair and powder blue dress adjusting her diamond earrings. She said in a calm voice, "Are you going in my direction or am I going in yours?"

"I'm so sorry," I apologized. "Your wheels must be ball bearing. I had skates like that once. You couldn't stop until you were at the bottom of the hill."

"Roller skates. Indeed. What is that charming outfit you have on, Child?"

"I'm a Marine, Mam."

"How delightful. Do you reside here?"

"No, Mam!. I'm stationed at Quantico, but maybe I've missed the last train, I guess."

The elevator had come down at least ten times, no twenty times. My Captain did not step out on any of them.

"Montgomery will drive you, my dear, to the railroad station if you wish."

The elevator made many more trips. Still he did not come down.

I waited and waited and chatted with the sweet old dowager whose husband had been a Congressman from Maine many years ago who lived alone in this hotel.

"Yes, Mam. I do have a family. A father and a mother and sisters."

Why didn't he come down after me? He'll never find me. He doesn't know my right name. Why did I play that silly game and lie?

The room clerk didn't have any Captain John Walker registered. Could the room be under another name? He hadn't noticed a Marine with sad soft brown eyes. He would hold the message and make inquiries. Their register was confidential and he couldn't look.

I gave the elevator one more glance and accepted Montgomery's kindness. I don't know how long I would have hung around in hopes my Captain would come looking for me if I hadn't had the offer of a chauffeur driven limousine to drive me to the Union Station.

The last train to Quantico was late as usual and I had plenty of time. I dragged myself into the USO Lounge, aware of every step, realizing my new G.I. pumps had begun to hurt. As soon as I walked in, I kicked them off with great relief.

"Oh, my aching feet!" I groaned aloud.

I heard snickering. Two soldiers grinned at my condition. Both of them had crutches and I joined in their laughter at my misery.

I recognized their sleeve patches. "You're the Fifth Army boys that beat the Italians!"

One of them made room for me on the couch. He lifted his wooden leg, very proud that he could get around as well as he was doing. I agreed: it was remarkable.

He said, "A German 88 had our names on it at Salerno. We were pretty lucky at that. We missed out on Cassino and Anzio. But a fellow has to be really crazy to join the Marines. I hear they really have it rough!"

His buddy said, "Yeah! A Marine has to take a picture of the Jap before he shoots him."

"We heard that a combat photographer goes along with each Marine squad of thirteen men."

"That's pure scuttlebutt," I said. "Marine photographers and writers are no rear echelon troops as the journalists from the Army's STARS AND STRIPES are. They are Marines first. Just so you have the *word*! There is only one photographer and one correspondent assigned to each battalion just to make sure the story gets back straight, not second hand, and to make sure the right guys get the credit. The Marines have to take the pictures first or else Army would get all the credit for what the Marines did."

"What do they feed you Marines? You're as *Gung-Ho* as the rest of them!"

"Women in the service. I can't see it."

These were fighting words that would rile up any military woman and they knew it.

I said, rather loudly, "I'm just as anxious to get this war over as everyone else is. Most of us Women Marines want nothing more than to have our men home, have babies and keep house."

"A woman's place is in the home," yelled a sailor from across the room.

"So is a man's. We can't have those babies by ourselves," yelled another service woman, a WAAC sitting in another chair.

That exchange woke up some of the other servicemen and women.

The USO hostess had to leave her desk and shush everybody but no one paid any attention to her. She retreated to her desk.

The Fifth Army soldiers brought out pictures of their wives and children.

"You're pretty lucky guys," I said. "I don't have anyone special waiting for me."

"We sure are. The war's over for us. Good Luck, Marine!"

They hobbled off to catch the train back to their hospital.

As I walked through the crowded train looking for a place to sit or stand, a woman shoved her ticket at me and asked me if she were on the right train for Richmond. I checked it for her and reassured here that is where this resurrected 1890 coach of the R F & P was going all right.

An old man wondered where the men's toilet was and I turned him around toward the opposite direction.

Another woman with two kiddies hanging on to her wanted me to escort her to the dining car and hold one of the kids. The baby was scared of me and started to cry. The mother looked at me with irritation and said, "I'll find it myself."

When another man stopped me and asked, "Miss, do you have any pillows on this train," I realized what was happening.

"Look, I am a Marine! Not a train porter," I informed everyone loudly.

A Shavetail Marine offered his seat but he was so exhausted I couldn't accept it. I did notice his tie. It was a violet-beige color exactly the same shade as my new Celanese khaki shirt. We traded ties right there and then, like a brother and sister.

Thereafter, whenever I heard the statement that "the men don't want us in the Marine Corps" I remembered this Marine who gave me his tie.

The train was so packed with returning servicemen, that one sailor made room for me to sit on top of his suitcase in a boxcar that had a casket and funeral flowers on it. Three other swabbies and a Chief Petty officer shared it with me. They also shared their apples.

The Chief asked conversationally, "Why are you returning to camp so soon and on a Saturday night?"

"I'm *sack happy*," which is Navy talk for being tired. I wasn't about to tell him my troubles and the wasted week-end.

He was very nice. "You can use my room to sleep in," he said.

I thanked him kindly and told him I had only three quarters of an hour's ride to Quantico and I was getting off before he did since he was going to Norfolk which was below Richmond.

He renewed his offer. "It's not true that Navy doesn't like the Marines and will screw them every chance they get. You're safe with me."

The hoots and hollers that greeted his *snow-job* made the train ride fun as the other swabbies teased him about his clumsy approach. The rest of the ride was spent listening to their hilarious ideas of the best strategy on how to win Women Marines.

The pain of losing my Marine Captain filled me with an unexpected let-down. I felt a disappointment and a certain sadness. I was aware of this loss in the middle of all this camaraderie. How could this misery be so strong so soon? Why had I missed my chance? Maybe it's true that I didn't know a good thing when I saw it.

I looked for Blanche all day Sunday and Monday She must have returned very late. I was so relieved to see her at the bulletin board that I bounded over to talk to her.

She was wearing dungarees with the letter P stenciled on the back and was reading the new notice the Duty NCO had tacked up: It read:

To Women Marines
Out Of Bounds
Lanie's Puka Bar and the total area on 9th Street

"I'm sorry, Blanche. I won't say anything, if you don't," I said.
"Shove off!" She barked, walking away from me. She was restricted to the barracks.

I tried to sympathize with her although I was breaking a rule talking to a *PAL, Prisoner At Large,* but she wouldn't have anything more to do with me. Me! Her only friend in the barracks.

I decided to spend a couple of days at my old barracks hanging out with my old buddies until I got my bearings. I needed their companionship until I decided exactly where to go for the rest of my furlough. There were many empty bunks since so many Marines had gone home for Christmas.

I had called home, but when Mama told me how much snow they were having, I decided I'd rather stay in Virginia.

Besides, the galley was planning a bountiful Christmas menu with turkey and all the trimmings for those Marines who were staying in Quantico for the holidays. Christmas dinner in the mess hall with my buddies instead of my family would be fun because they were my family now as well. Maybe more so. I could confide to them feelings and secrets I'd never tell Mama and Dad.

Sherry came bubbling into the barracks with a fistful of letters. That was how she received mail from her husband. She wouldn't hear for months until his submarine came up for air, then she'd be deluged. "He's crossed the Equator again!" They had a secret code which the censor had not caught on to and he was able to let her know when he had seen action by writing that he had cut himself shaving and had drawn blood. This meant they had sunk more Jap ships and other submarines.

Fenton sensed something had gone awry with my week-end. "What happened in D.C., Terry?"

"Remember when I said I would *know*? I thought I'd know it right away. But I didn't recognize it until the elevator closed on us and he was gone."

"What do you know? Do you want to start from the beginning?"

"His name is Captain John Walker, I think. I don't think he lied. I was the one who lied. You know, like the recruiting poster. That is all I know. And I know I'm in love. And I lied to him. I told him I was Lady Jane Greystoke. It was funny and romantic at the time. Now I'm miserable."

Smokey, the baker, on her way in from serving the last chow, stopped to listen. Texas did too. So did Belle, the projectionist at Post Theater. So did Lorry.

A private conversation was impossible to have in a squadroom. Even a whisper could be picked up by sharp ears somewhere down the line. Any deep dark secret became barracks gossip scuttlebutt fast and eighty women knew what eighty other women were doing at any given time because of the grapevine.

I began the whole story over again because my squadmates had missed the important opening sequence of my love story. I was beginning to relish my role as the sad heroine and all the attention and advice I was attracting.

Gerry, more cynical now that she was married to her corporal from Post Stables, said, "There is no such thing as love at first sight. It is a good thing you didn't go up to his room. You would have been disappointed."

Belle, the projectionist at the post theater, who cried at practically every love song that came on the radio because it would remind her of some old ex-boyfriend, interrupted my story to tell Gerry she was wrong as could be. "I've fallen in love at first sight a dozen times."

Sherry heard that across the room and stopped long enough to disagree completely. "If you have been in love a dozen times, Belle, then not once was it the real thing."

Lorry said, "How can you love someone you just met? You should be friends first. Like you and Spero are friends. That's very special."

It irritated me that she would bring Spero's name into this discussion of *Love At First Sight*. This was no time to talk about faithful beaus, good friends, or pen pals who were like a Savings Account in the bank at 2% interest.

"Look, Lorry. My Captain is a ride on the roller coaster. Spero and all the others are a ride on the merry go round. It's not the same thing. My captain knew what he was doing. He knew how to kiss."

Smokey's many marriages, all annulled, backed up her experience with men, giving weight to her advice. "It's respect that makes the world go around not horses. Remember, respect. If he doesn't respect you, he'll cheat on you, and beat you up. I know."

Fenton scolded, "Terry! You didn't even find out what religion your Captain is. Religion is the most important." Fenton was in love with an Army Captain and gave fifty cents weekly to the Roman Catholic priest to say a Novena of extra prayers to plead with God that the man she loved back home for the past four years would convert to her religion so they could marry.

"There are no atheists in fox-holes. Of course, my Captain is religious," I vouched for a lost love I knew nothing about.

"If you really love him, you can always change to his religion. Most Protestants don't care who they marry. Episcopalians are fussy. They don't cotton to Baptist or Assembly of God. It's more logical for the woman to switch to a man's faith. After all, it is Adam who had the seven ribs. So it's right that a woman cleaves unto the male. You'll have to switch." said Lindsey.

"A piece of paper doesn't hold people together. It's faith, trust and love. If you have that, you don't need marriage at all. You can say your vows in the boondocks or in a hotel suite. That's what I should have done in the first place." Those were Smokey's last words.

"Why don't you write to him and let him know how you feel, Terry? It worked for me," said Moonbeam who had forgotten she heard those words from me first.

"Moonbeam, I don't even know where he's stationed. There must be hundreds of Marines with the name of John Walker. He might as well have told me his name was John Smith."

"God works in mysterious ways. If it is meant to be, it will happen," said Fenton who had faith to spare.

It was I who lacked it.

I returned to Washington two times. Had lunch there. My heart jumped every time I saw a Marine officer. It was silly and stupid of me to pine away for someone whose face was getting blurred in my memory. Were his eyes brown or hazel? His hair was straight, I think. After all, he had his hat on most of the time.

I took a street-car to Lanie's place and retraced our route. Her boarded windows had painted snow on twin mountain peaks, dancing native girls in leopard two piece outfits and a setting Caribbean sun. Business was bad. No one in her bar. MP's and SP's patrolled it often. When she saw me she chased me out. Said she didn't want any jinxes around her.

I went straight to Arlington Hall, Virginia where Women Marines were billeted to see my old Boot Camp buddy, Shauna who was the records clerk and a likely person to know whether someone had been looking for a "Jane Greystoke". Marine Corps Headquarters seemed to me a most logical place to look for a lost Woman Marine if someone really wanted to find one.

She was very discouraging. "Bunkie, forget him. There are two thousand WR's working here at Headquarters. If you didn't give him your right name, it's a lost cause," she said with sympathy. "D.C. is crawling with Marine officers. You'll find another one."

Several times, I thought I caught a glimpse of him at the PX and once standing at Colors next to Iron Mike at Post Headquarters. Of course, it wasn't he. I had wished him to be there. That's all. I understood mirages now. But time does make memories and images fade.

Love at first sight was a fact of life. I know. I had seen it in the movies often enough. It could happen to anybody. Falling in love, keeping love, losing love, pining away for love, finding love, seemed to be the theme of all the songs, the movies, the short stories and novels. Boy meets girl; boy loses girl; boy gets girl. Finding love, happy ending; losing love, sad ending. It was an old story. It was happening to everybody in this war. It had happened to me. What was going to be my ending?

Living with hundreds of girls at a Marine Post meant I was never alone. That helped take my mind off my lost love. There was always someone to talk to who had equal problems of loneliness and loss.

Life and limb were at stake in the war. Of course, I wasn't in the same sorority as the women whose loved ones had been killed or whose men were prisoners, but no one ever made a comment that I hadn't known Captain John long enough to question the depth of my passionate feelings. There was always some one willing to listen. No one, other than my cynical bunkie Gerry, ever pointed out that John Walker and I hadn't spent enough time to even know each other much less be "in love". There were so many love affairs consummated after the shortest acquaintance that being in love was reason enough to run to the altar, the nearest Justice of the Peace or hotel room.

Pining for a loved one was acceptable and epidemic, even if it were for someone that one had known for only two hours.

I now looked for Marines that bore a resemblance to my captain as a way of holding his image alive a little longer in my memory. I realized with time, his face and the way his body and arms around me felt would fade until he was gone forever. He had begun to merge in my mind into the Marine I first saw in the recruiting poster.

It was also true that a busy mind doesn't have time to mope and brood. Life at Quantico was exciting, busy, rewarding and full of people. The scenes were ever changing and stimulating. The diversions were many.

A detachment of one hundred and fifty Marines returned from Londonderry, Ireland, marching in with a bagpipe band as they reported into the Post.

The Women's Trick Drill team was practicing on Lyman Field at the time and they timed their steps to the bagpipes.

A company of Officer Candidates in full battle dress marching from one area to another also picked up the rhythm of the Scottish music.

Yes! If one had to pine away, the Marine Corps Post of Quantico was the place to be. I visited the Marine Corps Museum on the second floor in Quantico and saw a Mameluke sword. It had a curved ivory handle and a Cross hilt. I got sloppy sentimental just at the sight of it. I was glad Gerry wasn't around to see me wipe a tear from my eye. She would have said I was enjoying my misery too much.

Richmond, Virginia

The small towns and cities of Virginia that surrounded Quantico were filled with memories of another era. The opportunity to see some of the early settlements of what made America great would never be more propitious.

I retreated to the historic past and went sight-seeing. The remainder of my ten day furlough was spent visiting the countryside with its soft rolling green hills and the Civil War battlefields. A short bus ride took me to Richmond, Virginia, where I stayed at the elegant, venerable and respectable Hotel Jefferson which had beautiful columns in the lobby and magnificent ceilings. I ate dinner in the charming dining room where Negro waiters wearing black suits and white aprons served me Southern fried chicken with biscuits and gravy on beautiful hand-painted china on white tablecloths.

I caught myself pining away, playing dumb games with myself, pretending that I was on my honeymoon and my handsome Marine captain was sitting across from me in this beautiful setting with its potted plants and lovely mahogany Southern furniture. As I walked around looking at the magnificent old Southern mansions, I imagined we lived in one of them.

I fell in love with Richmond as suddenly as I had fallen in love with my own recruiting poster Marine. I vowed that someday, I would return and stay and stay and stay and never return to the snows of Tonawanda.

Good-Bye To Captain Bungle And All That

I usually dreamt in color and always remembered my dreams in detail upon awakening. Each night my sub-conscious mind told me stories while I was asleep and I enjoyed them. But not on the morning I returned to duty.

I awakened with tears in my eyes as if I had been crying in my sleep, when the Duty NCO yelled *"Hit the deck!"*

As usual, I was the only Marine in the squadroom, the rest having departed for duty. I had tip-toed in at 1:00 A.M. to make the

6:00 A.M. reveille. Since I had been on furlough it didn't matter how late I came in. If I hadn't been on liberty, I would have had to be in by 11:00 P.M. sharp as everyone else.

I tried to recall the dreams but they had flown from memory. I skipped morning chow; missed the women's bus purposely and walked to duty at Post Garage, humming a song left over from my dream.

I had the craziest dream last night
Yes I did
I never dreamt it could be
Yet there you were in love with me

At the Bugler's call for Colors, I stood at attention with my hand in a salute as the flag of the United States was raised on a pole so high you could see it waving from a distance. A surge of pride rushed through me, reminding me that I was married to the Marine Corps. How satisfying and fulfilling it was knowing my country needed me.

I was returning to duty at Motor Transport, rested, filled with new resolve to attack those Kardex files and straighten out that inventory once and for all, determined to find those missing *generators* that were giving me so much trouble. The crisp day was glorious, the sun shining as usual, in this wonderful State of Virginia, with no evidence of the flurries of snow that had fallen the week before. No salt on the roads. No slush. Wonderful wonderful Virginia.

My new mood of dedication must have been obvious. The men in the warehouse greeted me by name for the first time as I passed the open garage-warehouse doors. They smiled and waved.

Someone had cut sprigs off the holly bushes and had decorated my Kardex files with the red berries. A Coca-Cola was on my desk to welcome me back after my furlough of ten days. No one in Post Garage had ever bought me a Coca-Cola before. Tears welled in my eyes. I could only stare at the gifts. I didn't know whom to thank.

The lieutenant was nowhere in sight. I could hear and see Captain Bungle in his office making lots of noise, drawers opening and closing, banging away. I waited for his buzzer to signal me.

He emerged finally. I put on my brightest cheeriest smile for him.

He snarled at me. "I knew you were a trouble maker from the moment I saw you."

I actually thought he might hit me.

Off he waddled, carrying his personal desk name plaque, framed autographed picture of Vice-President Wallace and his personal decanters of whisky.

I stood at attention and watched him climb into a jeep. The driver was staring straight ahead but there was a smile on his face.

Captain Bungle had been relieved of his command to await his honorable discharge.

I took the sprigs of the holly and the bottle of Coca-Cola out to the warehouse to thank the Marine who had given them to me. I was ready for a new romance. But it wasn't just one person that had decorated my file cabinet. It was the gang, the whole squad, that had done it.

"Here's our wonder girl! Our own *Kardex File Running Inventory Supervisor!*"

The men yelled it out but it didn't sound nasty anymore. It was shouted as a hurrah.

Joe, one of the mechanics who had been particularly unfriendly, now came up to me, actually put an arm on my shoulder and turned me around to face the very pallet I had parked my butt on several times.

He pointed to it.

"Here's that *GE 15 generator*. You've been walking around one of them all this time."

I stared at the one ton piece of machinery that had turned my shins black and blue every time I bumped against it. The very one I'd leaned against or sat upon when I was so exhausted looking for it, right under my nose.

"You mean that machine that is bigger than a house that has been in my way blocking everything is what I've been looking for all this time? That? That is a *GE15 generator*? What is it used for?"

"That is a field generator! A GE15! That baby lights the important tents in the field. The Mess Tent, Field Hospital, the General's Tent, that's what. It makes all the motors go. This little ole' machine generates the electricity for a full battalion of 2000 Marines on bivouac."

There was no way any one could have missed this monster of a machine. Yet I had. I couldn't be that blind. "Where is it marked GE15?"

He pointed to some tiny numbers on the machine right next to where I sat and had leaned against. No wonder it had seemed so funny when I asked if the generators were all gone. It was like sitting on top of the point of Washington's monument and asking where is it.

"There's supposed to be two of them. Where is the other one?"

"Where else? In Fredricksburg! Along with half the parts from Post Garage," said Steve.

"The Captain never said we had a Marine detachment there," I said which started everyone talking and laughing at once.

"There isn't! Everything went to the Captain's own garage. He kept his taxis and trucks in top condition at the Marine Corps expense."

"The *bastard* was stealing the Corps blind!"

"That sleaze put a freeze on all promotions!"

The men thought my questions were so amusing and my astonishment so appealing that they clustered around me falling all over themselves to ask what chances they had for a date. That was my first clue that the ice jam of friendship had been broken in Motor Transport for me.

The second cloudburst of understanding of a major change in the weather hit me the minute I walked into my Motor Transport barracks.

When I stopped to read the bulletin board four girls from topside squadroom smiled and greeted me by name, not by the title of "Corporal". One patted my back affectionately.

My squadroom bunkmates were having their usual fun and games, hillbilly music on loud, two of them waltzing with roller skates, arms around each other like Russian bears.

When I walked into the squadroom they picked me up easily in a bear hug and zoomed me right down the runway of the squadroom giving me a ride.

The attitude of the whole squadroom towards me had changed completely and instantaneously.

They claimed I was responsible for getting rid of Captain Bungle and credited me with his departure. How could I take credit for his departure? The long and short of it was that Captain Bungle blew the whistle on himself.

Captain Bungle's retirement was greeted with dancing in the Post Garage and the barracks. I was toasted in orange soda, Coca-

Theresa Karas Yianilos

Cola, coffee and chocolate milk. When I walked by, they serenaded me with Judy Garland's song;
Ding Dong!
The witch is dead.
The witch is dead!
Ding Dong! The wicked witch Is dead!

Ratings, frozen so long on his desk, were released immediately and sent up the chain of command for approval. Ear-banging, bucking or dating, or shacking up with the captain no longer was the only way for a Woman Marine to earn promotion to PFC or Corporal at Motor Transport.

"You mean all of you thought I got these corporal stripes by *shacking* up with an *officer?*" I cried, protesting my innocence.

That hadn't crossed my mind. I had mistaken their rejection for jealousy. I remembered Sherry's and my accusations against Sergeant Ellice Stukey and I felt very guilty. Everything seemed to go around in circles and the law of retribution kept coming back to haunt me.

They didn't believe me that there were good honorable commanding officers throughout Quantico.

I protested. "Not every officer is like Captain Bungle. You should have known Colonel Buse. He rewarded the Women Marines for their work and treated all of us as daughters!'

"That's a *sea story* and a long *snow job*, Terry but, we love you for it."

Many women Marines had been given only one assignment and had remained at the same duty post throughout their entire Corps career. They had no way of judging what made a good commanding officer as I had.

Their assessment of all commanding officers based on their experience of how Captain Bungle had conducted his command made me very sad and frustrated. I could not undo in a few days what he had done over the year. One rotten apple could tarnish a whole post of good dedicated Marine commanders. His actions had splashed mud on many fine conscientious men.

I remembered Colonel Buse and his military manner; and his accessibility to the men and women under his Command. He respected us as ladies and considered us Marines.

Now I had a greater appreciation for the efforts of General Torrey who had tried to neuter the gender factor in the Marine Corps with his general orders against fraternizing by insisting that we were Marines first, and men and women second.

Loyalty to Corps and Country was the glue that kept the Marine Corps into the tightly knit family that was its strength for hundreds of years.

Poor Captain Bungle. Yes, poor greedy Captain Bungle. I felt sorry for someone that obtuse and stupid. He had missed the whole point of what made for esprit de corps which was the heart and soul of the Marine Corps. He never realized that by honoring the Corps he would be honoring himself. He never understood what the words in the Marine Corps Hymn really meant: *to keep our honor clean.*

He had missed the opportunity to participate and add his name to its illustrious history. Each and every Marine who had ever served, in peacetime and wartime, from 1775 to the present in 1945, had donated a part of himself. America was safer because of Marines who had been willing to lay down their lives to protect the United States from harm. Captain Bungle was only interested in protecting his check book and bank balance and wouldn't lay down a dollar, much less his life, for his Country, his Corps or his fellow Marine.

Yes, I did feel sorry for Captain Bungle. He had no honor.

Captain Bungle had stolen more than a generator or auto parts. He had muddied the motto *Semper Fidelis.* Because this was wartime, Captain Bungle got his honorable discharge and never had to account for his actions.

For the present, that satisfied everyone except the women who didn't think he got what was coming to him. Short of hanging or castration, they would have liked to have seen his buttons cut off his uniform in view of the whole women's battalion.

Captain Bungle was ushered out of his command and discharged not because of his treatment of the Women Marines but for reasons much more serious to the Marine Corps. He was caught red-handed stealing government property and his signature on the requisition for thirty thousand dollars worth of generators was exactly the evidence that was needed to hang him. If this wasn't wartime, he would have been given the brig instead of a small ceremony and an honorable discharge. The Marines handled their own dirty laundry.

There were Women Marines in Motor Transport who hadn't been shipped out, although they too had signed the petition against Captain Bungle. Now they acted as if I had saved them from white slavery, hugging me and saying how they knew I had bigger fish to fry all along.

Theirs was the second petition that didn't do what the signers had intended. I remembered the petitions of Barracks-Two against the two Women Marines accused of being lesbians which also did not bring about the reform the WRs had sought. I came to my own private conclusion that the tools of democracy did not work in the Corps as they did with elected officials in the government. The Corps did not have to answer to an electorate.

Every enlisted person in Post Garage and Motor Transport barracks knew what had been going on but there was no way for an enlisted person to make a complaint and by-pass the Captain according to the rules of the chain of command.

Captain Bungle was ranking officer in the next link in the chain and he had the authority to pass on with recommendations any letter from a rank below him. He could ignore them also, and that's what he did, especially those requests from Women Marines.

Remember what the D.I. in Boot Camp said? First came the dogs, then the 'niggers', then the Women Marines! That was the order of enlistment and exactly Captain Bungle's attitude. He considered the Women Marines as *camp followers* to be approached at his will.

He was the worst kind of Marine. Since he was a Volunteer Specialist, a wartime concoction, the Corps could take comfort that he wasn't a "real" Marine with the hard core training which regular Marines received. Unfortunately, he besmerched all the fine Volunteer Specialists who had left their civilian jobs and businesses to volunteer their services to the Corps to win this war.

I was sure Captain Bungle was not typical. He was a bad apple in any service.

A group of Women Marines tried to by-pass him and go past the chain of command. They were shipped out to Parris Island as trouble makers. The men had closed ranks. Protecting the Corps was the first order of the day. Individuals didn't count. They never did in the Corps. The Corps had to be protected foremost.

Marine Corps rules didn't allow sub-ordinates to skip-hop and jump over their commanding officers, even if he were a *bastard*.

How can a military organization win wars if the officers weren't obeyed without question?

I now understood the subtle remarks I had heard every now and then from battle scared Marines—how an officer had better earn his men's respect and admiration, because if he pushed too hard or gave unreasonable stupid careless orders that endangered the squad or platoon he'd be a casualty of a sniper's bullet.

That was also the first time I heard the term *"friendly fire"*. It was explained to me how in the course of war some of our men were killed and maimed accidentally by miscalculations from our own troops. When it happened, it was "friendly fire". A bullet in the back? Friendly fire.

The new *KARDEX FILING SYSTEM* filing system had been purchased by the Navy to stop pilfering and stealing. It was supposed to be a foolproof system of inventory. The inventory I was taking of the seventy-seven thousand automotive parts would show the Navy exactly what material was missing so they would be able to take the proper means to prevent theft.

That little questionnaire I had filled out when I joined with the innocent question of what kind of job I held in civilian life told them I was a *Kardex Running Inventory File Clerk Supervisor*. That is how the Marine Corps found me.

I was on a secret assignment. But no one had told me about it.

I just did what was natural and in doing it, I did my duty. I was the cannonball that blew Captain Bungle out of the water.

While I was on my short leave in Manassas and in Richmond, a team of Naval and Marine Corps investigators from Depot Supply in Philadelphia converged on the Post Garage to find out why Quantico Post was missing *two, generators,* worth thirty-thousand dollars. When Depot Supply received the requisitions signed by the Commanding Officer Captain Bungle himself, it brought down the whole Quartermaster team on the first military plane.

Of course, they found both *generators,* one in Fredricksburg and the other one here at Post Garage where it had been right under my nose all the time. How ironic! If I had known there was even one *GE 15 generator* I never would have written an order for the other one at all and Captain Bungle could still be sitting at his desk. Good riddance!

"You mean they found other stuff in his garage at Fredricksburg worth thousands of dollars? I wondered if they found his etchings too?" I said.

"His etchings? Did he give you that old moldy hairy line too?"

The Women Marines of Motor Transport sent that remark down the line of bunks and the laughter flowed in waves as one WR heard it after another.

"Terry is a straight dope. She didn't even know what etchings were? Yeah! Old Bungle fed her that same line." That seemed to endear me to them even more.

When I found out that etchings were pictures on the wall, I was disappointed. I would never have gone to Fredricksburg with Captain Bungle in the first place, and certainly not to look at black and white pictures. How dumb did he think I was?

The change in my relationship with my squadroom was amazing. Overnight my bunkies had nicknames: There was Stretch, my six-foot tall bunkie under me, Angel (she came from Los Angeles), Minnie, from Louisiana who had a soft Cajun accent, Swanny with the straight hair bob, and Ginny from Virginia. Their friendship made all the difference in the world. No longer was I anxious to dash over to my old Barracks-A at the end of the day. I didn't need to. Living in Motor Transport barracks had become pleasant and comforting.

My squadroom had become true bunkmates, with androgynous names. Stephanie, became Stevie, Georgia was George, and Jacqueline was Jackie. A few were named for their classification. It was almost like Boot Camp where everyone was called by their State. I had found another group of squadmates I could call buddies, with whom to share chocolates, food, snacks, police duty and trips to the PX, Quantico Town, Post Theater and the Slopschute.

I was happy once more with women I could call my friends. They were willing to listen to my story of my romantic night with my handsome recruiting poster Marine, Captain John Walker.

My bunkies in Barracks-A had become bored with my repeated tale of my lost romance. As soon as I began to describe once more the magnificent ball where Walking John and I had danced under the mistletoe, they lost interest and made silly Navy jokes.

"Terry, how about looking under a rock to find him? Under *Rocks and Shoals,* that is!"

They thought that was a particularly funny since it was a pun. *Rocks and Shoals* was the Bible for the rules and regulations of the Navy and Marine Corps which all officers had to memorize and abide by.

My new squadmates in Motor Transport were more sympathetic and not the least bored. They took to stopping at my bunk to tell me what to do to find my lost Captain.

Minnie, who drove the 6 x 6 trucks and always had her radio tuned to Grand Old Opry sat on my bunk to give me some down home Cajun advice.

"Corporal, Honey, did you ever hear the story of "Evangeline"? What happened to youh all—it's the same tragic tale. Evangeline was torn from the arms of her true love. She left her homeland in Acadia—that is someplace far North, in Canada, I think—and spent her whole life looking for the man she loved. She walked thousands of miles and finally got down to our parts in the Bayou."

"She found him there?"

"Sort of. There was this fellow, Henry Longfellow, who wrote a poem about her. But he tells it wrong. He says she finds him when they are both old and he is dying in a Yankee City but that ain't the truth of it. What he done was marry up with a Cajun woman and had a passel of kids. Sure, he's old and so is she. He don't even recognize her. So, Corporal Honey, don't go waiting on him too long. There's plenty of crawdads in the swamp."

Several weeks went by without a new CO in Motor Transport. Work was carried on with a new lieutenant in charge. No one minded nor felt the loss of Captain Bungle. Everyone cooperated and things ran smoothly. We had become a close-knit unit just as a combat unit which carries on to the last man to win the objective even after the captain, lieutenant and others in command are shot down.

Motor Transport had finally found its esprit de corps.

It was almost like being back in Post Service Battalion. Informality and friendliness filled the garage and greetings were exchanged with laughter and joking while the work was getting done. I was able to do more in that time than I had during the months before.

I went to a Post movie every night with a different Marine from Motor Transport. It didn't matter that they had ranks of private and private first class. I took my dates to the NCO Club afterwards as my guests for a beer as other non-commissioned had taken me when I was a private. It amused them to be taken to a club they couldn't get into by themselves by a Woman Marine.

The evening went by fast with all the jokes about the Women Marines taking over the Marine Corps. Usually everyone in the Slopschute got into the conversation, some stopping at the table to join us, others throwing their comments across the tables. It was all very friendly in a family sort of way. I was ready for a new romance and once again, I sized up new Marines I met and eyed them for any possibility of a deeper relationship.

I was no Evangeline who would pine away forever.

Post Quartermaster–Spring 1945

We worked hard preparing for a new commanding officer of Motor Transport. I was particularly proud of how much I had accomplished with the cooperation of all the men in the garage. I had even washed the dust off the Kardex file cabinets and decorated it with flowers that grew on the side of the post buildings. Quantico had been landscaped beautifully. There was always a bush or a tree in bloom and spring arrived early in Virginia.

As soon as I stepped off the WR bus, the garage mechanics threw a warning at me before I entered my office."

"There's a new CO in the office. Watch your step, Terry. He's the whole Marine Corps Manual. All rules and regulations."

I straightened my cotton hose. I tugged down my girdle. The boys did not whistle nor make funny jokes. Not this time. This was G.I. time.

I heard a stern voice say, "Send the corporal in."

I smoothed my uniform and made sure the four buttons down the front and all those on the flaps of the pockets were snugly in place. I combed my fingers through my hair to fluff it out, squared my shoulders and went in to meet the new commanding officer of Motor Transport. His name was already painted on the glass door. Would he be like Colonel Buse?

I stood there at attention.

My new CO said curtly, "Corporal, I have heard all about you. The report is right here. Take it and present your transfer papers to the major at Quartermaster, Post Depot Supply. *Dismissed!*"

I did an *about-face* and rushed to the *head* very aware that the eyes of the men and women of Post Garage followed me. They could say nothing. It was a new day at Motor Transport, a new CO.

I walked as proudly as I could with my head held high out of Post Garage, away from the men who had brought me flowers and Coca-Colas, from the Kardex File System, from a job I had done cheerfully despite my distaste for the assignment. I had won the friendship and respect of the men the hard way which made it all the more difficult to leave them. And now I had lost another battalion. I left my second duty post for good, this time with a dark cloud over my head.

I had rocked the wrong boat and had made waves in a very big pond.

My brisk pace took me past buildings I had never seen in a part of Quantico where I had never walked before. I could hear my heart pounding and the heels of my regulation oxfords hitting the road at the same time. There were no sidewalks and landscaping at this end of the post. Row upon row of large concrete buildings with huge doors on one side where trucks rolled up to the platforms loomed before me.

The wooden sign painted in Marine Corps colors of scarlet red with golden yellow letters, read:
Quartermaster—Post Depot Supply

I entered a side door and presented my papers to the commanding officer, a Major.

He read them carefully, put them down and inspected me very carefully as if I had two heads. I stood at attention for what seemed a very long time.

Then he spoke in a very stern voice.

"Corporal, I am going to keep an eye on you. I am going to watch you every minute. You are not going to make trouble for me as you did over in Motor Transport."

I did an about face and was escorted out of the office with the staff sergeant at my heels. She took me to an office where there were thirty desks and thirty Women Marines with thirty typewriters. There was one desk, alone in the middle, sort of isolated from the rest. That was mine.

I sat down at it and waited for work to do. None was forthcoming. I spent the whole day sitting there. Everyone around me clacked away at their typewriters but I was allowed to remain idle. I wasn't given one sheet to type. The young Women Marines would glance at me surreptitiously every now and then but no one came near me.

That was it. That was my first day at Quartermaster Depot of Supply.

I took the bus back to the barracks where I sat in the lounge in a daze and tried to sort out what was happening to me and figure out what I could do about it.

The news of my transfer out of Post Garage and into Quartermaster spread throughout the barracks. Women from other squadrooms came into the lounge to comfort me. The whole evening was spent discussing the mysteries of Marine Corps promotions and recognition, who got the medals and who didn't, who got the sack and who stayed. Women Marines didn't get any medals. If I could have been fired, I believed I would have been. In the Corps, a Marine didn't get fired. He or she got transferred.

Once again, in the middle of this satisfying commiseration I was called to the Duty NCO office and was devastated at her instructions.

"Get your gear and move to top-side of Barracks Two. Report to the Duty NCO, Company B. You are to billet there."

My squadmates moaned and groaned with me and helped me pack. Without changing their clothes, Stretch, Minnie, Jackie, Angel, and a couple of others picked up my sea-bag, all my books, my bowls and kitchen equipment.

"What is all this, Terry? Salad bowl, kitchen knife, olive oil and oregano? Where did you get this white cheese?"

"I get so bored with the galley serving plain lettuce and bottled dressing. I miss my Mama's Greek Salad. I make it for myself. Greeks own the Riverview and A-I restaurants. They make Feta cheese and gave me some. But I'm leaving Spero's latest box of chocolates for all of you. His aunt sent it to me."

Once again, I had to leave my new found comrades. The rapport and solidarity that we had gained through the trials and tribulations of the past months were torn asunder.

This time, I knew enough not to make any loud complaints about my transfer when I walked into my new barracks. I wasn't about to make enemies with any more stupid thoughtless remarks. I had learned my lesson. But, it wouldn't have mattered if I had. These girls wouldn't have minded anything we said.

The Women Marines in this squadroom stepped aside as our procession entered Barracks Two.

My new squadmates offered us uncertain smiles of welcome.

They had bunched up into small clusters and watched wordlessly as we, *Old Salts* that we were, marched in and claimed a bunk nearest the door. They stood respectfully as they surveyed us, taking in our salty old insignia, our worn uniforms that had a sheen from so many pressings. They noted the men's sheep skin jackets and the men's boondocker boots of Motor Transport's mechanics and truck drivers. They listened to our Navy slang that rolled off the tongue so naturally. Our nonchalant attitude was less than G.I. sharp but, like the fighting Marines who had returned from the Pacific, none of us cared. We had served. We had done our duty. We were good and we knew it.

My new squadmates in Barracks Two were fresh Boots, *Class 1 clerk-typists* who had been assigned to Quartermaster only recently. They were the last of the training battalions out of Camp Lejeune as the Women's Reserve quota of 18,000 women and 1000 officers had been reached.

I looked around and saw that once again, I was out of my league. I looked at their fresh eager faces and groaned inwardly. They all reminded me of Lorry as she was when I first met her, eager to participate, young and inexperienced, anxious to be part of the pulsating life of the Corps.

And I was tired. I didn't want to be anybody's mentor, big sister, den mother nor teacher. Just the thought of having to adjust to new friends and new bunkmates was exhausting to contemplate.

Yet that is exactly the role that my new squadmates expected of me. The Boots in Barracks Two treated me with the kind of respect and reserve that a non-commissioned corporal deserved. They came to me for direction and advice and stood at attention when I talked to them. When I approached a cluster of them as they stood around the bulletin board, their eager young faces, filled with fresh *Gung-ho* esprit de corps, became serious and they parted with military correctness. If I walked into the room they made way for me.

Suddenly I felt quite old. I had been in the Corps over a year and a half. It had been a long time.

I needed to see Gerry, Sherry, Lorry, Fenton, and the rest of the *Old Breed.*

I returned to my first squadroom in Barracks-A to visit my old bunkmates, but things had changed there as well. It wasn't the same.

Gerry went home on a *four-ninety nine.* Her Post Stable husband had managed to achieve what she claimed was impossible. He had made her pregnant. She no longer was there with her cheerful cynicism to chide me for playing Scarlett after Rhett walked out on her.

"Get a live one, Terry! Forget the ghost! He can't make you pregnant!" With that flip remark Gerry Adams was gone and out the door.

Moonbeam showed up waving a piece of paper and claimed a rabbit had died and that gave her a *four ninety-nine* too. Her Marine beau, the one from Arkansas to whom I had composed all the love letters for her, had proposed and within a short time she was married, pregnant and gone with all the jugs for the moonshine her Paw liked to make by the light of the Missouri moon.

Moonbeam hugged me gratefully, and said, "You did it! You made me get pregnant! Ah never told him it was you wrote the letters. Do you mind?" Of course, I didn't mind. "Now, you keep writing to your Captain, hear?"

What Captain? Oh! That Captain! That was months ago!

Blanche never spoke to me again and seemed to be on permanent police duty. She hated the Marine Corps and wore a sour look on her face most of the time. She applied for an early discharge and got it in two weeks.

Fenton, after a four year see-saw engagement, broke off with her Protestant fiancee when he wrote he had stopped taking catechism lessons. She no longer wore the diamond ring. She had given it back.

In a short time while on furlough in Boston, she met and married an Ensign, in a full Catholic ceremony, she in a white gown and he in *dress whites*, with crossed swords over their heads as they emerged from a church. She had been promoted to sergeant and that seemed to appease her ambitions.

Lorry was still at Post Service Battalion in one of the offices. She had not made any waves and had stayed at the same duty station. She was now an *Old Salt* and carried herself with confidence and the certainty that came with experience and age. Her bunkmates hurried to catch up with her whenever she walked to the PX, Quantico town or to work.

Sergeant Major Jordan and Major Emery had retired and all the people I had known at H-barracks were gone to other posts or to the Pacific. Only Staff Sergeant Ellice Stukey remained and she was queen of H-Barracks. No one defied her nor tried to knock her off her perch after what happened to me and Sherry.

Sherry was transferred to Post Headquarters where her abilities as a stenographer and secretary were finally appreciated and she made sergeant. She planned to apply for a discharge as soon as her Submarine Lieutenant came home. She could do it just by announcing her marriage. The rules of fraternization were always enforced.

I hadn't heard from Spero for over two months. One day at mail call I received a dozen letters at once that had been held up by the censors. I was so relieved and happy to finally hear from him after two months that I did not even return the greetings from my young squadmates who were impressed with my deluge of envelopes.

The tone of his letters had changed. His infantry division, the *Timberwolves* had moved through Germany so fast that he hadn't been able to write for weeks. So many parts of his V-Mail were blacked out, that if I hadn't been reading in the newspaper that the 104th Division was fighting outside of Cologne, I wouldn't have known he was in danger as I traced the route of the First Army through France, Belgium, Holland and into Germany.

For a short time his company rested in a little town that had been abandoned by the German population and finally he had been able to sit down and write to me.

The Duty NCO showered me with his letters at mail call.

They were filled with longing and affection and the words "I love you" were written hundreds of times. War and distance had made him realize he cared very much and he made all sorts of extravagant promises that didn't sound like him at all. We would go dancing, to every new movie, to concerts and plays. We would kiss and make love and listen to our favorite songs together. For now, all he could do was listen to the Big Bands that played on the radio, close his eyes and dream he was with me. He could imagine he was home, back in the good old United States when he heard the music and songs of Benny Goodman, Glenn Miller, Jimmy Dorsey, Tommy Dorsey, Duke Ellington, Artie Shaw, Frank Sinatra, Dinah Shore, Helen O'Connell, and Bing Crosby. He wrote down the words from one of the Ink Spots songs to express his sentiments:

If I didn't care,
Would I feel this way?
Would my every prayer begin and end with just your name?
Would I feel this way
If I didn't care for you?

I knew Spero was a man with two left feet, who didn't dance, who didn't like the classics, who had taken me to only one play at the Erlanger Theater in Buffalo, because I had the tickets. I wrote back and pretended to believe he and I would really do all those things after the war was over.

His letters were also filled with longing for home, for his family, for Buffalo, for life before the war. He didn't write about babies, four-burner stoves nor refrigerators.

Several of my other home town pen-pals hadn't written to me in a very long time.

One day, my sister sent me a clipping from the Tonawanda News that brought me news of death. My very first high-school boyfriend, the one who was a Paratrooper in the 82nd Airborne, had been killed in the Normandy invasion on June 6. I cried for the young boy that had taken me to the senior prom whose only dream in life was to buy a car. He was only twenty years old. Now he'd never get that car. I cried and cried, first that he had lost his life and then again because he never got that car.

Another letter arrived from Mama with more sad news. Our friend and neighbor, Mrs. Martin's son, Henry, little Squirtball, had been drowned when his ship was hit by a Jap kamakazi. He was only nineteen years old. How ironic. He had joined the Navy, because he thought it was the safest place to be.

My heart was sorely tried that day. I cried for him and all the Marines and soldiers to whom I had said good-be.

I cried for Spero too.

And I cried for my handsome Marine Captain about whom I had woven so many fantasies. Maybe he was gone to the Pacific again.

My heart was heavy.

I buried myself in the boring stack of paper work that I was given to type, the orders and disbursement of supplies and corre-spondence that ran Post Depot Supply. The harder I worked the more work I was given. The sergeant had forgotten I was labeled a trouble-maker and the major no longer looked at me nor watched me with apprehension. Quartermaster Depot Supply was not the kind of work place where there was any kind of joking or pranks. It was an eight hour day of toil.

I needed to see familiar faces and so I returned to Motor Transport garage to say "hi" to everybody.

I was greeted with joy and friendliness. They fell all over themselves in their eagerness to show me the orderly garage which no longer had broken down vehicles cluttering the place. Proud as they were of the improvements they had accomplished, I couldn't care less for vehicles. It was their faces I wanted to see. It was reassuring to greet male buddies again, men with whom I had worked, and to see that they hadn't been shipped out. There was a lot of hugging and ruffling of each other's hair.

Three of the Motor Transport *gyrenes* asked me out on a date. They were some of the very same Marines who had given me such a hard time over the generators. The story of what happened to Captain Bungle had not died down as usual scuttlebutt did on the Post. We relived it over again.

When they all came to pick me up for the Post Theater and discovered we were a foursome, no one really minded. We were all Marine buddies, weren't we?

I was glad I made this mix-up. It was much better dating one fourth of a squad. We walked in military cadence to the Post Theater and they chanted their Boot Camp songs, which were so different from ours.

I wished my old bunkies were here. I didn't want any more changes in life. I wished Spero was here. He was always so comfortable to be with even though my knees did not buckle when he kissed me as they did with my phantom Captain Walking John who had known how make a girl melt in his arms.

I turned and laughed at a joke I hadn't heard one of my Marine escorts say. They were having fun competing for my attention, enjoying putting each other down. Their offers of undying love for me became more and more extravagant as each one suggested loudly for all to hear, how to throw the others overboard so we could be alone. They were having so much enjoyment with their own male companionship they never noticed my attention was miles away. I was only a foil and straight man for their wit and jokes.

We sat in the Post Theater. It was crowded as usual with every seat taken. As soon as the lights dimmed, I felt fingers inching across my knees coming from each side towards the middle of my lap. The hands met in the middle and the boys on either side of me were content to hold on to each other caressing and being caressed in return, playing finger games.

It was too precious to resist. I patted my hair and from the corner of their eyes, each Marine on each side of me realized the hand he was caressing wasn't mine. They slapped each other furiously and couldn't let go fast enough.

At first, they didn't think the joke was so funny, but by the time we reached the Tap Room, it had become hilarious as they teased each other

"If you expect to hold my hand again, Mac, you better get rid of those dish-pan hands. For Christ sake! Get some hand lotion."

"Look who's talking! You've got the hands of a walrus!"

"I wouldn't touch you again if you drank the damn hand lotion straight out of the bottle!"

The next day it was the story of the Post Garage and had made the rounds all the way to my old Barracks Three.

Stretch, Minnie and Angel from Motor Transport barracks came over the next night to laugh about it and share the joke all over again with me. It felt wonderful to be raucous and loud with the women of Motor Transport squad who looked so rugged and Marine Corps in their sheep-skin jackets and boondockers.

How beautiful they were! How confident and regal they were, their strength and maturity evident in the way they moved. How wonderful to be with these dedicated hard-working accomplished Women Marines who could strip an engine in no time and put it back together, who could drive monster trucks in the pre-dawn freezing temperatures and still have enough energy to roller skate, dance and drink beer with the best of them.

I longed to be back in Barracks Three with my old Motor Transport bunkies who roller skated down the middle of the room.

They departed and left me to the quiet tranquillity of my new billet. The women in Barracks Two did not roller skate in the squadroom nor did they play country music.

Week-ends were the worst. The Post and all the barracks emptied out as everyone went out on liberty. To stay on the Post on a week-end when you didn't have duty was as bad as admitting you had no date on a Saturday night. I turned on my radio, but the songs of Glenn Miller made me only sadder. My favorite band leader—our whole country's favorite music man—had become another casualty of this war. Captain Miller's plane was lost over the English Channel and after several months, he was declared dead.

The faces of my dear old friends and the boys back home who would not return from this war remained to haunt me.

I pressed my uniform and headed for Washington D.C.

Love And War–Washington D.C.–Spring 1945

Washington D.C. was the most exciting city in the world. Just walking down the streets and visiting the stores could dispel any clouds of sorrow and boredom. The sidewalks were crowded with uniformed men and women. Music blared from restaurants, night clubs and shops. Despite gas rationing, the roads were filled with the cacophony of cars, buses, street-cars and taxis which added a contrapuntal rhythm to the noise.

I decided to make this trip a small liberty and stay overnight, at the same house in Georgetown where Spero and I had spent the last night of his furlough. It would be comforting to relive that memory.

I made a record at the Free Pepsi-Cola Center which I addressed to Spero. I sat at one of their desks and wrote a Pepsi-post card to every person on my list, to my sisters, friends, Mama and Dad, Colonel Buse and Mrs. Buse.

As I wandered about, I began to feel a niggling nagging pressure to go visit the Hotel Washington again. It had been months since my last adventure there.

My desire to relive the moments with my ghost, Captain Walking John (*I had begun to call him that in my memory*) was so persistent that it didn't make sense. The face of my Marine poster lover had blurred and softened in my memory. I was no star-crossed "Evangeline" after all. It was no longer any fun to be the heroine in a play of unrequited love. I couldn't remember what he looked like and that bothered me.

Being flirtatious didn't faze me because that was what a pretty girl should be. It was fun, harmless and men liked it. Fickleness, on the other hand, denoted a character flaw. When I tried to bring my lost captain to mind, all I could see was Buster Crabbe or John Wayne. Even his hot kisses had cooled in my memory. Gerry was right. It was being "in love" that I was after, just as the song went:

It's love I'm after
I don't want to be a millionaire
I only thing for which I care
Is love

But the feeling of wanting to visit the site of my great romance again stayed with me. It didn't go away at lunch, and it lingered like the taste of onions long after I had made the rounds of the shops.

I felt a pull so strong, a call so irresistible, a mental telepathy message bouncing back so hard that I knew I had to do something about it.

I hopped a street car and was offered a seat by a sailor who started a conversation as he clung to the strap above me. Cute as he was, I wasn't in the mood to have my fading memories interrupted. I turned down his invitation to go to the USO in D.C. and dance the night away. I wanted to go to another dance with a ghost.

Like poking a tongue into an aching hole in a tooth to see whether it would hurt, I had to go to the scene of our last dance one more time.

Maybe this feeling of loss for what might have been would go away if I sat in the lobby and watched all the beautiful people. What was so silly about that?

I was stunning in my *Marine Corps Dress Whites*. I was just as attractive as the smartly dressed civilian women in their flowered patterned dresses that were patrons of the Hotel Washington.

I too was smartly dressed in my summer two piece white cotton gabardine jacket and skirt, crisp with gold buttons and Marine insignia, my green corporal stripes, green hat trimmed with white cord, my green covered shoulder purse swinging at my left side, my hands demurely covered with white gloves and smart white pumps and rayon stockings on my feet. No, I was not out of place at the Hotel Washington. I could hold my head high, proudly. I was a United States Marine.

I entered the lobby. The potted palms were still there. The lobby was filled with beautifully dressed women and men in uniforms, sitting on couches and milling about. My heart jumped when I saw the back of a Marine officer who reminded me of my lost Captain, but I turned away quickly not anxious to get caught in that silly game. I could hardly remember his face. Thinking I'd recognize him from the back of his head was really stretching it. All Marines in uniforms looked alike.

The tall doors leading into the ballroom were closed. I walked over and tried the handles to open them just to look inside one more time and remember the most wonderful night of my life. The carved heavy doors gave way and made a loud noise as I slipped inside. They clanged shut and I waited a few seconds with my back against the door to see if anyone had heard, expecting to be chased out any moment.

The room was cavernous. Gilt chairs were stacked up against the wall like wallflowers waiting to be asked to dance. The mistletoe was gone. The chandeliers were turned off and the room was in semi-darkness.

I was alone. I closed my eyes and once again hundreds of people filled the grand ballroom with laughter, music and dancing.

I sang a few bars of a melancholy song and danced by myself into the center of the room.

Will I ever find?
The boy on my mind

Theresa Karas Yianilos

The boy that is
My ideal

Somewhere, the door creaked open and footsteps came up behind me. I turned to apologize for my intrusion when two arms enfolded me and held me tightly, frightening me at first. Something deep inside me responded with recognition to the familiar feeling and fragrance of his Marine uniform almost before my conscious brain told me it was him.

His body swayed with mine. I was startled at the reality of the mirage. If I were going to hallucinate like this, I would not do it with closed eyes. There was absolutely no end to this dream. I felt his arms around me and I knew I didn't want the illusion to disappear. I held on so tightly and returned kiss for kiss. I began to tremble and held on more dearly. There wasn't one thing I could think to say.

I could only whisper his name.

"Walking John. John Walker, John Walker."

"Jane Greystoke." He nibbled on my ear as he whispered the name I had given him so carelessly.

That silly name. I repressed the nervous giggle that came out of nowhere. That dumb name I had given him so flippantly, so flirtatiously.

What was he doing here? Did he live at the Hotel Washington? Was he billeted here?

"I don't understand. How did this happen? How are you here?"

This time I wanted some answers. He wasn't going to get away without telling me where he came from this time.

"I couldn't believe my eyes when I saw you open those doors. It's fate, my own little Lady Marine. Pure fate! Do you believe in fate?"

Of course, I believed in fate.

Fate led me to the recruiting poster of Walking John in Buffalo, to Lanie's bar and her toilet, to the Hotel Washington and the mistletoe of Oklahoma, and to this Marine who came from California. That cinched it for me. The coincidence of our ever meeting again affirmed my belief that we were meant to be together.

I was overcome by the romance of this real life fairy-tale movie I was living. I was every heroine in every pulp magazine love story I had ever read by the light of a flashlight under the covers in my bed.

We stood there in a tight embrace, trading kisses, kisses that were different. His lips would barely touch mine yet electric impulses raced through my body until I almost cried for a closer stronger pressing of our lips.

His hands caressed my hair, and held me as we danced to music that wasn't playing in this beautiful empty ballroom, just like Fred Astaire and Ginger Rogers.

My head came to his shoulder and his face was against my hair as he spoke softly but so firmly, "I don't care how many Marines you've been with. I am your last Marine!"

So he thought I was fickle with many beaus and lovers?

How could I tell him it was otherwise?

I would have to prove it. I knew I could.

He held on to my hand tightly this time.

"I lost you the last time, but I'm hanging on to you, my special Little Lady. I know a good thing when I see it."

My God! Mama's exact words!

"So do I," I said.

He held my arm and together we walked into the lobby. He wasn't as tall as I remembered him to be. Somehow in my fantasies he had grown a foot.

He grinned and propelled me into the little hotel gift shop and said, "We'll do this right."

He went straight to the tiny jewelry counter where there were displays of engagement and wedding rings, bracelets, lockets and Zippo cigarette lighters.

I held my breath in astonishment and wondered if he'd ask me to choose which one I wanted.

He pointed to the large box of chocolates, a bouquet of flowers and a large wine bottle with silver wrapping on the shelves behind the counter.

I carried the flowers. He had the other stuff.

He had the use of only one hand as he opened the door to his suite.

"I have been *up the pole* since the night I sighted you *adrift.* I hadn't made sure you were *secured* the last time we met," he said. He was still talking Navy. He had not forgotten how I scrambled Marine Corps sea-going language.

"I knew you were the one after you pulled me out of that toilet and helped me get away from the MPs." I said, still in awe over the coincidence of our fateful reunion.

"When did you know?" I asked softly, taking it for granted he felt the same. He must. His kisses told me this was forever.

"Know what?" he asked, his head bent over the keyhole. The key was sticking in the door and he gave me the heavy bottle, the box of chocolates and the flowers to hold while he fiddled with the lock.

"What you just said," I said.

He waited for me to elaborate and he was concentrating so hard on the key that I had to remind him of what he had just said.

"That I was your special lady. That you'd hang on to me."

"I hadn't moored you properly the last time. That was bad sailing on my part. Will you forgive me?"

When he smiled at me like that, I would forgive him anything.

"At first, your bars scared me," I confessed. I was still apprehensive and afraid of breaking the laws of fraternization just as if I were a green Boot straight out of Lejeune. Did I really expect old General Torrey to come creeping up the hallway right here at Hotel Washington? Silly of me, but there it was.

"You certainly didn't act it when we met. We had heard about you girls in the Pacific. Then when you came right out with it and said you wanted to come back here with me to my hotel, I knew I found me a prize. And when you kissed me under the mistletoe in front of all those Oakies, well—."

"I thought you kissed me first!"

The door gave way and we were in his "suite". I wasn't the same nervous little girl from Tonawanda any more. I did not pull away. I'd seen "suites" before.

He grabbed and picked me up easily, heavy bottle and all.

"Now there's more than one way to chart a course through the *Rocks and Shoals*. The night is just starting," he said.

In all my fantasies and dreams, I hadn't gotten this far.

His caressed me gently as he carried me lightly through the living room into the bedroom and gently flopped me onto the bed as easily as Rhett had picked up Scarlett and carted her up the stairs in that famous scene where she got pregnant. Now love was happening to me!

He wasn't breathing as heavily as I and he was doing the carrying. I knew if he had a horse, he would have ridden off into the sunset like John Wayne with me him hanging on for dear life behind him.

The moment was magical. If Mama could only see me now. *What am I saying? I hope she can't see!*

He kneeled beside me, picked up both my hands and kissed each one of my fingers and then the center of my palm and looked soulfully into my eyes. Charles Boyer couldn't have done it any better.

He was very experienced in his love making.

His hand caressed my leg down to my ankle until he came to my G.I. white regulation dress pumps. He took them off and let them fall and rubbed my legs, stopping at the thighs. He nibbled my toes and the tingle went right through me and raised the hairs on the back of my head. No one ever had done that to me before. He kissed the back of my neck just above the collar line and tickled the lobes of my ears. My brain shut down. I let the emotions roll over me like the gentle waves of Lake Erie.

I opened my eyes and looked directly into his. He hadn't closed his eyes as I had when he bent down and kissed me, first on the eyes, then the temples and finally gently on the lips. He didn't rush me. He was slow, considerate and very knowing. Somewhere in the back of my mind, thoughts registered and I chased them away. *How did he know just what to do? He was so experienced, so sure in his movements. There must have been other women in his life before me. Who were they? Where were they? How many were they? Did I care?*

He helped me take my jacket off and even tried to unbutton my skirt when he placed his arms around me.

I excused myself to undress in the bathroom. I really didn't know how to handle this part very well. It was one thing to throw off your clothes in the barracks before eighty girls and run half naked to the showers before another girl got one of the few shower stalls. It was another thing to strip before a man.

There was no graceful sexy way I could get out of my G.I. girdle. Putting one on and taking it off required some clumsy contortions. I wasn't about to let this elegant Marine see me go through those gymnastics.

I marveled at the new fire-cracker sparkles going through my body. I had emotions that I never knew were there. Waves of confusion hit me hard as I had urges I didn't recognize. I was in deep water that was over my head.

If he was to be my last Marine, was I to be his last Marine too? Was that a proposal or a proposition?

"We'll wet down this occasion with a real toast. Stand fast! Don't move!" he called as he bounded into the other room of the "suite".

The phone rang. He picked it up and I heard him say, "Cast off, Mac. This compartment is full!"

I heard the pop of a cork as I returned from the bathroom where I had hung my uniform. The cotton twill fabric in my dress whites wrinkled very easily. I hadn't brought an iron. I was wearing my rayon slip and it clung to the curves of my body which no longer was held in with a girdle and bra. I was barefoot.

My Captain stood in the doorway holding a champagne bottle and two glasses. He had placed a box of chocolates next to the pillows and smiled wamly, welcoming me back from my trip to the bathroom.

The moment was filled with romance, sophistication and seduction. Soft hotel music flowed from the wall. The lamps cast a soft glow into the room and the drapes were drawn against the twilight. The night was still early. Daylight still remained of the day. What a day! It felt like midnight and it was only six o'clock.

He handed the glass of champagne to me and we smiled at each other as I took a gulp. It was sour. I didn't like it any better than the beer I had at the Slopschute.

"Do you have a Coca-Cola?" I asked.

"Is this your first glass of champagne?"

He seemed so incredulous at my naiveté that I suddenly felt very shy, very provincial, like the very small town girl from Tonawanda that I really was.

I took a chocolate and bit into it to cover my confusion.

Spero's family made better chocolates.

The thought came into my mind unbidden and I had a knot in my stomach where there was none before. Spero's St. Bernard's face floated before me, like an apparition at a seance! The poor inexperienced dope hadn't known how to kiss me the first time he tried it in the ice-cream truck I had to show him how to do it right.

And then another thought raced through my head as I thought of poor Henry Martin and his warning about *Spanish Fly* in a girl's drink. He had mentioned beer. He hasn't said a word about what champagne did to a girl, whether it made her want *it*?

Is this what seduction and lust was like?

Doc's disembodied voice whispered her oft-repeated warning, *"Carry a condom!"*

I didn't have one of those things. *Did he? Should I ask?*

All my mother's dire warnings started to crackle in my head like the static of bad reception in a cheap radio, each platitude canceling out the other.

No man will buy the cow if he can get the milk free.
You never know a good thing when you see it!
You never know a man until you sleep with him!
You'll come home pregnant!

My reflection bounced back from the dressing table mirror.

I was standing there in my white slip.

My slip was white, not black.

In the barracks, enlisted women who were shacking up with officers began buying expensive exotic underwear. In their black silk slips, bras and panties they stood out like blackbirds in a flock of doves.

Suddenly, I didn't want to become a blackbird.

I was a white dove and I felt like a pigeon.

I excused myself.

He stood there smiling and raised his glass to me as I made a return trip to the bathroom. His gesture told me we had all the time in the world.

On the hook on the door was my uniform. I had been very neat. I slowly put on my dress whites.

When I entered the room, my Marine Captain was on the bed without his shirt, and he looked so virile with tight muscles that rippled so impressively that my breath stopped just at the sight of him. My Marine recruiting poster hero knew he looked manly and handsome, my every movie hero from Clark Gable to Jon Hall to Buster Crabbe to John Wayne. His hardened muscular body was a beacon that could attract every moth that came against him.

And I was going away from him.

I found my pumps.

The smile fell off his face.

"I'm sorry," I said. "I don't want to be a blackbird."

The last words he said as I closed the door were, "A blackbird? What the hell does that mean?"

He didn't open the door after I had shut it as gently as I could. I wondered; if he chased after me would I have the strength to keep walking or would I go back into the room? I really didn't get the chance to find out.

My Captain didn't know my name and I never did get the chance to ask him what his religion was. Fenton was the only one who really wanted to know anyhow. I had a suspicion he wasn't Greek Orthodox. Maybe he was an Episcopalian.

My big romance had floundered on *Rocks and Shoals* after all.

Once again I was standing before the elevator in the Hotel Washington looking at the arrow. It pointed *Down*.

Marine Barracks Quantico–May 1945

For a few weeks after my encounter with my Captain John Walker, I had strange nightmarish dreams but they went away and left me with some new and disturbingly speculative thoughts. One bad dream was persistent and remained long enough for me to remember it upon awakening.

In this same dream, I found myself wandering through a beautiful large estate with many bedrooms, each more sumptuously furnished than the other. As I went from room to room that was always filled with a crowd of elegantly dressed people, none of whom I recognized, I would spot the face of my Captain. I could feel the rush of relief when I saw him. As I approached him he turned his back in a gesture of rejection. It was then I noticed there were signs everywhere, even floating in a large pool, in the red and gold colors of the Marine Corps, that read "Out Of bounds."

What did my dream mean? Was I regretting walking out on my captain? Not really. I had been as frightened of his expertise in love making and my lustful response to it as I was of breaking Marine Corps rules and regulations.

I realized that what bothered me more were the rules of fraternization that had placed me in the category of a second-class citizen. They were the same rules that I had accepted readily and without question when I had entered the Corps.

The Corps had a two-class system, perpetuated by history and tradition, which placed enlisted in one class and officers into another.

Rank had its privileges. I didn't care for that division. I had felt the separation and had seen the inequalities.

A two-class society was fine for England. For me, it was un-American. I had earned an A in my American History and Civics classes. I had memorized the Declaration of Independence...*we hold these truths to be self-evident, that all men are created equal...They have inalienable rights to life, liberty and pursuit of happiness.*

I had grown up believing in the American Dream where every girl could marry the prince and live in a big house. The Marine Corps rules would never allow any Cinderella to marry the prince, even if the glass slipper fitted, if he were an officer and she were enlisted. *Out of bounds. Out of bounds. Out of bounds.*

My negative attitude from my dream persisted.

At least, as a civilian, I always believed if I met a doctor, a lawyer or an Indian Chief with a college degree he wouldn't have been prevented from proposing to me because I had not attended a university. American literature abounded with stories of men who had married their secretaries, sales girls, waitresses and beauticians, even their mistresses. For thousands of years, men had proposed to women who won them with their beauty, charm and brains. Inequality made for happy marriages. Men liked girls who weren't as smart or as rich or as educated as they were. It was a fact of life, pounded into every girl's head by mothers, teachers, friends, the movies and magazines. Men didn't make passes at girls who wore glasses.

Once she was married it didn't matter what a female did or was before or where she was born. A Mrs. before any name wiped the slate clean. Once married, she got his name, his money and could be called Princess if he were the Prince, and live in the castle.

Maybe it wasn't the English way, since the Duchess of Windsor never got to be called Princess, much less Queen, but it certainly was the American Way.

Our American Navy and Marine Corps had been formed in the tradition of the English Navy but I came to the conclusion that certain English customs should have been left in England and never brought to our shores. Just as Captain John Smith made work respectable by demanding that English gentlemen pitch in with their own hands to produce food and shelter in America's first colony of Jamestown, the men of the Navy should have had the same kind of foresight.

The more I ruminated over my lost love, the madder I got at the Marine Corps. I couldn't direct my blame at any one person or officer in the Corps. That made it all the more difficult, since it was the tradition and the demand for blind obedience that made me upset. So much that was undemocratic and unfair in the Corps hid behind military rules and customs which assured their perpetuation.

The Corps had instilled discipline and loyalty in me and had given me esprit de corps and made me *Semper Fidelis, Always Faithful*.

It had also done one other thing.

It made me think of myself as 'enlisted'.

I hadn't had low self esteem when I came into the Corps, but somewhere along with military bearing, esprit de corps training and protocol, I had been taught that I had to look for a symbol on somebody's shoulder to determine where they and I stood in the hierarchy of human beings and how far below them I was positioned.

Would that prejudice stay with me the rest of my life?

What were the insignia I had to look for in civilian life?

I was still lost in a sea of desks in the Quartermaster Department at Post Depot Supply. I had come to accept my duty as an 8 to 4 job. I just didn't punch a time clock and I was wearing a Marine uniform instead of a pleated skirt and bobby socks.

The major and the sergeant had changed their minds about just letting me sit there in the middle of the room with no work to do within the second week of my transfer there from Motor Transport. Now, as corporal, I had more than enough work to do, typing up supply orders, dispensing toilet paper throughout the bases and other vital necessities to run a war. I returned to the barracks every night exhausted, too tired to eat at early chow at 4:30 p.m., going into Quantico town or the Hostess House for a snack after I had taken a long nap. I lost more weight.

I was no longer plagued with romantic illusions about a Marine whose face I could not recall. The whole episode had retreated into my memory as just another movie I had seen.

In my most quiet moments of reflection, I was smugly satisfied with myself, happy I hadn't given up my virginity to a stranger.

If Mama had known her lectures had taken root she would have been very happy. But, of course, I could never tell her.

Events swirled about me that commanded all my attention. Each day brought more portentous war news that affected each and every one of us.

In March the Marines took Iwo Jima at a bitter cost. We lost over four thousand Marines and counted over seventeen thousand wounded. The Fourth Division had paid a terrible price. Over five thousand killed, but no one could confirm that. Someone had leaked the figure and the whole Post of Quantico knew another Pacific Island in the march towards Japan had been secured at a great cost of Marine lives. The picture showing the planting of the Stars and Stripes on the top of Mt. Suribachi was on every front page and for a little while the news of what the Marines were doing overwhelmed the news from the European Front.

Quantico was almost a ghost town, bereft of young men. True to his word, General Commandant Vandegrift had done what he had promised when he took command of the Marine Corps in January 1944:

"There will be two kinds of Marines, those going to the Pacific and those who have been overseas. "

Quantico was filled with over-age Marines, and those recovering from battles.

The battle for Okinawa had begun and the newly formed Sixth Division was fighting there. Women Marines, almost twenty thousand of us, had fulfilled our role in this war finally by freeing all combat Marines that were available throughout the Corps. Enough men were released to make up a full division, and that was the Sixth Division.

On the twelfth of April 1945, President Roosevelt died. United States and the Allied nations went into mourning.

The flags in Quantico and throughout the nation were at half-mast. You could see the flag pole next to Iron Mike from any point at Quantico. The whole Post grieved for a man who had been loved by the people he had served, as President of the United States for four terms, from 1932 to 1945 and as Commander-in-Chief of a World War from 1941 to his death. Recent photographs showed how gaunt he had become in that service. There were always people who had been against Franklin Delano Roosevelt, but the enormity of the tragedy of losing our leader, just when victory was so near, silenced all voices.

Marines cried openly. No one apologized for having red eyes and visible tears. Our country had lost a father. His death was a personal loss to each Marine. The Corps had lost a good friend in President Roosevelt. He had always made his preference for the

Marines known. When he spoke of the Marines he used the pronoun, "We", and referred to himself as a Marine. I mourned and grieved a long time after that day.

Our Post emptied out as everyone went to Washington D. C. for the funeral parade. The train was on time but I had missed it which forced me to take the later one. I arrived to see the end of the cortege going down Pennsylvania Avenue.

The Women Marines were represented by a large contingency of us from the Women's Reserve Battalion of Arlington Annex. The Commandant's Own Marine Corps Band marched to a very slow cadence with the measured beat of the drums. The crowd was united in its loss and only a hush and quiet greeted the casket as it passed.

President Harry S. Truman was now our Commander in Chief. I remembered the little man who had stopped me on my way to Boot Camp to ask if the Corps were taking in children. I also remembered the comment he made to his wife that the propaganda machine of the Marine Corps was as good as Stalin's. It was a long time ago. Was it only fifteen months? I had the feeling President Truman didn't like the Marine Corps very much.

Mussolini died in April too. He had been shot by his own people, the Italian Partisans, and they strung him up alongside his mistress. His own countrymen rejoiced.

The next day Hitler committed suicide with his mistress whom he married just before their death. The most evil man this century had produced was gone. He had left as his legacy, a continent in smoldering ruins. No one mourned him.

Only Japan's Emperor Hirohito, and his malevolent Premier Tojo, the architect of Japan's aggression, remained of the Axis. Both these men were now the target of our full military force and had to be eliminated from the face of this earth.

All of America's vast war effort focused towards that goal. The Marines were to be part of an assault in the Pacific as the Armed Forces consolidated their efforts towards attacking Japan itself.

On May 7, 1945, Germany surrendered formally to the combined Allied Forces, the Americans, and the Russian Army. The next day on May 8, headlines on newspapers shouted:

V-E Day! Victory in Europe!

Everyone went wild.

The Post celebrated with dancing, kissing and hugging. Parties were held in every recreation hall in every barrack in Quantico. Beer flowed liberally at all the Slopschutes and clubs. The joy could not be contained. There was chanting and snake dancing with arms linked together on the street and sidewalks. Everyone greeted everyone else with the *V For Victory* signal, forefinger and middle finger straight up. Marines kissed for no reason as all except we were all so happy.

While the nation gave a collective sigh of relief, the pace on the Marine Posts quickened. Every Marine knew the job still had to be finished. Marines still had to fight for more islands in the Pacific. They would be shedding more blood.

Japan stood alone.

Their military regime, headed by Tojo, refused to surrender unconditionally and Japan rebuffed several overtures from our government. The writing was on the wall; they couldn't possibly have any hope of winning this war they had started, yet the Japs fought all the harder. The Japanese showed no sign that they would ever surrender. It was obvious to every Marine, from the *grunt* to the Commandant, that Japan had lost the war in the Pacific but they continued to fight to the last man.

It meant more Marines would die.

The hate for the Japs was strong in every Marine. There was no admiration for the courage of the Japanese soldier and his willingness to die and take a Marine with him if he could when he was sent to his ancestor. The Jap was considered sub-human, who couldn't think for himself, who followed orders blindly to his death, even in the face of insurmountable odds.

Every Marine knew that job was still unfinished and there were more islands that had to be won.

All our country's resources and our victorious Armed Forces were directed towards the Pacific and mainland Japan.

The war was over in Europe and soldiers were coming home. For the Marines, it was business as usual. The war had not ended for them.

In Europe, the cleaning up had started. People started to return to their bombed out villages.

General Eisenhower returned in June to a ticker tape parade in New York. The Army prepared to send the boys back on the troop ships that had taken them there. Some of its rules were relaxed.

The letters from Spero no longer were blackened out. A few that were written on stationary rather than V-Mail came through without being censored and they included photographs. He wrote how the American infantry had met the Russians outside of Berlin. One of the letters had a pin from a Russian soldier's uniform that was given to him in comradeship when the two armies met at Berlin.

His Division, the 104th Timberwolves of the American First Army, had entered Berlin first and they had captured it.

But, the American soldiers were ordered to retreat and back track and wait two miles outside Berlin until the Russians coming from the East could catch up. It was timed for the two Armies, the Russian Army from the East and Spero's First Army from the West to march into Berlin together and meet in the center of Berlin (*at the point which later became the site of the Berlin Wall*).

When I saw the newspaper photographs of Russians and Americans together in triumph, it bothered me that our victorious Army, with my Spero, had to share the credit. I knew the Russian people suffered and had fought valiantly, but when you are first, you should be given the credit and prize, and not have to share it. But, I suppose it doesn't work that way in war.

Spero's letters included pictures that he had taken on his march through Germany. One particular batch was so frightening and strange that I put them aside without showing them to anyone. They were photographs he had taken of cords of bodies of nude skeletons, which were stacked up like firewood in great piles, and left lying on the ground everywhere in grotesque positions. Some of these skeletons, wearing shredded parts of striped pajamas, actually were standing up as if they were still alive.

I didn't understand what I was seeing. Had he visited a cemetery? Why were these bodies lying on the open ground unburied?

A short time later, the obscenities of the Nazi Death Camps and the Concentration Camps filled the front pages of every newspaper, magazine and newsreel in the country. Our nation was shocked by the horror of the revelations.

Our armies had liberated thousands of prisoners in Germany. The survivors in these camps told their stories to the soldiers who had rescued them, one of whom had been my Spero.

Millions of men, women and children had been killed by the Germans over the four years of war. The Germans had practiced mass genocide and carried out, through acts of wholesale murder, Hitler's edicts and national program to cleanse the Aryan race. The Nazis gathered people from all the captured nations along with anyone who had Jewish blood in them, including German nationals, and put them in Concentration Camps throughout Germany and Austria. They shot, hanged, and buried their prisoners whether they were alive or dead, in ditches they were forced to dig themselves. The Nazis did other acts of violence that were too inhumane to contemplate in a national effort to achieve this goal. They gassed these unarmed civilians thousands at a time, burned their bodies in crematoriums that had been built for just such a purpose in order to expedite the extermination with Teutonic efficiency.

The second time I looked at the pictures that Spero had sent me I was able to understand what he had recorded. I recognized what the crematoriums were and what they did and I knew the naked standing skeletons were people who were barely alive that he had rescued.

I realized Spero was one of the fighting soldiers that had liberated some of these unfortunate souls and my heart went out to him. I had become so proud of him.

In June some of our European Armies came home and we all rejoiced with the women in the barracks whose loved ones were on that first boat load. Every day women returned from mail call and waved letters jubilantly proclaiming the news that their men were on their way home from Europe.

The silence of those Women Marines whose loved ones had been killed or wounded was louder than the hurrahs. The women whose men were still prisoners of the Japanese found new strength to hope.

Theresa Karas Yianilos

Spero, A Hero Returns–Summer 1945

I had always loved mail call. Over the past four years, I had gathered a few pen pals and my name was shouted with great frequency which elevated my status with my squadmates who were always impressed by my mail. They would groan when my name was called again and again and it was fun to let them think that all my letters were from beaus since some of them were from companies answering my coupons I had clipped out of magazines.

Now, a new anxiety had surfaced to pick at me as the mail clerk handed me more letters, a dozen at a time.

All the sailors and soldiers, whose morale I had been worried about for four years, to whom I had written cheery loving letters now wrote they were heading my way on their way home. I realized belatedly that some of them were looking forward to being with their Marine girl-friend who had been so steadfast and had waited.

What had I written? What had I promised?

My chickens were coming home to roost.

Spero's letters were filled with page after page of anticipation. He couldn't wait until he could return home to his beloved Buffalo and his beloved Marine sweetheart. It was only a matter of weeks, days, hours.

The first chicken to come home was Spero. Somewhere overseas he had changed to a fighting rooster.

When I saw Spero as he jumped off the Quantico train, my heart did a cartwheel and it began the craziest kind of pounding. I realized suddenly that my affection for him was strong enough to be called love.

He was gaunt; his hair had thinned out at his forehead, and his eyes were sad, hurt and held an expression of wariness as if he expected someone hiding in the bushes or around the corner of the building to pop out at him. He limped a little.

Lost in the pain of seeing someone I cared for looking so tired, so thin, so fragile, so lean when he should have been round and comfortable, I hugged him and kissed him with abandon and joy.

His relief that I had waited for him encased both of us in a warm blanket of emotion and love. There was no embarrassment this time as he returned my kisses with passion right there at the Quantico station.

He was so vulnerable and scared. I hugged and kissed him with great affection and much tenderness, stopping to embrace him and kiss him again as we walked. My total happiness and relief to have him at my side, safe and whole, was overwhelming. I was so grateful he had come through the European fighting unscathed that my soul cried out to him and I said a prayer of 'thanks' to God just in case He was listening.

We sat there on the bed in the Hostess House, with the door closed, and I held his hand while he talked and talked about us. We kissed and caressed each other, surprised at how natural it all seemed to be together again.

He didn't want to talk about the war. Nor did he want to tell me about the photographs but stupidly I asked him to explain what they were.

The fighting in Germany had been intense and when it was over, only two men had escaped being a casualty from his original platoon in the 104th Infantry Division. He was lucky enough to be one of them and grateful his frozen feet had recovered.

As new men joined his infantry company he was put in charge. One day, while in pursuit of Germans, his outfit marched into the countryside where they discovered an installation of buildings surrounded by electric fences which had been abandoned by the Nazis who had fled as the American troops closed in on them.

Nothing in all their experience had ever prepared the American infantry men for the sight that greeted their eyes. Nothing would ever be able to erase that sight from any one's memory who saw it. It haunted Spero when he returned to Quantico and for the rest of his life.

In the middle of a field, out in the German countryside, Spero and his men had stumbled into Nordhausen.

Nordhausen was a chamber of horrors, a Concentration Camp where slave labor was used to build bombs. Within the walls were thousands of starving and dying prisoners, mostly, Greeks, Jews and others who had been made prisoners and slaves. They had been without food or water for weeks and those who were still alive were too weak to stand.

Spero spoke to the Greeks in Greek, which was a language he had learned as a child and to the Jews in German, the language he had flunked in college.

People who were little more than skeletons with parched skin stretched over bones, had kissed Spero's hands and feet as he shared food with them which they couldn't hold down because they hadn't eaten solid food for months. The Nazis had departed so hurriedly that they had left thousands of bodies stacked like cords of wood without cremating them in the near-by crematoriums.

His Infantry Division was moving so fast towards Berlin that the burying was left for the Allied rear echelon troops to do.

I regretted asking him questions that dredged up such terrible memories. The price that he paid for such experiences, which he was able to submerge when he was awake, surfaced while he slept. When Spero took a nap, his body would jerk fitfully and he cried out in his sleep. I hugged him as tightly as I could which seemed to quiet him down. He clung to me even as he slept.

The clouds of war hung over our reunion.

His thirty day furlough was all too short. The time that remained was more precious than gold. He would have to report to his 104th Division in California in thirty days to train and prepare for the coming invasion of mainland Japan.

"Then it is true?" I said.

"Yes, it is. We are getting ready to attack Japan itself. The Army announced that there will be one million casualties," Spero said casually, too casually.

The United States had announced that the Armed Forces would assault the islands of Japan in autumn of 1945 with an attack force of two million men. A projection of the death of one million men was being publicized as a known probability. The Army was preparing the American public for the worst.

Japan had never signed the Geneva Accord which called for the fair treatment of prisoners of war. They had killed, tortured, starved and beheaded prisoners including Americans they had captured. Very few Marines of the garrisons that had been captured at China, Wake Island, Guam, Corregidor, Bataan and the Philippines had survived their merciless cruelty. The Japanese soldiers had killed two hundred thousand Philippine people, men, women and children for resisting them and helping the Americans.

Their attitude was a reflection of what their society believed. Japanese people considered life an interim condition before death and joining their ancestors. The code of bushido placed "personal honor" above life. "Saving face" was part of that code. Dying to preserve that honor was the solution and it didn't matter whether the death came from suicide or at the hands of another, whether it came in battle or alone with a knife against the belly. The Japanese code mandated death. There was no other choice available, no negotiation possible, no compromise, no individual choice nor decision allowed. Each man, woman and child was a warrior who would fight to the death if so ordered by the Emperor no matter how futile the gesture or hopeless the cause.

Within the context of this philosophy, it was entirely possible that the Japanese nation could commit suicide before surrendering when the Americans invaded their homeland. They had done that on the island of Saipan much to the horror of American Marines who could not stop women and children as they plunged over the cliffs to the rocks below.

Unlike the German women who had been kept out of the war and weren't allowed to work in the factories or shoulder arms, the Japanese women had participated in their war and would fight side by side with their men. The slaughter that was projected for both Japan and the United States was beyond anyone's comprehension.

In June 1945, while the Army sent the American boys home from Europe on one troop ship after another, other American boys, the Marines, Army and Navy, fought on and finally secured Okinawa at great cost of Marine and Army lives.

Okinawa was the island nearest to Japan. It was to be used to launch the assault. It was the last island that needed to be won. The Japs had fought all the harder although they knew they had lost the war.

The United States now occupied all the Pacific islands it needed to launch an assault: Guadalcanal, Bougainville, Tarawa, Peleliu, Tinian, Biak, Saipan and Guam, Iwo Jima and now Okinawa. All these little islands in between, in the South and Central Pacific had been fought for at heavy losses to the Marines.

The Army and Marine Aircraft fought together for the Philippines and General MacArthur had returned as he had promised he would in October of 1944.

The strategies and policies of the Joint Chiefs of Staff had accomplished what the President of the United States had ordered them to do: Win this war. This they did with the total commitment of the Marines, the Marine Air Squadrons, the Navy and the Army and their Air Forces.

The Generals and Admirals had won the admiration of a grateful nation. General Dwight D. Eisenhower and General Douglas MacArthur had become heroes to the American people.

When Okinawa, the last island in the Pacific Theater of Operations fell, America had the bases from which to launch and supply its ships, planes and men and the land from which to launch the thousands of planes that would bomb mainland Japan and support our troops.

The last Naval Battle was won and sea lanes had been cleared of Japanese ships and submarines, many of which went to watery graves.

The invasion plans were common knowledge. Unlike the elaborate plans that had shrouded the opening of the Second Front and the invasion at Normandy, our intentions were published in the media. They were not a secret. Sometime in autumn, America was going to strike. Japan was given plenty of warning.

If military personnel of such low rank as Spero and I knew of the plans, then the Japanese people must know what the future held for them as a nation. Still the Japanese military refused to surrender.

The Americans were forced to attack the Japs right on their own home base. They would do this with the largest invasion armada the world had ever seen.

And Spero was going to be among those two million men.

He knew what going overseas this time meant. He had the same fatalistic attitude that I had seen in Marines who were being sent back to combat a second time.

There was nothing I could say or do.

His luck had held in Europe. He was pessimistic about his fate in Japan.

Our moments together became bitter-sweet. He had been lucky the first time in Europe. He was more resigned to his fate now. I could only comfort him by talking about the future as if we had all the time in the world.

We avoided talking about the war and the immediate months ahead. We talked about houses, furniture, children, food, clothes, friends, movies and songs. We gossiped about members of our family. His clan was enormous, his cousins many, including one that had been my best friend.

As we talked about the future we realized we were using the pronouns "our" "us" and "we." There was love, respect, trust and friendship between us. We went to the same church. We had "necked", kissed, hugged, slept in the same bed together, ate from the same plate, and had shared colds.

The time had come to find someone to marry us. Spero did not propose formally. He had considered himself engaged since the night we had slept together. We simply agreed that if we didn't waste any more time, we could turn our furlough into a honeymoon.

I didn't want to bid farewell to the Corps yet I no longer was torn between the choice of a career and wifehood and motherhood. Oh, yes, motherhood. I equated marriage with immediate pregnancy and that meant a *499 Medical Discharge*. Yet we both knew that we had made a spiritual promise to each other that would mean a lifetime of commitment. We believed marriage was forever.

We placed a long distance phone call to Colonel Buse in Charleston, South Carolina and his voice a thousand miles away was as strong as ever. I had kept my promise to him that I would tell him when I found the right one.

"Colonel Buse, I am going to marry Spero. We are going to Richmond to find a Justice of the Peace. There's no time for publishing banns so we can't be married in church this time."

He said, "Congratulations to you both. You made a good choice. He's a fine lad, Terry. My best to both of you."

Mrs. Buse was so delighted for us that I could hear her tears over the phone.

We went to the PX and bought two gold wedding bands for four dollars apiece.

Spero and I hailed the courier from Post Headquarters in his jeep and he remembered us from the year before. He drove us to near-by Manassas for a license and blood test and joked along the way.

"You know that the Civil War started right here in Manassas? Sure you want to go through with this? Sure you want to marry this Dogface?"

Theresa Karas Yianilos

"We'll never fight," I told him in a bridal flush of certainty. "My Spero is so agreeable. He says whatever makes me happy makes him happy."

Yes, being friends was the most important ingredient in a marriage. Respect, trust and love were also up there at the top of the list. And having the same religion.

My squadmates were thrilled and perhaps relieved that the saga of my love affairs was coming to a Cinderella end. They quickly threw a small shower party together in the lounge and I went through the ritual of opening presents. I laughed when I saw the rayon floor length night-gown the Motor Transport squad had chipped together to buy at the PX.

"You know, I don't wear anything when I sleep," I said.

"You need a nightgown on your wedding night," they insisted.

I didn't agree but I took it with me, just in case.

We took a train to Richmond, Virginia where a Justice of the Peace married us at the City Hall. The train rolled by just as the Judge started to speak and I didn't hear his words. When he stopped talking and looked at me, I said "I do" which must have been the right answer because the paper his clerk gave us said we were married by the authority of Prince William County, Richmond Virginia, that was vested in him.

We ate our wedding lunch at a restaurant near the City Hall. It was noon on a Saturday and we were the only patrons in this very elegant spacious dining room filled with tables draped with white tablecloths. All it served was sea-food. I ordered Maryland fried crabs which I ate with some difficulty because Spero had entwined his finger with his wedding ring on his left hand with mine and wouldn't let go. I still wore the corsage of white orchids on my dress white uniform that Spero had bought from the hotel florist before the ceremony. I knew it wasn't regulation and I was out of uniform but I didn't care.

As we were sitting there, the maitre d' brought over a bottle of champagne in a silver bucket with the restaurant's compliments.

We looked at the bottle and watched as the waiter went through an elaborate routine of opening it. The cork popped off and by some quirk I caught it. I put the cork in my purse to save in my scrapbook.

382

Theresa Karas Yianilos and Spero J. Yianilos
Wedding photo: Richmond, Va.

Spero and I exchanged glances. We preferred Coca-Cola. We looked at the filled glasses and took one sip to please the maitre d' who waited for our approval. It was champagne all right.

"Do we have to drink this whole bottle? How did they know we were newlyweds?" I whispered.

"I don't know. Must be the white orchids you're wearing on your uniform. Just take a couple of sips to be polite."

We entwined our arms and clinked glasses and kissed just as we had seen it done in the movies. The maitre d' and the owner applauded and came over to congratulate us.

Our total wedding party consisted of the two of us and the two of them, the waiter and the owner. It was wonderful.

The Jefferson Hotel was the same as before, but now I was staying with someone who cared for me and whom I loved. I no longer had to eat dinner alone. The candlelight, the fine china and the attentive waiters made as much of an impression on Spero as the fact I had known about this hotel.

"How did you know to come here?"

I did not explain my fantasy crush on a Marine officer who had been only a ghost that had wandered in and out of my life. There are some things wives should not tell husbands. I do not remember if that piece of advice had come out of my mother or if it was one of my own original thoughts.

Our stay at the historic Hotel Jefferson was everything a honeymoon should be. I did wear my new night gown with the rosebuds for two seconds, but I ripped it off when Spero said his mother had one just like it. When I giggled that his size 40 boxer shorts weren't any better, he did likewise. We skinny dipped into our mahogany four poster nuptial bed.

Still, on the second day of our honeymoon we both realized something else was necessary. We went to a bookstore and bought two books. I selected a guide book on sex titled MARRIED LOVE written by a doctor and Spero bought THE JOY OF COOKING. We both had a lot to learn since it was the first time for both of us. I never did buy nor carried condoms and neither did Spero. We would go through life teaching each other how to make love and how to cook. We would accept whatever fate God had in store for us.

We wandered about Richmond and visited the sights, the beautiful old houses, the gardens, the shops. I, dressed in my summer greens and he, in his tailored pressed khaki's were just two ordinary servicemen, yet we attracted smiles from friendly Virginians who seemed to know we were newly-weds.

I brought up the subject of how beautiful Richmond would be to live in after the war. It was my second choice of where to settle and start a family, next to California, of course. I had not given up my dream to live in the Far West under palm trees, but the beautiful city of Richmond was enhanced by the glow of a wonderful honeymoon.

We had our first argument on the third day of our honeymoon.

"We have to go to Buffalo," announced Spero. "We have to tell our family we are married and we'll have to do it again in church."

He didn't ask me. He told me. He said it with a tone of firm certainty that made it clear he considered the decision final. My sweet husband had a silent streak of stubbornness I hadn't noticed before.

Go back to Buffalo? To that bleak cold dreary city? It was too hot in the summer and too cold in the winter. There was no in-between. There were better places in this world to live. My vote was for Richmond or California. But I didn't even get a ballot.

Just as I had not been given any choices in the Marine Corps when I took the oath of allegiance, it seems I had been disenfranchised when I said "I do" to the judge.

Spero didn't feel any need to discuss something that was inevitable. He insisted that we had to return to Buffalo first, and then we would face what the future would bring. He spoke quietly and softly, so it took a good half hour before I realized we were in the middle of an argument and disagreement.

And it was I who gave in first. It seemed the sensible thing to do in view of our situation.

After all, he was going to Japan and I was going back to Quantico. He was still a soldier and I was still a Marine. Uncle Sam was telling us where we were going to live. We weren't telling each other.

We could fight about this later when we were civilians. He thought my "okay" was an agreement but it was only a postponement of an argument that would go on for thirteen years.

PART SIX

Wedding Bells And Victory Bells:
Buffalo, New York–August 1945

Our wedding date was set for August 12, 1945. It was a date the whole world would remember.

Our furloughs were extended one week. Both the Corps and the Army proved equally accommodating to our requests for more time to get re-married in the Greek Orthodox Catholic and Apostolic Church. The Archdiocese had expedited the *Banns* because we were military. Spero's father was a major contributor to the church and that might have had some influence also.

My CO had checked with my major in Quartermaster who gave his approval to allow me to miss seven more days of hard work. It seems he had noticed my devotion to duty. Perhaps it was his way of being sorry for calling me a 'trouble maker'.

Spero's own CO, General Terry Allen himself had given his consent. Spero had served with him from the beginning of the 104th Timberwolves and was one of two of the fighting men in his company that had pulled through without being a casualty. He remembered Spero very well because he was one of the few in his division who could speak German. The captured Nazis would clam up to anyone who looked Jewish but they gave up information readily to the Aryan blond haired American with blue eyes. Little did they know Spero was of Greek ancestry who could trace his lineage back five hundred years in a little church in the Peleponnesus in his father's village.

August in western New York State is the nicest month of the year. The leaves are a bright green; the trees are full and lovely; the flowers are all in bloom: the skies are the bluest they would be for the entire year; the days are hot, and the sudden rain and summer showers refreshing and welcomed. The weather was so beautiful that it blocked memories of other times when there was no mercy shown to man nor beast.

We went to Buffalo and Tonawanda to be married in church and go through the elaborate Greek Orthodox ceremony with all our families in attendance. We would have a wedding dinner. His clan numbered well over a hundred. Mine was small and it included my sisters, father, mother and a few friends.

Mama was beside herself with satisfaction and vindication. It was a day of triumph for her. I not only had made a great catch, but I had served my country, kept my virtue and didn't *have* to get married. It would silence the wagging tongues forever and put those who had criticized her for 'allowing' me to join the military in their place.

My wedding dress was my dress whites uniform and Spero wore his Army khaki's.

He had requested that I remove my corporal's stripes for the wedding since he was still a private. The idea that my two stripes would make him lose face in his family's eyes was logical.

I had seen his mother and I understood perfectly. Spero's mother rarely smiled as befitting the wife of an important man, whereas his stern father said very little, as befitting his position as the patriarch of the family clan. Spero was the next in line, the eldest, the heir apparent. It would not be fitting for his wife to out-rank him at the altar.

As I snipped at the threads with my tiny cuticle scissors I wondered why he never had been promoted. Here he was a University man, short of six months towards his degree, having served in the Army's Specialist Training Program where they had sent him to the University of Wyoming, University of Chicago and the University of Illinois, where they had given him a horse in the Cavalry and a rifle in the Infantry, and made him Military Intelligence who interrogated Nazis, yet they never gave him rank. Finally, I asked him if he knew why. He said he did. He had never volunteered and would not order anyone to do what he didn't want to do. He wouldn't have made a good officer. I couldn't image any Marine telling me that but, he had returned alive and that was all that mattered to me.

My best friend and maid of honor, Helen, who was also Spero's first cousin took care of all the arrangements. We saw no reason to hang around Buffalo before the wedding. She encouraged us to spend the few days we had remaining of our furlough to take a small trip to the family cabin in the woods at Allegheny Mountains State Park.

It was true, we had to part the day after the ceremony and go our separate ways, me to Quantico and he in the opposite direction to California to train for the invasion of Japan. Every moment alone was precious.

While we waited for the *Banns* to return from the Archdiocese we slipped away to an isolated cabin in the nearby beautiful Allegheny Park and continued of what was left of our honeymoon. It never occurred to us to ask permission from anyone.

There was no running water, no electricity, no neighbor, no radio, no newspaper. The freedom of running around out of uniform, even nude in the little creek behind the cabin was exhilarating. We had shut out the outside world. For six days there was no war. Just us. We were creatures of the forest living under a mushroom.

Thousands of miles away a real lethal mushroom cloud exploded that changed the world. We knew nothing about it.

We returned Saturday afternoon barely in time for our wedding rehearsal.

We were scolded by his clucking aunts, his silent disapproving mother and the priest who rattled off some words in Greek as if we were naughty children who hadn't come into the house when we were called the first time.

We had shocked the community because we had not asked permission from the priest when we took off for our petite honeymoon before the ceremony. Until we went through the Greek Orthodox church ceremony, we weren't considered married by him or his family.

The priest reminded me of the drill sergeant in Boot Camp. It's hard to take someone seriously when you don't understand half the words, whether they are *"won up a reep"* or ecclesiastical Greek.

Spero lost his consternation when he saw the laughter dancing in my eyes during the chastising lecture. I thought the whole thing was funny, and too incongruous for words, considering the fact that we were part of the Armed Forces under military orders rules and regulations.

The scene was ridiculous. Here we were, the two of us, having to stand politely and listen to admonitions about punctuality and obeying the rules of the church. I was a non-commissioned officer in the Marines, and Spero, was a fighting soldier, getting ready to kill Japs. He had killed Germans and had taken prisoners many SS Nazi Germans who wore the tattoos of two lightening bolts on their arms, who had the skull and crossbones on their helmet and insignia, who had terrorized all of Europe and were responsible for the death of millions.

Frankly, we considered ourselves as an old married couple, and were going through this second ceremony to please our parents. But according to our priest, we were living in sin since our church did not recognize marriage by a Justice Of The Peace in the State of Virginia. But, as he explained to us, this was war-time, the priest was making an exception by giving us communion to expiate our sins. Communion meant drinking wine. It was red and sweet. Thank God! It wasn't champagne.

While we were making love in the woods, away from radio, newspapers, and people, a world event occurred which would affect our lives forever.

An atom bomb had been dropped.

The topic at our pre-wedding lunch was of war and the new bomb—a bomb to end all wars.

"It's called an atomic bomb. It's a hundred times bigger than anything we ever had before."

We didn't understand what an atomic bomb was. There had been thousands of bombs dropped in this war.

"So what does one more bomb matter?"

"We have dropped bombs every night. German cities are reduced to rubble but it didn't force the Germans to surrender. American foot soldiers, like my Spero here, still had to invade Europe and slug it out from city to city."

"There's nothing left in Belgium, Cologne or Berlin," said Spero. "Europe and England are in rubble."

A new bomb was old news. The word, atom, meant nothing to me. Spero would still have to go overseas and fight the Japs on their homeland soil.

"Is it worse than a V-2? You could hear a V-1 bomb coming. The V-2 s didn't make any noise until they landed and exploded."

"England didn't give up when the German air-raids devastated London and Coventry. They just went underground to live in shelters One bomb won't make the Japs surrender."

Theresa Karas Yianilos

"This one is supposed to be a thousand times bigger."

"Last week, they dropped this atom bomb on Hiroshima, a city in Japan the size of Buffalo. There's nothing left for miles."

"Russia declared war on Japan the very next day."

"It's about time. What took them so long?"

"President Truman announced on the radio that we dropped a second atomic bomb on Nagasaki. They say that hundreds of thousands of Japanese in both cities were killed, maimed and burned in a matter of seconds."

"We didn't start this war! What did they expect?" I said. There wasn't an ounce of compassion in me for the Japanese who had started this war.

"It is true. Kaltenborn said it on his radio program last night that Japan will surrender now," spoke his father firmly.

Wouldn't it be wonderful if that were true? Spero had orders to return to California, where the infantry outfit was training in the desert outside of San Luis Obispo to prepare for the invasion of Japan.

"If Japan surrendered it would save millions of American lives and Spero wouldn't have to go fight in Japan. He been away from home four years now. Enough is enough." I said.

"From your mouth to God's ears," said his Mother.

Everyone at the table put their thumb and two fingers of their right hand together and made the sign of the cross.

On Sunday, August 12, 1945, Spero and I were married again. This time it was done properly, with family members as witnesses, instead of a receptionist, in the traditional and elaborate Greek Orthodox service which left no doubt whatsoever that we were joined together for good.

Instead of a judge saying words we couldn't hear because of a train passing by, we stood before a priest dressed in heavily embroidered gold robes with a large hat and an even larger gold cross who held a gold and gem encrusted icon in his hands. He placed wreaths on both our heads which were joined together with a ribbon and smeared olive oil on our foreheads as he sang the ancient sacrament of the wedding ceremony in Ancient Greek.

I didn't understand a word of it because I didn't speak Greek, ancient or otherwise.

Once again I nodded my head at the appropriate moments and never understood the vows I was promising to obey.

We entered church thinking that we had only twenty-four more hours of our married life left to live. The invasion of Japan loomed before us. There was no room in our crystal ball for anything else. It took precedence over any other peek into the future.

As we left the church, our church bells rang out. Then we heard car horns, and other church bells chime in as shouting and blaring radios rang out the joyus news.

Newspaper headlines gave us the best wedding present in the world.

JAPAN SURRENDERS
V-J DAY
VICTORY OVER JAPAN

Our wedding day had become *V-J Day*.

There would be no invasion.

Spero's life had been spared. We thanked God right there on the steps of the little Greek church that was built to resemble a small Parthenon. We turned and hugged each other wordlessly and stayed in that position a long time. Our wedding guests embraced each other, made the sign of the Cross and beamed as tears and laughter were shared with kisses.

The priest said, "Blessings on all of us." He said it in Greek and English.

Japan signed the surrender on August 14.

General Douglas MacArthur accepted it formally in Tokyo Bay two weeks later.

The next day, I took the train alone to go to Washington D.C. and then on to Quantico. Spero's ticket read Chicago, Los Angeles and then a bus to Camp San Luis Obispo.

My train took me away first.

We kissed good bye with the whole clan looking on. The competition for his attention was quite fierce but I could be generous. After all, I'd have him all to myself in California.

I would fill out my Request For Early Discharge as soon as I returned to Quantico. We would be together in two weeks.

The Duration of World War II finally had a date.

Theresa Karas Yianilos

Demobilization, Quantico–September 1945

I reported for work to Post Quartermaster and discovered that Quantico had changed into a bee-hive of frenzied activity. In twenty-four hours, Quantico had been transformed from war-time to peace-time demobilization.

The Staff Sergeant said to me, "Where have you been, Corporal?"

A roaring Niagara Falls of paper work had inundated every office.

Every woman and man was submerged under the task of demobilizing four-hundred and eighty-five thousand Marines and all the nineteen thousand women Marines.

The Corps would revert to its pre-war all-male all white strength in the shortest time possible.

A points system was set up. Marines in the Women's Reserve who had served the longest were discharged first. By September 1946, all women would be discharged and the Women's Reserve disbanded. The Corps would be rid of the women in a year.

I filled out the formal form titled *Request For Discharge* for myself adding to the blizzard of *Requests* on my desk.

The Corps had become lenient about letting Women Marines go if they sought early discharge. I fully expected to be out and on my way to Camp San Luis Obispo to join Spero in California in two weeks. That didn't happen.

As attrition began with more and more desks emptying out, the Sergeant heaped up the paper work. She was discharged and released before I was. As one of the last of the non commissioned officers, I was put in charge of the very office where I had once been a pariah.

The deluge continued without respite. I typed up hundreds of letters of *Request For Discharge* and sent them up the chain of command, to be signed by commanders throughout the Post. They were returned promptly within two weeks.

All but mine.

September became October and the leaves of Quantico turned to their magnificent colors of red and gold. November started to peek around the corner of my calendar. Still my discharge seemed to be held up somewhere.

392

Spero wailed twice a week, spending some of our future nest-egg on long-distance calls. "Where are you? Why aren't you here?" Ironically the very men who had fought the enlistment of women in their Marine Corps also didn't want to give us up. We had been the best help they ever had.

Some of the *Requests* were delayed as commanders tried to hang on to us as long as they could. How ironic that the major asked me to stay at my duty when once he had labeled me "a trouble maker".

But I longed to be a civilian again, with all the inalienable rights of an American citizen.

No more rules of fraternization, having to salute those human beings who were superior to me by the powers invested in the Corps. No more having to *request permission to speak*.

No more *out of bounds* signs that told me I wasn't good enough to walk certain streets, eat at certain clubs, visit certain buildings.

Was all that discipline I received in Boot Camp for naught? I was ready to slough off my military skin like a snake in spring. Once a civilian always a civilian?

I was more than ready to trade my uniform and my typewriter for an apron, a maternity dress, a four burner gas range and a Westinghouse refrigerator.

My discharge came through three months after my V-J Day wedding.

By then, many of my original bunkmates had gone. The squadroom was half empty. The women were playing musical beds taking over those bunks that they had always coveted. A few of my good old Motor Transport squadmates were still here but most of my bunkies from Barracks-A and Motor Transport had said their last good-byes to me. Each day brought more farewells as women walked off the Post, boarded the train and melted back into the small towns and villages from where they had come.

When I came in waving my discharge, my bunkies gave me a going away present. We had one last squad party in our lounge. As I said my farewells to them, I kissed each and every one.

I hugged my sisters, with whom I had shared a life. Bunkies and squadmates with whom I had been billeted in the two years of my Marine Corps service had come together for one last time. Many faces were missing but there they were, my bunkies of Barracks A,

Theresa Karas Yianilos

my old squadmates of Barracks Three Motor Transport, and the youngest Boots from Barracks Two, topside who did not have enough points to get early discharges.

We were all about to share one more thing in life. We were all going to be veterans. Veterans of World War II. Veterans of The United States Marine Corps Women's Reserve.

Nineteen thousand women, enlisted and officers alike, would be bonded forever with the knowledge that out of the millions of women in the United States, they had come together in 1943, 1944 and 1945 to serve their country.

We were few and we were proud! No one could take that away from any of us.

We cried and let the tears show. We signed each other's autograph books and made promises to write and keep in touch crossing our hearts in the long-ago childhood gesture. I hugged Lorry and our eyes met in a last gesture of sisterhood and friendship. I would always be her buddy.

I stood at the Quantico station for the last time, tasting the coal dust in the air, and waited for the train to take me to Washington D.C. on the first leg of my journey to my new life. My heavy sea-bag was beside me. The *Ruptured Duck,* the symbol of my discharge, was sewn on the left side of my winter greens. My eyes blurred with tears as I focused on the scenes I wanted to photograph into my memory for the last time.

The autumn air in Quantico was crisp and tangy with the first nip of winter chill, but the sky was as blue as ever. Would I ever return to my beloved Virginia? To Washington D.C. which had been a magical city, a city of excitement and adventures.

But a new life beckoned. I was now a wife and had made new vows to honor. I was no longer a corporal. Still when an officer came along side of me to wait for the train, I saluted him automatically. He looked at my *Ruptured Duck* and I realized I didn't have to do that anymore! Would I ever stop thinking of myself as an enlisted who had to pay homage to a superior?

Then I boarded a DC-3 for my first plane ride for the twelve hour trip to Los Angeles with several stop overs. Phoenix was the first city of the American West that I saw. The red and tan colors of the desert could be seen from the airport where we stretched our legs.

California, Here I Come–November 1945

Quantico was forgotten as the warmth of the hot California sun beamed on me the minute I stepped off the plane in Los Angeles. If this lovely summer weather was typical of Southern California then it was all true. This was a golden land.

As the bus drove into downtown Los Angeles, towards the railroad station, my head spun from one side to another as I gulped in the sights.

The Pacific Ocean was awesome in its vastness, its expanse overwhelming in its endless horizon, in the grandeur of its beauty. On the other side was Japan and China, Okinawa, Saipan, Iwo Jima. The combat map of Post Service Battalion swam in front of me as I saw the real ocean for the first time. Huge white waves rolling towards shores were beautiful and graceful as they broke upon the sand. This was the Mother Ocean that pushed out of the cradle all the amphibious vehicles that the Marines had taken into her arms. It would take a little while before I could look at the Pacific Ocean and not see Higgins boats and Landing Craft Vehicles filled with Marines plowing between its pounding waves.

The flora in parks and landscaping was lush and verdant. I saw plants I didn't recognize, trees I had never seen before, palm trees that towered and roses in bloom, in November.

Buildings were of white stucco with red tiled roofs. The poorest neighborhoods had trees, flowers and greenery. A person could be impoverished in California and still live well. How could anyone be unhappy here?

Spero and I would have a chance to start life here and whatever happened, life would be wonderful. Pangs of guilt assailed me when I remembered so many to whom life had been denied as I basked in the glory of my dream come true. I was here. Here in California. I would never be unappreciative again. I vowed never to argue or fight with Spero again. We had been spared. To do otherwise was to tempt fate.

Theresa Karas Yianilos

The train station at Los Angeles was the beginning of my last leg of my journey up the coast of California past Santa Barbara to San Luis Obispo.

Everywhere I looked I saw something familiar. I knew this land. I knew this train station. The building was of Spanish Colonial architecture with hand painted tiles and tile roof. I had seen it many times over and over in all the cowboy movies I had watched for two decades. John Wayne himself had walked on these tiled floors.

While I waited I walked across the street to a little Mexican village called Olivera Street and ate delicious food called tacos and burritos. California was also a foreign land where people spoke Spanish and music had a Latin beat. I loved every new experience. I had come to the promised land. I was here to stay.

God had been good to me and I didn't know why.

Spero grabbed me as soon as I stepped off the train and kissed me hungrily, in front of everyone who had ridden on the train with me. This time, there was nothing shy about his greeting a military person wearing Marine Greens with a ruptured duck symbol as he showered passionate kisses on me right at the San Luis Obispo railroad station. He stopped long enough to let me thank the soldier who had helped me carry my heavy sea bag and we all grinned with happiness. We walked arm in arm and I fell into step with him. I couldn't help that. I would walk in cadence forever after. It would make me nervous to be out of step.

I never saluted the officers we passed on the way. That was one military custom I was happy to toss away.

Spero was anxious to show me our first home, proud that he had been able to find a place for us in a town that was filled with military families. He had rented a spacious room in a large house that very morning for one dollar a day. That was half of his private's sixty dollars a month private's pay.

I did not own one piece of civilian clothing. I'd have to go shopping. Our nest egg was very small but the whole world lay before us. Our life together was about to begin right here in California. My dream had come true. I looked at the blue sky above San Luis Obispo and sighed in utter joy and contentment.

For six glorious weeks, we had one continuous honeymoon where we made love every night, and followed the directions in the book on MARRIED LOVE by Dr. Swopes.

We read the recipes in the cookbook THE JOY OF COOKING and planned elaborate gourmet menus which I was going to prepare after he was discharged from the Army as we ate the 99 cent Family Plate Specials at the Golden Dragon Cafe.

We visited the Franciscan Mission and took long walks throughout the neighborhoods, picking flowers and leaves from bushes that were still green in the month of December. My happiness was so complete that I often held my breath in suspension as I basked in the delight of new sensations.

I reveled in the sensuous touch of nature, in the hot noon sun on my head and shoulders, the aroma of roses, orange and lemon blossoms, the exotic look of the orange and blue Birds of Paradise flowers, the pink and white oleanders, and the taste of the sweet pulp of palm dates which I picked off the ground to nibble. For breakfast, we ate oranges I stole off citrus trees which had been planted as street trees. I even loved the cut on my hand from the sharp spiny cactus when I discovered the cactus apples were edible.

We went sight seeing, taking buses into the country-side. We sat in our room reading, listening to the radio and talking.

Spero, who had taken care of himself for four years suddenly stopped doing it and turned the job over to me. All the housework was assigned to me. I enjoyed shining his shoes, ironing his shirts and doing the laundry.

That's what I did in the Corps. Only there, it was called PD, police duty.

He also loved magazines and was a voracious reader. LIFE, TIME, POPULAR SCIENCE were as important to us as our MARRIED LOVE. The magazines ended up in the strangest places, including the bathroom. None of them were ever thrown away and I was shocked at how much of our budget was spent on them. I was a book person myself and never knew Spero was such an avid reader of magazines. They piled up in the short time we lived in that one room.

One day he brought home a batch of magazines and newspapers and made a profound discovery. He had been part of history. He became very excited.

"I *worked* on the atom bomb! I helped break the code!" he shouted. Spero never raised his voice and when he did I jumped up to look at the pictures he showed me.

"When? How? What are you talking about, Spero?"

"Here are the guys I worked with at the University of Chicago! My professors! There's Dr. Enrico Fermi. There's Dr. Leo Szilard."

Spero had indeed been one of the men who had worked to develop the atom bomb.

For the first time he learned why in the year of 1942 he had been transferred from the cavalry into ASTP, the Army Specialist Training Program. When Army tests showed he knew how to do mathematics and calculus they sent him to the University of Chicago where he joined other university students who had been drafted into the Army. They were given a series of mathematical equations and integrals to work on.

They were told they could not discuss their work and when they left the campus, they had to remove their uniforms and wear civilian clothes to give the appearance they were regular students.

No other explanations or restrictions applied.

Every day, as soon as they finished and reached a solution to the problems given to them to decipher, the "students" would turn their papers in to the professors in charge, two of whom were the now famous Dr. Fermi and Dr. Szilard. They were free the rest of the day to play handball in the squash courts behind Stagg Field, which was where the football games were held.

The team of physicists broke the atomic code which led to the making of the bomb at Los Alamos, New Mexico. How much of that success was expedited by the students such as Spero was conjecture. All he knew, was that he had spent a year working on the problem without realizing it.

"Our papers never were corrected that we handed in to Drs. Fermi and Szilard. Now I know why. All they cared about was whether we all got the same answers."

Spero fell into a reverie of memories. "I played hand-ball on the courts behind Stagg Field, right where the first atomic pile was built and didn't even know it was there."

"Wasn't the place guarded?

"Sure it was. Round the clock. But the guards didn't carry guns. They even wore raccoon coats from the nineteen twenties they found in the old lockers when the cold got down to below freezing. Our dorms were right across the stadium and I could look right into the area where we played hand-ball. I worked on the bomb and never knew it!"

"Didn't you ever suspect anything?"

"Nothing. Everything was so casual. The doors were left open sometimes and there was nothing in there but graphite bricks. That's where they worked with the uranium. We could have been blown up if anything had gone wrong."

It was true. As tidbits of details came out about the Atom Bomb and pictures of the physicists who worked on it appeared in the newspapers and magazines, of how these men had beaten the Germans in the race to build the atom bomb, Spero knew he had been one of the few men who had participated in that contest.

Spero never mentioned this again after the initial shock of discovery. He didn't mention his part in the atom bomb scenario to anyone else.

Spero did not talk about his war experiences. He never mentioned the Nordhausen Concentration Camp he had liberated and the thousands of bodies that had been stacked like cords of wood.

He preferred to forget that he aimed his rifle at Germans some of whom he had hit. They had been shooting at him at the time and there was nothing else he could do.

Only at night, when he was asleep, did he talk. I would hug him tight until he stopped trembling and kiss him awake, which he never minded. Our honeymoon had just been extended in California.

For six weeks, I played at housekeeping, cleaning and dusting our room so often that it could have stood a captain's inspection at a moment's notice. There wasn't a *kitten* to be found as the dustballs used to be called by the duty NCO. I reveled in my role as the little wife, walking Spero to the bus stop each morning when he went to camp, and waited there for his return at the end of the day.

We never had an argument nor a disagreement. Life was wonderful. All was right with the world. How could I have been so obtuse not to have seen what a perfect husband he would be? I wore the four dollar gold ring and still had no diamond but I had him. I basked in the life of matrimony.

Mama was right! I didn't know a good thing when I saw it. Maybe at first I didn't! But at least, I caught the train before it left the station. I got on the boat before it sailed.

Quantico and the Corps were left far behind as the horizon of life stretched before us. Spero was in the process of being discharged. We had saved a little money; we had our health, our youth, our education. This was the United States. We could do anything we wanted to, live and work anywhere we liked.

Then God dropped the other shoe.

San Luis Obispo, California 1945
Top: Theresa Karas Yianilos and Spero J. Yianilos
Discharged and leaving California for Buffalo, N.Y.
Bottom: The California Mission at San Luis Obispo

Homecoming–December 1945

WESTERN UNION: Dec. 15, 1945 Buffalo, New York
Spero come home. Your father very ill. Family needs you.

Ten words. Telegrams always had ten words. And they crumpled my world into little pieces. I did not want to go back to Buffalo.

"You said we were going to buy cows and start a dairy in California," I reminded him.

"You said you were going to go back to school and finish college," I pleaded.

"You promised we would live in California and not go back to Buffalo. We can find jobs right here," I protested.

We argued. We discussed. We fought. But the decision was never mine to make. The part of the marriage ceremony I didn't understand when the priest spoke them in Ancient Greek to which I had agreed were the vows that said I would cleave unto my husband and obey all his commands. The marriage contract was as air-tight and irrevocable as the enlistment papers I had signed for the Marine Corps.

To Spero, the return to Buffalo was a matter of honor, a filial obligation he had to pay. He had to comply.

I understood that. Really I did. I loved him for his integrity and honesty which made it all the worse. I couldn't win this argument. It was time to pay homage to our family and meet our filial responsibilities.

Spero and I came to an agreement.

"Okay. Family can have one year only of our future. After that, we were going to return to California."

Spero made a solemn promise.

I realized I had placed him between a rock and a hard place, as my Texas bunkie, Lindsey, had always said when she had a difficult choice to make. I knew in my heart, that as eldest son, Spero had to help the family in their hour of need.

"I agree to living in Buffalo on one condition. As soon as we can, we are going to return to my golden land. One year. That is all you get. Then I will hold you to your promise."

Spero once again promised and gave me his word. I believed him.

Theresa Karas Yianilos

"We will live in Buffalo just long enough for me to straighten things out and take care of Dad, and to do what I can to help. After all there's my younger brother. He's coming home from the war too and he will need me. It shouldn't take but a few months."

I remembered my vow to God. That is when I threw in the towel and resigned myself to the inevitable.

What about Spero's college that had been interrupted by the war? He had only one more year for his degree. We could talk about all this later. First, we had to return to Buffalo.

Nevertheless, I made one last appeal to remain in California as we stood before the telegraph office, but I lost. He sent the dreaded ten word message:

Arriving by train. Home on Sunday. Love. Spero and Theresa.

The train took five days from San Luis Obispo to Buffalo, New York.

I left a sunny California day with a temperature in the seventies and an azure blue sky that was filled with floating white cumulus clouds. I departed from a land where flowers bloomed in December and stepped into the worst snow-storm of the century to hit Western New York.

We returned to a winter wonderland with icicles dripping from the bare branches of the trees and white banks of snow forming tunnels along the shoveled streets. The salt that had been sprinkled on the snow had begun to turn the new falling snow into dirty slush in the road and sidewalks. The temperature hovered just above zero. The chill factor was below zero.

In my new white California-chic coat from Bullock's I looked like a polo bear lost in a sea of black furred seals. What was warm enough for a chilly night in California didn't hold back the refrigerator cold of this part of the United States. I would need a fur coat and I hated the thought of it.

As usual, at this time of year, Bing Crosby's voice singing WHITE CHRISTMAS filled the air with sounds of joy, peace on earth and good will to men. Spero got his four year old wish for a white Christmas.

I adjusted my attitude and put on a smile as the family came forward to greet us.

Seeing Spero's joy as his whole clan enveloped him in a family welcome did little to temper my unhappiness in having to return. He was oblivious to the depth of my misery. My stomach was queasy and I couldn't hold anything down. This was the last place on earth I wanted to be.

I hid my feelings behind smiles as I accepted the family's greetings. It was Spero's homecoming.

They were so happy he was alive and had come through the war without a scratch. Only I knew about his nightmares where he cried out and awoke in a cold sweat and had to be hugged and loved until he was tired enough to sleep again. The war in Europe had left scars but they were all on the inside where they didn't show.

We had come home, home to Buffalo. Buffalo was where we would start our life as civilians. Our military adventures were over and we had survived.

My husband, my man, was by my side. I knew many women who were not that lucky. I was not without deep gratitude to God. I had reviewed the pros and cons of our return as a bookkeeper would do a balance sheet, debits on one side, credits on another, while the train clickety clacked its way to Buffalo.

I had exchanged one set of vows for another. I could think of our return as a temporary transfer. For better or worse. This was the worst part. Didn't Spero promise it was to be for a short time before our return to California? The thought sustained me from the time we were picked up at the train by his father and mother and throughout all the home coming festivities and family introductions.

There was no question of where we were to live. Even if there had been one single apartment or room available in Buffalo, we wouldn't have been able to take it without hurting his family's feelings. As it was, the critical housing shortage in the United States made it a foregone conclusion that we would live with his parents. There was no other place to live anywhere. Buffalo was no different than any other city across the face of the land. Not a single home had been built during the four years of the war. The hordes of demobilized armed forces were gobbling every inch of living space throughout the country. Young married couples were forced to move in with Mother and Dad and we were one of those couples.

"You will live in Spero's old bedroom. Please, consider my house the same as your house. There is plenty of room. It's a big house, all brick," his mother added proudly as we drove to her house.

She spoke in measured tones, each word enunciated precisely, her voice low and soft and her cadence slow. She never raised her voice and she always said "Please" and "Thank you". Now I knew where Spero had learned his good manners. She rarely smiled but when she did I would be suddenly reminded of Sergeant Ellice Stukey which was ridiculous since they didn't look alike in the least.

I looked around at "our" home. Her elaborately carved 1920's mahogany furniture and her choice of colors gave me an attack of instant claustrophobia. She preferred somber colors of maroon, ochre brown and deep forest greens. Her straight back stiff chairs were covered in scratchy fabrics of velour and mohair. The windows were draped in damask and brocades to prevent the sunlight from coming through to fade the expensive fabrics. Sunlight in Buffalo? Such a precaution was unnecessary. *How soon can I get out of here?*

My favorite colors were red, yellow, blue and white: the colors of the Marine Corps. My house would have blue carpet, white walls, blue and white curtains, and yellow or red dishes—linens and cottons—painted or unstained furniture—clean simple lines. I had decorated it in my mind countless of times.

I thanked her for her kind offer of hospitality with my usual smile. Immediately, I remembered Spero had chided me for doing that. I had to say the actual words.

"Thank you," I said in a low well modulated voice mimicking her tones and speech pattern unconsciously exactly as I had done to the Boots who had Southern accents.

"You are welcome," she said in her low well modulated voice.

I expected to hear her say in Jenny Mae's voice, "Are you funnin' me, bunkie?"

Of course, she said no such thing. She thought I was talking normally. I would have to curb my mimicry or I'd be sounding like her. No one shouted in her house. Nor did they sing nor play the radio, I later discovered.

Spero's family was very large. The house was full of people; it looked like a big party but it was only a formal family dinner. The dining table in his mother's two-story large brick house held 24 people; the large kitchen table accommodated the younger generation.

Would I be expected to cook for this huge clan? The prospect of having to entertain this horde was appalling to me. I had planned intimate candlelight dinners for two. This dinner party was a scene out of a Cecil de Mille movie. I had better learn how to cook very fast, as I calculated the number of different dishes that had been prepared to welcome us. Just looking at the groaning table made my stomach turn over again and the acids grumble.

Everyone wanted a piece of Spero's attention. They did their utmost to welcome me as well. Each aunt and each cousin piled another spoonful of food on my plate. My facial muscles began to hurt from smiling my thanks.

"Eat. Eat. You don't need to worry about weight. You can use a few more pounds. Didn't you eat those chocolates we sent you?"

I looked at the food on the loaded plate and my stomach rebelled at the sight. Suddenly I felt green.

I, who had always such a voracious appetite and had been such a chow-hound in the Corps couldn't look at food without a wave of nausea. I would rather have been offered a sour pickle.

The same nausea had hit me at breakfast for three straight mornings now. I hadn't been able to eat my bacon and eggs after I had ordered them in the train's dining room. The train ride and the thought of returning to Buffalo had truly upset my digestion.

I stood up to leave the table and with no warning nor apology I pushed my chair back and bolted out of there.

I made it to the kitchen sink just in time to up-chuck in front of everyone.

When I returned to the table, I was apologetic and contrite, mortified beyond belief, unable to meet anyone's eyes. I couldn't even look at the food which everyone had gone to so much trouble to prepare.

"I must have gotten the flu," I said weakly.

"Oh, you'll be fine," said one of the aunts.

Spero's mother, aunts and the older women smiled at each other knowingly.

Spero's aunt leaned over and patted my stomach. "It is only for a few months. It goes away," she said kindly.

Suddenly, right then and there, out of the blue, I knew what was wrong with me.

Mama was right after all.

I had come home pregnant.

Theresa Karas Yianilos

PART SEVEN

San Diego, California–September 5, 1992

The Marine Band from the San Diego Marine Recruit Depot resplendent in Dress Blues played *THE MARCH OF THE WOMEN MARINES*. I hadn't heard that song for years yet the music could still stir an emotion that made me stand straight and tall, almost at attention. My posture had not been this straight in five decades. I hadn't forgotten how to 'chest out' 'shoulders back'.

The Marines were playing for the banquet dinner of the 1992 Convention of Women Marines Association which was being held right here in my own beloved city of San Diego, California, where I had lived with my husband and our three children for the past thirty-five years.

I looked about me. I saw women who were veterans of many wars. My age group represented World War II and we had the largest numbers. There was, surprisingly, one woman from World War I, in her ninetieth year, who received resounding applause. She did not stand up from her wheel-chair.

The ladder of ages spread through the years.

Several members who had been part of the group called "the magic thirty" stood up to take their bows. The magic thirty referred to the number of women of the Women's Reserve who had joined during World War II, who were never discharged at the end of World War II, as the rest of us. They had gone on to serve a full thirty years. They were discharged sometime in 1973-1974.

Many women who had joined after 1948, when the women were no longer Reserves but regular Marines, had been able to make the Corps a full career and retire after thirty and twenty years of service with full pensions. They had served during the Korean and Viet-Nam Wars. When we talked about the war, they asked "which one?" That group was quite large as well.

Most surprising were the young women, in their twenties, the Marines of today, who were on active duty, who had served in Desert Storm in the war against Iraq. These were the women who were carrying on traditions that we had begun, so long ago in 1943, almost fifty years ago.

Former Women Marines with husbands or their escorts entered the huge ballroom of the Town and Country Hotel in Mission Valley in the heart of San Diego. The grand room was filled with round tables that would seat over a thousand people.

My head swiveled as I looked at faces, searching for someone familiar, hoping to recognize the young women behind all those years of maturity. Where were my buddies? My bunkies? The young girls with whom I had served?

Women were now part of the Regular Marine Corps since nineteen forty-eight and were no longer *Reserves* as we had been. No longer were they called WRs or Woman Marine. They were now known as Marines. No more nicknames nor initials for the women who had joined the Marine Corps of today.

Younger women, in their twenties, who were on active duty, wore the dress blues that were a copy of the men's dress uniforms. I was sorry to hear that the beautiful dress whites we had worn in World War II no longer were part of the uniform but these new uniforms looked every bit as gorgeous and distinctive. But, were we ever so young? So thin?

"We are all so old," I said to Spero.

"Not you! You look the same. My bride has the same brown curly hair. These ladies all have white hair!" Spero said.

"That's because I dye mine, darling. I haven't seen my true color for thirty years." I enjoyed his extravagant compliments every time he said them. I loved his calling me his "bride" after forty-seven years of marriage. I teased him about not wearing his glasses when he looked at me.

He didn't dare muss my hair and ruin my careful grooming that had taken me months to achieve. Ever since I was told that my old buddies, whom I hadn't seen for almost fifty years, were coming to San Diego, to La Jolla, where we had retired, I was in a frantic state of preparation, not knowing what to do first, re-cover the couches, buy new plumbing fixtures, have the kitchen re-painted or lose fifty pounds. It was too late to start the Richard Simmons exercise tape and *Deal A Meal Program* which had lain in my drawer for a year. I went on a *Slim-Fast* liquid diet and managed to slim down eight pounds which I regained at all these hotel lunches, banquets, cocktail hours and open house hospitality rooms.

Theresa Karas Yianilos

Anyone who has ever attended a reunion or a convention knows that the best part is meeting old friends from the past.

The year 1992 had disappeared during the past six days of this Women Marines Association Convention. I had been transported back in time. It was 1944 and 1945 again and old memories became as fresh as today as we remembered our youth and our tour of duty. We compared war stories and told them over and over, asking questions of each other to confirm facts that had faded in the mind like the old photos in our albums.

I met my contemporaries, former Women Marines who served during World War II at Marine bases across the country. They too were in their seventies, had gained weight and had aged. We were like mature trees, no longer saplings. Our trunks had girth and the passage of time could be counted on the rings of lines on our faces.

Seeing three of the former Directors of the Women Marines brought the esprit de corps feeling from the depths of my heart.

I searched for the face of my Captain Katherine Towle, the one who had spent that cold rainy night on guard duty with me. She had been promoted to Colonel and served as the first Director of the Women Marines after the war from 1948 to 1953. But I was too late. She had died in 1988 in California where she had retired.

But, my very own commanding officer with whom I served in Quantico in 1944 and 1945, Colonel Julia E. Hamblet, was there. I was a young girl again, rendering a salute to one of the most beautiful women Marines in the Women's Reserve. In her seventies, she was still as stunning as when she was Commanding Officer of Women's Reserve in Quantico in 1944 and 1945. Colonel Hamblet became the Director of the Women's Reserve in 1946 to 1948, and went on to become the Director of Women Marines in 1953 to 1959.

The women clustered about her and the curtain of years parted. I found myself remembering her words; instructing us how to be the best that we could be, as Marines and as women. It was a lesson I had carried for fifty years.

I was surprised at the welling up of tears and the rush of emotion that engulfed me at the sight of Colonel Hamblet. After all, I was a seventy-year old lady and a lot of water had gone under the bridge since I had been a twenty-one year old filled with hero worship over my commanding officers. I could feel her warmth, compassion and love for all of "her" Marines all over again. In a rush of affection, I asked permission to greet her with a hug.

Colonel Margaret Henderson, who had been Director of Women Marines, from 1959 to 1964, and Brigadier General Margaret A. Brewer, who was Director of Women Marines from 1973 to 1977 attended our San Diego Convention.

The faces of those who had served with them reflected great joy in seeing their Commanding Officers again. They clustered around them, and there was much chatter and patience as each Marine waited her turn to talk to her own Commanding Officer who had come from many miles away to attend the convention.

I saw tears in their eyes and I realized they were experiencing the same feelings as I.

Colonel Barbara J. Bishop, who was Director of Women Marines in 1964 to 1969 had canceled out at the last moment and her girls milled around, disappointed but hopeful they would see her at the next convention.

Colonel Jeanette I. Sustad, who had been Director in 1969 to 1973 had passed away and the conversation centered over her loss at such a young age.

Time had not changed how we felt about our officers. The women's Corps had never been large. We had a closeness and rapport between us, officers and enlisted alike. The women who grouped around them had a hunger and a need to touch their former commanding officers and share remembrances. All three former Directors who had been retired for many years, Julia E. Hamblet, Margaret M. Henderson, and Margaret A. Brewer, recognized this need. They stood there and greeted, with a warm graciousness, each and every former woman Marine who approached them. These women were now in their sixties, seventies, and even eighties and the cord of love and admiration they held for their commanding officers had not frayed by one thread.

They were all dedicated women who had left their mark upon us. They had been our big sisters, our mothers, our teachers. These women who had been our commanding officers had been a bulwark. They protected and gave succor. As Directors, they had seen to it that the transition from civilian to military had been made as smoothly as possible within the restrictions of rules and traditions that had been enacted for an all male Corps. They never lost sight of their goal to protect the welfare of the women in the Corps when it was a Reserve and not part of the regular Corps. They concentrated on measures to

Theresa Karas Yianilos

see that the Corps utilized the capabilities of the Women Marines effectively.

What a coup for our chairman, Kay Miller, who hovered over every part of the festivities and had worked the whole year to make it a success.

Through her dedicated efforts, the Commandant General had come down from Washington D.C. to address the group and a popular actress who played a woman Marine on a television sit-com gave a small speech.

Young women Marines who served as Color Guards carried in the flags. Handsome men Marines escorted the officers of the Women Marines Association to their places at the head of the table. The Marine Band played music that caused old vibrations of patriotism.

And a quartet of singers, dressed in the clothes and hats of the nineteen forties sang songs from the war years in the manner of the Andrew Sisters.

"Where have you been?" said Olga Bullock, Kay Miller and Betty Noble to me simultaneously filling me with guilt at my lack of participation in bringing about such a successful affair. As officers of the San Diego Chapter of the Women Marines Association these women had worked tirelessly for decades to enlist veterans like me into this organization that now numbered over three thousand women Marines.

"I'm was one of the lost women Marine veterans," I said. "But, now I am back!"

There wasn't much time left in life for me to find my old bunkies. So many were lost. Only three thousand women Marines had found the WMA and had become members. Where were the rest of the thousands of women who had served as women Marines during the past fifty years?

The first thing I did was read every name on the list of those attending the WMA Convention. I posted a note on the bulletin board fishing for lost mates whose names I no longer knew.
Anyone. Looking for my squadmates.
Quantico 1944-1945 Terry Karas.

Fenton, Zoe, Sherry and Moonbeam answered.

410

We were amazed to find each other together again, three thousand miles from where we had lived and were stationed. The first few moments were spent searching each other's faces for the young girls behind the mature women. It didn't take but a few moments for the years to peel away and we were chattering away as the bunkies we were.

There was a lot of catching up to do. We all had our life stories to tell each other.

They all remembered Spero and particularly, his chocolates. We had a lot of years to catch up on the news of each other.

Spero and I were nearing our fiftieth year of marriage and we still wore the wedding rings we had bought at the PX in Quantico.

We celebrated our last wedding anniversary at a Japanese restaurant in San Diego. As we lifted the food with chopsticks, in a restaurant decorated with banners that had the very familiar round red sun on a white field, I was reminded of the symbols I had seen on Japanese aircraft.

"Did you ever think in August 1945, as you were getting ready to kill Japs, that forty-seven years later, our favorite foods would be *Sushi, Udon noodles, Katsu Chicken* and *Sukiyaki* and the Japs would be buying half of California and Hawaii real estate?" I said.

"Lower your voice. You can't call them Japs anymore," he said.

The fact we were still married amazed me.
Our early years had been filled with conflict and bickering.

Spero And Theresa: The Early Years

We had moved out to California after thirteen years of my constant efforts and pleadings to pry Spero out of Buffalo.

In 1958, I won that battle at last and we drove from Buffalo, New York to San Diego, California in our 1956 Plymouth station wagon with our three children and one St. Bernard.

Spero's dad died in 1946 after a lingering illness and we never returned to San Luis Obispo in the twelve months deadline I had given Spero. The responsibility fell upon my husband, as the eldest son, to carry on the family chocolate candy and ice-cream business. My dream of returning to California never faded, but as time went on, like a distant star, its glow became dimmer as parenthood, work and going to college took up every bit of energy we both had.

Each year he renewed his promise, first made in San Luis Obispo, that we would move to California. I believed him. In the meantime, we gave birth to three children, built a California ranch home out of California redwood and attended classes at the University of Buffalo.

I had started school because I needed to take a few psychology courses to cope with three babies. Under the GI Bill of Rights, education was one of my benefits and there for the taking. University classes were relaxing, easy and recreational, a wonderful respite from my household chores and baby talk. At first I sat there, enjoying the lectures as I once did movies, listening to the sound of talking adults who could enunciate, who said whole sentences instead of one syllable words of "wee wee" "pooh pooh" and "no no".

After a few years of taking only classes just for fun, the Dean called me into his office and suggested that I declare a major and go for a degree. It had never entered my mind. Since I seemed to like history I was invited to join their American Studies program. It was the first time such a degree was being offered in the United States and I was very fortunate. Until that year, there had never been a University degree that was devoted solely to the study of American history, literature, religion and politics. Up to this time, bits and pieces of American subjects had been part of the total presentation of the English story with the emphasis on England.

Once again, fate had taken a hand in my life. Had the Dean suggested that I concentrate on the history and literature of England, I would have refused and gone back to doing the dishes. My experience in the Marine Corps with the Navy's rules of fraternization and the chain of command had left me with a great distaste for the traditions of England's segregated two-class society of upstairs and downstairs people.

The idea of learning all about my country which I had served with so much patriotism appealed to me very much. The classes I had been given in Boot Camp on the history of the Corps had only whetted my appetite for more American history. I entered the program with great enthusiasm.

Fortunately, I lived five minutes away from the University and could dash home between classes. My darling sisters had grown up enough to stay with me and baby sit.

Spero concurred with me completely and cooperated fully.

With our degrees, my Bachelor of Arts in American Studies and his Bachelor of Science in Business, Spero and I now had tickets to go anywhere in the United States and start any new career we wished. There was nothing to keep us in Buffalo. Still he balked, stalled and made excuses for several years.

Then something happened that made me realize our lives were slipping away. We had been confined to the house with snow blocking the front door for one solid week. One day, our garbage collector told me he had sold his business and was moving to Florida. From the bottom of my memory came the old dream of living in the sunshine of California.

As soon as spring arrived, I packed up the three children and their clothes in the 1956 Plymouth station wagon and put the keys in the ignition. I was heading West.

Spero saw the look of determination on my face, turned the chocolate business over to his brother and told me to move over. He did the driving, and we followed the Oregon Trail just as the pioneers did in the eighteen fifties to California.

We chose San Diego, the southern most city in the United States, for our new homestead deliberately because of its benign climate, beautiful beaches and palm trees.

We left traditions behind and became Californians.

Movie Stars And Marine Generals–La Jolla, California– September 1958

We found La Jolla, a suburb of San Diego, which was an elegant little village famous for its wonderful climate, exclusive homes, beautiful beaches and charm. It was a small town where everyone knew each other, similar to Tonawanda in many ways, where the life style was casual and friendly yet very cosmopolitan. People came here from all parts of the world and they spoke in educated tones of English interspersed with French, Spanish, English accents, Dutch and Chinese.

Spero thought it would be more fun to run a toy shop than to start another candy company. So our family opened a toy shop we named THE PRINCE AND THE PAUPER in 1958 on Girard Avenue which was the main street. We sold exclusive imported toys and stuffed animals which were made in France, Germany, England and Europe. We did not stock toys made in Japan at first. I was very prejudiced against the Japanese and considered their products junk.

Movie stars week-ended here, down from Beverly Hills. They stayed at the La Valencia Hotel which was just around the corner. Famous faces, easily recognized, could be seen strolling Girard Avenue and they often come into our exclusive shop to play and buy. I learned to serve the film stars with aplomb, never letting on that I knew who they were.

It was not true that movie stars were not as beautiful off screen. They were more glamorous. It was difficult to restrain a gasp of recognition at Elizabeth Taylor and Eddie Fisher, at Caesar Romero and Raymond Burr, but, it was gauche for a La Jollan to gush at the sight of movie stars. They came to our town to get away from the fans and be just like real people to shop and walk into stores like ordinary folks.

The day when John Wayne walked into our shop I became so flustered that Spero took my hand gently and firmly and told me he'd take care of Mr. Wayne. Together they selected the right toys for his children and grand-children and from then on they became friends and he told Spero to call him "Duke".

At one of the museum openings, we were seated with Bob Crosby and his lovely wife, June. We had a lot in common. Bob had been a Marine also and June and I were interested in food and both of us had written cookbooks. June's cookbook SERVE IT COLD had been published the same year as my THE COMPLETE GREEK COOKBOOK was by prestigious New York firms.

"Bob Crosby," I said. "I love your music and your 'Big Noise From Winnetka' is one of my favorites. But I have to tell you the truth. Your albums are no substitute for a diamond ring."

"How's that?"

"In 1943, after months of telling me how much I meant to him, and leading me on to expect a diamond engagement ring, Spero gave me your album HOLIDAY INN with Bing Crosby's song, WHITE CHRISTMAS in it instead."

"Do you still have it?"

"Yes. It is still in the Hope Chest!"

"That album is a collector's item. It's probably worth as much as a diamond ring today," he exclaimed excitedly. "You know, when we put that song in the picture, we didn't think much of it. When it hit so big, we were all surprised."

June was delighted with my comments. "Bob is so much nicer than his brother Bing," she said.

It was the start of a friendship that lasted for thirty years.

San Diego was also known as a Navy Town because so many Navy people and Marines retired here.

I found we had bought a house right smack in what would have been marked as "Out of Bounds" on any Marine Corps Post.

Our old California Ranch house in La Jolla was in a beautiful section of town that faced the Pacific Ocean.

My neighbors were Marine Corps Generals.

They were all famous men of World War II whose names were known to every Marine that had ever served in the Corps. They had been immortalized in the history books and were heroes. They were men I had served under and now these living legends were neighbors to whom I waved 'hello' as they walked their grand-children or dogs or took their morning constitutionals.

That was when I discovered that I had never recovered from the rules against fraternizing and had been left with a permanent enlisted mentality.

I never told any of my famous Marine Corps neighbors that I had been a Marine corporal. Although we were now civilians whose children and grand-children played with each other, I felt instinctively that the chain of command was still intact.

The chain of command and the rules of fraternization had been instilled in me very deeply. I could not shake off the attitude that I would be censured for my behavior or rejected if my true rank was unmasked.

Spero was amused at my request to keep my former status a secret and at my preference that I be known as just a housewife. He never thought of himself as an Army private. His service in the Army had been an interruption in his life and had not left a mark. He never thought of himself as a former soldier; he didn't join any veteran's organizations and if he heard derogatory remarks about the Army or military life, he'd be the first to agree they were true. He never became sentimental when he saw a soldier as I did when I saw a Marine.

But I still thought of myself as a Marine. I defended the Corps at the slightest umbrage. *Once a Marine, always a Marine.*

General Philip Torrey, himself, the old Commanding General of Marine Barracks Quantico, had retired in La Jolla. I had gained weight and he never remembered he had met me once as Colonel Buse's Courier and I never reminded him on the few occasions we met.

Parris Island's commanding general A.H. Nobel's wife, who lived right next door, liked to play her opera records very loudly so she could hear her music as she gardened outside. Well, I never had the courage to ask her to reduce the volume because I had sleeping babies in the house.

War hero, Admiral "Bull" Halsey's grand-daughters attended school with my son and they went to dances together. When the old Admiral, himself, came to pick her up from my son's birthday party, I held my hand right hand behind my back so I wouldn't salute and give myself away.

Marine General Holland Smith lived up the street. He turned out to be a dear man whose heart was heavy with the sorrow of the loss of so many men in World War II. When I read his book CORAL AND BRASS I was indignant all over again about the injustices that had been done to the Corps during the war because of inter-service rivalry and the jockeying for authority and power.

When another neighbor, retired Army Chief in World War II, General Joseph T. McNarney, came into our store with his wife to buy toys, Spero was afraid my facial expressions of disapproval would alarm a good customer and he made me go back into the storeroom because he was afraid of what I would say.

General McNarney epitomized, for me, the kind of inter-service rivalry at the highest level that made me ache for the Marines who had fought in the Pacific War. I remembered the biggest gripe of the Marines who returned from fighting in Guadalcanal and Peleliu. They had cursed the powers that didn't give them enough support, in men, materials, supplies, landing vehicles and ships. Despite what was shown on the newsreels and narrated by the commentators the Marines had been shorted more than once in the Pacific Theater of War.

It was General McNarney's memorandum to Admiral King early in 1942 which influenced the entire participation of the Marine Corps in World War Two. It was his suggestion, which was ratified by the Joint Chiefs of Staff, which served to keep the Marines out of Europe and confined them to the war in the Pacific which was supposedly the smaller operation, while the greater Army amphibious divisions and the major land forces were sent to Europe to deal with the Germans who were perceived as the larger threat.

General McNarney continued his efforts after the war to consolidate the Corps into the Army. He had come close to succeeding because President Truman was in accord with his military philosophy. Yes, I remembered also what President Truman had thought of the Marines and history had proven my suspicions to be right.

Spero teased me about my anachronistic *esprit de corps*.

"World War II is over," he said. "We sell imported toys made in Germany and Japan. Japanese and German factories have been reconstructed and rebuilt with American money. Aren't you ever going to forget you were a Marine?"

That was when I called him a 'dog-face'. Army would never understand the Marines. *Once a Marine, always a Marine.*

One day, I read in the San Diego Union that Mrs. Thomason was in town to dedicate a destroyer that had been named in honor of her husband, Colonel John W. Thomason Jr., who had died in the Pacific in 1944, two decades before.

I still regarded him as America's literary genius. His book JEB STUART was required reading in schools. I was convinced he would have been as well known as Hemingway had he not confined most of his works to stories about Marines. The Corps and the Navy realized how fortunate they had been to have had such a brilliant talent in their midst. and had named streets on Marine Posts and a ship after him. One of his sketches of the marching World War One Marine, in leggings and helmet, had been made into a recruiting poster that had been distributed throughout the United States. My Walking John was now framed and hung in my one of the rooms in my home.

I invited Mrs. Thomason to lunch with me and was thrilled when she accepted.

As I prepared exotic recipes from the Greek cookbook that I had written, I remembered Sergeant Ellice Stukey's frustration and her look of fury that I had not stepped aside and let her take charge over our famous visitor, Colonel Thomason, when he walked into our office so unexpectedly. I giggled while I cooked. Wouldn't Ellice have a fit if she knew I was preparing a fabulous lunch for his wife? I wish Sherry were here. We could really laugh about Ellice now. At the time, when Ellice had triumphed, it had hurt very much.

My literary aspirations had never been completely submerged by wife and motherhood. True, I never wrote any screen plays nor the great American novel as I had planned in the outline of my life. Instead, I had become the best gourmet cook in the whole Yianilos clan, as good and maybe better than Spero's mother, aunts and uncles. I had cut down so much of the oil and sugar that went into them that even Spero preferred my cooking above that of his mother's. She accused me of "Americanizing" the recipes. But if CocaCola could take out the sugar and bring out Tab, so could I.

I put all our family recipes into one big book THE COMPLETE GREEK COOKBOOK which was published by a prestigious New York firm. It turned out to be a national best seller which made me the Julia Child of Greek cooking in San Diego. I donated many hours preparing dinners for the various museums as fund raisers and gave cooking demonstrations to many groups, small and large.

With great confidence, I prepared some of my best and most favorite recipes from my book to honor the wife of the literary giant whom I remembered so well. My only regret was that my Colonel wasn't here as well.

I served luncheon in the shade of the olive tree that grew in the center of the patio of my California-Mexican-Colonial home. We couldn't have asked for a prettier, more pleasant day, not too warm with just a soft breeze. The view of the blue Pacific Ocean and the tropical flora that filled the garden due to Spero's horticulture expertise gave me a feeling of utter contentment. I had never stopped asking God why he was so good to me.

Mrs. Thomason arrived with Mrs. Lemuel Shepherd, the wife of a retired Commandant General, who happened to be one of my La Jolla neighbors. They were elegant gracious women who carried themselves with dignity. Mrs. Shepherd was just as I imagined the wife who got to live in the beautiful historic commandant's house in Washington D. C. would be. I didn't dare ask her about the tea set under General Archibald Henderson's portrait. I came away from the Corps curious if that story about it falling down the day the women were signed into the Corps was true or something cooked up by General Holcomb for a laugh.

I had dressed up elegantly as well but I was without any jewelry. I had smeared butter on my emerald ring as I made the *Baklava*. My lapis lazuli and gold beads had banged against the blender as I made the *Caviar Tarama* so I had to take them off and forgot them on the kitchen counter. My guests arrived just as I was taking the hot pans of *Spanakopitta* and *Moussaka* out of the oven and they caught me with an apron over my silk dress.

I could hardly contain my pride in the honor of being able to offer them Greek hospitality. We talked over *ouzo* and *Mavrodaphne* wine and demi-tasse cups of Greek coffee about Mrs. Thomason's husband and his genius in writing and art.

We talked a little about the Women Marines and how much we had contributed to the war effort.

They assumed because I had been stationed at Quantico, I had been an officer in the Women's Reserve. I said nothing to correct that impression. After all, twenty eventful years had passed since the time I had been a lowly corporal. When they asked me about my experience, I told them I would never forget that I had been a Marine and I never regretted joining the Corps.

The wives of Marines were as much a part of the Corps as the Women Marines, but they didn't get any medals for their service. We were all sisters. Later, when I received a thank- you note, I found a membership card enclosed as a thank-you gift that announced I was now a member of the Command Museum at the Marine Corps Recruit Depot in San Diego.

I had not planned it but the Marine Corps was still a vital force in my life.

I resided in a city where seeing Marines on the street was a common sight.

Marine Corps Recruit Depot was in San Diego and Camp Pendleton was thirty miles away at Oceanside.

La Jolla was only a few miles away from the Top Gun School of the Marine Air Squadron at Miramar Air Station. The jets flying overhead in close formation was a daily spectacular sight.

I had taken my grand-children to see the Corps Silent Drill Team perform on the parade grounds at Recruit Depot and to hear the Commandan't Own Band, resplendent in their red and white

Theresa Karas Yianilos

uniforms, march and play, when they came here from Washington D.C.

My son-in-law's father had been a major in the Marine Corps and had been with the Marines who had accompanied General MacArthur in their return to the Philippines at Leyete in October 1944. Our dinner conversation often centered around the history of the Corps and our wartime experiences.

Once a Marine, always a Marine!

The Family Tree

About Mama and Dad. Mama died in her sixty-third year two years after Dad died of a heart attack. She was heartbroken when he was gone which surprised me since all they did was bicker and argue. She would talk about him and complain about something he had done just as if he were alive and had gone to the corner to the saloon for a couple of hours. I realized that she had loved him very deeply. Strange, how you can be next to love and not see it.

In my sixth decade, I could look in the mirror and see that I looked like Mama more than any of my other sisters. Under apple trees, apples fell. That was another of her sayings and I was truly an apple that had fallen under her family tree.

My mother-in-law lived to be eighty-six years old. Each year, for thirty years, she arrived to stay with us in California for six weeks in the guest room I had prepared just for her.

While she was with us I tried to speak in a low well-modulated polite manner but several times I lost control and raised my voice to Spero which distressed her greatly. Well bred wives did not challenge the head of the house. *How can a unit function without respect for the chain of command? Husband is the captain and wife is the mate. Children are the enlisted crew! Dog, cat, bird, turtle, fish fall in proper order. Aye, Aye, Sir! Permission to speak, Sir! By your leave, Sir!*

Oh, yes! About my sisters! I didn't ruin it for them after all.

Two of them married doctors. The youngest, Elaine Faith, became a college teacher, museum curator and councilman.

Mary ended up owning parcels of property in California and held a post at the University of California, Davis. Sister Theocly grew to be tall, thin and beautiful was widowed early in life. She married

420

a millionaire who owned chocolate shops, See's Candies. For the short period of their marriage, our house was filled with boxes of chocolates and I gained weight for which she refused to take the blame.

Among all my sisters' progeny, there is a doctor, an architect, an art teacher who pilgrimages yearly to Florence, Italy, an executive in a lecture-bureau who deals with famous people daily, an auto executive and a real estate broker who juggles career and family.

My children? Well, my one daughter became a lawyer who maintains her own home and office and has given us a beautiful grand-daughter who has inherited my personality. *Under apple trees!*

My son became a writer and a business man, yet he finds time to cater to our seventy-year old infirmities, takes us on trips and makes certain our needs have been met. He addresses us by our first names, which many find strange. He has requested that we phone him at work every day so he won't worry.

My oldest daughter has a kind, generous and permissive nature who laughs a lot. She loves plants and animals which cause her dad a little consternation when he visits her and is greeted with enthusiasm by two St. Bernards, a poodle, several Salukies, a dozen cats and birds. She married a brilliant physicist who is very dear to us and is the mother of three wonderful children who always close each telephone conversation with the words, "I love you, Yia Yia and Papoo." That means grandmother and grandfather in Greek, the only two words they know of that language. They are learning Spanish in their private schools, not Greek nor Latin.

This is the 1990's and California is now a state on the Pacific Rim with Mexico as her closest neighbor.

She is an excellent hostess and at one of her parties, two old men, my Spero and the famous Dr. Edward Teller, who developed the atom bomb, sat by themselves talking about the days both of them were at the University of Chicago, working with the same people, in the same place to split the atom in 1942.

Other than at that time, Spero never discusses his experiences in the war. We have sent the photographs he took in 1945 when he liberated Nordhausen, the Concentration Camp in Germany, to the Holocaust Museum in Jerusalem. We were told they were able to identify some of the people through computer enhancement.

My son-in-law is the most honest man I have ever met and so is his brother who is Congressman Duncan Hunter (Republican-CA) which gives me a direct line to register any complaint I have. My latest crusade is to make the Veteran's Hospital put gynecologists on their staff. In the year 1992, many Veterans Hospitals in the United States, including the one at San Diego, here in La Jolla, still do not have a gynecologist on call or on the staff to service the women veterans. There are urologists on twenty-four hour call for the men to take care of their male infirmities but no gynecologists. The women should not be treated with anything less than the same equal care.

I hope I can bring about that change.

Reunion Of The Old Breed

The joy of seeing old bunkmates, of having one more chance in life to be together, to renew the esprit de corps we shared when we were young was a gift none of us had expected at this point of our lives.

Stories of five decades of living tumbled out of us, as we chattered away, catching up on news that was old but unknown to us as we reminded each other of events long past, people long dead and spoke of forgotten names. Behind the faces of these old women were the young girls with whom I had served. It took only seconds to get past the facade that time and life had wrought.

Fenton was still lovely, still prim and dressed in a soft violet silk pleated dress. She wore a large diamond and a plain gold band. She had spent her life doing good works and was a docent and active in several museums in Boston. Her Catholic ensign, whom she had married on the rebound, had made millions on an invention that he patented. The Cardinal of Boston was her personal Confessor. She had been to the Vatican and had an audience with the Pope.

Sherry and her husband, now a retired professor from the University of Indiana, had made this trip out West just to be with me. We had kept in touch all these years but this was the first time we had met since the war. She stayed at my home and we visited until the wee hours of the morning. She had lived the academic life, that of a professor's wife, in Bloomington, Indiana. But now she and her husband were moving to Kentucky where he had inherited a farm. Sherry had changed very little. The extra weight was becoming and she too was a grandmother several times over. Her daughter looked exactly as Sherry did when she was a young woman in the Marine Corps. I thought the photo was that of Sherry, as a matter of fact. The family tree lived on.

Zoe, my buddy, was the only one in the Buffalo Platoon that had served at the duty station she asked for, Camp Pendleton, California. She still towered over all of us and her posture was straight and tall. She had changed very little. She chided herself for having gained weight but it was minimal. Her hair was still blond and soft, her smile the same, her face unlined. She had married a Marine and had a child but her husband died two years after the war. She left California, a place she loved, returned to Buffalo and spent the rest of her life raising her child and taking care of her aged parents who were now in their nineties. She complained that they thought of their seventy year old daughter as a young woman. I could see why. Her calm nature had kept her youthful.

Moonbeam came to the convention dressed in a mini skirt. Her pink blond hair was short on top and fluffed out at the sides and she had many rings on her hands. She no longer saved gallon jugs. The Ozarks had been left behind a long time ago. Voice lessons had gotten rid of her Missouri twang.

She gave us a synopsis of her life as she played with the ice in her Perrier.

"I moved to Los Angeles and took violin lessons on the G.I. Bill after the war while my husband baby sat. I never returned to Missouri but my Paw moved out West after my Maw died. He started selling corn whiskey in a small bar in Santa Monica. The revenue officers never bothered him there on Ocean Boulevard like they did in Bear Hollow back in Missouri. I helped him a lot in the bar and when he died I took it over. Gene Autry came along and offered me a lot of money for the property. He built his big hotel right there."

Her husband? What happened to him?

"He ran off with a hippie bar-maid. We've been divorced for years. He's living on the beach in Venice and pumps iron. Besides I've got a live-in boy-friend who's twenty years younger than me."

"That sure beats Cher and Elizabeth Taylor."

Having a young boy-friend was the latest status symbol in Southern California and Moonbeam had embraced a young lover as well as other new philosophies. She believed in fortune tellers, tarot cards, astrology and numerology.

"So now I travel to Reno and Laughlin to play the slot machines for fun! I won thirty-nine thousand dollars last year after my psychic told me to keep dropping silver dollars in the fifth machine in the fifth row. Have you heard anything that mystifying?"

I didn't believe in psychics but, yes, I had a story that was more mystifying.

I began it with, "Do you all remember Lindsey? Remember how she was the spitting image of Gary Cooper?"

"Sure we do. What ever happened to her?"

"Let me tell you the strangest story. In 1955, ten years after the war, Spero and I and the three kids were crossing the United States, going from Buffalo, New York to Los Angeles on Route 66. When we got to Texas I told him all about Lindsey and how she was the only Texan I ever knew and how she looked like Gary Cooper's sister. Well, I told him that at least twenty times because it takes two days to drive through the Texas Panhandle until Spero threatened he'd stop the car the next time I repeated it and abandon me right there in Texas.

Now we were in New Mexico, in a little dusty town. It was three o'clock in the afternoon and I saw this little cafe right on Route 66.

I yelled, "Stop! Right here!" All of a sudden I had an irresistible hunger for a hamburger.

Spero didn't want to eat then. We had planned an early dinner at an auto club recommended restaurant in the next big town which was our usual practice and he wanted to stick to our plan.

This place looked like a dive and it had no AAA sign. I made such a fuss, that he parked diagonally right in front of the restaurant and we went inside this cafe.

It was empty except for the two people sitting at the counter, a man and a woman in a black dress. She was over-weight and not too tall. I sat in a booth facing the door. I glanced over and saw the woman's profile. It looked like—no—it couldn't be. I was sure it was.

I yelled "Lindsey! Lindsey! Lindsey!"

Spero grabbed my hand and tried to make me sit down. "Sit down! Stop yelling!" There were no other customers except these two people and still he was embarrassed because I had raised my voice.

The woman turned around and got off the stool and came over and looked at me for a moment as I stood there. Then we hugged as she recognized me. "Terry? Terry from Quantico!"

We were so surprised that all we could do was look and stare at each other.

My being there and her being there, at that same minute, in New Mexico, a state neither of us lived in, was too impossible a coincidence to believe. It scared us both. It was too too weird. Just too strange. I couldn't explain it and neither could she, so it made us uncomfortable as if there were a big puppeteer in the sky pulling strings.

The circumstances of how it happened didn't explain the coincidence any better. Neither of us frequented this route. It was a one time thing for both of us.

Lindsey lived in Odessa, Texas and was returning from a Los Angeles Trade Show where she and her husband had gone to sell his new model motor home which is what he did for a living as a dealer in recreation vehicles. He had made this same trip alone for the last five years, but this time, she had come along because she was able to get a baby sitter to watch her three babies and could get away.

And this was my first time in this town. We were moving out to California and using the old wagon trails as a history lesson for the children. And that is how come we met in this out of the way cafe in New Mexico."

"Was she the same Lindsey?"

"Yes and no. We were happy to see each other, but our meeting like that scared her. And I just was so shocked I couldn't think of much to say. We caught up on what we had done the last fifteen years. She had three babies. So did I. She worked with her husband. So did I. We exchanged addresses and went on our way. I have never met any other Woman Marine that I have served with in all the years. Not before, not since."

My old bunkies agreed that the coincidence of meeting Lindsey like that was inexplicable! They had never met any of the girls they had bunked with. No one could top that story. Few of us met other women Marines accidently that we had served with. We had all melted into the population of the United States from where we had come. The odds were simply too great. Twenty thousand women had served out of the millions. Spread that number across the United States and what you got was a mathematical miracle. The coincidence of this meeting has never stopped astounding me. It has led me to remember how much a role the fates played in shaping my life and brought me to a belief that our lives were determined by greater forces than we were capable of understanding as human beings. That force wasn't necessarily Catholic, Greek Orthodox, Protestant nor Jewish.

Moonbeam said, "It's your higher power, Terry."

Ellice Stukey was honored In Memorium at the services which were held for those Women Marines that had passed away. The setting was the historic and beautiful Mission de Alcala at San Diego, which was one of the restored Franciscan Missions on the Camino Real that had been founded by Father Junipero Serra in 1769 A.D.

She would have loved the solemnity of the occasion and seeing her name printed on the beautiful brochure. How sad she couldn't be here to take charge of the whole affair. Sherry and I giggled at the thought and the years melted away. We were no longer in the Mission Church but at Post Service Battalion H-Barracks plotting to do away with an ear-banging obnoxious controlling female. We stopped laughing as we remembered how we ended up doing ourselves in. It still bothered us after all these years that righteousness had not prevailed.

I was the one who had kept up with our Colonel Buse.

"Our family stopped twice on our way to Florida during the children's school holidays at Christmas to see him at his home in Charleston. Our beloved fun loving Colonel Karl Buse lived to a ripe old age as a real Southern Colonel, drinking mint juleps in his antebellum home which was filled with original furniture from the Civil War period. Mrs. Buse belonged to the Daughters of The Confederacy and always called him The Colonel which rankled him enough to make him drink another mint julep because he hadn't made general before he was retired. Tears came to his eyes when I kissed him and told him I loved him and what a wonderful commanding officer he had been to all of us."

Everyone remembered Chick, the Marine who looked like my twin brother. Chick had been sent to London after I had replaced him. He brought home an English bride. Like me, he had found romance. We wrote for a few years, but after our third child our correspondence drifted to an occasional card then nothing.

Lorry married Cookie after the war and they bought a farm in Maine. She kept in touch all these years, by letter and by phone. One day she sent me a hat that was made of camouflage material with a brim that played *THE MARINE CORPS HYMN* when it was pinched. I took it to the luncheon of the Women Marines Association and it made all the girls laugh.

I lost touch with Gerry. After one of her twin babies died she divorced and left the small town she had moved to after she was discharged. My letters were returned to me. She never joined the Women' Marine Association and there was no way I could ever find her. That was the fate that befell most of us. Friendships disappeared into the fog of time. So many stories were unfinished, so many fates unknown. My heart ached to see her again.

Yet here we all were, gathered together again, almost fifty years later for the biennial convention of the Women Marines Association. The year 1993 would be the Women Reserve's fiftieth anniversary. Where had the time gone?

We had been Marines who had served in a perilous time, who had answered our country's call to arms. We were once young and lithe, filled with dreams, illusions, and aspirations some of which did come true.

We commiserated and talked about the major changes that had occurred in the Corps. New opportunities now allowed career possibilities for this new generation of women Marines. They had advantages our generation never got. We had broken the ground and were the pioneers of today's liberated woman Marine.

"Do you know that Women Marines not only are in the regular Marine Corps, but they can stay in after they are married and get pregnant? They actually have maternity Marine uniforms. They even have maternity camouflage outfits!"

"That's not new. They've been able to do that since 1975. The laws today allow the woman Marine the same rights as the men, the same allowances and benefits, privileges and rights. She can have dependents, husband and children. And she gets time off to have her child and still retain her military career," said Fenton, who still was the historian of our group.

"Ever since 1976 women have been allowed to enter all the academies to become officers in West Point and Annapolis. Women can be generals and admirals now. Our last director was a brigadier general," Fenton added. It still rankled she hadn't become that officer she had wanted to be.

"We've come a long way, Baby," we chorused.

"Remember when Terry fell in the water during that exhibition the men put on for us on that field trip in Boot Camp and all we did was watch and they had the fun?"

"Well, now the women go through field training exercises and get weapons familiarization lessons. They actually learn how to use those rifles. Remember how we got to shoot once and that was it?"

We groaned. Our exercycles were stored in our garages along with our best intentions never to lose our Marine Corps figures.

"Where have those girls gone who were so slim with all the tight muscles from drilling gone?"

We patted our well padded bodies and smiled at our girth and at each other. We saw only the young women we once had been. Fortunately, old age brings an acceptance of the changes in life that allows contentment.

"Remember, my being accused of being a lesbian when I didn't even know what the word meant?" I said.

The incident had been such a minor one, that I had to refresh their memories of what had been very painful to me.

"Things are so different today. Anything goes. It seems the only choice we had then was to get married and get out of the Corps or stay single. But today, the field is wide open. Single mothers, significant others, ex-lovers, gays coming out of the closet and marching for their rights."

"We all were in the closet then. If a girl were unmarried and pregnant, she had to go out of town to hide the fact and have her baby secretly. No one ever said the word "homosexual". Now they are shouting it and the democratic candidate for President, Bill Clinton, has promised to let gays in the military."

"This may be 1992 but, he'll never win with that campaign promise. If Clinton had served in the Armed Forces, he never would have made that promise. He just doesn't understand how little privacy you have in a squadroom or barracks."

"The gays are in the military already. If they don't flaunt it and can keep it quiet and to themselves, it could work."

"Remember the two lesbians who were in Barracks Two? If they had been discreet no one would have ever said anything or signed a petition against them. But their conduct was unacceptable. It tore the squadroom apart. Today's gays are much more militant and arrogant. Gays will never be accepted in the Corps."

The idea seemed far-fetched and the subject didn't interest us. Who wanted to waste time talking about something that was only a political campaign hot air speech?

We turned to another topic that dominated the news for a year. Sexual harassment was an issue that had touched every woman who had ever served in the military. Fifty years of women in the Armed Forces beginning with the year of 1942 to 1992 could attest that sexual harassment was not new.

The newspapers of 1992 and 1993 were full of the scandal of sexual harassment known as the Tailhook Incident. It dominated the news almost daily for months. For the first time in history, the plight of military women was being examined by the public. Columnists, psychologists, news commentators on CNN, PBS, CBS, NBC, ABC, Fox and Turner Broadcasting Networks and experts in the fields of social, legal and the military professions pontificated on television and radio on the subject of sexual harassment in the military. Some of them did not know what they were talking about.

Congress responded to public pressure and started a Congressional investigation of the incident. For the first time in fifty years, the American public was interested in what happened to its military women and the men in control of the military had to give an accounting of themselves. It was long overdue.

What had brought all this about was the annual convention which convened in Las Vegas in 1991 by the Top Gun Association of jet-fighter pilots

Liquor had flowed liberally and was consumed to excess. The hi-jinks of young virile men who were Navy and Marine officers disintegrated into unacceptable behavior. They confined their carousing to the third floor of a hotel but any female that was unfortunate to find herself, through invitation or accident, had to confront a corridor lined with silly young drunken men who had exposed their privates and thought it was funny to grab at parts of the women's bodies who were forced to go down the hall just to get out of there.

Scores of women who had attended that convention, many of whom had been military, including an admiral's aide, complained about the incident and of the sexual abuse they had encountered.

For almost a year, nothing was done about the complaint that had been filed by the admiral's aide. Her letter was shuffled around and stalled somewhere in the ladder of the chain of command which had been a successful ploy that had worked for years in the military.

After the media became interested in the salacious parts of the story and Congress became involved to the point where they set up investigating committees, a great clamor went up about the cover-up as if that were the greater crime. Concern about sexual harassment in the military became a hot topic for analysis as if it were a new phenomena.

Cover-ups were not new. Sexual harassment was not new. It had been going on for decades. We, women Marines, had experienced it in the 1940's. Many of us remembered bunkies that had been transferred because of cover-ups when they had made complaints or had signed petitions.

We told of our experiences and one of the women at the next table, moved over and said out of the blue, "We had the worst officer in the Corps. His name was Captain Bungle and he hit on every WR that came into his command. He never promoted anyone unless they shacked up with him."

"Were you in Motor Transport? Quantico 1945?" I asked.

"Quartermaster. But we knew what was going on in Motor Transport," she said. "There was this captain that hit on all the girls and finally, he was caught red handed. I seems that this WR ordered some very expensive equipment which he okayed and put his signature on it. He had to resign after that!"

I stood up in my astonishment to hear someone else tell my story. I cried, "That was me! I'm the WR that got rid of Captain Bungle! You know, I had begun to wonder if I had dreamed that had happened."

More women Marines of our era and age joined our group and pulled up chairs to reminisce with us.

The topic of sexual harassment was the hottest one of the year. We shared our experiences.

We agreed that most of us never experienced any sexual harassment during our whole period of enlistment.

"Either the men were different and it was a different era, or we just didn't recognize what sexual harassment was. We dealt with it. It never got out of hand with me. You? Did any of you get into trouble?"

"I never had any problems with the men. They were always gentlemen. Sure they flirted and teased but nothing to worry about."

"You could always say no. They'd walk away and there'd be no trouble. We never had to contend with the stuff you hear about today!"

"Sure, there was some of it, but we learned to handle it with a sense of humor or to turn it aside or to our advantage. We did not have to deal with the violence and outright abuse that the women in the service today have to deal with."

A few of the World War II women veterans who had been at Camp Pendleton and at Parris Island, remembered otherwise.

"Of course, there were rapes and sexual incidents, particularly when alcohol was involved. Especially during the celebrations of V-E or V-J day, or when the men knew they were being shipped out to the Pacific Islands and were angry, hostile and aggressive. We used to carry hat pins because the Marines would grab your crotch or breasts when we were packed on the trucks going into town from Oceanside to San Diego. We used to call them cattle cars."

"We rode those trucks from Baltimore to Washington D.C. on liberty and that never happened to us!"

"What is sexual harassment anyway?"

Our generation did not know what this new generation was talking about.

Several women at our table had difficulty comprehending the why and wherefore of the Tailhook story or how it happened.

What were the women doing there on that third floor in a hotel in Vegas? Maybe the men had misunderstood and didn't realize the women they had harassed, propositioned, grabbed and leered at were legitimate military women! Maybe they thought they were the other kind of women who were notorious for cruising the Las Vegas hotels looking for men whooping it up at a convention.

In our continued naiveté, we ladies of another generation raised under the double standard, were still giving the men the benefit of the doubt.

The New Breed

That was when a table of young women Marines who were the Color Guard at this convention interjected themselves into our conversation. They were all sergeants and were magnificently impressive in their dress blues. We were flattered and delighted they wanted to join us. They had been listening quietly to us old veterans.

"The Corps now gives courses on *Sensitivity Training and Sexual Harassment.* Everyone in the Corps has to attend these lectures. Men do not know what constitutes sexual harassment and these courses define it for them. Some of them actually think we women like being propositioned and hearing comments made about our body parts. And they think that "No" means "Yes" or "Coax me"."

"What about the word *BAM*? Do you ever hear it anymore?" I asked their group in general.

Their reaction to my question was one of puzzlement.

"What does it mean? We haven't heard that word."

"That is what the men called us in World War Two. It means *Broad Ass Marines.*"

The reaction of these young women was immediate, strong and belligerent.

"If any Marine used that term I'd have him up on *Charges* for sexual harassment so fast that he'd get a *BCD* before he knew it," said the twenty-two year old corporal

"No one ever uses that word. That is what sexual harassment is all about. We will not be belittled," said the staff sergeant who was about twenty-eight years old.

"Every military women's group had a nickname!"

"Not any longer. No more nicknames since the nineteen seventies. We are just Marines. Not Woman Marine, not WRs, just Marines. We don't use Waves or Wacs either. It's soldier or sailor."

"Why did you women allow the men to call you BAMS?" Their voices held a note of censure that was directed to all of us for having been so meek.

The young women did not understand that there was no place to go to complain in 1943 to 1945. There were no women's groups, no support systems at that time. We had lived in a man's world.

I wanted to know about the rules that bothered me fifty years ago, that still could stir up resentment within me.

"Are the enlisted still forbidden to date the officers? Are the fraternization rules still in effect in 1992?"

"Absolutely," the Sergeant said. "It is a very serious offense and carries a discharge. Furthermore, a private, corporal or sergeant cannot date staff or above!"

The implication of what she said stunned me.

"You mean enlisted can't date enlisted? That is ridiculous. "

"That's right. The lower ranks cannot associate with the upper ranks.

That was incomprehensible to me. What about inalienable rights to pursuit of happiness? Love couldn't be denied because of a symbol on a sleeve. I recalled all the staff sergeants I had dated when I was a private at Quantico and how thrilled I was to be taken to the Staff NCO Club. They had done wonders for my self-esteem and my esprit de corps. Nothing had made me feel more accepted into the military fraternity than that invitation. A staff sergeant asking a private out was like a senior in high school or college asking a freshman to the big game, or a senior partner in a firm asking a junior to join him at lunch in the executive dining room. There was no quicker way to ensure loyalty, Semper Fidelis.

I voiced my concerns to the young women and my point of view did not mesh with theirs. They listened politely.

The oldest one with the rank of staff finally spoke frankly.

"It makes sense, in one way to prohibit social mixing between the first three pay grades with the staff. That rule prevents the older guys from hitting and monopolizing the pretty young Marines who come in. They are easily impressed and usually naive."

She continued, "But, you are right. It does make it difficult when you have a staff rating and you work with officers all day long and then when the week-end comes we have to separate. Most of the time we have more things in common and are more compatible with the officers. The enlisted men who have the same ratings as we do are younger by as much as five to eight years. Generally, the women who are staff are older than the men with the same rank. But still, we can't date the officers or even socialize or let our families intermingle socially even when we have the same interests, like boating, tennis or golf."

I remembered the lovely nights I spent with the Colonel and Mrs. Buse, the evenings at Major Emery's house, and the nights Sergeant Major Jordan and his wife I spent, cooking supper together, trying to keep the gravy from going lumpy. The Corps had been one big family then within the rules of fraternization.

How sad I was about the Corps of today that was frozen into the narrow confines of a two-class society with such rigidity.

"What about combat? How do today's women Marines feel about going into combat?"

We asked a question that had been on all our minds.

We seventy-year old veterans remembered the blood spilling of the Pacific War. We had joined the Corps to 'Free a Marine to Fight' before we even knew what the price was going to be to win the Pacific Islands from the Japanese.

Perhaps, the place for young women was no longer confined to the home, but certainly, the battle field was not the place either.

"Combat status means promotions and ratings. It's not about fighting and dying. Today's Corps is high tech."

The young Marines explained carefully.

The *Cold War* is over. Without combat status, we don't get the pay hikes. Without combat status, we don't get the promotions, the pay raises, the money, and big pensions."

They were united in their consensus. Combat ratings meant equality. Without access to that rank, there could be no equality. "Promotion at the top ranks depends on the experience of command. Women are barred from combat and combat related fields. That's where the majority of the jobs are."

Yes! The Marine Corps had changed and one look at these dedicated Marines told us more changes would be forthcoming.

It had taken fifty years for a support system to develop that would help military women deal with problems they encountered in the Armed Forces. Women now were able to call upon a support system that was composed of women's organizations, women's media, women in Congress and women in the medical and legal professions. There were more women in Congress now, women who listened and would take action, who gave speeches that were televised to the whole Country, who could propose bills in Congress to bring about changes legislatively.

Women's organizations have been formed by women which seek equality in all areas of our culture. Many of the women in the service are black. The Civil Rights movement in the past decade now give these women a voice in what happens to them. It is up to them to use this voice in or out of uniform.

We reviewed their options and ours. Their lives in the Marine Corps were different from ours in so many ways.

Each of us had a point to make.

"Today's media is responsive and will enter any fray, particularly if it smacks of discrimination or hints at scandal."

"The Civil Rights movement has splashed over into the military world. Where at one time, the military woman had nowhere to turn other than the chain of command, today's military woman now has a place to go with her grievances if that chain of command breaks down. Charges of sexual harassment and discrimination no longer can be hidden in the 'military good old boys' club'."

"The women Marines of today are part of the liberated educated generation that had grown up in a hi-tech society."

There are substantial differences in our generations.

"Our generation smoked cigarettes to show we were liberated. These women Marines reject cigarettes and have turned to nuitrition and body building to preserve their good health."

"We tried to avoid confrontations with the men. This generation meets them head on. They are smart enough and angry enough to go after their legal rights."

"We found our identity as wives and mothers and when the war was over, everyone of us returned meekly to our kitchens and learned to master the plethora of cleaning compounds and new appliances which the advertising industry was so clever in convincing us we had to learn."

"Today's Marine doesn't lose her own identity when she marries and becomes a mother. She is still a Marine and is both."

We had been pioneers in a woman's movement.

Now we were Veterans.

As we stood up to remember those with whom we had shared lives we touched again those secret places in our hearts where fear, love, joy and sadness come together.

The Women Marines Convention came to a close.
The Marine Band played the *MARINE CORPS HYMN.*
We all stood up to sing except those who were in wheel chairs.

When they played the *MARCH OF THE WOMEN MARINES,* even those women who had crutches and canes, stood tall with tears running down their cheeks as they sang loudly:
Marines!
We are the women members of our Fighting Corps
Marines!
The name is known from burning sands to ice bound shores
Marines!
We serve that men may fight on land and air and sea
Marines!
The Eagle, Globe and Anchor carry on
To make men free

We said our good-byes and made promises to meet in Williamsburg in 1993 and in DisneyWorld in Orlando in 1994.
The Field Music from Beyond would soon play *taps* for many of us and we knew it. We were being mustered out of life a few at a time by that Commandant in the Heavens. Perhaps at the next reunion the memorial brochure would have my name on it.
I held on to my bride-groom's hand and together we waved good-bye to all my buddies and bunkies of Quantico and Camp Lejeune.
We called out one last time to each other.
"SEMPER FIDELIS!"

Molly Marine
The only statue honoring WWII Women Marines in the United
States which was erected in New Orleans.

For information about The Women Marines Association,
write to:
P.O. Box. 387, MCB, Quantico, VA 22134-0387

THE MARCH OF THE WOMEN'S RESERVE
Words And Music

March of The Women Marines
(Official March of the Marine Corps Women's Reserve)

Words by
EMIL GRASSER
Conductor

Music by
LOUIS SAVERINØ
U. S. Marine Band

Bel.Bd.No.113

THE MARCH OF THE WOMEN'S RESERVE
Words And Music

Theresa Karas Yianilos

THE MARCH OF THE WOMEN'S RESERVE
Words And Music

Bel.Bd.No.113

440

THE MARCH OF THE WOMEN'S RESERVE
Words And Music

Marine Corps Language, Slang, And Navy Words

Abaft of In back of
Aboard To be there on the station, on duty or ship
Adrift To be loose, not made fast, not tied down
Aft Toward the stern
Alive, *look alive* Be alert
All Hands Entire crew
APC All purpose capsule, an aspirin
Asiatic Eccentric, a little crazy, out of touch with reality
As you were To remain in the same position; keep doing what you were doing
At ease Relaxed attention, no talking, keep one foot in place
At-taen—hunh Attention: stand straight and still
Awn awp reep A marching cadence saying "One up reach-reach for your left",
Aye Aye Sir/Mam Required official reply that an order is understood and will be obeyed

BAM Outlawed slang acronym for Women Marine used by male Marines meaning *"Broad-Ass Marine"*, considered a term of sexual harassment
Barracks A building housing enlisted quarters
Bars Officer's insignia made of silver or gold
Bastard Term for someone who is unpleasant, mean, unfair or grouchy
Battalion Consists of 3 recruit companies, 550 women each company, total of 1650
BCD Bad conduct discharge
Bear a hand To help someone, hurry with support
Beating his/her gums Talking about unimportant things
Beer busts A gathering where beer flows liberally
Belay To rescind an order, to make fast
Below Beneath the deck; the first floor
Bill An organization sheet or chart
Billet A place allotted an individual to sleep; assignment
Binnacle list List of those excused from duty because of illness
Black tie, black shoes Slang for Navy officer
Blouse Marine Uniform jacket, not a shirt
Blue coat Slang for Navy officer
Blues Dress or undress blue uniform worn by enlisted; red stripe down leg is on uniform worn by NCO's
Boondockers Heavy field shoes or boots with high tops that come to the ankles issued to the men
Boondocking Walking in the woods; making love in the woods
Boondocks The woods, fields, or jungles (from the Tagalong Philippine term *bundocs*)
Boot New recruit who is undergoing initial training
BOQ Bachelor officer's quarters, out of bounds to enlisted personnel
Break out To unpack; to unfurl; to arouse

443

Brig Ship's prison; confinement on post
Broad Uncomplimentary slang for a female
Bucket of beer A pitcher of 1 1/2 quarts.
Bucking To ingratiate one's self for promotion
Bulkhead A wall
Bumps Two long wails on a trumpet for 5 minutes to mess call
Bunk Bed, made of metal with a mattress, single or one bed on top of another to accommodate two
Bunkmate, bunkie One who sleeps above or below or in the same room or tent
Bust To reduce in rank

Cadence count The beat or timing in marching called out by the drill instructor and sometimes sung out by the troops. Verses are usually original with each group.
Carry on Continue with whatever you are doing
Cast off To let go; leave port; depart
Chanting Verses sung in a sing-song manner in time to marching rhythm
Charge of quarters Duty non-commissioned officer responsible for billets
Chicken A naive Marine in his teens with a baby-face, inexperienced and young
China Marines Marines who served in Tientsin and Shanghai, China during the 1920's and 1930's
Chin strap Part of officer's cap, formerly worn under chin
Chit An IOU to officer's mess; a receipt
Chow Food, meal
Chow hound One who eats with gusto, a gourmand
CG The Commanding General
CMC The Commandant of the Marine Corps
CO The commanding officer
Colors National ensign or flag, to stand at attention in a salute
Commando Guerrilla soldier; infiltrator: a derisive term when combined with other terms, e.g.: barracks commando
Company A military unit of 165 persons
Company officer Captain, first or second lieutenants
Compartment A room or a locker
Corps Marine Corps
Corps and country calls To depart because of other responsibilities
Crap out To fail; to lose
Crumb, crummy Untidy or dirty person; one who does not keep his/her word
Crying towel Unsympathetic term for complaints or complainers; e.g.: wipe your tears on the Chaplain's crying towel

Deck Floor or ground; to knock someone down
Deck court Special court held for minor infractions of rules; enlisted punishment can be reduction in rank; solitary confinement; loss of pay or liberty
Deck, *hit the deck* An order to stand up immediately from sitting or lying position
Devil dogs Name of respect given to Marines at Belleau Wood during World War I by Germans
DD Dishonorable discharge from the Corps,
DI Drill instructor at recruit depot
Doc Navy hospital corpsman, not a doctor

444

Dogface Derogatory term for an army enlisted man

Doggies Derogatory term for army soldiers

Dog tags Identification tags of metal with name, serial number, blood type, date of tetanus shot, and religion stamped on it

Dope Any kind of information; sight setting and wind correction for a rifle under certain conditions

Doping off Loafing; avoiding work

Dowse Put out the light; cover with water

Dungarees Cotton work clothes, worn by enlisted Marines, also called fatigues or utility

Duty NCO Non commissioned officer in charge of barracks

Eagles The insignia of a colonel

Ear banging Flattering talk, attempting to curry favor with a superior

Eight ball, *behind the eight ball* Unfortunate individual who can't do anything right

Emblems U.S. Marine Corps emblems or Corps logo, adopted in 1868, frequently called Globe & Anchor; seen in many forms as insignia, pins, painted or printed on flags, posters, fabric

Ensign National flag; junior Naval officer

Esprit de corps The spirit of comradeship, loyalty and brotherhood among Marines

Establish a beachhead To land on a shore and take over; to take command of a situation or relationship

Extend To lengthen a contract to stay in service

Fall out To assemble for formation

Field boots Heavy leather shoes with higher tops issued to men, worn by women who drove trucks, worked in mess

Field commission Officer who was promoted from enlisted ranks to commission during battle

Field day Cleaning time, can be a few hours or a full day

Field hat Broad brimmed hat of felt with four dents in crown for men. For women, it was a cotton hat round top with stitched brim.

Field music Drummer or trumpeter, person who rings ship's bells

Field officer Colonel, lieutenant col., major

Field scarf Regulation Marine Corps uniform necktie for men; for women it was the red muffler worn with trench coat

First sergeant Senior non-commissioned officer, wears six stripes, three above and below

First lieutenant Officer, wears a silver bar

Flag officer Rear Admiral or higher

Flatfoot A derogatory term for sailor or soldier

Fouled-up A mix-up, something gone wrong or awry

Four F (4-F) A category in the draft which excluded any male from involuntary service for reasons of physical impairment or other circumstances

Four ninety nine (499) Regulation order number mandating a medical discharge for any pregnant woman Marine

Fruit salad Campaign ribbons, decorations worn at left breast

Furlough Vacation time from duties, 10 or 30 days

Theresa Karas Yianilos

Galley Kitchen of a mess hall or mobile field kitchen
Gangplank fever Tired of being aboard ship or in service
Gangway Make way for officers; ladder to board ship
Gear Equipment, personal effects
General mess Enlisted men's eating hall
General officer Brigadier, Major and Lt. Generals
General Order An order that applied throughout the Corps
GI Government issue; strict interpretation of military rules
GI party Everyone available to clean up to conform to strict standards
Gizmo or giz A thing, a gadget
Globe and Anchor Marine Corps Emblem with American Bald Eagle facing left, wings outspread, perched on top of half a globe of the world with the continents of North and South America showing, pierced in the center by an anchor with entangled (fouled up) rope. Eagle faces the direction of the anchor.
GO 20 Navy Dept. General Order #20 which stated that any Marine who was incapacitated from performing his duties through carelessness, intemperance or misconduct would be subject to a court martial if he were absent from duties for more than 24 hours. Replaced by Articles 15.
Gooney bird stare A shocked, glazed look in the eyes, common among men returning from battle
Goon squad New recruits who haven't received their uniforms and look awkward in civilian dress
Goldbrick Someone who is lazy
Greens Marine Corps winter wool uniforms
Grits Hominy, always served at breakfast
Gung Ho Chinese word meaning "pull together", Marine connotation to be "over anxious"
Gunner, Gunny Marine Gunnery Sergeant, warrant officer
Gyrenes Slang word for Marines, a combination of GI and Marines

Hack Officer's arrest; to be under arrest
HAM Half-Ass Marine, a term of derision used by Women Marines to counter the *BAM* acronym
Hands, all hands All members of a command
Hard-charger Zealous professional Marine
Hash mark Service stripe denoting four years of service
Havelock A plastic protective rain covering for WR hat
Head Toilet, shower room, dressing room
Hill, *Go over hill* To leave without permission; to desert
Hit the deck Get out of bed feet on the floor
Hold Lower portion of ship; basement; cellar;
Holiday Blemish; imperfection; open space storage area

ID card Identification card, to be carried always
Inboard Toward the center
Iron Mike Statue of World War I Marine in front of old Post Headquarters in Quantico
Irish pennant Loose end, untidy

Joe, joe pot Coffee, coffee pot

Keeled over Fainted, fell down, surprised or shocked
Khakis Summer service uniform for men; woman's shirt
Kittens Dust or lint as it balls up on the floor
Knock it off An order meaning "shut up", to stop talking or making any noise or action
Knobler An opportunist; a conniving person
K-rations Canned or dehydrated foods, sent overseas to armed forces or given out in the field

Lad Term of address for any enlisted marine regardless of rank or age used by officers
Ladder Stairway
Latrines Toilets
Leatherneck Traditional name for Marines who once wore high leather neck-bands on uniform jackets
Leave Special permission to be absent from ship or station; liberty
Liberty A period of days when person is given free time, can be 72 hours; does not count against furlough time
Liberty list A list of enlisted entitled to liberty, posted on bulletin board, to be signed
Lights out The hour at which all lights are turned off
Lock up To confine to brig or quarters; under arrest

Mail call When mail arrives and is passed out
Main deck First floor of a building or ship
Main Gate Main entrance to base with posted guard
Mameluke sword A sword carried by officers; has cross hilt and ivory grip; worn during formal ceremonies; traditionally used to cut wedding cake; officers ordered by Navy in 1942 to contribute their swords to metal scrap drive.
Man aboard A cry of warning in women's barracks when a male is on the premises, such as a repair man
MARCORPS Abbreviation for U.S. Marine Corps Headquarters, Washington DC.
MCWR Marine Corps Women's Reserve established, July 30, 1942, founded Nov. 7, 1942, enlistment opened Feb. 13, 1943
Mast Navy equivalent for *Office Hours*
MCM Marine Corps Manual, a guide book
Mess Where meals are served for officers
Mess hall Where meals are served for enlisted
Mess duty Service for one month in the kitchen, mandatory for each private and private first class and corporals.
Mess sergeant Non-commissioned officer in charge of enlisted mess hall
MP Military Police: in 1943-44 jurisdiction over Marines was held by Army & Navy MP's
Music Short form for field music; specifically the field music assigned to the guard of the day
Mustang An officer who earns his commission up from ranks

Theresa Karas Yianilos

Muster To fall into ranks in designated places; to assemble a section and determine absentees

Navy time Knowing how to tell Navy time was mandated in the Marine Corps. Going around the clock, 00 and 12 are added to make the P.M. hours: e.g.[12 noon, 1200], [1:00 p.m., 1300], and so on up to midnight which read at 2400. The 0 prefaces the AM. numbers so [1:00 a.m. becomes 0100], [2:00 a.m. is 0200].
NCO Non-commissioned officer
Nervous in service Slang for a desire to return to civilian life
Non-rated Not of non-commissioned rank, a private

Old Man Familiar for commanding officer
Old Marine Corps Prior to 1939
OOD Officer of the day
OD Officer of the deck
Officer's country Quarters for officers only, marked by "out of bounds" signs to enlisted
Office hours Occasion when commanding officer awards, praises or blames, hears special requests and awards non judicial punishment
One brew A person who can't hold his liquor
Old Corps The Marine Corps before 1940
Outboard Toward sides; away from the center
Out of bounds An area that is forbidden to enlisted
On the double To run or march at a fast pace
Overhead Ceiling of a room or compartment aboard ship

PI Parris Island, South Carolina, Marine Corps base
Paid off Discharged at end of enlistment
PAL Prisoner at large; slang for person who is restricted to barracks or post
Pass over To omit an officer from the promotion list; by promoting another junior to his rank
Paymaster Disbursing officer who writes the checks
PD Police Duty, to clean up
People Enlisted Marines; one's subordinates
Pick up To promote an officer previously passed over
Pipe aboard Announcing an officer aboard ship by whistle
Pipe down An order to keep quiet
Platoon About 28 Marines, women or men
Platoon sergeant Non-commissioned officer in charge of recruit platoon
Pogie bait Candy
Police To clean up
Police Gang A group assigned to clean up
Poncho Rain cloak
Port Left side
PX Post Exchange: a general/department government store for military personnel

QM, Quartermaster Supplies the base with everything needed to run that base.
Quarters Living accommodations on base or government housing

Raider A member of the Raider Battalion, World War II
Raider cap A green utility cap, very distinctive
Railroad tracks Insignia of captain of double silver bars
Rank happy A person who is impressed with his/her own rank
Rated man Any non-commissioned officer
Rating A person's rank
Read off To reprimand severely
Red lead Refers to red stripe on pants of men's blues allowed to corporals and above
Regulation Strictly according to Marine specifications
Retread A Marine who has become unfit for combat duty and is assigned to desk duty, or one who has re-enlisted after having served once
Reveille Morning call to wake up, between 4:30 A.M. and 6:00 A.M. depending upon the command
Rifle The weapon of a Marine. Never called a gun.
ROC Reserve officer candidate
Rocks and Shoals Articles of Navy Regulations
Rock happy Someone who has become eccentric, bored or out of touch from being assigned for too long a time at a remote station or island.
Runner Messenger
Ruptured duck A gold insignia issued to discharged service personnel, as a patch to be sewn on a uniform or a gold pin to be worn on the collar: an emblem of an eagle with wings outspread encircled by a ring in gold thread on a diamond shaped khaki green back ground.

Sack Bed
Sad bastard One who is in trouble and is sorry
Sad sack Person who can't do anything right; one who is caught in a web of his own making
Salt, old salt, salty Experienced old time Marine; anything made green and antique from salt spray
Savvy Well informed; someone who knows the score
Schupper A large mug used for beer
Screw Raped; cheated; taken advantage of
Scuttlebutt Rumor: hear-say, gossip; drinking fountain
Sea bag Canvas duffel bag issued to enlisted Marines
Sea going Shipboard duty
Sea going bellhop Slang expression for Marines because they were assigned duty aboard ships
Sea going language Slang and vocabulary used aboard ship
Sea lawyer Any Marine who gives advice without being qualified and who lacks expertise
Sea soldier An amphibious soldier, Marine
Sea story A tale, usually prevaricated or exaggerated
Secure To complete a job or exercise; to leave or cease work or drill; to make fast
Secure, *Time to secure* Quitting Time
Semper Fidelis Marine Corps motto meaning "Always Faithful"
Semper Fi Shortened form of Marine Corps motto used as greeting; Parody of the motto; denotes lack of spirit translated into "Hooray for me, I've got mine. You get yours," "I'm aboard. Pull up the ladder".

Sergeant major Senior non-commissioned officer
Shack up To live together; to sleep together or share quarters
Shack job A sexual relationship primarily for a limited time with no commitment
Shape up or ship out Conform or resign
Shavetail A new second lieutenant
Shook Dazed, groggy, to be shocked
Shoot the breeze Chat casually of inconsequential matters
Shove off To leave; an order to go
Sick bay Dispensary
Sick bay soldier A malingerer, one who constantly goes on sick call to avoid work
Sick call To go to report an illness, first thing in the morning when ailments are
    reported and treated at sick bay
Side arms Weapons worn by Marines; creamer and sugar containers on the table
    at mess
Sight in To aim at a target; zero in
Silver leaves The insignia of a lieutenant colonel
Skipper Familiar for commanding officer
Skivvies Men's undershirt adopted by the women as nighties and for wear with
    dungarees and mess pants
Slop down or up To drink beer in quantity or to eat without table manners
Slopshute A beer hall for enlisted
Smart Snappy appearance or posture
Smoking lamp A light usually located at end of the room, which when on, indicated
    smoking was allowed
Snafu Slang for the phrase, "Situation normal, all fouled up" meaning it's common
    for things to be confusing
Snap in or to To break in a new job; to conduct exercises with a loaded weapon
Snow job To lie or exaggerate purposely and knowingly
SOS A breakfast dish of creamed chipped beef on toast served frequently. The
    initials were an acronyms for *Shit on a Shingle*, a term that was not picked up
    by the women.
Sound off Give your name and rank
SP Shore patrol; Navy policemen who patrolled military and civilian areas and had
    jurisdiction over Marines as well as sailors
SPARS Women's Auxiliary of Coast Guard, motto of Coast Guard "Semper
    Paratus"
Spit and polish To be extremely neat and clean with adherence to the minutiae of
    all things military
Spit shine To shine leather to a mirror brilliance
Squad A unit in the Marine Corps
Squadroom A room with eighty or more bunks; A barracks room where privates,
    privates first class or junior NCO lived together
Square away To put things in order
Square off To arrange yourself in proper position; stand and account for yourself
Staff NCO Non commissioned officer in first three pay grades; includes staff
    sergeant, gunnery sergeant, First Sergeant and sergeant major
Stand by Prepare and remain in readiness
Stand fast Stay where you are; don't move
Starboard Right side
Survey Medical discharge; to dispose of an item because it is no longer serviceable

Swab To mop up or wash down

Swab detail A duty to wash the floor, or deck or the area

Swabbies A slang term for sailors

Swagger stick A stick carried for effect by officers and staff NCO. Usually made out of rosewood with silver tips for commissioned officers and brass for the non-commissioned.

Taps The notes of music when it's time to retire

Tell it to the Chaplain An expression denoting a lack of sympathy

Tell it to the Marines An expression dating from the time of King Charles II of England. It means, "if the Marines say it's true then it must be so, for they go everywhere, see everything and do all".

Trade school boys Nickname for officers who attended military colleges: Virginia Military Institute, Citadel, Annapolis, West Point

Train in To terminate a drill

Turn in To go to bed

Two block To tighten and center a field scarf

Uniform of the day The proper uniform to wear according to posted regulations for the day. Winter or summer uniforms to be worn upon the date ordered, not according to individual's preference or climate

Up the pole Abstaining from alcohol in any form

Very well Reply of senior to junior officer

VMI Virginia Military Institute, a military school, many of whose graduates went into the Marines

WAAC(S) Women's Army Auxiliary Corps: women in the army in World War II

WAFSP Women's Air Force Service Pilots

Walking John Traditional nickname for the Marine Corps sergeant in blues who is forever marching on recruiting posters

Wardroom Officer's Mess room

Watch Officer Any officer standing a duty watch

WAVES Women's Accepted for Volunteer Emergency Service; women who joined the Navy in World War II

Wet down To serve drinks in honor of one's promotion

Whites Marine Corps dress uniform, all white worn by Women Marines and officers, both Marines and Navy

Windward Side exposed to weather, pronounced "wind-ard"

Word The final say so; an order; a rumor

Working over Severe reprimand

WR(S) A shortened name for United States Marine Corps Women's Reserve in the Marine Corps from 1943 to 1948

The War In The Pacific, 1941-1945

Six Marine Divisions fought in World War II. The Women Marines freed 20,000 men to fight. The Sixth Division was formed due to the 20,000 women that joined the Women's Reserve. Total casualties of U. S. Marines were 86,940.

Date	Battleground	Wounded	Killed
1941			
12/7	Japanese attack-Pearl Harbor	1178	2403
	Marine casualties	69	109
12/8-10	Wake Island		449
	garrison surrendered		
12/10	Guam	150	
	garrison capture		
12/2-23	Bataan & Corregidor		
	garrison capture		
12/8-5/6/43	Philippines		
	Philippino civilians killed 10,000		
12/10	Battle of Badoeng Strait		
	China—the 4th Marines lost		
	Makassar Straits, Java Sea,		
	Sunda Straits		
	Aleutian Islands, Dutch Harbor		
1942	**South Pacific Theater**		
2/15	Fall of Singapore		
2/19	Battle of Coral Sea		
5/4-8	Battle of Midway		
8/7-9	First Savo Battle (Naval-Air)		
	The Solomons Group		
	(Capture and Defense of Guadalcanal)		
8/7-9	Tulagi		
8/10-2/9/43	Guadalcanal Is.	2619	1584
8/17-18	Makin Island Raid (Gilberts)		
8/23-25	Battle of Eastern Solomons		
10/11-15	Battle of Cape Esperance (Naval)		
10/26	Battle of Santa Cruz Island (Air)		
11/11-15	Battle of Guadalcanal (Navy-Air)		
11/30 -12/1	Battle of Tassafaronga (Naval)		

Date	Battleground	Wounded	Killed
1943			
2/2-3	New Georgia-Kolambangara		
2/9	Guadalcanal secured		
	Supply lifeline to Australia now assured		
2/13	**Recruiting for Women Marines begins**		
3/26	Battle of Komandorski Is.		
6/30-8/31	(Aleutians) North Pacific		
	New Georgia-Rendova Vandunu		
	Segi-Viru, Rendova Munda,		
	Rice Anchorage-Enogai, Bairoko-		
	Tetemara & Tombi	28	
7/5-6	Battle of Kula Gulf (Naval)		
8/15-10/27	Vella Lavella Occupation		
11/6	Treasury Island Landing		
10/27-11/3	Choiseul Is.	14	11
10/3	Funafuti (Ellice Islands)		
11/1-12/15	Bougainville	1418	423
	Purata Island		182
	Piva	71	39
	Cape Torokina	93	17
11/20-12/8	Tarawa Operation (Gilbert Is.)		
	Buariki Is.	59	32
	Tarawa Atoll		
	Betio Island	2391	990
	(New Britain)		
12/26-3/1/44	Cape Gloucester	1083	310
	Russell Islands		
	Pavuvu, Banika Islands		28
1944	**Central Pacific Theater of Operation**		
2/15-19	Green Island Landing (Kavieng)		
1/31-2/17	Kwajalein and Majuro Atolls		
2/17-3/2	Eniwetok Atoll (Ellicell Islands)		
	Roi,Namur, Kwajalein Atoll,		
	Eniwetok Atoll, Ennubirr,		
	Parry Island	1100	536
	Rabaul (14,718 sorties-air strikes)		

Date	Battleground	Wounded	Killed
3/6/44	New Britain	**1083**	**310**
	Talasea		
	Marianas Group		
6/15-8/18	Saipan	13,208	3426
6/19	Marianas Turkey Shoot		
	(Naval and Air)		
7/21-8/15	Guam	7122	1919
7/24-8/10	Tinian	1571	328
9/15-10/12	Pelelui (Palau Is.)	6526	1252
	(Army casualties)	1185	208
	Ngesebus Is.		28
10/20	Leyte, Philippines Landings		

Gen. MacArthur returns with the Grace of God and a few Marines.

10/24-26	Battle of Leyte Gulf		
	(Naval, Marine Air)		

1945			
2/19-3/16	Iwo Jima	17,328	5931
	doctors & corpsmen		738
4/1-6/21	Okinawa	13,523	2834
4/12	President Roosevelt Dies		
5/8	Germany Surrneders V-E Day		
6/21	Okinawa Gunto Occupied		

Last island needed from which to assault mainland Japan is secured. U. S. announces plans to land with a force of 2 million men in 1945. Military regime in Japan refuses to surrender. The ENGOLA GAY departs on August 6, from Tinian Island, to drop the Atom Bomb.

8/6	First Atom bomb dropped on Hiroshima
8/9	Second Atom bomb hits Nagasaki
8/12	Newspapers headlines read Japan surrenders
8/14	V-J DAY

BIBLIOGRAPHY

Bailey, Gilbert P. Cpl. USMCR. *Boot*, New York: Macmillan, 1943
Bradley, Omar General USA. *Bradley, A Soldier's Story*, Rand Mcnally & Co. 1951
De St. Jorre, John. *The Marines*, New York: Doubleday, 1989
Doukoullos, Ellen Stone and Bonnie Smallwood Medin. *Musical Women Marines*, U.S. Copyright TXu 75-525, 1981
Have They Come A Long Way. DAV Magazine, April 1992, pg. 12-14.
Heinl, Jr., Robert Debs Colonel. *Soldiers Of The Sea, The U. S. Marine Corps 1775-1962*, U.S. Naval Institute, Annapolis, Maryland, 1962
History Of The Women Marines 1946-1977, History and Museums Division, Headquarters, U.S. Marine Corps, Washington, D.C.
Home Of The Commandant, 1956, Leatherneck Assn., Washington, D.C.
Hough, Frank O., Major USMCR. *Island War*, New York: J.B. Lippincott Co., 1947
Krulak, Victor H. Lt. General, USMC (Ret), *First To Fight*, New York: Pocket Books, Simon and Schuster, 1991
Lawless, Chuck *The Marine Book*, New York: Thames & Hudson, 1988
Letter Of Instruction #489, Commandant USMC, Headquarters Marine Corps, Washington D.C., July 16, 1943
Manchester, William. *Goodbye Darkness, A Memoir Of The Pacific War*, Boston: Little Brown & Co., 1979
Marine Corps Women's Reserve In World War II, Marine Corps Historical Reference Series, No. 37, Historical Branch, G-3 Division, Headquarters, U.S. Marine Corps, Washington D.C., 1964
McMillan, George. *Uncommon Valor, Marine Divisions In Action*, Washington Information Journal Press, 1946
Millet, Allan R. *Semper Fidelis, The History Of The U.S. Marine Corps*, New York: The Free Press, Div. of Macmillan, 1991
Montross, Lynn. *The United States Marines*, New York: Bramhall House, 1959
Presidential Commission On The Assignment Of Women In The Armed Forces, U.S. Government Printing Office, 1993
Schneider, Dorothy and Carl J. *Sound-Off, American Military Women Speak Out*, New York: E.P. Dutton, 1988
Smith, Holland M. General, USMC (Ret) and Peter Finch. *Coral And Brass*, New York: Charles Scribner's Sons, 1949

Stremlow, Mary Col. USMC (Ret.). *Coping With Sexism In The Military*, New York: Rosen Publishing Group, 1990

Sulzberger, C. L. *The American Heritage Picture History Of World War II*, New York: American Heritage-Bonanza Books, 1966

Thomason, Jr., John W. *And A Few Marines*, New York: Charles Scribner's Sons, 1943

U.S. Marine Corps Women's Reserve, Camp Lejeune New River, N.C., yearbook, 1944, U.S. Marine Corps

Uris, Leon. *Battle Cry*, New York: G. P. Putnams, 1953

Utilization Of American Military Women In Operations Desert Shield And Desert Storm, Aug. 2, 1990-April 11, 1991 Division of Public Affairs, Headquarters Marine Corps, 1991

Women Marines In The 1980's, Division of Public Affairs, Headquarters Marine Corps, October 1986

Yianilos, Theresa Karas and Spero James Yianilos. *Private Letters, Diary And Correspondence*, 1942-1945

About The Author

Theresa Karas Yianilos is a graduate of the University of Buffalo (now SUNY) and has taught several courses at the University of California at San Diego. She was born in Warsaw, New York, of Greek parentage. She married Spero James Yianilos of Buffalo, New York, in Richmond, Virginia on July 1, 1944 and again, in the Greek Orthodox Church in Buffalo on August 12, 1945. In the year of 1993, the fiftieth anniversary of the Women Marines, she and Spero James Yianilos celebrated their forty-ninth wedding anniversary. They have three children, and four grand-children.

Mrs. Yianilos has written several books and many articles. Her best selling cookbook titled **THE COMPLETE GREEK COOK-BOOK The Best From 3000 Years Of Greek Cooking** was first published in 1970. It has become a classic throughout the United States and in Greece. Noted cook and television personality, the Frugal Gourmet, Jeff Smith, recommends it with high praise in his book, THE FRUGAL GOURMET COOKS THREE ANCIENT CUISINES.

Her second book **GREEN WORLD**, a gardening book for the home gardener, was written with co-author Spero Yianilos, a noted horticulturist in Southern California, who is an expert on palm trees and sub-tropical flora.

Both books are currently published and are available from the La Jolla Book Publishing Co., P.O. Box 569, La Jolla, California 92038.

Mrs. Yianilos moved from Buffalo, New York with her family in 1958 to La Jolla, California, where she maintains a botanical garden of sub-tropical plants. She has received awards as a foremost ceramic artist whose tile murals are installed in many homes, hospitals and restaurants, including Scripps-McDonald Hospital in La Jolla, Kaiser Permanente Medical Center, San Diego and nine operating rooms in St. John's Regional Hospital, Oxnard, CA.

Her crusading activities in the La Jolla community have been written about in the local newspapers and she was dubbed "The Palm Lady" for her efforts in preserving the palm trees in San Diego. Mrs. Yianilos continues to fight for her country and community.

To order a copy of

WOMAN MARINE

A Memoir Of A Woman Who Joined
The U.S. Marine Corps in World War II
To "Free A Marine To Fight"

by
Theresa Karas Yianilos

Fill out the form below and send it to:

WOMAN MARINE A Memoir   (ISBN 0-9621142-4-3)
La Jolla Book Publishing Co.
P.O. Box 569
La Jolla, CA 92038

NAME: _____

Address: _____

City: _____

State: _____ Zip: _____

Send check or money order : $19.95 per copy
Add: Shipping & Handling $3.00
Add: 7.75% Sales tax for CA residents $1.52

No. books ordered: _____ Amount enclosed: $ _____

Please, inquiry for quantity orders
Other titles available by Theresa Karas Yianilos
THE COMPLETE GREEK COOKBOOK The Best of 3000 Years
Of Greek Cooking $12.95 + $3.00 S&H
GREEN WORLD, The Home Gardener $12.95 +$3.00 S&H